RECAPTURING THE OVAL OFFICE

RECAPTURING THE OVAL OFFICE

NEW HISTORICAL APPROACHES TO THE AMERICAN PRESIDENCY

EDITED BY BRIAN BALOGH AND BRUCE J. SCHULMAN

CORNELL UNIVERSITY PRESS

Ithaca and London

Published in association with the University of Virginia's Miller Center

First published 2015 by Cornell University Press

First printing, Cornell Paperbacks, 2015

Printed in the United States of America

Library of Congress Cataloging-in-Publication Data

Recapturing the Oval Office : new historical approaches
   to the American presidency / edited by Brian Balogh
   and Bruce Schulman.
      pages cm
   Includes bibliographical references and index.
   ISBN 978-0-8014-5372-4 (cloth : alk. paper)
   ISBN 978-0-8014-5657-2 (pbk. : alk. paper)
   1. Presidents—United States—History—20th century.
   2. Executive power—United States—History—20th
   century. 3. United States—Politics and government—20th
   century. I. Balogh, Brian, editor. II. Schulman, Bruce,
   editor. III. Skowronek, Stephen. Unsettled state of
   presidential history. Container of (work):
      E176.1.R297   2015
      352.23'509730904—dc23   2015008963

Cornell University Press strives to use environmentally
responsible suppliers and materials to the fullest extent possible in the publishing of its books. Such materials include
vegetable-based, low-VOC inks and acid-free papers that
are recycled, totally chlorine-free, or partly composed of
nonwood fibers. For further information, visit our website
at www.cornellpress.cornell.edu.

Cloth printing   10 9 8 7 6 5 4 3 2 1
Paperback printing   10 9 8 7 6 5 4 3 2 1

Contents

RECAPTURING THE OVAL OFFICE

Confessions of a Presidential Assassin

BRIAN BALOGH

As an undergraduate, I did not major in his-
tory.[1] In fact, I only took one history course, which I vowed would be my
last. Although the professor was a towering figure in his field and, as I later
learned, a gracious and generous colleague, the focus on the presidency to the
exclusion of other elements within the political universe, not to mention the
vast world that lies beyond politics, was stifling. My reaction was not based on
a sophisticated knowledge of the new social history that was gaining ground
in history departments in the early 1970s when I was in college. Rather,
it was the gut reaction of a naive twenty-year-old who sensed that there
was more to history than presidents and their outsized personalities. Besides,
hitching the nation's history to its president at the very time that the Watergate hearings were exposing Richard Nixon's high crimes and misdemeanors
did not seem to be a wise choice. Upon graduating from college, I worked
at the grassroots level for a community-based organization that was fighting
for more equitable utility rates for poor people and then worked in a series
of government positions in Massachusetts and New York, ultimately directing several income maintenance programs for the New York City Human
Resources Administration. At age thirty I enrolled in a PhD program in
history at the Johns Hopkins University. Social history dominated the field,
spawning work that explored race, class, and gender. By the mid-1980s, informed by anthropology and eventually literary criticism, the new frontier

was cultural history, which moved the field even farther from magisterial accounts of presidential administrations toward the generation and reception of ideas, behavior, and customs by average Americans and marginalized groups.[2]

As a former New York City welfare administrator scrambling to understand how and why Americans created durable bureaucratic regimes despite longstanding antagonism toward "big government," I latched onto the few shards of political history that remained afloat in a sea of social and cultural history. One fragment was the "organizational synthesis." Pioneered by historians who were also interested in social structures—Samuel P. Hays, Ellis Hawley, Robert Wiebe, Louis Galambos—this approach to political history credited large-scale shifts in social relations and the political economy—industrialization, urbanization, professionalization—with causal agency.[3] The roots of the organizational synthesis were grounded in the broader shift to social history, even as its practitioners remained focused on top-down outcomes. Another band of historians focused more exclusively on the recent history of public policies forged by the modernizing twentieth-century American state.[4] Scholars like Edward Berkowitz, Martha Derthick, and Michael Hogan demonstrated that programs ranging from social security to the Marshall Plan were worth studying in their own right.[5]

Political history was a dying field then, but historical approaches to politics were thriving in the social sciences. "American Political Development" focused attention on the state as an independent actor, or at least one that was capable of adapting to broad social changes, at times even inducing some of those changes. The rise of "APD" offered important methods and analytical tools to historians interested in politics and public policy. More importantly, it reassured them that somebody was listening.[6]

What all of these scholars shared was a skepticism about the kind of history that focused exclusively on the Oval Office. Even Steven Skowronek's *Building a New American State*—a foundational text in the APD literature that dealt extensively with the Progressive Era administrations of Roosevelt, Taft, and Wilson—was animated by the clash between an older polity built around parties and administrative institutions in the military command, fiscal sinews, and transportation networks of the twentieth-century state that were constructed in response to the pressures of a modernizing society.[7] The key argument in the seminal synthetic work in the organizational school—Robert H. Wiebe's *The Search for Order*—credited a rising professional middle class and the bureaucratic mechanisms of "continuous management" with far more agency than the individual actions of TR and Wilson.[8]

It was not simply social and cultural historians who reduced presidents to bystanders in the march of history: It was first and foremost several generations of political and policy historians who abandoned the Oval Office. That is why presidents remain on the outside looking in at the historical profession today, even as political history has rebounded within the academy. Several generations of political historians had quite self-consciously constructed an approach to their topic that displaced the "presidential synthesis" forged by the likes of John Morton Blum, John Milton Cooper, and Arthur Schlesinger Jr.[9] I had joined a team of presidential assassins intent on taking out the chief executives around whom much of the century's political history had been framed.

We succeeded. Our triumph was most pronounced in the field of twentieth-century political history, arguably the very period in which presidents were most influential. Graduate students, buffeted by a powerful current of history crafted from the bottom up and trained by a generation of political historians who forged careers by dismantling the presidential synthesis, were discouraged from writing about the presidency. For twenty years I warned graduate students against writing dissertations centered on a presidential administration or the presidency. Although my advice was based on instinct and anecdotal evidence from the career paths of scholars who were either courageous or foolhardy enough to write about presidents, a recent review of hiring patterns confirms my suspicions. Of the roughly seventy first books (the product of dissertations) published by twentieth-century U.S. historians currently teaching at the top fifteen history departments over the past two decades, only one deals largely with the presidency.[10] And that one, Fred Logevall's *Choosing War: The Last Chance for Peace and Escalation of War in Vietnam*, came in the field formerly known as "diplomatic history"—and even that one we actually counted as only half about the presidency. The presidency was an island unto itself, just as isolated from mainstream political history as it was from currents in social and cultural history. As such, diplomatic history never relinquished its interest in the executive branch and presidents themselves, as work by Robert Dallek, John Gaddis, and Mel Leffler, among others, demonstrates. As a result of this continuity, what is now a field of study called America and the World and the history of U.S. foreign relations, which has since reconnected with mainstream currents in the historical profession, can serve as a model for reintegrating the presidency into twentieth-century political history as well as U.S. history more broadly.

It is time to take study of the presidency off the endangered species list elsewhere in the historical profession, and it is essential that a new generation of political historians lead the way. That is because dissertations and the monographs they become are the basic building blocks of the profession. A generation of work lost at the beginning is a generation lost forever. Now is a propitious time to integrate the presidency into cutting-edge historical scholarship because we know so much more about the context in which presidents operate and the structures that guide, and often limit, their actions and beliefs. That is because over the past thirty years social, cultural, intellectual, and more recently, economic historians have developed and mined rich fields of inquiry. The histories of African Americans, gender, workers, the environment, and consumption, to name just a few subfields, have thrived.[11] These studies have illuminated the social and cultural environments in which presidents operate.

No doubt, initially much of this new energy came at the expense of political history and especially scholarship on the presidency. Recently, however, scholars working in social and cultural history and a range of some of the other new subdisciplines have brought politics back into their work.[12] Meanwhile, the subdiscipline of political history has witnessed a renaissance. The history of U.S. foreign relations has also incorporated a number of new approaches, expanding its global perspectives to examine America and the world.[13] At the same time, legal historians have drawn on the methodologies of social and cultural history to explore the ways in which the law shapes day-to-day activities and common understandings.[14]

The essays in this volume model the scholarly possibilities for "bringing the presidency back in," situating the presidency in literatures that have displaced it over the past thirty years. Social historian Robert Self, in his penetrating analysis of presidents' ability to harness and domesticate the energy that fuels social movements, illustrates the integral connection between the bottom-up politics of the street and the Oval Office. Economic historian Michael Bernstein's savvy explication of the ways in which presidents failed to consider the exceptional historical conditions that undergirded the influence of economists from 1945 through 1975 demonstrates the historically contingent power of expertise. Political historian Gareth Davies's essay on the evolving role that presidents play in responding to disasters captures nicely the crucial role that shifting responsibilities between the states and the national government, on the one hand, and public expectations, on the other, play in dictating the chief executive's response to hurricanes, floods, and other acts of nature. Historian of religion Darren Dochuk's incisive narrative about "oil patch" spirituality that seeped into presidential politics during the New Deal and continues to fuel debate today connects the worldviews of presidents to a broad range of public policies. In these and the other essays in this volume, this book illustrates what is possible when materials from the Oval Office are deployed by scholars who are *not* specialists on the presidency.

There are promising signs that junior scholars are already testing the presidential "no-fly zone." Kathryn Brownell, an assistant professor at Purdue University and an author in this volume, has synthesized popular culture and presidential history in her analysis of the ways in which celebrity has reconfigured the nation's highest office. James Wilson, a scholar in the Office of the Historian in the U.S. State Department, just published *The Triumph of Improvisation: Gorbachev's Adaptability, Reagan's Engagement, and the End of the Cold War.*[15] Wilson has continued an older tradition that balances presidential agency and personality with the more structural factors that undergirded the Cold War. These examples from the ranks of junior scholars, combined with a recent spate of scholarship on the presidency from senior scholars ranging from contributors to this volume, Frank Costigliola and Bruce Schulman, to David Greenberg, James Kloppenberg, Dan Rodgers, Tom Sugrue, Sean Wilentz, and Julian Zelizer, suggest that this is an auspicious time to capitalize on the historical context that was often missing in the presidential synthesis and that has been honed by the historical profession over the past thirty years.[16]

While internal historiographic opportunities explain some of this resurgence, exogenous factors explain far more. The electrifying victory of America's first African American president is certainly one crucial catalyst. Making up for the decades-long neglect of the history of racial relations had pointed historians toward the grass roots and the cultural interstices of history. Obama's election and, perhaps more remarkably, his reelection offer an opportunity to write about racial politics through the highest office in the land. With (at this writing) Hillary Clinton the odds-on candidate to win the Democratic nomination in 2016, the same can be said for gender. Two other factors have redirected attention of historians of all stripes toward the Oval Office. The first of these is the recent fascination with globalization (in spite of its centuries-old role in American life). As the focal point for America's interactions with the rest of the world, the Oval Office looms far larger in the lives of Americans who are attentive to such global influences. Second, decades of growing income and wealth inequality have raised fundamental questions about the kind of society that the United Sates is becoming. Questions like this, just as the battles over the shift from an agrarian to industrial economy at the turn of the twentieth century and America's permanent military deployment abroad during and after World War II indicate broad-gauged debate that is often best interpreted through an examination of America's highest office.

Bringing the presidency back into the mainstream of historical scholarship has important implications that extend far beyond the ivory tower. As

Stephen Skowronek argues in his essay in this collection, the intellectual community in the twentieth century has played a crucial role in defining the possibilities for and limitations on presidential power. "The presidency might never have attained the power and position it now holds in American government," argues Skowronek, "without a broad and influential cadre of public intellectuals committed to its development and capable of lending legitimacy to its transformation." Progressive interpretations of history were a crucial ingredient in this mix, pitting democratizing movements, given voice by newly empowered presidents, against the strictures of an outmoded Constitution. More than half a century later, an equally committed intellectual insurgency in the wake of Vietnam and Watergate helped rein in the imperial presidency. Once again, historians and a cohesive interpretation of history were pivotal factors in the debate. Arthur Schlesinger Jr. and other key architects of the presidential synthesis, normally not shy about presidential prerogative, now charged that Richard Nixon had exceeded the limitations that historically had governed executive power.

This book signals historians' reentry into a discussion that for too long has been left to political scientists, the public intellectuals labeled "presidential historians" by the media, and, most recently, legal scholars. Bringing *historians* back into the debate is likely to reshape the very definition of the powers at the president's disposal by emphasizing the long history of debate over the nature of the office. Underscoring this historical perspective will likely undermine any notion of the progressive expansion of the powers of this office. Because the actual authority of presidents has rested in part on a shifting intellectual consensus, not simply judicial interpretations of the Constitution or the personalities of the individual occupants of the Oval Office, historians do not simply chronicle the history of that office. The historical framework they craft can play an important role in determining the course of that history. Of course historians themselves are hardly immune to the influence of the times in which they write. Contemporaneous events will no doubt continue to shade the historical examples and tendencies that historians privilege when they contextualize the presidency, just as they did for Charles Beard and Arthur Schlesinger Jr.

The essays in this volume also model ways to address the gap between academic historians and those "presidential historians." These public intellectuals, including Michael Beschloss, Doris Kearns Goodwin, and David McCullough, do extensive research and craft evocative narratives about presidents and their legacies.[17] What distinguishes presidential historians from academic historians is that the former do not engage the voluminous scholarship on their topic. Rarely do presidential historians delve into deeper structural questions or plumb the historical context that scholars are inclined to examine. For their part, because academic historians have been heavily invested in explicating complex social, cultural, and economic structures, they tend to understate the possibilities for individual agency—at least when it comes to presidents.

The tension between agency and structure provides the organizing principle for this volume. Part I, titled "Balancing Agency and Structure," includes three essays that introduce this central tension. Are presidents the architects of the world they operate in or prisoners of that world? Is the presidency largely defined by the individuals who occupy it, or are all presidents restricted by larger forces and structures that limit their actions? Part II, "The Social and Cultural Landscape Presidents Confront," addresses the social, cultural, intellectual, religious, and economic structures that presidents face and examines in greater detail the interaction between the Oval Office and these factors. And Part III, "The Presidency and Political Structure," examines the political structures that shape the presidency.

As Bruce Schulman notes in the conclusion, a number of the essays in this book chart a "third way" that promises to bridge the agency/structure divide. Eliminating the top-down/bottom-up split between social and political actors, they take a page out of "presidential history" by deploying more narrative "microhistories" of individuals. In contrast to heroic accounts that credit the protagonist with herculean agency, however, these scholarly accounts "embed subjects within their contexts, to illuminate broader structures rather than obscure them." It is our hope that these examples of presidential history, which draw on the structural context in which presidents operate, will capture the attention of popularizers, encouraging them to draw on a broader range of historical scholarship when crafting their powerful narratives.

Making history whole, deploying that history as part of a broader intellectual discourse that influences the nature of the presidential power itself, and narrowing the gap between the presidential history that millions of Americans read (and view) and the scholarship that chronicles the historical context in which presidents have operated—all of this will require a sustained initiative, and this is true even if this volume achieves all of its objectives. Although we do not have any formula for ensuring its success, engaging graduate students in this initiative is essential. If the next generation of historians bring the presidency back in, and if the job market responds positively (as I believe it will), the historical profession can look forward to reaping the full benefits of its investment in social and cultural history. With a bit of luck, the nation will also benefit from a more nuanced understanding of its history as Americans continue to debate the parameters of the president's power.

PART I

Balancing Agency and Structure

The tension between agency and structure in the history of presidential administrations and the history of the office of the presidency itself generally pits the talents of the incumbent and his capacity to mobilize the accoutrements of political power against the constitutional constraints on the power of the office. That those constraints echoed larger fears about the dangers of distant centralized authority to a fledgling republic grounded this legal structure in deep cultural and political soil. While this is political scientist Stephen Skowronek's point of departure, that context merely serves to introduce a far more original and penetrating exegesis of the relationship between presidents and the structural constraints of the office. Scholarly conceptions of the history of the presidency, Skowronek argues, have been a powerful agent in interpreting and indeed shaping the prevailing structures within which presidents operate. Skowronek identifies a period of remarkable consensus about the basis of modern presidential power—one that shifted the debate from a formalistic balance among the three branches of government to one that decidedly enhanced presidential power at the expense of the other two branches. That consensus was grounded in the work of Progressive historians and political scientists. By reaching outside of the Constitution to the capacity of presidents to speak for national public opinion and drawing on expertise intended to serve all three branches of government, the self-conscious Progressive project built a durable basis for expanding the reach of the presidency without relying on presidential prerogative. Post-Progressive scholarly critiques, starting in the era of Vietnam and Watergate, pointed out a series of intractable problems with this source of authority, problems exposed by presidential actions that were clearly out of step with public opinion and congressional determination to use experts of their own. His essay concludes with a discussion of the current state of affairs in presidential studies, in which the break between "modern" presidents and those who preceded them in the nineteenth century has been challenged. Each scholarly movement is the product of its time, shaped by factors ranging from industrialization to the speed of communications; Skowronek makes a strong case for the agency of intellectual communities in the centuries-long struggle to adapt the structure of politics to the needs of the nation. In that spirit he welcomes historians back to the study of the presidency but warns those returning to the fray to understand themselves as a community of scholars and to take stock of where they stand in relationship to others who have taken part in this high-stakes enterprise.

Frank Costigliola introduces a third element into the analysis of the give-and-take between presidential agency and the structural constraint on presidential influence—contingency. Examining the transition from Franklin D. Roosevelt to Harry S. Truman in the months immediately following Roosevelt's death in April 1945, Costigliola points to a rare "plastic" moment in international relations precipitated by the end of World War II. FDR died just at the moment that deference to the commander-in-chief had been enhanced by wartime secrecy, a Democratic majority in Congress, and the sudden acceleration of the war's end due to the decision to use atomic weapons in Japan. Beyond America's borders, Costigliola argues, such critical junctures for reordering foreign relations in the twentieth century can be counted on one hand: August 1914; November 1989; September 2001. The confluence of Roosevelt's death and a rare opportunity for presidential agency propelled another relatively contingent factor to the forefront: personality. Costigliola distinguishes the divergent personalities of each occupant of the White House during this drama by comparing their self-confidence and their comfort level with difference—both gendered and cultural. He concludes that Roosevelt's extraordinary self-confidence and ease with difference, when contrasted to Truman's need to prove himself to others and distrust of difference, ended up mattering. At stake was nothing less than the future of the international system. Costigliola suggests that had FDR mentored Truman while he was still vice president, or had FDR lived a few more years, the rupture in the alliance that ultimately became the Cold

War might have been avoided or at least mitigated. His essay sheds a new perspective on a fierce debate among students of foreign relations. It also offers a valuable framework for demarcating the course of presidential agency over the history of that office. Scholars must be attuned to critical junctures and consider how presidents handle these rare moments. In doing so, they will benefit by weighing the personal characteristics that are formed long before presidents set foot in the Oval Office.

Economic crises, like critical junctures in international systems, present another kind of opportunity for presidents to assert their agency in a context relatively unconstrained by prevailing structural constraints. One of the most distinctive tools available to presidents in the twentieth century has been rhetorical—shaping and controlling the story of what happened, who caused it, and what needs to be done to restore the nation to economic health. Alice O'Connor compares presidential responses to three of the most devastating economic calamities of the twentieth century: the Great Depression of the 1930s; the Great Inflation of the 1970s; and the recent "Deep Recession" begun in 2008. O'Connor recounts the key components of Franklin D. Roosevelt's and Ronald Reagan's transformative responses and questions why such a gifted orator as Barack Obama has failed to craft a similar transformative narrative and policy response. O'Connor concedes that the degree of difficulty is higher for President Obama, who operates in a far more bitter and evenly divided partisan environment and has inherited a permanent electoral campaign footing (going back to Reagan) that slices and dices constituencies in ways that undermine broad ideological appeals, even to a president's own base. Yet O'Connor ultimately places the blame squarely on Obama himself. President Obama failed to craft a compelling explanation for the crisis and, perhaps more importantly, has refused to embrace an overarching public philosophy, perhaps fearful that doing so would alienate key constituencies. Second, O'Connor argues, President Obama has failed to delineate a broad vision of economic citizenship comparable to Roosevelt's "forgotten man" or Reagan's call to release the economic power of individual citizens by getting government off their backs. Finally, in O'Connor's opinion, President Obama has simply aimed too low. Both Roosevelt and Reagan proved transformative because their narratives contributed to an ambitious set of policies that sought to make the impossible inevitable. In light of Steve Skowronek's provocative claim that the very scope of presidential ambition is defined in part by the degree to which a united intellectual community can craft the historical justification for the kind of ambition that O'Connor is calling for, might the long absence of historians from the field of presidential studies be another, albeit indirect, contributing factor?

CHAPTER 1

The Unsettled State of Presidential History

STEPHEN SKOWRONEK

Historians contemplating a return to the study of the presidency will want to think about what has been going on in their absence. Presidential history is vital to work in a variety of disciplines, and recasting that history has been a central concern of many for some time. Alternative renditions of the broad sweep of affairs are now readily available, and they seem to be accumulating at a rapid clip. If energy and creativity are indicative of the state of a field, presidential history has been thriving.

By these same indicators, however, the historians' input has sorely been missed. Storylines are proliferating because a long-dominant understanding of the relationship between past and present has lost its grip and because precepts essential for reassessing that relationship have been thrown up for grabs. Efforts to revise the conventional wisdom began decades ago, but scholars find themselves today farther than ever from a shared framework for discussion or a common understanding of the nature of the problem. I doubt that the return of the historians can remedy this situation all at once or all on its own, but I do think that their absence from the debate has made it easier for the rest of us to assume our scattered positions. By the same token, it seems to me that historians contemplating reentry into the field face a threshold question: Do they intend merely to stake out a bit of ground for themselves, or do they intend to deploy the tools of their trade to recast the terrain more broadly? Stated differently, will theirs be just another voice or will it be a clarifying voice?

"Presidential history" encompasses a number of related enterprises. It might be useful at the outset to array the literature along a continuum, with the history of the *presidency* on one side and the history of the *presidents* on the other. There are no stark divides along this line, no clear demarcations where questions about institutional structure end and questions about the agents begin. How the history of the institution is narrated depends a lot on how the contributions of individual incumbents are interpreted, and how the contributions of individual incumbents are interpreted depends a lot on how we understand the institution and its place in the larger governing scheme. Nonetheless, each pole anchors a distinct set of concerns.

Not long ago, the history of the presidents appeared the more imperiled of these projects. The turn to social and cultural understandings of the past stigmatized "great man" approaches to the American experience and laid siege to their narrow conception of politics. But work at this pole has proven resilient, and in recent years its public profile has been soaring. Whatever its limitations, the history of the presidents claims a clear and compelling unit of analysis, and that is no small asset. Incumbency is easily delineated; even the broader construct of a presidential "administration" has relatively clear boundaries. Presidents appear one at a time for a set term, and their tenure in office has a straightforward narrative structure. They are selected in elections that periodically mobilize and crystallize national sentiments. They represent the nation, both internally and externally, as high officers of state. They hold potent powers, the exercise of which becomes the focal point of national political contention and invariably changes politics moving forward. In the end, when achievements and failures are assessed in summary form, each agent encapsulates a unique episode, and each episode becomes an emblem of its time.

No one today will defend a presidential "synthesis" of American history, but the history of the presidents appears to have adjusted to its status as one point of access among others, and it continues to demonstrate its capacity to ferret out issues that bear more or less directly on present-day concerns. Interest in interrogating, reconstructing, and redeploying the reputations of our presidents seems inexhaustible, and far from undermining the program, the controversies sparked by these ever-changing depictions are precisely what sustain it. No doubt, the safest bet for a group of historians seeking to reengage with presidential history would be to join the work at this pole and pull a broader range of social and cultural issues into its orbit.

The chief concerns of this essay lie at the other pole of research in the field, the history of the office. The issues encountered on this side of the continuum are harder to tame. The history of the presidency reaches back to the early formation of nation-states and the operation of executive power in monarchical empires, and it sprawls forward from the American Founding across more than two centuries of political change and institutional reform.[1] In this history, the unit of analysis is the primary sticking point. The rejection of executive independence during the American Revolution and its rehabilitation just a few years later in the Constitution created an office of uncertain character and scope. Of all the Framers' improvisations, this was the most inscrutable. Scholars have long tried to divine "general political tendencies" from the reverse double flip that produced the American presidency, but the issues that beset work on the history of the office today are a sobering reminder of the opacity and irresolution of that founding sequence.[2]

The objective in narrating a history of the office is plain. It is to account for the creation over time of a "presidency-centered" system of government out of a republican tradition deeply suspicious of executive power. Research scouts the relationship between the "modern presidency" at the heart of our contemporary regime and the executive office as it was originally framed by the Constitution. No one doubts the critical significance of this relationship or the urgency of the issues that the development of the office poses for American government as a whole. Everyone is aware that the presidency continues even now to expand its reach.[3] But an assessment of the distance traveled from the point of origin—of the development of the presidency conceptually, operationally, and constitutionally—is only as sturdy as its premises, and present-day controversies have been amplifying the noise at the foundations.

The remarkable thing, perhaps, is that a modicum of consensus once did hold sway over these matters. Then again, the presidency might never have attained the power and position it now holds in American government without a broad and influential cadre of public intellectuals committed to its development and capable of lending legitimacy to its transformation. Between the publication of Woodrow Wilson's *Congressional Government* in 1885 and the publication of James McGregor Burns' *Presidential Government* in 1965, scholarly work on the development of the presidential office employed and elaborated a common understanding of historical problems and latter-day priorities.[4] A shared reading of the relationship between past and present created this field of research, and a timely program for accommodating old institutional arrangements to new governing demands deepened its appeal. Scholars closely tied to the events they were describing set the "rise" of the presidency within a historical framework that was acutely diagnostic, powerfully prescriptive, and sweeping in its conception of the development of American government and politics at large.

It seems unlikely that another construction of the history of the office will attain the commonsense status of the Progressive paradigm. But it is equally unlikely that the work of recasting that history will soon shed its programmatic thrust. Situated between the muddy origins of the office and its sweeping powers in contemporary government, scholarly work on the development of the presidency remains deeply implicated in the controversies that swirl around its operation. This is an instance in which structure so expands the play of agency as to include as a vital component of their interactions the many different communities of scholars currently at work trying to make sense of them. For historians about to reenter this field, the only thing more valuable than a full view of the lay of the land will be a clear sense of their own purposes, of what they themselves have to bring to the table.

The Progressive Paradigm

The Progressive paradigm was constructed on a critical assessment of the Constitution as an instrument of modern government. The foundations of this critique were laid in Woodrow Wilson's blistering assault in *Congressional Government* on the notion that the powers of the nation-state should be divided and held in a timeless balance.[5] The mechanical equilibration of separate authorities was, Wilson claimed, an ideal already antiquated by the time the Constitution made it fundamental law; the Framers' decision to formalize the division in writing was, in his view, "a grievous mistake." It was not just that the written format had locked in an institutional framework that was operationally clumsy and politically conservative. More troubling were the structural distensions and distortions brought about by the changing nature of demands on government. The Progressives' charge was that the Constitution's ingrained checks on concerted action had come to thwart the organic adaptation of government to the exigencies of national development.

At the heart of this critique lay a keen appreciation for the nationalizing thrust of the Union victory in the Civil War and a practical concern that the social and economic transformations of the post–Civil War era had caught American government flatfooted. The urgency of reform was conveyed in apprehension of a developmental impasse, of a mismatch between the organization of state power and the emergent organization of national life, and these anxieties were not easily allayed. They persisted in the face of all evidence of this state's success, seemingly indifferent to the government's achievements in negotiating a string of extraordinary challenges during the first half of the twentieth century. Harold Laski rearticulated the Progressives' angst on the heels of America's triumph in World War II: "A government does not prove its adequacy because it can transcend its own principles in an emergency; its adequacy is born of its ability to prevent the outbreak of emergency. That is the test by which the relationship between the president and Congress must be judged. At the least, there are grounds for grave doubt whether [American government] can meet this test successfully."[6] Richard Neustadt beat the same drum at the height of the Cold War, arguing that "politics as usual" in American government had run afoul of a new age in which crises had become routine.[7] Any reversion to the normal operations of the American system would have to be assiduously resisted, Neustadt warned, for concerted national action was no longer just a sporadic demand.

The turn to the presidency followed on this critique. Progressives identified the presidency as a latent solution to America's developmental problem, an office that had, in its early history, signaled its potential to overcome the obstacles to concerted action and national direction interposed by the original constitutional settlement. This idea may be traced back to Wilson's protégé, Henry Jones Ford. Like Wilson, Ford fretted about the separation of powers and its tendency to enshrine petty bossism in the high affairs of state. But in *The Rise and Growth of American Politics*, Ford pointed to pregnant paradoxes in the promulgation of the Constitution: On one hand, the precautions the Framers had taken to check legislative supremacy with the conservative counterweight of an independent executive "were so effectual that Congress was made an incurably deficient and inferior organ" of national government; on the other hand, by crafting the executive office to contain the powers of the Congress, the Framers had unintentionally positioned the president to become "the master force in the shaping of public policy."[8] For evidence of the presidency's potential to supersede the Constitution's narrowly conceived executive role and to provide direction to the polity as a whole, Ford pointed to the presidencies of Andrew Jackson and Abraham Lincoln. In short order, Theodore Roosevelt elevated that pairing into a "Jackson-Lincoln school" of presidential leadership, a way of thinking about power that he contrasted with subservience to constitutional formalities (the "Buchanan school") and that he elaborated into his own "stewardship theory" of the presidency.[9] Wilson picked up the point in *Constitutional Government in the United States*.[10] Revising his earlier dismissal of the presidential office for lacking the wherewithal to hold its own ground, he now celebrated incumbency as a test of personal skill in overcoming constraints: "His capacity will set the limits."[11] Ford's theme reappears time and again, for example in Walter Lippmann's portrait of the Congress as "a group of blind men in a vast, unknown world" and in Neustadt's famous juxtaposition of the "clerkship" role assigned to the president by the Constitution with present-day demands for the president to assume a leadership role.[12]

Two premises seem to compete in these formulations: one, that the Constitution thwarted necessary action; the other, that the Constitution did not stand in the way of its own reconstruction. The tension between these two claims is elaborated in all latter-day criticism of the Progressive paradigm. The Progressives imagined a fundamental change, "a new declaration of independence," an overthrow of "the monarchy of the Constitution."[13] They wanted to invert institutional relationships as they saw them laid out in the original structure, and, as we will see in a moment, they acknowledged the scope of their ambition by providing a new legitimating framework for presidential power alongside the formal arrangements of the Constitution. But their contention was not just that the old forms needed to be reconstructed; it was also that responsiveness could supersede "formalism" altogether, that reconstruction need not be a belabored, episodic affair tied to the Constitution's imposing amendment procedures. Progressives' designs for the presidency reflected their broader interests in replacing doctrine with performance, originalism with pragmatism, literalism with realism, structure with agency. The reconstruction lay as much in this new approach to governance as in the substance of the changes anticipated, and that distinction did not go unnoticed. Consider the discriminating demur from Franklin Pierce of New York. Pierce accepted the Progressives' diagnosis: "I do not . . . consider our Constitution, framed a hundred and twenty years ago, well suited to the needs of our existing government." But he rejected the Progressives' cure: The Constitution's "rigid provisions are an obstacle to popular government, [but] they should be radically changed by amendment, never by construction or usurpation."[14]

All of this points to the importance of a third pillar in the Progressive paradigm: popular sovereignty. Progressive history arrayed constitutional stricture against the democratization of the polity, and it linked forceful assertions of presidential power to great democratizing movements. Ford set the frame for this argument as well: In electing Andrew Jackson, the people "lay hold of the presidency as the only vehicle sufficient for the exercise of their sovereignty."[15] In the great democratic advances of the nineteenth century, the presidency represented "the work of the people breaking through the constitutional form."[16] Identifying the presidency as an instrument of popular rule, the Progressives linked the construction of a new presidency-centered government to the creation of a more vibrant national politics and a more responsible democracy.[17] To be sure, they did not have much use for the received forms of popular rule. Progressives identified the party machinery as outmoded reinforcement for localism and particularism, and they rejected the aggregation of public opinion from the bottom up. Still, the invention of parties and the prior association of presidential power with successful partisan insurgencies were integral to the Progressives' project. That history indicated that presidential power could be safely liberated from its constitutional straitjacket and hitched in a more open-ended fashion to democratically determined purposes.[18]

The pivotal role assigned to the presidency in the construction of a new, less encumbered democracy was derived from its singularity as a national office. As the president represented the whole, he was the one most likely to respond to new expressions of the interests of the whole. By tying the president's powers more directly to public opinion at large, Progressives sought both to magnify them and to make them more responsible. As Wilson put it, "His is the only national voice in affairs. Let him once win the admiration and confidence of the country, and no other single force can withstand him, no combination of forces will easily overpower him."[19] Public opinion was, in the Progressives' view, eminently practical; it could not be "hypnotized and scared into accepting traditional constitutionalism as the final word in politics."[20] By the same token, public opinion took on considerable importance in the Progressive worldview as a regulator of governmental action. To render constitutional relationships malleable, the president would need to mobilize popular support and to articulate public opinion. The Progressive president would cut through blockages in the institutional system only insofar as he was able to capture and convey "the common meaning of the common voice."[21] Institutionalizing leadership of this sort, making the mobilization and articulation of public opinion an integral part of the incumbent's job description, recast the authority of the office. The constitutional clerk was transformed into a political leader by harnessing the powers of the office to a different system of accountability. Theodore Roosevelt pushed this point to its logical extreme when, at the height of the Bull Moose campaign, he endorsed the recall of presidents who had lost the confidence of the people.[22]

The final pillar in the Progressive paradigm—its repositioning of administrative power around the authority of experts—was similarly conceived. Over the course of the nineteenth century, administrative positions had become the linchpin of state operations in America, and the Progressives saw plainly the central role they played in the interactions among the branches and levels of the constitutional system. They depicted the old order as a patronage machine that kept the national orientation of the presidency submerged in congressional and local interests, and they asserted time and again that nothing new could take hold in American government until that machinery was dislodged. But eager as they were to cut party ties to administration and to liberate the presidency from the party bosses, Progressives remained wary of the separation of powers. Their ideas about collective responsibility were different than those incorporated into the patronage state, but they fashioned their new bureaucracies to accord with a similar preference for power sharing. (Consider in this regard Neustadt's famous depiction of the constitutional design as a system of "separate institutions sharing powers.")

Just as surely as they wanted to elevate the authority of administrative experts and to break from the patronage state, the Progressives sought to ease inter-branch conflicts and promote in their stead institutional coordination and cooperative management. The patronage system was to be superseded by another equally attuned to the extraconstitutional values of "unity and harmony."[23] In these respects, administrative authority and public opinion went hand in hand in the Progressive framework. Both instruments aided the cause of presidential leadership by making it at once more effective and more collective. On both counts, Progressives externalized the rationale for constructing a presidency-centered government: The modern president would not direct affairs at will; he would orchestrate the work of the whole according to commonly recognized and externally verifiable standards. The value of mediation in the Progressive construction of modern presidency is notable today for what it avoided—a simple invocation of prerogative. These, after all, were the reformers who riddled American government with independent boards and regulatory commissions. In their quest for consensus and cooperative management, Progressives repeatedly violated hierarchical principles of executive organization. When Roosevelt's Commission on Administrative Management recommended consolidating the new bureaucracies under presidential control, James Landis, a leading proponent of Progressive administration, recoiled. He repudiated the commission's report for its retrograde formalism and recommended, as a first step in thinking about modern administration, a break from antiquated, fetishistic attachments to the notion that government had to be compartmentalized into three, and only three, branches.[24] The Progressive president was not to be in charge of administration so much as he was to be surrounded by administration and informed by administrators speaking with authority of a different kind. Administration was to be repositioned in government as a repository of independent agents capable of deriving the public interest objectively and of impressing it on Congress and president alike. Replacing the binding ties of party with the binding ties of administration was an encompassing project which extended deep into society itself. The new guidance system was, like the old, organized outside as well as inside the formal structure of the government. The Progressives' "parastate"—think tanks, graduate schools, information clearing houses, churches, and professional associations—was both a refinery for distilling public opinion into practical programs for action and a recruitment pool for administrative personnel who would carry the ideology of national service into governmental affairs.[25]

Though the President's Commission overreached with proposals for hierarchical command and control, other premises—that the president needed "help," that help should take the form of "honest brokerage" and "neutral competence"—were more widely accepted. By "institutionalizing" the presidency around these norms, Progressives sought to anchor executive direction of the whole on the common ground of reason and knowledge; the "presidential branch," like the bureaucracy at large, was to be professionalized and to that extent collectivized. The constituent parts of the new Executive Office—the Bureau of the Budget, the Council of Economic Advisors, the National Security Council—provided the forecasting, planning, and monitoring services required to bring all relevant authorities onto the same page and to coordinate their actions. President Truman famously resisted the creation of the NSC, viewing it as an insult to the constitutional independence of the president within his own sphere. But the independence of the president was not what the Progressives were after. Charles Merriam, a member of the Brownlow Commission, elevated the value of "prudence" over autonomy and pluralism over hierarchy.[26] The prudential ideal was served by drawing the leader out of the narrow confines of his office, impressing him with all viewpoints, and keeping him abreast of best practices. Full engagement with others was the essence of the Progressive presidency. As Richard Neustadt saw it, the modern president was ill advised to rely on his constitutional position alone. He had to be political entrepreneur. He had to rely first and foremost on his persuasive skills; he had to convince relatively independent actors in a variety of different spheres to follow his lead.

Post-Progressive History

The Progressive paradigm rode a sea change in the functions and operations of American government. Culturally, it helped make sense of the "rise" of the presidency, and it offered assurances that the break with traditional practices was essential to the further expression of shared values. Analytically, it bifurcated presidential history, setting modern practices off from older ways of governing. It stigmatized received conceptions of power, accountability, and responsibility; recast governmental operations around the promise of leadership; and reconceived the political and institutional foundations of legitimacy.

Through the middle decades of the twentieth century, criticism of the Progressive paradigm followed fairly predictable lines. Conservatives from the 1940s through the 1960s invoked the original Constitution against the specter of bureaucratic regimentation and unwarranted executive imposition. They defended the formal design of the government as protection for congressional prerogatives, limited government, and the representation of local interests.[27] Progressives took these criticisms in stride. The promise of a new democracy and an enlightened administration offered a full and potent rebuttal. More worrisome were the concerns voiced by Edward Corwin about executive overreach in wartime and its implications for the future of constitutional government.[28] These concerns acknowledged much of the developmental teleology the Progressives had established, and as Progressive expectations of presidency-centered government became harder to square with the actions of presidents themselves, demurs of that sort grew louder. Still, there was no fundamental rethinking of the Progressive paradigm until the Vietnam War.

We can now date this turn precisely. On April 27, 1967, the leading light of progressive historians, Arthur Schlesinger Jr., wrote in his journal: "The irony is that all of us for years have been defending the presidential prerogative and regarding the Congress as a drag on policy. It is evident that this delight in a strong presidency was based on the fact that, up to now, strong presidents in American history have pursued policies of which we approved. We are now confronted by the anomaly of a strong presidency using these arguments to pursue a course which, so far as I can see, can only lead to disaster."[29] A few years later, Schlesinger published *The Imperial Presidency*, a history of presidential power laying out the dynamics of executive aggrandizement and institutional overreach that had led the Republic, step by step, into a constitutional crisis.[30]

Schlesinger's sober second look at the history of the office punctuated important disciplinary shifts. The encompassing community of scholars that had constructed the Progressive paradigm was scattering. Historians were already well along in debunking the Progressive story line, and replacing it with New Left and corporate-liberal interpretations of power. Among political scientists, Schlesinger's soul searching resonated more deeply, perhaps because it was harder for them to change the subject. Setting out to determine what had gone wrong with the great transformation, political scientists recast presidential history around the theme of shortfall, around the failure to realize Progressive aspirations.

Reeling from the traumas of the Johnson and Nixon years, this work turned the focus of criticism away from the Constitution and directed it toward the modern presidency itself. In these new assessments, it was not the Framers who had made a "grievous mistake" but those latter-day reformers who had treated the structure of the Constitution as if were fungible. But because this was largely a shift in the relative values assigned to the old arrangements and the new, many of the key assumptions of prior thinking about presidential history were carried into the new critique more or less intact. By and large, these studies did not take issue with the notion that categorical changes in the demands placed on government in the first half of the twentieth century required a reconstruction of some sort, nor with the notion that the presidency was the natural centerpiece of this reconstruction, nor with the notion that the history of the office was discontinuous, with modern practices departing categorically from traditional practices. The difference was that Progressives had written their history with eyes forward, as a story of possibility, while the post-Progressive histories were looking back to explain seemingly deranged results. Summary judgment of the Progressives' handiwork was rendered by Theodore Lowi: "power invested, promise unfulfilled."[31] What had been the institutional solution to America's developmental problem was recast in these histories as the central problem of the day.

The new disposition brought structure and agency together with grim diagnostics. Explanations were suffused throughout with the irony of good intentions and a not-so-subtle sense of betrayal. Scholars pointed to high but flawed ambitions, to a reconstruction rife with unfortunate tradeoffs and unintended consequences, to a "Second Republic" categorically different from the first but unable to stand its own test of legitimacy.[32] The critics deflated the reputation of Woodrow Wilson and rehabilitated the insights of James Madison.[33] They exposed the limits of pragmatism as a standard of rule, underscored the difficulties of adapting old forms to new functions, and lamented values forever lost in the transition from traditional to modern operations.

The new thinking was derivative, in the sense that it took its cues from what the Progressives had promised. Nonetheless, it was comprehensive. It tested the Progressives' brief for the modern presidency conceptually, empirically, and theoretically. In no small measure, this testing became a proving ground within political science for new "historical-institutional approaches" to thinking about political development more generally. Presidential history appeared the perfect site for investigating problems of transition; analytic leverage was drawn from the identification of generic difficulties that are likely to complicate any negotiated shift from one institutional ordering to another.

For example, Jeffrey Tulis's *The Rhetorical Presidency* posed the problem of "layering."[34] Tulis credited the Progressives with a powerful critique of the Constitution and a timely reconception of the presidential office. The problem, as he saw it, was that Progressives did not follow through and replace the constitutional scheme outright. Their confidence in institutional adaptation and their innovations on behalf of a new democracy overrode sober consideration of the obstacles they faced in reorienting the old governmental system around presidential leadership, public opinion, and programmatic direction. As it happened, their reforms left in place arrangements of power that had been promulgated to prevent exactly what they were trying to promote. Because new practices and expectations were simply layered over the old forms, modern presidents were left "to inhabit an office structured by two systemic theories."[35] Modern practices subverted inter-branch relations as they had been inscribed in the original frame, and the original structure of inter-branch relations subverted modern methods of inducing programmatic action.

Terry Moe lighted upon a similar problem, the problem of conversion.[36] The Progressives wanted to foster greater cooperation in government by building up intermediary institutions that would operate on the basis of neutral competence, objective diagnosis, expert prescription, and service to the government as a whole. But converting the old system of institutional divisions and checks on power was a daunting task, and Moe saw that the projection of the president into a new position of prominence in democratic politics had made the change all the more difficult. As the governing responsibilities and public exposure of the presidency increased, so too did the pressure on the president to perform and deliver results. Because the new system juxtaposed a term-limited president against a permanent bureaucracy, the incumbent's demand for "responsive competence" overwhelmed Congress's interest in, and provision for, neutral services. Agencies that Congress had installed in the Executive Office to coordinate and harmonize the operations of government were gradually redeployed by presidents to promote their own interest in political vindication, and the informational advantages they afforded became tools of presidential manipulation. What Moe called the "politicization" of the modern presidency entailed the downgrading of presidential offices organized around professional standards and the expansion of presidential offices that ran on political ambition alone. That shift evoked an in-kind response. Congress began to dismiss the findings of fact presented by the president's administrators and to create a counter-organization under its own control to provide expert guidance, professional advice, and surveillance services. Congressional budget committees, the Congressional Budget Office, the special prosecutor, the installation of inspectors general throughout the bureaucracy—all of it served to redraw the lines of institutional combat and to turn the new bureaucracy into a battleground for political control.[37]

Sidney Milkis pointed to another problem endemic to a systemic transformation of institutional operations: the problem of displacement.[38] He observed that when Progressive reformers did manage to dislodge institutional arrangements vital to the operations of the old order, basic values were traded off, and in the long run, the capacities that were lost proved to be as significant as those that were gained. Try as they might to cast "enlightened administration" and leadership of national opinion as democratic substitutes for the traditional party ties, the Progressives' program undercut institutional connections that had linked federal power to local participatory organizations. Building up administrative power without providing the electorate with an equally potent mechanism for holding that power to account created an executive that was dangerously out of balance. Worse yet, the progressives left the polity disengaged just as the government was coming to exercise more direct control over social and economic life. When the party democracy of the nineteenth century was superseded by the presidential democracy of the twentieth, one set of limitations was replaced by another.

Empirical findings accumulated alongside this inventory of developmental problems, and these too pivoted off progressive assumptions. Post-Progressive political science scrutinized presidential efforts to mobilize national sentiments, to "go public" in generating support for action in the Congress, to foster a concert of power out of an institutional system built on checks.[39] The book titles tell the tale: *At the Margins: Presidential Leadership of Congress*; *On Deaf Ears: The Limits of the Bully Pulpit*; *Power without Persuasion*; *The Myth of Presidential Representation*.[40] The post-Progressive critique of the development of the presidency offered a point-by-point refutation of the ideas and aspirations that had guided thinking about the office from Wilson to Neustadt. Showing that the limitations of original constitutional structure were not so easily finessed, this critique forced to the fore some hard questions about change over time: Will arrangements carried over from the past always thwart and distort the designs of institutional reformers? At what point does the insinuation of new ideals into old institutional arrangements place the entire governmental system at cross purposes? Does the modern presidency have defensible foundations or any principled coherence at all?

The vulnerabilities of this line of scholarship were equally significant. Pointing out the shortfall from Progressive standards sufficed as a common project for the field only so long as no one was proposing alternative standards for evaluating the operations of the modern presidency. Moreover, documenting the derangement of "new ways" placed a heavy burden on contrasts drawn with the "old ways." That is to say, attributing a more principled coherence to American government before the rise of the modern presidency disrupted things all but invited closer scrutiny of those halcyon days of yore.

But most troubling of all, the post-Progressive critique did not point beyond the intractable problems it exposed. Elaborating on all the pitfalls that are likely to accompany efforts at a systemic reordering of institutions did little to encourage further talk of remedial action. The post-Progressive critics did not propose going back to the government's original ideals, for they thought that the Progressive reformers had been essentially correct in their diagnosis of the limitations of the old order. Nor did they offer a clear way forward, for their central insight was that institutional tinkering creates as many problems as it solves. Lacking faith in reform but unwilling to disavow it, the critics constructed a history of hand-wringing dilemmas.

A Seamless History of Presidentialism

While disillusioned Progressives were disabusing us of faith in the modern presidency, other scholars were contemplating a far more radical revision of the progressive paradigm, one that would dispense altogether with the idea of a "modern" office distinct in its foundations and organization from "traditional" practices and constitutional norms. This was, in part, "thinking outside the box," an attempt to advance the field by breaking down the analytic categories that had long organized research. But it was also an attempt to repackage the subject. No longer presented as a critique of the Constitution and the thinking of the Framers, the power of the modern presidency was recast as an expression of original principles and an affirmation of the formal constitutional design.

The bifurcation of presidential history into modern and traditional periods, a common feature of Progressive and post-Progressive scholarship, served to call attention to the novelty of the president's power and position in contemporary American government.[41] Dissolving that divide has become a way of preempting second thoughts about the wisdom of the departure. Demonstrating that there was no categorical change, that the way things are now is much the same as they have always been, serves to bolster faith in an office that otherwise looks like it has fallen into a perpetual state of controversy. David Nichols gave the myth-busting of post-Progressive scholarship this new twist by taking aim directly at *The Myth of the Modern Presidency*.[42] Nichols argued that Progressives and their critics had seriously misconstrued the office of the presidency as it is found in the Constitution and, by extension, had misread the relationship between original forms and current practices. Going further, he chalked up the latter-day disappointment with presidential performance to extraneous norms and standards carried into analysis by Progressive reformers themselves. Presidents, he concludes, can be labeled "modern" only to the extent that "they fail to live up to expectations created by the 'modern presidency.'"[43]

There are now several different strands of scholarship revisiting the early American presidency to reconfigure the relationship between the present and the past. In political science, much of this work has an open-ended cast; it expresses a newfound willingness to put the rationale for a modern-traditional divide in the history of the office to the test. For example, John Woolley charges that the "modern presidency" construct has become a methodological crutch, an excuse not to examine earlier practices more carefully. He looks forward to a more candid assessment of whether and to what extent modern practices are in fact a departure from traditional norms: "The bodies of research available suggest *none* of the following: a dramatic change at some specific point in time, dramatic reduction in the variability among modern presidents, or enduring enhancement—or decline—in the influence of modern presidents."[44] Woolley's recommendations follow the canons of good science: expose assumptions, discard those that cannot be supported, expand the data base.

Progressives were aware of precursors. Indeed, they cultivated the reputations of Hamilton, Jackson, and Lincoln and incorporated their examples into what they hoped would become a new standard. Extending the emergence of modern practices backward in time and filling in the gaps can go a long way toward blurring historical divides, even when the intention is to describe the cumulative result as the construction of a new and different office.[45] Along these lines, recent scholarship has detailed the premodern development of presidential claims to an electoral mandate, backfilling the president's connections to programmatic action from Jefferson to McKinley.[46] It has reached back to the nineteenth century to trace the long-term processes by which institutional norms and expectations now associated with "presidential government" were created.[47] It has examined the practices of "proto-modern" presidents who sought to define a leadership role for the office before that role became institutionalized.[48]

Safe to say now, there was no "dramatic change at some specific point in time"; there is no clear demarcation between "old ways" and "new ways." But while some are smoothing the developmental timeline, others are leveling it. History-as-development now competes with history-as-just-more-of-the same. Along these lines, Daniel Galvin and Colleen Shogan argue that most telling tests of the distinction between modern and traditional practices lie in close examination of leadership by the lesser lights of the nineteenth century. They find that John Tyler, James Polk, and Rutherford Hayes all politicized executive branch operations and centralized power in a quest for administrative control, and they conclude that these practices, lamented by the post-Progressive critics as products of the twisted course of twentieth-century institution building, are "neither distinctly modern nor particularly extraordinary."[49] Mel Laracey offers a similar view of presidential communication. Questioning Tulis's claim that nineteenth-century presidents implicitly acknowledged a constitutional proscription against "going public," he surveys the many ways in which early incumbents impressed the public with their policy preferences and documents their extensive use of the partisan press, in particular, for this purpose.[50] Again, the implication is that there was no latter-day reconception of the president's role or reconstruction of the office. On these accounts, change reflects the new technologies available for advancing the presidents' abiding interests.

On the empirical side, breaking down the modern/traditional divide in presidential history is a research frontier and a work in progress. Identifying practices in earlier days that were functionally equivalent to what we observe today only goes so far in refuting claims that presidential history is about development and that the changes negotiated over time have been fundamental. One may well still ask whether those early cognates were more compatible with the Constitution's original design—less destabilizing to other institutions and relationships—than the practices that replaced them.[51] But this is only one front on which the bifurcation of presidential history has been challenged in recent years. The main line of action coincides with a concerted move by constitutional lawyers into the field of presidential history, in particular with the elaboration in conservative legal circles of the "unitary theory of the executive."

The unitary theory marks an abrupt turn back to formalism in thinking about the history of the office. It strips the case for presidential power of all latter-day appeals to realism, pragmatism, and invention, anchoring it instead in a few doctrinal claims about the "structural Constitution," that is, about the separation of powers and the prerogatives granted to each of the three departments.[52] In this recasting, sweeping assertions of executive power and presidential control in contemporary American government follow directly from the initial warrants of the office; they are consistent with the intentions of the Framers and the understandings of those who ratified their handiwork. The office did not have to catch up with the development of the nation; rather, the development of nation finally caught up with the capacious provisions for executive power in the Constitution. And because the political role assigned to modern presidents did not formally supersede the executive role assigned by Article II, there is no reason to apply new standards to its operations.

The unitary theory harbors a seamless history of the presidency, a history in which incumbents have proven their fealty to the Constitution by persistently defending the separation of powers and resisting the encroachments of other authorities. In the leading treatment, Steven Calabresi and Christopher Yoo have examined presidential power administration by administration from George Washington to George W. Bush to show that every incumbent—not just the strong or the great—has aggressively asserted his authority to remove and to direct executive branch subordinates.[53] Their point is that there has been no acquiescence in the derogation of these powers and that latter-day practices that have modified or qualified them are not dispositive. As Calabresi and Yoo observe, "The uniformity of the historical record . . . contradicts the claims of scholars who have argued that the growth in presidential power justifies Congress's placing greater limits on presidential control over the execution of the law."[54]

The unitary theorists are to the early twenty-first century what the Progressive theorists were to the early twentieth. They are a coherent and purposeful intellectual cadre possessed of an expansive conception of the president's governing role. They resemble their early-twentieth-century counterparts as well in offering a timely response to political developments in the nation at large. Their theory paced the rise of a conservative political insurgency out to recast the priorities of the national government and the electoral success of conservative candidates for the presidency. More generally, it has sought to accommodate the nation to the predilection of contemporary incumbents for independent action.

Because the new conservatives share with the old Progressives an expansive conception of the president's office, it is not at first clear what might have compelled them to write a new history and to tell a different story. The question calls attention back to the terms and conditions that Progressives attached to their advocacy and, in that sense, the new story line sheds fresh light on the meaning of the old. The Progressives had invoked public opinion to serve as a new foundation for presidential leadership, but that has little to offer ambitious presidents at a time when national opinion divides evenly or tilts against their designs. Progressives advocated intermediary authorities to foster collective responsibility and to bridge the separation of powers, but that has little to offer ambitious presidents at a time when the parties are polarized and governmental control is politically divided. The Progressives stood for flexibility, invention, and pragmatism in dealing with emergent problems of institutional design, but this license for experimentation was not restricted, and much of the creativity in the last quarter of the twentieth century was aimed at reining in perceived presidential excess. The unitary theory avoids these traps in the Progressive paradigm by pulling the powers of the modern presidency back into the Constitution and then advancing them anew behind timeless precepts of legitimate national government. The standards it sets forth for evaluating presidential powers are not only different; they also effectively invalidate the legitimating standards on which those powers had previously expanded.

There is, then, no simple way to situate the unitary theory in relation to the scholarly disputes of the twentieth century. Previously, the case for expansive presidential powers was externalized and placed on extraconstitutional foundations; now it is internalized and insulated from extraconstitutional authority. That cuts equally against the appeal of Progressives to supersede constitutional formalism with new thinking about democratic accountability and collective responsibility and against the appeal of twentieth-century conservatives who invoked constitutional formalities against the threat of bureaucratic regimentation and executive imposition. The new synthesis thoroughly scrambles the field: It locates the modern departure from original conceptions of the presidential office not in the expansion of its reach but in more recent efforts to limit and to control it. The result is an arresting marriage of formalism and constitutionalism with presidentialism and unilateralism.

The unitarians agree with post-Progressive critics that political development has led to a sorry derangement of American institutions, but they explain the wayward course of affairs very differently.[55] Problems were not created by layering a more powerful presidency over a governmental system designed with other ends in view; they were created by reforms that sapped the office of the independent powers that adhere to the Vesting Clause of Article II and to the president's oath of office. Indifference to the accountability and responsibility lodged in a unitary executive fostered the growth of a bloated and uncontrolled bureaucracy. Misguided improvisations insulated administrative officers from presidential direction, subjected the president to "independent" prosecutors, and compromised unified command and control of the executive branch. These problems were compounded by court rulings from *Humphrey's Executor v. United States* to *Morrison v. Olson* that have limited the ability of the president to "execute the office" and to assume responsibility for its affairs.[56]

This new disposition is acutely diagnostic, powerfully prescriptive, and paradigmatic in its reconfiguration of the relationship between past and present. But it is not a bid for scholarly consensus. The unitary theory is scholarly agency on steroids, a lawyer's brief addressed to judges who will hear cases in dispute; the intent is to "set the stage for several legal claims that presidents may want to make."[57] To do so, the theory doubles down on the most inscrutable moment in the history of the presidential office, the moment of its inception, and it stakes out an uncompromising position on the most sensitive points. In determining the scope and legitimate application of presidential power, John Yoo pushes discussion back to the history of the executive in England prior to the Constitutional Convention in America.[58] The theory boils to a set of historical claims about how that prior history of prerogative survived the Revolutionary sequence. The key assertion is that the deep aversion to the executive evident in the post-Independence interregnum was jettisoned during the promulgation of the Constitution and extinguished by the ratification debates, that in adopting a new government organized around separate branches, each endowed with the wherewithal to protect its own prerogatives, the American people repaired to, and in modified form adopted, common European understandings of what an independent executive entailed.[59]

Alexander Hamilton made a similar argument in 1793.[60] James Madison countered, arguing that the relevance of monarchical precedent to the American presidency was "a field of research which is more likely to perplex than to decide."[61] So it remains today.[62] In the new cottage industry of refutations, the histories of Louis Fisher are perhaps the best indicator of the current state of play. Fisher too invokes an uncompromising formalism, but his reading of the original design cuts very differently. In a history of the war power, Fisher reviews the evidence from the Revolutionary sequence and weighs it heavily against today's unitarians.[63] Finding that the overwhelming preponderance of war power was given intentionally to the Congress, he plows through the post-Constitutional history of presidential assertions to the contrary as an open-and-shut case of usurpation. Notably, Fisher's formalism is equally hard on progressive history; he sees no improvement in a bifurcated historical frame in which modern practices claim pragmatic ground and operate in accord with other standards.[64] As he presents it, Progressives and conservatives have each conspired to dislodge the Congress from its designated role as the keystone of the American constitutional system.

Pick and Choose

The unitary theorists have transformed the field of presidential history by exposing the doctrinal controversies at its core. This has sharpened the implications of foundational disputes, spurred a search for alternative formulations, and turned the field of presidential history into a mirror of the unsettled state of American politics at large. On the positive side, there is now less about the past that can be taken for granted and more that is open to fresh examination. Practitioners today are in full recasting mode. New story lines are appearing at such a rapid clip that it is hard to know which way to turn.

Consider two recent offerings, both of which repackage some familiar themes in strikingly new ways. In *The Executive Unbound: After the Madisonian Republic,* legal scholars Eric Posner and Adrian Vermeule express impatience with the resurgence of constitutional debates about the presidential office and propose a radical hyperrealism for thinking about the expansion of presidential power.[65] The authors draw on Carl Schmitt's critique of "legal liberalism"—of the failure of the rule of law to deal with the "state of exception"—to explain why formalism fails as a guide to the development of modern practices. Their historical argument is that public opinion has been the only effective constraint on presidential power; their normative argument is that in a robust democracy like ours, public opinion is the only constraint that is really necessary. This is Progressivism unhinged: It dispenses with niceties of constitutional design, turns opinion into the sole arbiter of power, and justifies presidential supremacy.

In *The Decline and Fall of the American Republic,* Bruce Ackerman offers a very different assessment.[66] Ackerman tracks institutional changes that have fostered extremism in the presidency and derangements of power throughout the executive branch. In light of his prior theorizing about the central role played by the president in the periodic regeneration of American government and democracy, Ackerman's turnabout is as stunning as Schlesinger's own volte-face a generation earlier. But Ackerman does more in this book than simply add his voice to the chorus of disillusioned Progressives. He is a discriminating critic of the development of the office, and he sees contemporary problems in their full variety. In one sphere, the military, he finds an officer corps emboldened by public respect for the authority of experts and the credentials of professionalism. Generals now routinely enter the public domain and assess the national interest in their own voice, and Ackerman reckons media solicitation of their independent judgment a threat to unitary command and control under the president. In another sphere, the Justice Department, he finds just the opposite. There, a thoroughly politicized presidency has compromised professionalism, undermined the independent authority of the government's lawyers, and turned neutral service into presidential power-mongering. As Ackerman sees it, the deployment of all the legal resources of the executive branch behind the president's constitutional pretensions now threatens the rule of law. Constitutional standards and Progressive values seem to be going haywire simultaneously in this formulation, but Ackerman refuses to throw up his hands in despair. Still a progressive at heart, he improvises a different remedy for each of the institutional perversions he identifies. His problem-solving patchwork is the most compelling aspect of the book, for now pragmatism and invention are enlisted to repair the damage to constitutional principles they had earlier worked to pull apart.

These are committed scholars. The positions they are staking out are deeply held, thoughtfully crafted, and worthy of careful consideration. But rather than reorder the field, position taking of this sort now exposes its disarray. Each formulation operates in its own political universe; each is a paradigm unto itself. All point to a way forward, but no one seems to be falling into line. Scholars are, at once, responding to the absence of clear standards of governmental action and demonstrating the difficulties of establishing any consensus on what they should be.

So what will the historians make of this rather urgent situation? Their newfound interest in presidential history could not come at a more opportune time. But the ambition to recast has been afoot for quite a while, and the results thus far have yet to add up to much more than a restatement of the problem. Much depends on how those now proposing to enter the field understand themselves as a community of scholars, how they perceive the historian's role and its relationship to the others with a stake in the subject. If there is traction yet to be gained in this field, it probably lies in establishing some common ground for discussion rather than in grand theorizing. The current division of labor among the disciplines may work against finding those synergies, but the best bet for discovering them lies, I suspect, with the historians' craft.

CHAPTER 2

Personal Dynamics and Presidential Transition

The Case of Roosevelt and Truman

FRANK COSTIGLIOLA

One of the major turning points in U.S. history was the death of Franklin D. Roosevelt and the replacement of Roosevelt by Harry S. Truman on April 12, 1945. Only days later, a confidant of Prime Minister Winston Churchill remarked: "We are waking up to the fact that Roosevelt's death has changed everything."[1] Gone was the experienced, charismatic, and cosmopolitan New Yorker who was gifted with extraordinary emotional intelligence but was also ground down by ill health. Now the occupant of the Oval Office was an inexperienced, insecure, and parochial former senator from Missouri who was blind to subtleties but who was determined to apply his formidable energy to the new job.

The transition from Roosevelt to Truman was a contingent event with plenty of serious and lasting consequences. The shift entailed a change in the personality of the nation's chief executive at a moment in history when the president enjoyed unusually wide agency in deciding fundamental issues—and when personality figured significantly in those decisions. Deference to the commander-in-chief in wartime, the secrecy facilitated by summit conferences in distant lands, the Democrats' majority in Congress, the public's unfamiliarity with most international issues, and the accelerated changes brought on by the ending of the war and the dropping of the atomic bomb all reduced the usual structural constraints on presidential action.

Roosevelt and Truman differed in their ability to adapt to the opportunities and challenges of this critical historical juncture. While Roosevelt was deeply self-confident and even believed himself to be a man of destiny, Truman suffered from various insecurities—about his height, his meager education, his precarious economic background, his past association with a corrupt political machine, and, most pressing at the time of the transition, his ability to handle the presidency.

A second personal difference had to do with styles of masculinity. An aspect of Roosevelt's broad charismatic appeal was his sinuous and complex gender identity. Thomas "Tommy the Cork" Corcoran, an insider who observed Roosevelt at work and play, later described him as "the most androgynous human being I have ever known in my life."[2] With an unknowable degree of intentionality, FDR sometimes acted in ways that his contemporaries described as feminine. His mellifluous voice, patrician air, and nonstop talk and gesture all connoted effeminacy. Yet his muscular upper torso, developed after contracting polio; his visible courage; and his aura of power also denoted masculinity as it was and is conventionally understood. Roosevelt felt comfortable around women and included them among his closest advisers and confidants. His more flexible gender identity, coupled with his confidence, expanded his repertoire of behaviors while enabling him to take a broader and more inclusive perspective on matters. Truman, by contrast, clung to a more narrow gender identity. He felt most comfortable with other men, particularly those he knew well. He recalled that from an early age, he had had to wear thick glasses. "That's hard on a boy," he later recalled. "It makes him lonely, and it gives him an inferiority complex, and he has a hard time overcoming it. . . . Without my glasses I was blind as a bat, and to tell the truth, I was kind of a sissy."[3] As an adult, Truman was called "little" so often that the word never lost its sting. In his memoir he interjected the subject of height into a discussion of foreign policy. Stalin "was a good six inches shorter than I am," he stressed, while Churchill was three inches shorter than Truman. "Yet I was [supposedly] the little man in stature and intellect!"[4]

The two presidents also diverged in how they reacted to cultural difference, especially in foreigners. As a boy Roosevelt had attended school in Germany and had traveled extensively on the Continent. He picked London for his honeymoon. As president, he enjoyed meeting European royalty, whom he cheekily insisted on calling by their first names. FDR believed that he could sway foreign leaders with the force of his personality—backed by the awesome power of the United States. Truman, after seeing war-torn Europe in World War I, could not wait to get home. On arriving back in New York in 1918, he wrote: "I've nearly promised old Miss Liberty that she'll have to turn around to see me again."[5] Although Truman did his best at the Potsdam summit with Churchill and Stalin, he never overcame his initial impulse: "I hate to go."[6] Afterward he shied away from further meetings with foreign leaders, even those from Britain or Canada.

These differences in personality proved crucial in shaping the nature and extent of the agency at the disposal of each president. The components of FDR's personality served as resources enabling him to craft a wartime alliance that he intended to continue into the postwar period. His emotional intelligence, flexibility, and comfort with cultural differences allowed him to sidestep the barriers erected by the touchy, suspicious, and brutal dictator in the Kremlin. The limits of Truman's background and repertoire of behaviors narrowed his options. The bounds of his personality inclined him against the political, cultural, and emotional risks of sustained engagement with the difficult, seemingly alien Russians. Truman's actions and reactions resulted in a dramatic and long-lasting shift in the international structure that limited the agency of subsequent presidents. In the end, his "good vs. evil" approach helped launch a Cold War that trumped presidential agency for decades to come, foreclosing potential critical junctures and thereby muting the impact of personality on foreign policy.

The differences in personality between Roosevelt and Truman constituted an endogenous contingency, in contrast to such exogenous happenstances as the collapse of Japanese power earlier than Allied leaders had expected. Although American voters had not elected FDR because they could discern his androgynous tendencies or his cultural sophistication, they did perceive and appreciate his flexibility, resourcefulness, and grasp of the big picture. These personal capabilities enabled him to craft New Deal reforms, to ramp up war production, and to plan global strategy. In contrast, Truman's small-bore vision hampered his ability to deal with the challenges that beset his administration. He managed to win election in his own right in 1948 by pitching himself as ordinary, yes, but also as a plucky, no-nonsense common man who had made good. Truman was similarly successful in persuading voters what he, no doubt, also believed: Problems with Moscow stemmed solely from Soviet aggression.

Nevertheless, despite the claims of Truman and his defenders, it was not foreordained that the wartime alliance would collapse. Nor was the all-out militarized struggle of the Cold War inevitable. Rather, the shift in leadership in Washington provided the impetus for these dangerous outcomes. The new president, anxious to prove to himself and to others that he was up to the job of president, resolved not to back down before the brusque Soviets. Truman's sensitivity about his own social standing probably encouraged him to look down at the Russians, who, he explained, "came from the wrong side of the tracks."[7] Roosevelt's self-assurance as a Hudson River aristocrat liberated him from the anxiety of having to measure every interaction in terms of his own pride and respect. Observing that Stalin seemed "too anxious to prove his point," Roosevelt concluded that the dictator "suffered from an inferiority complex."[8] He calculated that playing up to the former revolutionary's craving for respect by, for instance, traveling great distances to the Tehran and the Yalta conferences could reap substantive gains. More cosmopolitan than Truman, Roosevelt took in stride the cultural differences between himself and the Georgian-born Marxist-Leninist dictator. Indeed, FDR sought to align himself with the "oriental gentleman" in the Kremlin in a shared opposition to European colonialism.

FDR's background and experience made him confident that he could accomplish almost anything through persistence, experimentation, guile, and luck. When he had gambled, it had paid off. He had defied polio—and had disguised from the public the severity of his paralysis—to win six straight election victories as governor and as president. "Roosevelt weather"—the sunny skies that prevailed on his election days—had helped snare those victories. In dealing with Congress, he had pivoted to the right and to the left in securing landmark legislation establishing social security and labor rights that had strengthened his political coalition. He believed that he could transcend narrow ideological categories. He had brought the nation out of the Great Depression, or so he could claim. He had shepherded a war-averse nation into a world war and had led it nearly to victory on two global fronts. Of course, Roosevelt's optimism had also led him to overreach, as he had in his court-packing plan and in his effort to purge conservatives in Congress.

By the late war years of 1943–45, Roosevelt was confident—though not certain—that he could work with Stalin to sustain the wartime alliance. He believed that while a certain amount of rivalry and tension between the United States and the Soviet Union was inevitable, the two nations had concrete, overriding interests in common. They, along with Britain, needed to remain together in order to prevent renewed German and Japanese aggression. Roosevelt saw the Soviet Union as a postwar ally also in fostering the gradual breakup of the European colonial empires. He believed that those empires were a dangerous anachronism because they could permanently alienate the "colored races." To head off a future "race war," he believed that it was essential to line up the "partly Asiatic" Soviet Union and China on the side of the United States. A few days after Roosevelt died, his confidant Daisy Suckley jotted in her diary: "F[ranklin] did not have too much faith in Stalin, but he thought that he and Stalin looked at things in the same *practical* way, & for that reason there was much hope that Stalin would follow along."[9] To sustain this practical collaboration, Roosevelt planned on regular, intimate gatherings of the Big Three leaders, preferably in isolated locations such as the Azores. Such summits would constitute the beating heart of their informal organization as they oversaw the transition to a lasting peace and, eventually, a more democratic world order. With an almost boyish enthusiasm Roosevelt welcomed the secretiveness and sense of adventure that enveloped summit conferences.

While American history abounds with examples of presidents in foreign affairs exercising the agency denied them in domestic matters, the World War II era stands out as a time when the president—in this case, a supremely confident man with an outsized personality—enjoyed broad leeway in making momentous decisions reflecting his personal predilections. Moreover, Roosevelt aimed to reduce, at least for the foreseeable future, the structural limits on presidential power. Though FDR valued the United Nations Security Council as an institutionalizing mechanism for Big Power decision making, he privately dismissed the General Assembly as a talk chamber useful only for public relations and as a sop to the non–Big Powers. He agreed with Stalin that being small did not make a country virtuous. Truman, in contrast, valued having the "confidence of the *smaller* nations." Neither Britain nor Russia had that trust. "We have," noted the former senator, who regarded coalition building as morally superior to Big Power deals.[10]

The shift from Roosevelt to Truman would have led to changes in at least the tone of U.S. foreign policy, no matter when the shift took place. But, unfortunately, the Roosevelt-Truman transition occurred at a pivotal moment, when the future of international relations hung in the balance. The wartime alliance had come together only after Nazi Germany had declared war on Britain, then Russia, and then the United States. Germany surrendered a few weeks after FDR's death. The key issue then became: Would the wartime alliance stay together? Or would the coalition fall apart in acrimony and thereby threaten an even worse world war?

The months after Roosevelt died stand out as a critical juncture in world history, a turning point in many ways similar to August 1914, November 1989, and September 2001. At such critical junctures, the otherwise immovable, foundational structures of strategic imperative, political ambition, cultural habit, economic interest, and geographic location suddenly loosen their grip and, like the ground in a massive earthquake, temporarily become plastic. When contingencies are so important—when so much is up for grabs—the personalities of key leaders can make a decisive and lasting difference. In August 1914, the leaders of Europe failed to prevent the long, destructive war that none of them wanted. In September 2001, President George W. Bush and Vice President Dick Cheney decided to react to the terrorist attacks on 9/11 by launching a war in Afghanistan and planning for a war in Iraq instead of focusing on the international criminals, led by Osama bin Laden, who had actually carried out the attack. In November 1989, the endogenous contingency that someone with Mikhail Gorbachev's personality and ideas was in charge in the Kremlin, rather than yet another rigid Communist Party boss, allowed the Berlin Wall to come down and the Cold War to end suddenly and peacefully. So, too, who was in command during the critical months after April 1945 made a crucial difference for future developments. Although tension and rivalry between Russia and the United States after World War II were probably inevitable, a militarized, deadly competition between the two nations might have been avoided.

FDR believed that the Soviets' number one postwar aim was preventing another German invasion of Russia. He also concluded that, because of the movement of armies, Russian postwar domination of Eastern Europe after the war could not be avoided. He often said that, in the effort to prevent that domination, there was no point in going to war or in wrecking the alliance. Roosevelt wanted instead to work with the Russians, to engage them, and to bring them slowly closer to a Western system of values. For his part, Stalin also believed that preventing another German invasion was Russia's number one postwar priority. He repeatedly and publicly stressed that the alliance with America and Britain could hold together if the three agreed on keeping Germany and Japan under control and if they treated each other on an equal basis. Stalin expected that the Soviet Union would indeed dominate Eastern Europe, especially Poland—the invasion route into Russia used twice by the Germans and by Napoleon as well. But that did not necessarily mean excluding the Western allies. On many different occasions and in talks with different groups, both Communists and non-Communists, Stalin stressed, perhaps naively, that postwar Poland could have friendly relations with the United States, Britain, and France—as well as with its main ally, Russia. So there appeared a basis, Roosevelt and Stalin agreed, for a postwar alliance grounded in overlapping interests.

But such postwar collaboration was not a sure thing. Both Roosevelt and Stalin preserved other options. The United States might stay clear of Europe's politics and focus instead on the Western Hemisphere and on global air and sea power. FDR also kept in his vest pocket two ace cards to be played in the future—a postwar loan to help rebuild Russia and a sharing of control over the atomic bomb. Stalin held on to the option of going it alone, of seeking to spread Russian influence and Communist control in Eastern Europe and elsewhere, regardless of American and British opposition. Stalin realized, however, that his nation's chances of preventing a future German attack would be much stronger if he could keep Washington and London as allies. Winston Churchill was readier than either Roosevelt or Stalin to give up on the wartime alliance. He saw the emotionally loaded issue of Russian domination of Poland as a wedge issue that could be used to pry the Americans away from the Russians. As early as 1943, British postwar planners were outlining plans to make the western part of Germany an ally after the war and to use German troops in a possible future conflict with Russia.

Roosevelt expected the crucial test of the wartime alliance to come in the first years after the war. There would be a delicate transition period, during which relations with Russia might sour or might be put on a secure basis. He believed that the immediate postwar period would be, in other words, a critical juncture. During this period it would be necessary for leaders to manage contingencies, tamp down explosive emotions and rhetoric, meet regularly so as to cultivate good personal and political relations, remain open-minded about each other's foreign policy interests and requirements, and not allow smaller nations to play the Big Powers off against each other. A tall order! But necessary, Roosevelt believed, to head off yet another deadly war.

A key component of FDR's emotional intelligence was his instinctive attunement to the culturally and historically conditioned emotional tendencies—what we might call the emotional dispositions—of different countries. Emotional dispositions influence the particular anxieties and concerns of national leaders. U.S. officials (Roosevelt not included) tended to fret over whether others saw them as tough enough. The British, staggering to victory, seemed frantic to assert their national authority. The Soviets suffered and tried to overcompensate for anxiety about their status relative to Western nations. These trends were neither absolute nor exclusive. But like a computer operating system, such tendencies organized more or less inchoate concerns into a pattern of emotionalized political issues.

Russian status anxiety was fed by geography, history, and culture. Soviet officials, despite their proud nationalism, claims of superiority over the decadent West, and leadership of the world's first Marxist state, nevertheless yearned for respect: to be treated as equals and accepted for whom they were. When Roosevelt's emissary asked Stalin's representative what was needed for real collaboration, the Russian "stressed the necessity for mutual respect."[11] In contrast to Truman, Roosevelt's extraordinary self-confidence enabled him to extend that respect without feeling that he was humiliating either himself or the United States, which, after all, was still the most powerful nation in the world.

Thus far we have discussed the differences in personality that made Roosevelt more confident, adaptable, and willing to experiment and learn than Truman. Truman would also learn during his presidency, but the lessons he would imbibe only reinforced the breach between Washington and Moscow that opened during the critical juncture of 1945–46. While Roosevelt and Stalin believed that there existed mutual interests that provided potential for postwar collaboration, there remained a sticking point: the Russians' brutal behavior in Eastern Europe, especially Poland. Roosevelt, with only mixed success, tried to downplay this issue. Truman, in contrast, would seize on the issue as proof that postwar collaboration could not work.

Though the Cold War would eventually become a worldwide conflict, the quarrel that wrecked Allied unity in 1945–46 was the opposition of Washington and London to Moscow's domination of Eastern Europe. Having suffered invasion by Germany twice in less than thirty years, the Russians were determined to have "friendly" governments on their western border, especially in Poland. Given the longstanding hostility toward the Russians felt by many Poles, friendliness toward Moscow and democratic governance were antithetical tendencies. The fate of Poland was a highly emotional issue for all concerned—for Polish patriots determined to regain their freedom, for Russians convinced their blood sacrifice had earned them security, for Britons who had gone to war over Poland, and for those Americans who saw the issue of Polish independence as a matter of right and wrong. Moreover, six million Polish-Americans constituted a sizable voting bloc.

Roosevelt, characteristically, adopted a flexible and practical attitude toward this explosive issue. He adapted his stance to fit the harsh realities of realpolitik. Truman, partly because of his personality, saw the issue of Russian domination of Eastern Europe as a matter of good vs. evil. On becoming president, he determined that this was an arena where he could prove his decisiveness and toughness.

Like most Americans, FDR in the late 1930s was appalled by the land grabs that would spark World War II: Italy's invasion of Ethiopia and then Albania; Japan's move into China; and Germany's seizure of Austria, Czechoslovakia, and then Poland. In mid-September 1939, the Germans and Russians divided Poland. Soon afterward, the Russians demanded from Finland territory that they claimed was needed to bolster the defense of Leningrad. The Finns offered surprisingly tough armed resistance. This so-called Winter War won the sympathy of nearly all Americans, including FDR. U.S.-Russian relations became frosty.

But when Hitler attacked Russia on June 22, 1941, FDR saw in this exogenous contingency a chance to stop or slow down the hitherto unbeatable Wehrmacht. Roosevelt in mid-1941 remained unsure whether the United States itself would ever join in the fighting. But now, with the Red Army, the vast Soviet land space, and the coming Russian winter arrayed against Hitler, there appeared some light at the end of the tunnel. A shrewd gambler, FDR decided to send supplies to the Soviets. He did so against the advice of most of the U.S. military. Roosevelt had never been a fierce anticommunist. Unlike many of his peers, he had not succumbed to the Red Scare in 1919–20. Months after becoming president, he had ended the sixteen-year snub of the Soviet government and had sent an ambassador to Moscow. To ascertain whether Stalin would continue resistance against the rapidly advancing Germans, Roosevelt dispatched his right-hand man, Harry Hopkins, to talk with the Soviet dictator. FDR asked Hopkins to get a read on Stalin's personality and emotional makeup. Hopkins suffered such poor health that he did most of his work as Lend-Lease administrator from his bedroom in the White House. In sending Hopkins on that long, cold flight to Moscow, Roosevelt had acted on his belief, which was shared by many other leaders, that affect could be read as evidence of inner political intentions. Therefore it was crucial that Hopkins meet Stalin face to face, read his body language, and assess his emotions in order to get a good sense of whether the Kremlin chief would indeed keep Russia in the war. In that case, sending Lend Lease aid was a good bet. Hopkins made his perilous journey—on the return route observers thought he might die before reaching America—and reported that Stalin was determined to keep on fighting. Hopkins also told FDR that Stalin was "get-at-able"—that he had enormous respect for Roosevelt and that he was, despite his cruelty and his many crimes, approachable on a personal and political basis.

FDR assumed that relations with the Soviet Union would move forward largely on U.S. terms. In August 1941, Roosevelt, Churchill, and their aides drew up the Atlantic Charter. This outline of principles for the postwar world restated the ideals of Woodrow Wilson. There should be open-door political and economic relations. Land grabs were not legitimate. International borders and the makeup of governments should reflect the will of the people involved. There was even talk of human rights. Although the Atlantic Charter inveighed specifically against the sins of the Axis nations, its principles were also implicitly aimed at the territorial seizures of the Soviets. While FDR was never an all-out advocate of the Atlantic Charter, he saw the document as useful for rallying U.S. public opinion. Most Americans, after all, still opposed entering the fighting. The Atlantic Charter gave the nascent alliance a moral basis while offering an alternative to the harsh world order trumpeted by the Axis.

In mid-December 1941, when British Foreign Secretary Anthony Eden arrived at the Kremlin for talks with Stalin, it appeared as if the Germans and the Japanese might well win the war. One could hear the booming of German guns that had penetrated the suburbs of Moscow. Despite the perilous situation, Stalin insisted that the Germans could be rolled back. He wanted to talk with Eden about the postwar territorial settlement. The cynical war aims that Stalin laid out to Eden were the same list that the dictator would return to throughout the war and into the postwar period. He insisted on the borders that the Soviet Union had had at the time of the German invasion.

That meant regaining the territory that Russia had taken from Poland, Romania, and Finland in 1939–40 and keeping the Baltic nations of Latvia, Lithuania, and Estonia that the Soviets had annexed in 1940. Stalin proposed that Russia and Britain divide postwar Europe into spheres of influence. The British would have bases and pro-British governments in Western Europe, and the Russians would have bases and pro-Russian governments in Eastern Europe. By "friendly" Stalin did not necessarily mean communist. But given the hostility that Poles, Rumanians, and others in Eastern Europe felt toward Russia, "friendly" governments would have difficulty in being truly democratic. And given the Russians' ineffectiveness at indirect control in the manner of the Monroe Doctrine, Russian influence tended to entail the secret police and communism. These problems notwithstanding, there was probably political space, absent the Cold War, for much of Eastern Europe to have developed the kind of semi-independence finessed by Czechoslovakia until 1948 and by Finland for many decades.

FDR, in any case, did not worry very much about the prospect of communism in Eastern Europe. At nearly the same time that Eden was in Moscow, Hopkins discussed the consequences of Russia's beating Germany in the war. He voiced an opinion that likely reflected what he had heard Roosevelt say. Hopkins said that regarding Europe's going communist after the war, "he didn't care. . . . Either we could adjust to a communist Europe or we weren't worth surviving." Hopkins predicted that postwar Europe "would get the economics of communism but accompanied with civil liberties because the terrific pressure of capitalist encirclement would have been lifted."[12] The aide was being naive about the liberating effect, at least in the short run, of ending capitalist encirclement, but the key point is that the Roosevelt White House did not equate communist nations with enemy nations.

Nevertheless, FDR did oppose the spheres-of-influence approach that Stalin was laying out to Eden. That postwar setup would violate the Atlantic

Charter and, more to the point, would offend American public opinion. Eden's conversations with Stalin took place only a week after Pearl Harbor. Before that attack, most Americans had opposed getting into the war. Now most Americans wanted to wreak vengeance on Japan, not fight Germany. FDR dared not risk flouting American opinion by pursuing what could be condemned as a war waged to benefit Russian and British imperialism. Churchill also opposed the spheres-of-influence approach. The prime minister believed that the Russians, desperate for aid and for allies, would back down. Eden, in contrast, appraised Stalin's proposals as realistic and moderate. He recommended accepting them. But Churchill and Roosevelt overruled Eden. "It now looks as if the [Atlantic] Charter was directed against the U.S.S.R.," Stalin said sourly.[13]

Again in the spring 1942, when the British and the Russians were negotiating the terms of a treaty of alliance, Stalin brought up the borders of June 1941 and the postwar division of Europe. And once again FDR vetoed the deal. He dismissed Russian security and territorial concerns as "parochial." Meanwhile, beginning in 1942 and continuing into 1943, FDR tried to get a face-to-face meeting with Stalin. He believed that he could deploy charm and displays of respect to convince Stalin of his intention to pursue postwar collaboration. Stalin conditioned such a meeting on the Americans and British coming across with a second front—meaning an invasion of German-held France. With some hedging, Roosevelt and Churchill pledged such an assault for the fall of 1942. The Anglo-American leaders then postponed the second front until the spring of 1943, then the fall of 1943, then the spring of 1944. By late 1943, Churchill was still hedging about a costly cross-Channel assault. But Roosevelt, backed by General George C. Marshall and other U.S. military leaders, now insisted on launching the invasion by June 1944.

Roosevelt was adjusting to exogenous contingencies. He worried that the advancing Soviets, after retaking their June 1941 borders, might make a separate peace with the Germans. He understood the geostrategic consequences of the dramatic military victories at Stalingrad and at Kursk. It was clear that the Soviet Union would emerge from the war as a major world power. In contrast, China, led by Chiang Kai-Shek (Jiang Jieshi), was proving feckless as a military and political collaborator. Roosevelt and his military advisers saw Russia as a potential alternative ally in East Asia. The Soviet Union also seemed to offer a partial answer to another problem. The island-hopping campaign across the central Pacific was costing enormous casualties. Might the United States attack Japan from bomber bases in the Soviet Far East? Laying the groundwork for such bases was a major part of the mission that

Roosevelt in late 1943 assigned to ambassador to Moscow W. Averell Harriman. Another aspect of Roosevelt's global strategy focused on what he saw as postwar differences with London over India and the rest of the British empire. Churchill famously declared that he had not become the king's first minister in order to preside over the dissolution of the empire. Roosevelt regarded European colonial possessions as a dangerous anachronism and the Georgian-born Soviet leader as a potential ally in staving off a "race war."

A final element in Roosevelt's changing strategic perspective centered on Poland. He bristled at what he saw as attempts by the Polish government-in-exile in London and its supporters to play the United States against Russia. "I am sick and tired of these people," he said, referring to the émigré Poles. He asked the Polish ambassador: "Do you expect us and Great Britain to declare war on Joe Stalin if they cross your previous frontier?"[14] In contrast to what he had insisted in December 1941 when Eden was in Moscow and in contrast to what he had said in the spring of 1942 when the British and the Soviets were negotiating a treaty, FDR in the fall of 1943 told the Poles: "I really think those pre–June 22, 1941 frontiers are as [fair] as any."[15]

By late 1943, Roosevelt regarded the Atlantic Charter as more of a long term ideal than as a practical guide to immediate policy. As he put it, "You can't invoke high moral principles where high moral principles do not exist."[16] FDR was altering his viewpoint and his foreign policy objectives in light of changing global power realities. He did not abandon the traditional U.S. goal of an open, liberal world order. Rather, he calculated that this long-term aim could be achieved only by sustaining Big Power cooperation through the dangerous postwar transition period. Establishing an understanding with the Soviet Union and forging personal ties with Stalin now stood at the forefront of Roosevelt's postwar strategy. Confidence that he could probably secure these relationships flowed from his personality and from his assessment of the geostrategic situation.

At the Tehran summit conference of late 1943, FDR and Stalin reached out to each other, both in the public sessions and, evidence suggests, in a number of private tête-à-têtes. Roosevelt made a particular effort to show Stalin respect and thereby assuage the cultural inferiority complex he believed he had discerned. Stalin's aides were astounded at the extent to which the dictator made gestures indicating his esteem for Roosevelt. The president explained to the Soviet dictator that while "personally he agreed" with the pre–June 1941 border, he would like to see the Soviets take a bit less from Poland. Moreover, due to the 1944 election and the sentiments of Polish-Americans, he could not publicly endorse any arrangement with regard to Poland. Stalin said he understood.[17] Was this guarded statement

Roosevelt's only assurance regarding Eastern Europe? Stalin and his foreign minister, Vyacheslav Molotov, would later refer to a more specific commitment. FDR may have been more forthcoming in the private chats he had with Stalin where Charles E. "Chip" Bohlen, the official U.S. interpreter and note-taker, was not present. Harriman later reported that after Tehran, Roosevelt told him that he did not care if most of Eastern Europe went communist. A former ambassador to Moscow reported that Roosevelt had acknowledged listing for the Russians the "countries they could take over and control completely as their sphere—so completely that the United States could from this moment on have no further policies with regard to them—Rumania, Bulgaria, Bukovina, Eastern Poland, Lithuania, Estonia, Latvia, and Finland."[18]

Stalin, despite his brutality, cruelty, and inexcusably murderous behavior toward innocent victims in the Soviet Union and elsewhere, seemed committed to attempting continued Big Three unity. Partly through his own misdeeds, the Kremlin dictator was in a bind with regard to the fate of postwar Poland. He understood that only a Warsaw government bound in "friendship" with Moscow would forego revenge for the Katyn murders of 1940 and other crimes perpetrated on the Polish people. He also worried about Russia's vulnerability to yet another German attack. Stalin told Harriman: "Why can't the President leave Poland to us. Doesn't he realize that this is the invasion route?"[19] Simply controlling Poland would not solve the problem, the dictator believed. A limp Polish puppet could not help block a third lunge from Germany.

In a series of remarkable conversations with Polish communists, Polish noncommunists, and Western officials, Stalin argued that postwar Poland had to be not only "friendly" but also vigorous and linked to a larger alliance system. At a Kremlin reception for the Soviet-dominated Lublin Committee, he warned that "for Poland it won't be enough to have an alliance only with one state." The postwar German danger required "an agreement of four states: Poland—the Soviet Union—England—America."[20] Stalin told French leader Charles de Gaulle that history had proven that neither France and Russia, "nor any other two countries are strong enough to stay on top of Germany." Such containment required "a solid entente among the Soviet Union, France, Great Britain, and America."[21] Overestimating his ability to shape events, Stalin sought to square the circle: to secure a neighbor not only friendly to Moscow, but also independent, vital, and "democratic." He emphasized to de Gaulle "that *it must be Poland itself which closes the passageway*." Poland could not "be strong if it is not democratic. We have an interest in a strong Poland."[22]

Many Polish patriots, however, saw the Russians as an enemy worse than the Germans. In part because of the rape and pillage committed by Red Army soldiers as they tore through Poland, whatever "friendly" feelings toward Russia that might have existed among noncommunist Poles evaporated. Resistance forces, including the guerrillas fighting against the Soviets, hoped for British and American intervention on behalf of a truly independent Poland. Harriman later recalled that "much to Stalin's surprise and chagrin, he found that the Red Army was accepted not as a liberating force" in Poland or Rumania. Instead, "they were looked upon as a new invading force. And that hurt the Russians. That was an awfully, awfully upsetting thing for them to accept."[23] The Soviet-supported Lublin group would lose any free elections. Stalin came to realize that Russian control of Poland would have to be more naked and brutal than he had earlier expected. That brutality set the stage for tensions between Stalin and his Western allies.

Roosevelt, however, still determined not to let disputes over Poland destroy the far more important objective of overall postwar cooperation with Moscow. The February 1945 Yalta conference fleshed out the tacit deals outlined at Tehran. As at the earlier conference, Stalin and Roosevelt at Yalta each went out of his way to indicate respect for the other.

In talking with American journalists before the conference, FDR tried to make them understand what he had come to learn: that Wilsonian idealism was not practical for the immediate postwar era. "The Atlantic Charter stands as an objective," he explained, part of the upward curve of humanity "over these thousands of years," much like the Ten Commandments or the teachings of Jesus.[24] When newsmen on the voyage home asked FDR about the Atlantic Charter, he described it as merely "a beautiful idea." When "it was drawn up, the situation was that England was about to lose the war. They needed help, and it gave it to them."[25] He then dropped the subject. The implied lesson: Don't look to the Charter as a practical guide for the postwar world.

On March 1, 1945, Roosevelt delivered to Congress and the American people his report on Yalta. It was a curious and deeply personal speech. Harry Hopkins, Roosevelt's longtime partner in crafting big ideas and in selling them to the public, was too ill to help with the drafting. Exhausted after the long conference, FDR loafed on the voyage home. He procrastinated, as he was prone to do. Consequently, much of the speech was drafted by State Department officials and others who did not wholly grasp the President's vision for Big Three cooperation. Displaying his customary confidence, flexibility, and glibness, Roosevelt improvised. As he sat before the assembled Congress and the radio microphones, he ad-libbed key passages of the speech. Presumably speaking from the heart, he instructed Congress and the American people on what they had to understand in order for Big Three cooperation to have a chance in the emerging postwar era. Picking up on this extraordinary performance was the astute commentator and frequent Roosevelt critic Walter Lippmann: "Not for a long time, if ever before, has he talked so easily with the Congress and the people, rather than to them, and down to them."[26] The president warned that despite the power of the United States, the nation could not dictate the peace. He tried to lower expectations. He added qualifying phrases that toned down the Wilsonian boilerplate employed by the speechwriters. To a nation accustomed to simplifying foreign issues and to universalizing the American experience, Roosevelt ad-libbed that postwar issues were "very special problems. We over here find it difficult to understand the ramifications of many of these problems in foreign lands, but we are trying to." In a long addition, he instructed Americans on Russia's case for regaining its June 1941 border with Poland. He cautioned that the government in Warsaw would not be immediately, but rather "ultimately," selected by the Polish people. Yalta was "a compromise," he stressed. To give a sense of how the Soviets felt, he described the Germans' "terrible destruction" in the Crimea. Roosevelt emphasized "give-and-take compromise. The United States will not always have its way a hundred percent—nor will Russia nor Great Britain. We shall not always have ideal answers to complicated international problems, even though we are determined continuously to strive toward that ideal."[27] Unfortunately, Roosevelt diluted his message by mouthing as well the Wilsonian idealism inserted by the speechwriters.

Far worse, Roosevelt did not explain all this nuance and complexity to his parochial vice president. FDR believed himself a man of destiny. God would allow him, he was sure, to complete his task of winning the war and then managing the transition to a peaceful and stable postwar order. Roosevelt was overconfident about his ability to manage his precarious health. Upon learning in March 1944 of his severe heart disease, he drastically changed his lifestyle—cutting down on rich food, cocktails, and cigarettes and napping every afternoon. "I've worked it out," he assured a friendly reporter.[28] But Roosevelt had not worked it out enough.

His death on April 12, 1945, opened the door for influence by Ambassador Harriman. Angry and frustrated by the Soviets' brutal domination in Poland, Harriman was goaded also by what he was hearing from George F. Kennan. Kennan and other diplomats fiercely resented the Kremlin's policy of isolating them from normal contact with Soviet citizens and officials. Many of the Americans and Britons working in Moscow had grown skeptical about postwar collaboration with a government whose repressiveness they had experienced in this intensely personal way.

After Roosevelt died, Harriman, impelled by what a colleague observed as "hate" for the Russians, rushed to Washington to brief the new president.[29] The ambassador's clout was enhanced by what a collaborator called his "total ferocious dedication."[30] His determination could lead to distortion. Harriman "will exaggerate things, and know that he exaggerates them," an official observed. When called on it, Harriman would justify himself, saying: "Well, yes, perhaps, but you know, I feel very strongly about so and so."[31]

Harriman poked Truman at his most vulnerable point. He said that FDR's policy toward the Russians had rested not on a long-range plan to preserve the wartime alliance and achieve lasting peace but rather on shameful fear. Roosevelt feared the Russians, Harriman insisted. Proud and insecure, Truman quickly interjected that "he was not in any sense afraid of the Russians." Harriman then undercut the rationale for the alliance by presenting as a fatal contradiction that which Roosevelt had regarded as a fact of life. During the postwar transition, Moscow would seek both cooperation with its allies and dominance over its neighbors. The ambassador made still another alarmist claim: The Soviets lacked any sense of limits. They would advance to the English Channel if given a chance. Harriman concluded this influential briefing with a prediction that proved flatly wrong. Because the Kremlin "did not wish to break with the United States . . . we had nothing to lose by standing firm."[32]

In ensuing weeks and months, America's most influential "Soviet expert" argued these points to other top Washington officials and to leading journalists. These conversations helped make it permissible and habitual to talk about the Soviets not as fellow world policemen, as Roosevelt had most often depicted them, but as international criminals.

Roosevelt, understanding that cultural differences could doom the alliance, had played them down. Harriman played them up. Indeed, he inflated them. To Truman, who liked reading about Genghis Khan, Harriman warned that the Soviet armies rolling back the Nazis amounted to another "barbarian invasion of Europe."[33] A few weeks into his presidency, Truman banged his fist on the table, declaring: "We have to get tough with the Russians. . . . We've got to teach them how to behave."[34] He never moved far from that assumption.

Truman did learn during his presidency. He revised his initial enthusiasm for the destructiveness of the atomic bomb—"This is the greatest thing in history!"—after seeing photographs of the terrible suffering endured by the people of Hiroshima and Nagasaki. He overcame his reluctance to spend

U.S. money to revive the European economy. He came around to the necessity for a permanent military alliance. Indeed, his administration's implementation of atomic deterrence, the Marshall Plan, and NATO would become proud, lasting achievements. In these and in other respects, the Truman administration would adopt an assertive yet careful policy in dealing with Moscow. Nevertheless, Truman never transcended the limits of his personality. He remained oversensitive to slights, narrow in perspective, and ill at ease with most foreigners.

Even as Roosevelt's energy was ebbing in 1943–45, he tried to maximize his agency in foreign affairs by institutionalizing the structure of Big Three diplomacy. While extraordinary confidence led FDR to assume that he could manage the delicate transition to a peaceful and stable world order, that self-assurance also proved dangerous. He did not, despite his precarious health, take Truman into his confidence. Truman's personal limits circumscribed his response to the contingencies that aggravated tensions and rivalries with the Soviets. The many problems of Stalin's personality exacerbated the explosive situation. Personalities, then, were instrumental in the formation of the Cold War. The presidential transition between Roosevelt and Truman had such sharp consequences because the personalities of the two men were so divergent and because the shift took place during a critical juncture in history.

CHAPTER 3

Narrator-in-Chief

*Presidents and the Politics of Economic
Crisis from FDR to Obama*

ALICE O'CONNOR

On December 6, 2011, President Barack Obama
traveled to Osawatomie, Kansas, to deliver what the White House promised
would be a major address on the economy. This was to be a defining speech
for the Obama presidency. With unemployment stuck near post–Great Depression highs and the economy to a remarkable extent unrecovered from the
damage of the 2008 financial collapse, the administration was on the defensive against charges that its economic policies had only made things worse.
The president's recent, belatedly unveiled jobs bill had similarly bogged down,
amid the ongoing ignominy of debt ceiling debates and Republican obstructionism on any measures requiring additional taxes or domestic spending at
all. Now, Obama would take his case for economic recovery directly to the
American people. The speech would address what the president "sees as a
make or break moment for the middle class and all those working to join it,"
according to the press advance. It would also set the stage for his upcoming
2012 presidential campaign.

Judging from the considerable buildup in the weeks before Obama's trip,
the speech was to be a self-consciously historic one as well. This was confirmed by the long-awaited announcement, just days before the scheduled
event, of where it would take place. As the historians who had been quietly advising the president since the previous summer were well aware, the
choice of Osawatomie was significant not because it would take Obama to

red-state America, just a couple hours' drive from where his mother was born. Osawatomie was the place where, in 1910, former president Theodore Roosevelt made one of the most famous—and progressive—speeches of his career. Seeking to overcome the intra-party rifts that would later lead the Progressive Party to break away from the Republicans in 1912, Roosevelt had used Osawatomie's originally intended commemoration of radical abolitionist John Brown to summon the spirit of Abraham Lincoln instead. Laying out a reform agenda for what would come to be known as his New Nationalism, TR urged a more vigorous response to the nation's gaping, increasingly volatile economic divide, with measures such as tougher antitrust and fair labor standards and progressive income and inheritance taxes. For Obama's purposes, Osawatomie's reform spirit mattered more than the policy particulars. The New Nationalism envisioned a society "where everyone gets a fair chance, a square deal, and an equal opportunity to succeed," the White House noted in the advance packet for Obama's speech. In a phrasing that echoed Roosevelt's own, the press statement went on to promise that at Osawatomie the president would "lay out the choice we face between a country in which too few do well while too many struggle to get by, and one where we're all in it together."[1] He would also deliver a rebuke to his Republican contemporaries, rejecting their obstructionism in favor of the aisle-crossing reform tradition TR's Osawatomie speech called up, one determined to, in Roosevelt's own words, "equalize opportunity, destroy privilege, and give to the life and citizenship of every individual the highest possible value both to himself and to the commonwealth."[2]

In reality, Obama's speech resurrected many of the themes that had animated his own first presidential campaign, themes he had memorably developed in a widely praised speech he delivered at New York City's Cooper Union Hall in March 2008. Then, candidate Obama used the site of Abraham Lincoln's 1860 candidacy-making speech to invoke the spirit of another incontrovertible Republican president as he confronted the assembled titans of finance capitalism with the damage they were doing to the economy. Obama called Wall Street to task for the culture of greed and irresponsibility that would eventually lead to financial meltdown; the broken compact that left millions working longer and harder for less; and the relentless pursuit of deregulation, lower corporate taxes, and outsized profit that had sent the top 1 percent share of national wealth and income soaring to heights unseen since the eve of the Crash of 1929. Obama had also used that occasion to lay down the gauntlet for his own version of progressive reform, beginning with the need for a bigger, more constructive role for government in regulating the securities industry and in protecting the interests of consumers against powerful corporate interests.[3]

At Osawatomie, Obama assumed a more tempered tone, speaking broadly of the "you're on your own economics" underlying contemporary Republican obstructionism while laying out a recovery plan based on investments in education, "innovation," and infrastructure, to be paid for by higher taxes on the very wealthy. He took the opportunity yet again to remind listeners that the ideas he championed had a long tradition of support among Republicans who believed in an economic system that would meet the standards of "real democracy" by using government to maintain fairness and opportunity—and who, like Teddy Roosevelt, had been labeled socialists as a result. Most important, he offered an explanation for the problems that, nearly three years into his administration, continued to plague the economy and leave millions of Americans unemployed and insecure—an explanation meant to return the debate to the core issues Washington had been ignoring in its turn to the politics of austerity and debt reduction. The economic crisis, the president argued, did not start and end with the financial collapse of 2008. It was rooted in an older, more deep-seated pattern of technology- and globalization-driven job loss, declining wages, and rising inequality brought on by a decade of deregulation and top-heavy tax cuts. Inequality, the president concluded, was "the defining issue of our time." For this, his speech was greeted with varying degrees of enthusiasm on the liberal left: Liberal bloggers welcomed its populism; the *New York Times* said it "came as a relief." The speech drew more animated reaction in the Tea Party–inflected media outlets of the right, where it was roundly and predictably vilified as yet another sign of Obama's "Marxist" designs.[4]

But the president had another task at Osawatomie as well, one that called to mind TR's propensity for using the proverbial bully pulpit to get his way. With all focus in Washington on the politics of tax cuts and deficit reduction, Obama needed to re-take control of the basic economic narrative, if for no other reason than to remind the country that the Great Recession had not started on his watch. Like TR at Osawatomie, he needed to use the power of the presidency to act as the nation's narrator-in-chief, with an explanation of its economic problems and prospects, a statement of national objectives and policy, and a vision of national identity and purpose that could rally support for his own embattled program of economic recovery and reform. In this struggle the president faced a number of roadblocks, reflected in his own deteriorating relations with the Republican leadership as well as Washington's stalemate over deficit reduction.[5] Complicating the situation for Obama were growing signs of discontent on the left, crystallized in the appearance of the Occupy Wall Street movement in September 2011, with its own account of the economic anxieties and frustrations that had been gripping the "99 percent" of working- and middle-class Americans since well before the onset of the Great Recession. Obama gave a nod to the swelling tide of popular protest and Occupy's 99 percent formulation in his speech while keeping an arm's distance from the movement's call for more aggressive financial reforms.

In fact, Occupy's challenge hearkened back to criticisms that had dogged his administration from the start and called attention to what Obama would later recognize as his first term's "biggest mistake": the failure to provide, let alone maintain control over, a compelling economic narrative that would help put the country on the road to economic recovery and reform. "When I think about what we've done well and what we haven't done well," the president said in a July 2012 televised interview with CBS News six months after his momentarily triumphant Osawatomie speech, "the mistake of my first term . . . was thinking that this job was just about getting the policy right. And that's important. But the nature of this office is also to tell a story to the American people that gives them a sense of unity and purpose and optimism, especially during tough times."[6] By then, what might be called "the narrative of the president's failed narrative" had itself become conventional wisdom among friend and foe alike—including the messaging experts who would presumably have an influence on Obama's presidential campaign.[7]

Explanations abound for Obama's failure to command the Great Recession narrative, especially puzzling to commentators in light of his demonstrated capacity for soaring rhetoric and the enduring legacy of failed Republican policies.[8] The more sympathetic among them emphasize his pragmatic experimentalism, his professorial manner, his "post-partisan" attachment to consensus-building, and the bewildering nature of the economic crisis itself.[9] Sympathizers also point to the power of the simple, inaccurate, but well-organized counternarrative of government overreach and liberal entitlement that has animated Obama's Republican opposition. Others have come down harder, calling Obama to task for everything from political naiveté to Wall Street cronyism and, more fundamentally, for lacking the courage of his own progressive convictions—with some raising questions about whether indeed he had such convictions at all.[10] But Obama's narrative struggles also raise questions that go beyond the particulars of his personality and leadership style. Much like his ongoing efforts to draw on the political capital of historic predecessors, they invite us to look back at the experiences of past presidents in times of economic crisis but also to reflect more broadly on the historically evolving capacities of the presidency as an institution and of presidential leadership as a set of institutionalized practices operating in changing conditions of opportunity and constraint. In what follows, I draw on the presidencies of Franklin D. Roosevelt and Ronald Reagan to consider these questions of presidential capacity, in a discussion that focuses on the changing role and powers of the president as chief economic narrator over the course of the twentieth century and explores the developments in politics and political economy in order to understand why these powers have been diminished at a time when they are needed most. Economic crisis narratives figure centrally in this larger story, having been effectively deployed by both FDR and Reagan as tools of economic policymaking and presidential governance and, ultimately, for purposes of sweeping (if diametrically opposed) programs of political economic reform. By situating Obama's struggles within this longer historical trajectory, my discussion also touches on themes raised elsewhere in this volume and in the wider literature—of executive leadership in the face of divided government and political polarization—to explore the interplay between individual agency and structural constraint in determining presidential capacity to bring about political and economic change.

Crisis Narratives and Political Development

Crisis narratives occupy a central place in the history of American capitalism and appear frequently in the recurring cycles of panic, depression, and economic restructuring that make it as much a system of "creative destruction" as production and growth. These accounts come to us from a remarkably diverse and far-flung cast of narrators, ranging from the assorted preachers, artists, unemployed workers, and political gadflies who made telling the story of hard times their business in the nineteenth century to the professional mandarins of finance who appear on the airwaves and in congressional hearing rooms today.[11] Over time, the work of narrating crisis has involved an increasingly sophisticated array of conceptual, literary, visual, and communicative tools. Still, especially during periods of extended economic downturn, narratives have consistently served very basic social and cultural needs—whether for some semblance of order and explanation for otherwise bewildering events or for some way of giving voice and recognition to widespread experiences of pain and disruption. Crisis narratives can also perform important civic functions, especially when it comes to absolving victims and blaming perpetrators (or vice versa, as the case may be) and otherwise channeling social anxieties and resentments about destabilizing economic change.

Economic crisis narratives figure critically in the history of American politics and political development as well, as illustrated in the emergence and evolution of the role of narrator-in-chief in the presidencies that continue to anchor opposite ends of our polarized debates over economic policy. The New Deal presidency of FDR, with its promises of "freedom from want" and its Economic Bill of Rights, remains the standard-bearer for reform visions based on federal commitments to full employment, labor rights, Keynesian economic management, progressively redistributive social policies, and regulated capitalism. The presidency of Ronald Reagan, in contrast, is held up for its vision of individual freedom, personal self-reliance, and entrepreneurial, free-market capitalism and of anti–big government austerity as the road to recovery and reform.

And yet, despite their vastly conflicting reform visions, FDR and Reagan share important features as historically renowned narrators-in-chief. Both assumed office during historically bewildering periods of economic crisis as challengers to incumbents of notoriously failed economic policies. FDR and Reagan were also both seen as great communicators, uniquely able to connect with their vast radio and, later, television audiences with psychologically reassuring explanations of what had gone wrong and why. Both drew on recently popularized economic theories to educate the electorate in new or untried ways of getting back on course. In these and other ways, both used moments of crisis to introduce broader, ideologically driven reform agendas with varying degrees of success. Most important for purposes of this essay, what made FDR and Reagan effective narrators-in-chief was the recognition—their own and that of those around them—that narrative could be used as an essential tool of modern presidential governance and leadership: of presidential publicity, statecraft, and executive-centered reform. For FDR and Reagan, narrating economic crisis was thus not merely a rhetorical strategy, nor simply an opportunity to make the case for a "new" (at the time) unorthodox economics. It was an opportunity to cultivate a distinctive idea of presidential leadership and economic policymaking that would empower them to set the agenda for decades of reform.

The Public Presidency

When Andrew Jackson blamed the Panic of 1833 on the nation's elite central bankers and their allies in Congress, he was articulating an early version of what scholars refer to as the "public presidency"—the idea, that is, that the president is uniquely empowered to act in the name of "the people" and is responsible for defending the general welfare against the corrupting influence of powerful elites. Only through more recent presidencies, however, have scholars traced the emergence of this idea as a more formally recognized dimension of presidential leadership. On the level of political doctrine, it is most often associated with Woodrow Wilson and the Progressive project to make federal governance more executive-centered and democratic, with the president acting as protector of the public interest against corrupting "special interests" as well as a leader of public opinion. The concept of the public presidency has also become institutionalized within presidential politics, as seen in the increasingly elaborate efforts to measure and sway public opinion, to control relations with the press, and to keep pace with changing communications technologies. Most recently, "going public"—to create popular pressure for a president's legislative priorities as an alternative to negotiations with Congress—has been recognized as an increasingly important strategy of presidential leadership as conditions of ideological polarization and sharply divided government have become more and more the political norm.[12] Crisis narratives thread throughout this process as well. Theodore Roosevelt presented himself as the protector of "the average man, the average citizen" when he pledged "perseverance in the war against successful dishonesty" in the wake of the Panic of 1907.[13] Jimmy Carter spoke as "a president who is not isolated from the people, who feels your pain, and who shares your dreams" when he addressed the nation about a deeper "crisis of confidence" at the heart of America's economic woes in a famously botched (if misinterpreted) attempt to "go public" in search of support for his energy program in 1979.[14] But during the presidencies of FDR and Reagan, crisis narratives were most fully integrated into strategies of political leadership when they served more systematically to establish, and then to redraw, the parameters of the public presidency itself.

Thus, when FDR first addressed the nation as president in 1933, he offered a gripping account of national emergency that would also establish the kind of deliberately public leader he would be. Without minimizing the "dark realities" of deprivation and institutional collapse, FDR framed the Depression—and the obligations of his office—in moral and spiritual terms. Unlike the "generation of self-seekers" who had led capitalism so badly astray, FDR promised "a leadership of frankness and vigor" that would restore trust to a system brought down by "callous and selfish wrongdoing." Against an old order tied to the narrow pursuit of profit, he positioned himself as a leader who understood the moral and spiritual value as well as the material necessity of work. He used metaphors of war to call on the people for whatever shared sacrifice they could afford, but more forcefully to pledge his willingness to use "broad Executive power to wage a war against the emergency, as great as the power that would be given to me if we were in fact invaded by a foreign foe." Especially important, he placed himself squarely on the side of the people, standing with them in rejecting the "practices of the unscrupulous money changers" and offering assurance that they had "nothing to fear but fear itself."[15] FDR solidified this special relationship between the presidency and the people in the intimacy of his evening fireside chats, in which he took advantage of the popularity of radio to offer a running, plain-spoken narrative of the unfolding crisis and of how his administration would fix it—with the people's "intelligent support."[16] Within the first hundred days, FDR had made an unprecedented commitment to the public mission of the Progressive presidency, an achievement that continues to shape his historical reputation as a leader capable of using his voice to, as Harry Hopkins put it, "set in motion tremendous social and moral forces to combat fear and evil."[17]

But in narrating the Great Depression and its challenges over the course of several years, FDR also dedicated the presidency to an even more ambitious progressive reform ideal: a bold reconceptualization of the American public itself, in this instance based on a shared sense of grievance, a common understanding of core values, and a common stake in the success of the New Deal. For FDR this meant using the story of the Great Depression to shatter the national myths of laissez-faire and rugged individualism, to set up an object lesson in what he continually referred to as "our interdependence on each other." It meant locating the case for the New Deal in a distinctively progressive narrative of American history in which "the people" were up against a small group of "economic royalists" who by the Crash of 1929 had "concentrated into their own hands an almost complete control over other people's property, other people's money, other people's labor, other people's lives" and posed a threat to democracy every bit as profound as the "tyranny of political autocracy" brought to defeat by the patriots of American Revolution. As he launched his second presidential campaign, it meant reminding people that their shared economic and political struggles had taught them to think differently about government—and about their relationship to it—as something that worked with and on behalf of the American people to guarantee genuine "democracy of opportunity" by guaranteeing "equal opportunity in the market place."[18]

Under FDR's leadership, the task of defining the democratic public would only grow more expansive over time. As a candidate in 1932, he had spoken movingly of working on behalf of the "forgotten man at the bottom of the economic pyramid." But the economic citizenship he conjured in his Great Depression and New Deal narratives—and in his Economic Bill of Rights—was deliberately encompassing, reaching from the "one-third of a nation ill-housed, ill-clad, ill-nourished" of his Second Inaugural to the occupational republic he enumerated in a 1938 fireside chat seeking support for emergency federal spending and jobs creation during the depths of recession: "the farmer, the factory worker, the storekeeper, the gas station man, the manufacturer, the merchant—big and small—the banker who takes pride in the help he gives to the building of his community."[19] By then, the New Deal had devoted unprecedented agency resources to documenting the story of hardship and channeling it into a Rooseveltian idea of economic citizenship under the auspices of the Farm Security Administration, the Federal Theatre Project, and the Works Progress Administration, all part of what to this day remains an unmatched public investment in the cultural work of political and economic reform.[20]

FDR accomplished a lot within the framework of New Deal economic citizenship, from the passage of legislation establishing basic labor rights and social welfare protections to the forging of a lasting, if internally divided, political coalition. Nevertheless, the notion of an identifiable, interdependent economic citizenry proved more tenuous and controversial than other innovations of FDR's public presidency (such as the Office of the Press Secretary and the presidential radio address), as suggested by the fate of the New Deal cultural front. The FSA and the Federal Theatre Project were early victims of congressional red-baiting, as were projects that flirted with "un-American" ideas in other agencies. After 1941, federal resources for public representation and related efforts to forge a sense of national citizenship—economic or otherwise—were diverted into the war effort.[21] This general trend continued in a postwar political economy fueled by mass consumption and Cold War, when the semi-official language of economic citizenship turned on the virtues of free enterprise, mass affluence, labor/employer accords, and the achievement of a "classless" society from which the role of government was conspicuously absent. Nor were bonds of economic citizenship particularly encouraged by the expanding postwar welfare state, with its stigmatizing categorical divisions, heavy reliance on hidden forms of provision for the growing middle class, and racial and gender exclusions. The divided and "submerged" nature of social welfare provision would provide traction for appeals to economic resentment when hard times returned, as Richard Nixon would learn when he played the "Silent Majority" off against racial minorities and variously designated segments of the undeserving poor. Jimmy Carter's vision of economic citizenship was based on notions of socially embedded obligation and the common good, but the picture he presented in his crisis of confidence speech was of a citizenry mired in the pathologies of affluence and unable to find its way.[22]

What will forever mark Carter's as a historic speech, however, is the political opening it (along with many other things) created for Ronald Reagan's starkly revisionist understanding of economic citizenship, of presidential leadership, and of the nature of the crisis Jimmy Carter had failed to resolve.

Much as FDR had nearly fifty years before, Reagan expressed these understandings in the extended account of the "present crisis" with which he
opened his official tenure, in an inaugural that also set a dramatically altered
tone for the public presidency. The crisis itself could be boiled down to a few
basic propositions. The American people were suffering from "the longest
and one of the worst inflations in our national history." They were burdened
by achievement-sapping taxes. And the relentless growth of public spending
had "piled deficit upon deficit" thanks to decades of "government by an
elite group." All this added up to the formulation that would become the
defining principle of Reagan's presidency: "government is not the solution
to our problem; government is the problem." As representative of the people,
his role was decidedly *not* to put the power of activist government on their
side. It was to free them—and the market—from government's shackles, to
reverse the course the country had been on since the New Deal, and to restore Americans' "right to dream heroic dreams" once again.[23]

From the very beginning, then, Reagan cast his public presidency in a
distinctly individualistic, anti-statist language of economic citizenship that
could hardly be more different from FDR's emphasis on interdependence
and collective rights. The shared grievances it evoked were those of the op-
pressed taxpayer and the overregulated businessman; to the extent that he had
one, Reagan's forgotten man was the heroic entrepreneur.[24] It was infused
with a view of American history as a "struggle for individual liberty, self
government, and free enterprise throughout the world."[25] These differences
would only grow more pronounced once the economy started to move out
of the deep recession of Reagan's first two years in office and his core narrative shifted from crisis to reform. By the time of his Second Inaugural,
Reagan's theme of "renewal" had turned to talk of a "second American Revolution" based on a return to the historic principles of limited government,
self-reliance, voluntarism, economic liberty, and a revival of "the drive and
entrepreneurial genius that are the core of human progress."[26] Reagan was
even more triumphant upon signing historic rate-lowering (and flattening)
tax reform legislation two years later, which he celebrated as the demise of
the "un-American" progressive income tax and a return to "first principles"
of "faith in the individual, not groups of classes, but faith in the resources
and bounty of each and every separate human soul."[27]

Before then, though, Reagan's account of what he and others on the
right had taken to calling the "Great Inflation" had been the centerpiece
of a highly orchestrated strategy of "going public" that would also mark a
departure from earlier approaches to the public presidency. A reflection of
Reagan's determination to make the economy the "first, second, and third

priority" of his first hundred days, its goals were to build on Reagan's rhetorical strengths and populist appeal to set the terms of the economic policy
debate in Washington and to generate broad public support for the controversial package of tax and social welfare spending cuts he was trying to push
through Congress. Its two-pronged approach revolved around a "rhetorical
package" of strategically timed speeches on radio and television and public
appearances in key congressional districts, urging constituents to contact their
representatives to push passage of his proposals. To a far greater degree than
any of its predecessors, the administration paired this "outside" campaign
with a no-compromise "inside" stance, consisting of hard-line negotiating
tactics and parliamentary maneuvers designed to force action in Congress
and to take Democratic leaders by surprise.[28] When signing the landmark
tax and budget legislation in 1981, Reagan made it clear that he thought of
"going public" less as an isolated tactic than as an extension of his economic
and governing philosophy. The passage of the Economic Recovery Tax Act
and the Omnibus Budget Reconciliation Act of 1981 marked "a turnaround
of almost a half a century" of government growth, he told reporters, calling
it a victory for "the people of the United States who finally made it plain
that they wanted a change."[29]

As Reagan administration strategists came to discover after this initial
moment of triumph, however, even the most urgent and popularly appealing rhetoric could not overcome the limitations of going public as a strategy of presidential governance. As political scientist George Edwards has
persuasively demonstrated, targeted presidential offensives do little to sway
public opinion. Nor does presidential popularity provide much leverage
in Congress—indeed, in an era of growing polarization, it can have quite
the opposite effect.[30] Though ostensibly aimed at making divided government work, the turn to "outsider" tactics has more generally fed into the
heightening of mistrust and resentment that pervades "inside" negotiations.
Going public also carries strong likelihood of producing bad policy, as was
decidedly the case with Reagan's combination of drastic tax cuts, increased
military spending, and slashed social welfare spending in the face of deepen-
ing recession—from which the administration had quickly to retreat with
major tax hikes as deficits soared. From the standpoint of at least one cast
of political players, however, going public proved a resounding success. It
elevated the pollsters, media specialists, marketing consultants, and other political operatives who made up the presidency's public relations infrastructure
to an even greater level of influence than they had already had, hastening the
transformation of the public presidency into what journalist Sidney Blumenthal in 1980 called a "permanent campaign."[31] The result is a presidency

more institutionally structured than ever to govern with an eye to winning elections—and all the requirements of raising money and targeting electoral constituents that that entails. Like the anti-statism that also became signature features of Reagan's public presidency and approach to governance, it left a lasting legacy that would ultimately undermine presidential capacity to speak in the name of a unifying economic citizenship to a citizenry that might expect government to act on its behalf.

The President as Economic Policymaker

Presidential leadership is not about persuasion alone. It is also about having a policy agenda and the credibility to back it up. No one showed more awareness of this than FDR, when at the depths of the Depression he made it a point to assure the nation that, in sharp contrast to the "abdicated" leadership of the old regime, the New Deal administration was prepared to respond to the people's call for decisive "action, and action now."[32] Here again, FDR's intervention came at a critical juncture in the historical evolution of the presidency, when the threat of economic collapse made it possible to push beyond the old constraints to centralize responsibility for the management and intellectual direction of the economy in the executive branch. It was a critical juncture for economic narrative as well. As never before, narrating hard times would be an instrument of economic statecraft, a way of introducing new orthodoxies to replace the tired old ones, of shaping the conceptual and institutional apparatus of policymaking, and of exercising presidential authority over the terms of economic debate and reform.[33] As in the case of the public presidency, Reagan would join FDR in using this instrument of economic statecraft to great effect and in ways that would ultimately restrict the capacities of economic governance the New Deal had helped to launch.

For FDR, what only gradually (and hesitatingly) emerged as a new, Keynesian orthodoxy started out as a set of commitments—to government activism, to experimentation, to the eradication of the "evils" of selfish speculation, and above all to the ambitious project of putting people back to work. These were linked by his unwavering conviction that the philosophy of laissez-faire was intellectually and morally bankrupt. Beyond that, FDR was famously ecumenical in his own thinking, looking to an eclectic, often internally conflicting group of appointees for expertise and advice. The resulting state of uncertainty was to some degree reflected in his rhetoric, but it came through more clearly in a policy agenda caught between rival factions within the cabinet and competing explanations of the Depression's causes and cures. Until well into FDR's second term, what would only later be recognized as a Keynesian approach was but one voice among many, augmented by that of Keynes himself, writing from afar to urge more direct and ongoing deficit-financed public investment to get the economy back on a pathway to growth.[34] When Keynesianism finally did emerge as the basic framework for New Deal economic policy, it was in a comparatively limited, American-ized version that emphasized fiscal management over the kind of planned public investment Keynes was urging.[35] The deep and unexpected reces-sion of 1937–38—which Keynesians blamed in part on the administration's ill-advised effort to balance the budget with sharp spending reductions—was the precipitating event.[36] By then, they had Keynes's *General Theory* (1936) to back up their claims. But the Keynesian turn came more fully into view as the administration shifted its attention to mobilizing for World War II and, subsequently, to establishing the policy infrastructure for managing postwar stability and growth. Here again, presidential policy action spoke louder than presidential words, in commitments built into legislation and the burgeon-ing economic policymaking bureaucracy—to full employment, to national income accounting, to aggregate demand management—that bespoke a fun-damentally revised understanding of how the economy works. These insti-tutional anchors of a new economic narrative were most prominent in the Employment Act of 1946, which in addition to making employment the central objective of economic policy created the Council of Economic Ad-visors as the presidential office with central responsibility for carrying it out.

This is not to say that Keynesianism became official economic orthodoxy overnight. It would not be for another two decades, in the Kennedy and Johnson administrations, that the "new economics" would fully take hold. Nor can the shift to Keynesianism as the center of the economic policy conversation be attributed to presidential agency alone. Nevertheless, the gradually unfolding Keynesian revolution did engage the presidency in a far broader field of operation, with a wider array of policymaking tools and more opportunities to make key appointments than ever before. For presi-dents willing and able to use them, these newly expanded tools of economic statecraft represented an unprecedented opportunity to shape and establish the parameters of policy conversation about economic priorities, if not al-ways to put them into effect.[37]

Considered against this backdrop, the narrative reverberations—and the ironies—of Reagan-era economic statecraft come more fully to light. Reagan himself entered office as an acolyte of Milton Friedman's strict monetarist theories, having played no small part in popularizing a Friedmanite philoso-phy of free-market "democratic capitalism" in the syndicated radio addresses he broadcast between 1975 and 1979.[38] He also arrived with an avowedly

Friedmanite economic recovery and reform agenda, which claimed fighting inflation as its top priority, blamed government and labor "entitlements" as the cause, and made aggressive tax, budget, and regulatory cutbacks its fundamental tools. But in translating these precepts into policy, Reagan was bringing new ideological purpose—and momentum—to shifts in practice that were already underway and that under his watch would become more thoroughly embedded in the policy bureaucracy. Full employment, already sidelined in the inflation-ridden 1970s, would officially be jettisoned as a central goal of economic policy during the Reagan years, when policymakers embraced Friedman's view of unemployment as "naturally occurring" and not to be tampered with.[39] The primacy of inflation-fighting elevated the policymaking role of what for much of the postwar period had been a comparatively dormant Federal Reserve—and the banking interests it traditionally represented.[40] Tax cuts and deficit spending, now tied to the rhetoric of government failure, would be devoted to defunding and disabling the welfare state. What had once been the instruments of Keynesian economic statecraft would now steer an anti-Keynesian course in an effort to, as Reagan put it, "return the economy to its classical roots—to an understanding that ultimately the economy is not made up of aggregates like government spending and consumer demand, but of individual men and women, each striving to provide for his family and better his or her lot in life."[41] Thus, even as the specifics of his policy agenda (such as privatizing social security and passing a balanced budget amendment) fell short, Reagan shifted the prevailing economic narrative in ways that future presidents would find hard to undo. In the process he laid the groundwork—rhetorical as well as infrastructural—for a neoliberal economic agenda in which the values of promoting individual investment and risk-taking would prevail over those of economic security for all.

Obama's Challenge

More than any single factor, what makes us remember both FDR and Reagan as successful narrators-in-chief is that they presided during periods of political and economic turmoil and were able to use the powers of rhetoric and statecraft to launch sharply divergent programs of economic reform. They were, to use political scientist Stephen Skowronek's terms, presidents operating in political time, with the vision, the political organization, and most crucially the opportunity to push the polity in directions once deemed beyond the pale. "The Impossible Became the Inevitable," noted one Washington Post headline with reference to Reagan's tax reform legislation in 1986, as the president duly noted when signing the bill into law. As transformative presidents, FDR and Reagan also used narrative to operate in fiercely contested political space, where newly energized voices of protest were vying for political allegiance with competing narratives of their own. Two things proved critical as the presidents navigated this volatile narrative field. One was the absence of a well-organized opposition to defend the established regime. The other was their ability to align with strategically placed and organized change agents within the polity while also keeping more radical voices in check. Thus, when FDR zeroed in on the "economic royalists" and "unscrupulous money changers," he was not simply appealing to populist anger at the malfeasance of bankers and the gross concentration of wealth; he was also tapping into a decades-old reform discourse that sought more robust regulation over powerful trusts. Full employment, mass purchasing power, and freedom from want were cornerstones of Keynesian economic theory, but they were also demands around which intellectuals and activists associated with the labor and consumer movements had been organizing for years. And the concept of economic security at the heart of the New Deal welfare state managed to keep such grassroots initiatives as the widely popular movement for old-age pensions led by physician Francis E. Townsend at bay while responding to at least some of their core demands.[42] Likewise, Reagan's relentless attacks on government bureaucrats and welfare "cheats" fed an anti-statist reform sentiment cultivated in the taxpayer revolts of the 1970s as well as the more elite associational networks of the self-styled conservative counter-establishment.[43] Reagan joined a similar configuration of conservative movement change agents to give greater political voice to market interests and ideologies. Ultimately, these movement voices would prove difficult to contain.

Barack Obama ran on the promise that his would be a transformative presidency, and by the time he assumed office expectations were high.[44] Nowhere were these expectations more pronounced than in economic policy, where the reverberations of near-collapse had spurred talk of a long-awaited end to free-market fundamentalism and the advent of a "new" Obamanian New Deal.[45] Obama himself had spoken admiringly of Ronald Reagan as a president who "changed the trajectory of history" by correctly reading the country's frustration with the status quo.[46] And yet, though clearly eager to tap into the transformative capacities the presidencies of FDR and Reagan had come to represent, Obama has continually been frustrated in his efforts to exercise leadership as the nation's narrator-in-chief.

Thus, July 2013 found Obama once again preparing to "go public" with a series of economic speeches timed in part to avert a return to the politics of obstructionism when Congress returned from recess in the fall. This time there was no mystery about the site: Obama would open at Knox College in Galesburg, Illinois, where Abraham Lincoln had debated Stephan A. Douglas and where Obama himself had once given a historic speech—his first as U.S. senator—excoriating the "winner take all" economy and pledging a better future for the struggling middle class. In an advance email sent out to Obama supporters and the press, presidential adviser Dan Pfeiffer made it clear that the president would be invoking his own rhetoric more than that of Lincoln. The speech to come would demonstrate Obama's "consistent vision for the middle class," Pfeiffer promised, with a video montage of keywords from Galesburg I (2005), Georgetown (2009), and Osawatomie (2011) to illustrate the point.[47] The message was also an inadvertent reminder of something else. Nearly five years into his tenure and despite these repeated attempts, the president was still struggling to command the basic narrative of economic crisis and recovery—even after winning reelection with support from an electorate turned off by a mean-spirited Republican program of cutting back on social programs for low-income people, infamously pegged as the "47 percent of Americans" deemed dependent, non-taxpaying, and basically unworthy of concern.[48]

So how to explain Obama's ongoing struggles, and what do they tell us about the current state of presidential governance and leadership? Certainly Obama has encountered a number of obstacles that have diminished the public and economic policymaking capacities of the presidency. Some have to do with long-range political and economic developments that have only accelerated in the wake of Reagan's presidency: the encroachments of the "permanent campaign"; the incapacitation of fiscal policy in the face of congressional gridlock and divided government; the political empowerment of anti-statist ideologies; and the dramatic growth in inequality at the outer extremes and across the middle of the American economy. Other obstacles are of more recent vintage, foremost among them the coalescence of the Republican leadership into an opposition party that has turned massive resistance into a signature form of statecraft, replete with increasingly extreme strategies of repeal, nullification, budgetary brinksmanship, and credible threats of government shutdown. Although these developments are not unique to Obama's presidency, during his tenure the polarizing politics of resistance and opposition have reached modern-day heights of ideological and racial animosity. They have also made it that much more difficult to realize any part, let alone the potentially transformative parts, of his economic agenda.[49] Nor has Obama gotten much push from the grassroots in comparison to his predecessors and to their politically connected counterparts among the top 1 percent.[50]

But formidable though they are, these impediments only go so far in explaining Obama's struggles as narrator-in-chief. For all the political and institutional roadblocks hampering his economic policy agenda, Obama has also faltered at using the tools the presidency does have at its disposal, starting with an economic narrative that falls short as a strategy of transformative leadership in three major respects.

First is in its failure to provide a theory-based explanation of economic problems and prospects that provides a convincing story of what went wrong and charts a different course for the future—a new "new economics," as it were—while definitively repudiating still-entrenched orthodoxies of austerity and laissez-faire.[51] Obama's narrative invokes Keynesian principles, with its emphasis on rebuilding infrastructure and growing the economy "from the middle out." Behavioral economics is frequently cited as the basis of the administration's policy innovations—though more prominently of its campaign strategies.[52] But Obama has shied away from embracing any overarching economic or public philosophy in favor of an accommodation to various factions in the existing debate, leaving outsiders to guess about the firmness of his stated commitment to making job creation and inequality "defining issues" for his own policy agenda. This in turn has left the administration weak in the ever-important battle for political control over economic ideas and without a visible strategy for a significantly revised economic statecraft devoted to equitable, employment-driven growth.

Second is in the absence of a broadly inclusive vision of economic citizenship that recognizes and creates unity across the differences of class, race, and gender that exist within Obama's imagined "middle class and all who aspire to it." Especially notable is the invisibility of poverty as an issue in this formulation and of the needs and interests of the "forgotten" men and women at the bottom of the economic distribution who occupy the fastest-growing, lowest-wage segment of the post–Great Recession recovery—and who represent a potential vanguard in a more deeply progressive challenge to the "new normal" of inequality than Obama has thus far been willing to imagine or embrace.

And third is in its reluctance to articulate an ambitious—if necessarily aspirational—economic reform agenda along with an elevated set of expectations for what presidential leadership, in alliance with a democratically mobilized public, can achieve, despite the structural obstacles in the way. Thematically consistent though it may be, Obama's core narrative has been gradually calibrated to keep expectations in check, with a combination of sensible but modest proposals and a readiness to blame congressional gridlock for holding things up. This may be a reflection of Obama's instinct for moderation and political realism, but it also speaks to a deeper problem in his approach to presidential leadership: an unwillingness to take political risks, whether to embrace big economic ideas, to ally with and build coalitions for change, or to imagine alternatives that go beyond the boundaries of existing political possibility, but that in moments of crisis, as the examples of FDR and Reagan remind us, can sometimes be made to seem like political inevitabilities.

PART II

The Social and Cultural Landscape Presidents Confront

For well over a century, dating back to the Populist moment, the fate of presidencies often hinged on how well or poorly the president managed his relationship to social movements. Populism, labor mobilization, civil rights, and the New Right proved to be powerful forces that brought millions of passionate citizens into electoral politics and bolstered presidents' claims to speak for the entire nation—not simply its elites. But as Robert Self enumerates below, presidents must be careful about what they wish for. As Self puts it, "Political movements in American democracy are by nature disappointments in waiting." Self drills down into the case of Ronald Reagan, the New Right, and the struggle for the soul of the Republican Party since the Reagan era. Sweeping aside a public memory that worships Reagan from the far right of the Republican Party, Self chronicles the fierce battles that raged within Reagan's administration over issues like abortion and family values. Reagan's strategy of satisfying his right flank through the power of appointment—especially appointing judges—represented a "long game." It positioned advocates for the Christian Right inside the administration and the judiciary, paving the way for executive and judge-activated policy that would outlast Reagan himself. More importantly, however, Self documents the sense of frustration that failure to deliver in the short run produced among New Right activists. This pushed advocates even farther to the right and toward more divisive tactics. In a nation evenly divided along partisan lines, a morally self-confident group of true believers could make a big difference in Republican primaries, and over the next couple of decades it succeeded in pushing the entire party to the right. While the dynamic of each president's relationship to the mix of social movements he encounters varies, Self makes a convincing case for considering any president's relationship to the nation's social base, as articulated through social movements, a key variable in the success or failure of his administration.

Darren Dochuk asks why the influence of religion on presidential politics continues in the vein of the "imperial presidency," with set pieces about presidential prayer and conversion, long after scholars have placed other elements of the presidency in broader social and cultural contexts. Dochuk demonstrates in the essay that follows a more nuanced approach that maps the middle ground between religious and moral belief, on the one hand, and daily behavior, especially commercially driven behavior, on the other. Mapping the beliefs, geography, and institutions of "oil patch politics," Dochuk draws a line from wildcatting oil men, certain that God placed pools of oil on their land so that they could extract it efficiently, produce wealth for the nation, and demonstrate the true capitalist spirit in a world threatened by New Deal regulations and bureaucracy, to the worldview of President George W. Bush.

Replacing set scenes of Bush's singular conversion experience with a nuanced account of seventy-five years of the ideational evolution of evangelical East Texas oil men, Dochuk's approach effectively explains the president's simultaneous quest to open up drilling in Alaska's Arctic National Wildlife Refuge and to secure federal funding for church-based social programs. Strongly held religious views about "capture," whether referencing the gathering of God's natural bounty, the profits from that bounty, or souls, animated evangelical capitalists in taking on such specters as FDR's regulatory Department of the Interior, Truman's efforts to claim off-shore oil for the federal government, and the Kennedys' flirtation with national prerogative in lieu of states' rights. As Dochuk makes clear, any person or institution that sought to intervene between a believer and his god—whether church or state—and a land owner and God's bounty—especially the state—was working on behalf of the devil. George W. Bush was exceptional as a president in literally embodying much of this background. Dochuk's approach, however, opens vistas for understanding the religious environment that presidents operate in because of his careful attention to the organizations and institutions spawned by true believers and the millions of followers touched by this perspective, whether in Christian bookstores or in the pews of megachurches. The logic of oil patch politics explains the fierce defense of land and natural resources that every bit as much as abortion and the politics of sexuality has defined the past half-century of presidential politics.

If religious beliefs grounded in the political economy of a particular geographic region were one crucial contributor to a president's worldview—or at least the worldviews of key actors that presidents encountered—ideology, especially during America's Cold War, was another. Will Hitchcock explores the ideology of a president who was often said to lack one—Dwight D. Eisenhower. Ike's worldview was bounded by four bedrock beliefs: an American exceptionalism built on a unique relationship with individual citizens who voluntarily pledged their allegiance to the state in exchange for the state's protection of their collective security and right to remain individuals; fear of the tendency of that state to expand, thus abrogating individual rights; fear that other states might impose their ideological will or geopolitical influence on the United States through the alien ideology of Communism; and an abiding commitment to internationalism. Early in his administration, Eisenhower laid bare the sinews of this ideology in public statements and behind closed doors. His embrace of a massive nuclear deterrent to ensure America's place in the world embodied many of these ideas. Yet Eisenhower was not rigidly bound by his ideology: he could be pragmatic, even opportunistic. Such was the case with his decision to end the Korean War without achieving victory on the battlefield, and his outreach to the Soviet Union in the wake of Stalin's death. Hitchcock illustrates that when it came to the issue of nuclear strategy, the president was caught between ideological commitment and a more nuanced response to changing Soviet strategies around the globe, in some ways reaping the worst of all worlds when it came to adapting military strategy and reining in military spending. The lesson here for students of the presidency is that the difficult work of charting the influence of ideology on a president's worldview is worth the effort, if only to demonstrate that such ideational values may well serve as only one of many factors that influence presidential behavior.

Arguably, no group has overcome more social and political barriers in the twentieth century than African Americans. From a position that N. D. B. Connolly characterizes as "apartheid" at the start of the twentieth century, most African Americans have attained full citizenship. And presidents have been an important part of that story, although not always on the side advocating inclusion. Yet, in his essay, Connolly pursues a perspective that raises serious doubts about just how broad and deep these changes have been. By narrating the relatively static role assigned to (and assumed by) high-level African American appointees, Connolly exposes just how elusive the goal of equality remains. Whether it was beleaguered Eisenhower White House aide E. Frederic Morrow, a specialist in domestic policy who was constantly putting out fires with foreign diplomats denied service in the Washington, D.C., area, or leading foreign relations expert and Secretary of State Condoleezza Rice, who rushed back to Washington to deal with the racial fallout from Hurricane Katrina, skin color mattered at least as much as (and in some cases more than) expertise when it came to advising while black. When not putting out fires, Connolly demonstrates, the history of black presidential appointees over the past seventy-five years has yielded a consistent set of lessons. Such appointees are expected to demonstrate the racial sensitivity of presidents, regardless of party, and to fend off attacks from the left, in the case of Democratic presidents, by urging patience and inspiring hope in their brothers and sisters. Yet their most significant contribution to presidential politics, Connolly insists, is to "affirm the stories Americans tell themselves about themselves," stories of personal progress and obstacles overcome by these high-profile appointees. Connolly even suggests that with the election of America's first African American president, who ran on a platform of hope, some of the tasks and restrictions that once been outsourced to black appointees can now be handled "in house." Eschewing both the top-down framework that an older presidential synthesis assigned to race relations and the bottom-up approach that social and cultural scholars have deployed to explain many of the social changes of the past half-century, Connolly fixes his gaze squarely on race and place, noting that when it comes to African Americans in the White House, serious revision of the standard accounts is in order.

One of the conduits for distilling social, cultural, and technological changes in ways that presidents are forced to come to grips with the media environment in which they operate. Susan Douglas reviews the history of presidential relations with the media over the past century. Douglas charts key turning points in this relationship, such as the rise of radio, which provided a relatively unmediated, far more intimate connection between president and national audience; the emergence of television; and, ultimately, the arrival of the internet and social media. Rarely were presidents quick to figure out how best to capitalize on these changing technologies and the social practices in which they were embedded. Yet there were significant advantages for those first movers who did master the possibilities of the new media. With the overlay of multiple media forms and venues, presidents have had to pay increasing attention to the performative aspect of their administrations. While presidential tweets might be considered the

logical endpoint of a "rhetorical" presidency that began in the early twentieth century, presidents who have retained some control over their media
environments have required robust management strategies vis-à-vis the
media, along with the ability to personalize their message, no matter what
the outlet.

One of the themes embedded in the history of presidential negotiations
with the evolving media environment chronicled by Susan Douglas is the
emergence of presidential candidates as celebrities. Kathryn Brownell
examines that phenomenon in detail in her essay. She concludes that crafting a celebrity image was a conscious choice on the part of the Kennedy
campaign—one driven by Kennedy's need to demonstrate his electability
to traditional party bosses in an age when primaries were "beauty contests" and not decisive in procuring delegates. The young Kennedy had
few other options open to him, and the added element, given his choice,
of his family's extensive business dealings with Hollywood and familiar-
ity with California-style media-driven campaigns. Brownell points out that
for all the retrospective congratulations and emulation, Kennedy's choice
was not an easy one and was roundly criticized by leading members of his
own party, not to mention his opponent, Richard Nixon. Eight years later,
convinced that he had been defeated by style rather than substance, Nixon
took a page out of the Kennedy playbook and emulated some of the same
techniques, making candidate-as-celebrity a staple of American presidential politics. Brownell naturalizes the relationship between candidate and
media, framing such strategies as deliberate choices among many options
in a campaign and assessing the risks along with the benefits of these
choices. As such, she makes media strategy one of the standard tools for
assessing presidential power, as opposed to an exogenous factor subject
to technological breakthroughs, on the one hand, and the candidate's cha-
risma or personality, on the other.

CHAPTER 4

The Reagan Devolution

*Movement Conservatives and the
Right's Days of Rage, 1988–1994*

ROBERT O. SELF

At an early Republican presidential primary debate in 2011, eight candidates gathered under the wings of Air Force One at the Ronald Reagan Presidential Library to trade jibes and audition policies. The host, NBC's Brian Williams, observed that each of the candidates, many of them representatives of the right wing of the party, "would like to claim his [Reagan's] legacy." Williams oversaw what by the twenty-first century had become a regular, four-year ritual among Republican presidential hopefuls, the competition for Reagan's mantle, the right to position themselves as the recognized inheritors of his forthright conservatism.[1]

The art of politics, and perhaps especially the art of presidential politics, lies in the continual recalibration of public memory. Democratic Presidents Franklin D. Roosevelt and John F. Kennedy were posthumously lionized as liberal icons, despite the attacks each endured from liberals in their party while in office. So, too, with Ronald Reagan. The man whose legacy so many Republican politicians, including those from the farthest rightward provinces of the party, felt (and feel) they must claim was in his own day widely and at times pointedly criticized by conservatives, who charged him with insufficient enthusiasm for their agenda. "If it is 'morning in America,'" the conservative pundit at the Free Congress Foundation, William Lind, wrote in 1987, "the dawn proved false." Lind was among the gentler of the critics.[2]

Political movements in American democracy are by nature disappointments in waiting. The aspirations that collect millions of voters under an ideological banner are always imperfectly realized in the compromises and tradeoffs that constitute actual governing in a constitutional system of divided powers. In this regard, the forces massing on the right in the late 1970s were like most American insurgencies, regardless of political stripe, before them. The gushy nostalgia of post–Reagan era commemoration has obscured the wobblier reality of 1980s movement conservatism, in which success and failure were intertwined. Amid the ordinary catalog of political victories and defeats, however, what stands out about that era's movement conservatism—especially the Religious Right and what became known as the profamily and eventually the "family values" movement—is how central a narrative of defeat and victimization became to the movement itself.[3]

What interests me in this essay is not the extent or duration of the Reagan Revolution, whatever we may mean by that term. I am interested, rather, in taking the measure of Reagan's right-wing critics and assessing how movement conservatives imagined a post-Reagan political landscape. The essay concentrates on the period of intensive right-wing protest and mobilization between 1988 and 1994, what we might call the right's "days of rage." Having supported, and not infrequently battled, Reagan throughout his two-term presidency, a range of conservative critics launched into open revolt in these years against what they saw as the president's tepid commitment to their still-unfinished "revolution." Others, notably anti-abortion activists and conservative Southern Baptists, bolted further rightward less as a reaction to Reagan himself than in response to the general political environment, which they viewed as hostile to their aims. George H. W. Bush's ascension to party leadership in 1988 and the presidency in 1989 only amplified the anxiety of movement conservatives. They saw the Reagan-Bush handoff as something akin to a betrayal of the conservative revolution and a tacit return to the me-too centrist liberalism of the Eisenhower-Rockefeller years.[4]

Reagan's relationship to movement conservatives raises questions that lie at the heart of this volume. Political scientist Daniel Tichenor has written of the "uneasy yet pivotal partnership between the presidency and social movements." The space between "uneasy" and "pivotal" demands exploration. Presidents have at critical junctures in the modern history of the office both seized on and contained the radical impulses of social movements, on both the left and the right. Presidents confront, as Stephen Skowronek put it a generation ago, "several institutional orderings simultaneously." One such ordering is composed of "governing coalitions and party systems." Reagan depended on a governing coalition whose survival required him, as it had

Democrats Roosevelt and Lyndon B. Johnson before him, at once to invigorate and to domesticate the social movement energies swirling just beneath
conventional party politics. Once Reagan's presidency was over, his successor
proved a less adept manager of this delicate mandate.[5]

The Reagan coalition offers one instance of a more general principle
of social movements in American political and presidential history. In a
vast continental nation of hundreds of millions of inhabitants, with acute
regional, religious, class, and racial differences and governed through a profoundly decentralized majoritarian political system with only two competitive parties, social movements face considerable political constraints. So do
presidents, the de facto heads of their political parties. For social movements,
achieving meaningful political leverage—as the Populists discovered in 1896,
the labor movement in 1936, and the New Right in 1980—has depended
on their joining a fractious and ideologically diverse major party. For presidential hopefuls and presidents once in office, success and failure can depend on their management of social movement constituencies that typically
view the compromises and tradeoffs of traditional politics with suspicion or
contempt—consider, for example, the relationship between the New Left
and the Democratic Party between 1964 and 1972. American political parties, at least until the last two decades, have tended to be less ideological than
regional, religious, and racial, making them complicated, at best, and inhos-
pitable, at worst, vehicles for social movements.

The argument set forth here is straightforward. Having ridden a wave
of social movement mobilization to the presidency in 1980, Reagan proved
a more cautious and pragmatic politician in office than many movement
conservatives could countenance. Their narrative of betrayal would become
an essential feature of that movement and a spur to future mobilization.
Determined to outflank the Republican moderates who still dominated the
national party apparatus, movement conservatives of various stripes launched
a series of initiatives—the "days of rage"—that signalled their determination
to accelerate the party's, and the nation's, ideological transformation that had
begun in the mid-1970s. Their efforts in the half-dozen years in between
Pat Robertson's bid for the presidential nomination in 1988 and the Newt
Gingrich–orchestrated 1994 Republican takeover of the House of Representatives institutionalized a particular brand of internecine warfare in the
Republican Party, one that has shaped presidential politics in every election
cycle since then.

By "movement conservatives" I mean largely those activists and voters animated by what commentators later called "social" and sometimes "cultural"
issues. Their defining positions were opposition to abortion, homosexuality,

the Equal Rights Amendment, federal interference with public schools (on issues ranging from racial segregation to prayer), pornography, sex education, crime, and welfare. They might best be described as activists and voters appalled by what they believed to be a national moral decline that, in their view, the federal government had at best done nothing to arrest and at worst had actively abetted. Many such activists and voters supported other conservative objectives, such as lower taxes, increased military spending, and deregulation. Yet national moral decline remained their signal political banner, action to reverse that decline their presidential measuring stick. Movement conservatives constituted a critical constituency of the New Right, which also prominently included anticommunist hardliners and free-market fundamentalists, even as their organizers and political patrons contended that they *were* the New Right.[6]

Taken together, the events that constituted the "days of rage" bequeathed to the next generation of Republican presidential candidates what pundits came to call the "culture wars." The culture wars had many sponsors and diverse expressions in American life, but in presidential politics they were first and foremost a product of the quest to anchor right-wing commitment in a post-Reagan world. The range of issues embraced by movement conservatives after 1988 did not differ substantially from those of a decade earlier. What had changed, as the former Nixon aide and converted evangelical Baptist Charles Colson put it in 1988, was the passing of eight years under Reagan during which "most items on the evangelical social agenda [were] either defeated or shelved."[7]

In an especially telling exchange in the middle of Reagan's first term, the Moral Majority's vice president, Cal Thomas, sent an accusatory letter to presidential aide Morton Blackwell about the administration's "incremental" approach to conservative aims: "Incremental would be something one could hope for with a liberal Democratic administration." Blackwell wrote back with a simple rejoinder: "With respect to incrementalism, the fact is it works." On the heels of a 1982 *Newsweek* report that Jerry Falwell's influence in the Reagan White House was on the wane, Blackwell reassured the Moral Majority's followers that the preacher's access to the president was "undiminished." This sort of back and forth was common during Reagan's tenure, usually falling to senior aides to manage. The president himself stepped in at key moments, as in his thunderous speech to the National Religious Broadcasters convention in 1984, a critical juncture in his reelection positioning in which he endorsed a constitutional amendment guaranteeing school prayer.[8]

Public assessments of Reagan's shortcomings during his presidency typically remained respectful and restrained, if pointed. Early in the president's second term, when conservatives were already contemplating 1988, Paul

Weyrich, who did as much as anyone to draw evangelical ministers into Reagan's political orbit in 1980 and 1984, credited Reagan with having "held the conservative movement together remarkably well," but added, "despite his startling lack of accomplishments in a number of areas." Earlier, on the eve of the 1984 election, National Conservative Political Action Committee director Terry Dolan called the idea that "conservatives are running everything" nothing but "nonsense." He warned that "1986 is going to be a disaster for a large number of conservatives because of the Reagan Administration." (It was, with Republicans losing their hard-won Senate majority.) Fred Barnes, a senior editor at the *New Republic* and an evangelical Christian, concluded in 1988 that for the Christian Right, "very little has been achieved" under Reagan. "The sun is setting on the Reagan years," Colson observed in a 1988 column in *Christianity Today*, "and on the hopes of once-euphoric evangelicals as well." Nothing short of a feeling of dread crept over movement conservatives, especially evangelicals, during Reagan's second term. They worried both about minimal progress on their political agenda and whether after Reagan they would have even rhetorical support from a Republican presidential nominee.[9]

This essay considers the dilemma faced by movement conservatives in Republican presidential politics between the mid-1980s and the mid-1990s. Major developments in that decade, including Operation Rescue's anti-abortion protests, the conservative takeover of the Southern Baptist Convention, Pat Robertson's bid for the 1988 Republican presidential nomination, the rise of the Christian Coalition, and Pat Buchanan's presidential run in 1992, suggest that Reagan interrupted and contained but never fully resolved the struggle between centrist and right-wing forces in the Republican Party. After 1988, movement conservatives transformed their dilemma, born of their minority status, into a strategy: pushing presidential, and national, politics rightward not by swaying a majority of voters but by mobilizing a consistent 3 to 5 percent of the electorate. Within a nation more or less evenly divided and politically clustered around the center, that small percentage was often enough to win congressional elections and was certainly enough to command the attention of presidential candidates in Republican primaries and to secure a prominent place in the drafting of party platforms.

Political candidates and consultants alike concluded in the post-Reagan years that winning elections, and especially the presidency, required calibrating the culture wars at just the right temperature: too hot and the candidate risked burning his or her electoral chances, too cold and enthusiasm among crucial voters flagged. Thus in addition to temperamentally inclined cultural warriors—men like Pat Robertson, Pat Buchanan, William Bennett, and

Gary Bauer—a group of pragmatic culture-war managers emerged, party officials and Republican consultants—men like Lee Atwater, Ralph Reed, and eventually Karl Rove—who endeavored to temper and shape the enthusiasm and passion, and sometimes the ideological extremism, of the Religious Right. Indeed, for consultant-activists like Rove, culture war management became a lucrative full-time job.

Finally, whatever failures and compromises it endured, the New Right achieved the objective of insurgencies everywhere: It changed the terms of debate and placed its opponents on the defensive. Civil rights activists, feminists and other women's advocates, lesbians and gay men, and liberals generally found themselves on their heels for a long period after the 1980 election. They had to defend not just the legal and legislative gains of the previous two decades but the "rights" framework in which those gains were embedded. The Reagan coalition transformed the debate about the content of American citizenship from one about rights to one about government provision. The issue became not who deserved equal citizenship but what would the government provide and support, what would it guarantee. Once reframed that way, rights, which imply state obligation, increasingly yielded to free-market orthodoxy.

Nowhere was disappointment with the pace of change during the Reagan presidency more evident than among the most passionate foes of abortion, who took to the streets to stop a moral crime they believed politicians would not. Between 1979 and 1984, right-to-life activists, inspired by a radical posture of moral certainty, had begun to protest at clinics and hospitals, led by Chicago's Jo Scheidler. Scheidler's Pro-Life Action League initiated small protests at Chicago-area clinics in 1979, when such tactics were still considered too extreme by much of the right-to-life movement. Scheidler's "truth squads" drew on the example set by left-leaning 1960s-era activists, employing direct action to garner headlines and publicity for the cause.[10] The context was a series of political disappointments for the right-to-life movement in Reagan's first years in the White House. In July of 1981, just four months into office, the president appointed Sandra Day O'Connor, a moderate Sunbelt Republican who in 1970 had voted in the Arizona legislature to repeal her state's strict abortion law, to the Supreme Court. Letters from ordinary Americans and evangelical ministers alike poured into the Reagan White House expressing outrage at this missed opportunity. "Reagan Goofs!" the National Pro-Life Political Action Committee declared, calling the nomination "a slap in the face to all pro-lifers." The following year, still smarting over the O'Connor nomination and likewise over Reagan's reluctance, influenced by his centrist pollster Richard Wirthlin, to make a definitive pro-life statement to the press, the *Moral Majority Report* speculated that "old line Republicans think they have the New Right in their hip pocket." Hardly, the report continued. "There are several places we can and will go," including "home" on election day, "ensuring Republican defeats."[11]

Equally frustrating from the standpoint of right-to-life advocates and movement conservatives was Reagan's lukewarm stance on the various Human Life Amendments introduced in Senate committees that year. Anti-abortion stalwarts Jesse Helms and Orrin Hatch each sponsored versions in the Republican-controlled chamber. However, in a testament to the degree to which abortion was not yet strictly defined by partisan affiliation, Robert Packwood, a liberal Oregon Republican, led a filibuster against the Helms bill. Calls among the anti-abortion ranks for Reagan to intervene reached an intense pitch, but he stayed out of the fray and made only a modest, largely symbolic appeal. Reagan followed Wirthlin's polls, none of which showed that a majority of Americans favored anything like a right-to-life constitutional amendment. Reagan eventually diffused some of the right-to-life criticism by nominating dozens of anti-abortion judges to the federal bench during his eight years in office, nominating Robert Bork to the Supreme Court in 1987, and issuing key executive orders, such as the well-known "Mexico City Policy" forbidding American foreign aid to organizations that perform or provide information about abortions. These measures stilled some, though not all, of the right-to-life bridling, particularly as the realists in the anti-abortion forces recognized that the future of reproductive policy would almost certainly remain in the hands of the courts, where Reagan's judges (they correctly predicted) would prove invaluable allies.[12]

The Reagan administration's strategy was to play the long game with movement conservatives. President Jimmy Carter provided the close-at-hand cautionary tale. Embraced by evangelicals in 1976 as one of their own, Carter quickly and decisively reversed that affection once in office. Despite advice from his advisers, particularly his religious liaison, Southern Baptist Robert Maddox, to appoint a prominent evangelical to his administration or to make some other conciliatory gesture to the likes of Falwell and Oral Roberts, Carter kept evangelicals at arm's length. The political cost to him in 1980 has been well documented. Reagan, in contrast, brought evangelicals into his administration, where he gave (Bork, federal judges, Mexico City policy) and withheld (O'Connor, Human Life Amendment) in equal measure. Reagan's long game was far more ad hoc than it might seem in retrospect, and it evolved over time. Yet it is clear that his most decisive actions in support of the pro-life movement, with the exception of Bork's appointment, were those with the least immediate political cost.[13]

Despite, or perhaps because of, this pragmatism, in 1984 far-right disillusionment with both the Reagan administration and the abortion stalemate more generally intensified, and radical-fringe right-to-life forces surged past Scheidler's direct action. They turned to clinic bombings, arson, and gunfire. That year alone, there were more than thirty incidents, largely in the South and the Southwest. Two clinics in Virginia and Maryland were firebombed in February; two separate arson attempts targeted a clinic in Everett, Washington, in March and April; Molotov cocktails were hurled into several clinics in Texas in August and September; and bombings struck clinics in Washington, D.C., Georgia, and Florida. In most cases, the perpetrators remained unknown and were never apprehended, and right-to-life organizations denied complicity in the violence. But virtually all of the attacks targeted clinics where there had been extensive picketing and protesting by right-to-life activists, a coincidence exploited by pro-choice advocates.[14]

In this increasingly tense context, one of the many young conservative Christian activists inspired by Scheidler, an Elm Bible College graduate from upstate New York named Randall Terry, refocused the clinic protest movement. Terry founded Operation Rescue in 1986, not simply to stop abortions but also "to rescue the nation." "America still deserves the righteous wrath of almighty God," Terry would write. From 1987 to 1991, Operation Rescue advanced the front lines of the anti-abortion movement into new territory. A series of demonstrations in 1988, which took place in locations like Philadelphia, where 700 activists were arrested, and New York City, where 900 were arrested, concluded in Atlanta, site of the 1988 Democratic National Convention. In the "Siege of Atlanta," 1,200 activists, including Terry, were arrested. A serious and devoted student of civil disobedience, Terry understood that producing "tension in the nation and pressure on the politicians" (a quote strikingly similar to a line from Martin Luther King Jr.'s "Letter from Birmingham Jail") was a legitimate objective of protest. The anti-abortion movement's direct-action surge continued through 1991, culminating in the massive "summer of mercy" protests in Wichita, Kansas. Americans, accustomed to seeing left-wing protestors dragged off to jail, found newspapers and television news broadcasts suddenly filled with images of their right-wing counterparts facing, and embracing, the same fate.[15]

While Operation Rescue filled the streets and jails, pastorships were on the line in the struggle for control of the Southern Baptist Convention (SBC). Internecine Baptist warfare (there is no other word for it) was not in itself a product of disappointment with Reagan. But the outcome of that war decisively raised the stakes in the rightward march of evangelical forces in the late 1980s. Despite the prominence in the Religious Right of Southern Baptists Jerry Falwell, James Robison, and Charles Stanley, among other ministers, the SBC itself held for a time to the long and proud Baptist traditions of individual church autonomy and respect for civil liberties. For decades, the fundamentalist-versus-modern controversy that had split many other American congregations had been kept at bay in the SBC by what one historian has called a "grand compromise." Beginning in the late 1960s, however, fundamentalists, led by W. A. Criswell, pastor of a Dallas church, one of the largest in the nation, gained increasing influence over the organization and in the early 1980s moved decisively to win control of SBC agencies and its seminaries, the gateways to individual church pastorships.[16]

Fundamentalists cited doctrinal differences over "inerrancy" as the source of their mobilization, but few involved in the dispute doubted that shifts in southern, and American, culture lay at the heart of the struggle. Criswell and his allies charged that SBC seminaries taught modern, historical readings of the Bible rather than emphasizing scripture as the "inerrant" and infallible word of God. Only a return to inerrancy could save the Convention. Criswell ally and editor of *Christianity Today* Harold Lindsell penned two polemical books—*The Battle for the Bible* (1976) and *The Bible in Balance* (1979)—that encouraged the right-wing radicals. Moderate Baptist leaders, however, contended that the inerrancy controversy was a symbol of fundamentalists' deeper concern with abortion, feminism, and homosexuality—and perhaps, not a few suggested, even a reflection of their anxiety about the erosion of southern white supremacy. William Finlator, the liberal minister of Pullen Memorial Church in Raleigh, was among those who led the fight against the fundamentalist takeover. Baptists were historically "civil libertarians," Finlator emphasized, but the fundamentalists had decided that "unless you are against gay rights, unless you are against abortion, unless you are against obscenity . . . you're not a Christian." The Baptist seminarian and ethics professor Paul Simmons used even stronger words. Comparing fundamentalism to McCarthyism, Simmons called the Criswell-inspired conservatism within the SBC "a power-crazed authoritarianism, a win-at-any-cost ethic and a total disregard for personal values and religious freedom."[17]

By the late 1980s, what observers called the conservative "takeover" of the Southern Baptist Convention was nearing its completion. Among the first and most prominent casualties were women. A campaign by fundamentalists against the ordination of female ministers was successful, based on the "submission God requires" of women. Reproductive rights suffered a similar fate. Throughout the 1970s, guided by moderates, the SBC had staked out a flexible position that recognized the spiritual validity of "pro-choice" positions. By the middle of the 1980s, however, fundamentalists had replaced this moderation with one of the most rigid anti-abortion stances taken by an American religious group. Unyielding statements from the conservative

SBC faction in the late 1980s summed up a decade of bitter infighting. On the eve of the tenth consecutive year in which a conservative had been elected SBC president, Criswell said in 1988 that liberal Baptists were only a short step from atheists, secularists, and infidels: "A skunk by any other name still stinks."[18]

Among the forums where the moderate-versus-conservative Southern Baptist conflagration played out was *The 700 Club*, televangelist Pat Robertson's Christian Broadcasting Network platform (Robertson had founded the CBN in 1961). Robertson, a member of the SBC since the early 1960s, assisted the conservative faction in the mid-1980s during a critical SBC election. Three former presidents of the organization, conservatives all, appeared on his broadcast to stress the importance of reelecting then-president and archconservative Charles Stanley. And when Robertson declared himself a candidate for the Republican nomination for U.S. president in 1988, Stanley became a crucial supporter and adviser, a role he continued to play when Robertson founded the Christian Coalition in 1989. Robertson resigned his pastorship and membership in the SBC in order to run for the presidency, but Stanley continued to serve as his direct line to right-wing SBC ministers and their political constituency, tightening the critical sinews that connected Robertson the politician with the rightward lurch of the Southern Baptists.[19]

Robertson enjoyed a rapid ascent in the conservative firmament during Reagan's second term. In 1985, Weyrich and Richard Viguerie each authored enthusiastic endorsements of Robertson as Reagan's heir apparent. "As well equipped for the post-Reagan era as anyone in our midst," Weyrich wrote. "He will help finish the job that Barry Goldwater began and Ronald Reagan continued," Viguerie added. With the New Right's two behind-the-scenes brokers backing him, Robertson enjoyed newfound attention in official Washington circles between 1985 and 1987. For movement conservatives who worried that a George H. W. Bush or Bob Dole presidency would diminish, if not extinguish, the right's influence, the crusading televangelist appeared to be the perfect antidote (Viguerie's *Conservative Digest* gave an interview with Robertson the title "The Answer to America's Problems"). Even if unelectable nationally, which virtually all honest observers and Robertson advisers believed he was, a stirring primary challenge could further instantiate New Right issues and voters in the party's fold. Declaring that "as president of the United States, I am free to serve God as my conscience dictates," Robertson ran on a campaign of moral reawakening and the "family values" that had become the Religious Right's anthem.[20]

Much of the subtext of Robertson's rise in the imagination of movement conservatives was written in struggles over social policy within the Reagan administration. Bruising internal battles over HIV/AIDS policy, abortion, welfare reform, and a range of social policies related to the family pit right-wing administration officials, led by Education Secretary William Bennett and Undersecretary of Education Gary Bauer, against Reagan's centrist, pragmatic advisers, whose moderation extended the pattern set by James Baker in Reagan's first term. Emblematic of this internal warfare was the controversy surrounding Surgeon General C. Everett Koop. In 1986, Koop's scientific instincts triumphed over Bennett and Bauer's moralism in the Surgeon General's report on HIV/AIDS, which endorsed sex education and a massive public health response to the crisis. Withering right-wing criticism, including demands that Reagan fire the erstwhile conservative physician, descended on the White House, as Bennett and Bauer fumed. The following year, after completing a major study of abortion, Koop stunned New Right activists by declaring that having an unwanted child may be more psychologically traumatic to a woman than having an abortion. Bauer, who had directed Koop to undertake the study in the first place, was furious, along with key right-to-life movement leaders. "Fire Dr. Koop forthwith," the president of March for Life demanded.[21]

Administration infighting over Koop points to a larger set of issues regarding the relationship between presidents and social movements. The presidency as an office and the executive as a dimension of the state bestow on the occupant of the White House extensive resources for both invigorating and domesticating social movements. For members of Congress, votes on the floor are ultimately the most obvious, and scrutinized, measure of their fealty to constituents. But presidents have enormous powers of appointment. Much of the struggle between Republican political pragmatists and movement conservatives in the 1980s played out, as evidenced above, inside the Reagan administration, between competing sets of advisers. Bennett and Bauer, along with Patrick Buchanan, White House press secretary from 1985 to 1987, and Edwin Meese, who served in a variety of administrative roles, including attorney general, led the conservative forces in the White House. Reagan's political appointments thus to a degree contained, even if they failed to resolve, the key tensions within his coalition. There is an obvious delicacy to this strategy, because mere presence in the bureaucratic machinery offers short-term satisfaction only. Yet disappointment, too, is its own strange reward, since it offers a narrative of incompleteness, even betrayal, that energizes the injured to redouble their efforts.

A telling example was coincident with the imbroglio over Koop. When the evangelical and profamily right complained vocally in Reagan's second term that the president had abandoned their policy agenda, the president established the Working Group on the Family and handed it to Bauer. Under the auspices of Reagan's Domestic Policy Council, headed by Attorney General Meese, Bauer assembled a critical mass of the administration's conservative appointees, including Clarence Thomas, then chairman of the EEOC; William Kristol, who was part of William Bennett's brain trust at the Department of Education; JoAnn Gasper, the right-to-life activist then at Health and Human Services (HHS); and Dorcas Hardy, an HHS staffer and advocate of social security privatization. The working group combined the Religious Right's social conservatism with tax-cutting state retrenchment in its final report, entitled *The Family: Preserving America's Future*. The report remains a striking articulation of post-1960s movement conservatism's principles and objectives, many of which found their way into executive orders and congressional legislation in subsequent years. Yet once delivered to the president, it was subject to the same "incrementalism" that had so frustrated the Moral Majority in Reagan's first term. Incrementalism contained conservatives by directing their energies toward real, if vague, objectives and thus away from criticism of the administration. But it also empowered them, because Reagan placed a good deal of executive agency rule-setting in their hands.[22]

What the Washington journalist Sidney Blumenthal in 1984 had presciently called "the tumultuous succession crisis of 1988" took shape against a background of conservative anxiety and disappointment. Incrementalism was difficult to sell to fiery activists. The crisis had all the makings of a return to 1964, when Goldwaterites had stormed the Republican National Convention to swamp the Rockefeller centrists, or 1976, when Reagan nearly defeated President Gerald R. Ford for the Republican nomination. Yet in 1988 there was no Goldwater or Reagan on the horizon, no gold-plated conservative who looked capable of uniting center and right while having a legitimate chance to win the White House. Robertson won four states and 5 percent of Republican votes in the 1988 primary. The local dimension of his political operation scored key victories, most notably in Michigan, where his supporters gained control of the state party convention. Five percent of the vote and a growing local operation was enough to get the conservative Christian agenda written deeper into the Republican platform. But it was not enough to deny Bush the nomination, whose selection of the profamily political neophyte Dan Quayle as his vice presidential running mate represented one of his few, though not insignificant, election-year gestures to movement conservatives.[23]

Robertson's 1988 campaign deployed an insurgent strategy that would become another distinct feature of post-Reagan Republican presidential politics. The strategy, an old one in modern democracies, owed its revival in the 1970s to the right-to-life movement. In state and congressional races beginning with the 1978 midterms, right-to-life activists took advantage of the logic of American elections. The 50-percent-plus-one principle for deciding political races in the United States—commonly called "first past the post"—creates unique opportunities for vocal minorities. With an evenly divided electorate, elections are frequently decided by the shift of just 3 to 5 percent of voters and sometimes even less. Insurgent political movements need not convince 51 percent of voters. They must only sway (or frighten) enough people whose convictions are not fixed to create a 51 percent majority. By 1980, one anti-abortion organization boasted, "State after state had organized anti-abort [sic] constituencies that could produce a solid 3–5% of the vote." The same national polls in which a majority of Americans endorsed abortion rights also revealed that one-third of voters were willing to support a candidate who favored banning abortion—the soft underbelly of the nation's pro-choice majority. Right-to-life strategists could amass political influence, candidate by candidate and election by election, even in the face of a pro–Roe v. Wade national consensus. Deploying the 3 to 5 percent principle, right-to-life activists had chased virtually all pro-choice Republicans from the party by the early 1990s (as pro-choice activists endeavored to do the reverse in the Democratic Party).[24]

Once the parties had been largely—although it must be remembered, never entirely—purged of their abortion-issue minorities, a new election-cycle drama took hold. Republican candidates and officials had to appease their most ardent anti-abortion constituents without appearing to vault radically past the broad middle of public opinion, which since 1973 has favored some degree of reproductive choice. The Bush administration's response to the major abortion-related Supreme Court cases of his tenure represented early instances of this new pattern. In Webster v. Reproductive Health Services (1989) and Planned Parenthood v. Casey (1992), vocal Religious Right voices insisted on, and Justices William Rehnquist (Chief), Antonin Scalia, Clarence Thomas, and Byron White vociferously advocated, overturning Roe. And in Casey, as the president's advisers eyed the 1992 election, the Bush administration in fact filed a brief pushing to overturn the 1973 decision. The moderate Bush, who had a history of cautious support for abortion rights, thought it prudent to appease his family values critics. Even though in both cases the justices lacked the five votes necessary to overturn Roe, the rulings represented a dramatic narrowing of the accessibility of abortion—and thus a substantial, if "incremental," victory for anti-abortion activists. Yet in the internal narrative of the Religious Right, a limited victory was regarded as a defeat, fueling even greater passionate opposition to the moral turpitude of the nation's laws.[25]

The longtime conservative strategist Pat Buchanan rode this wave of discontent during his campaign for the Republican presidential nomination in the 1992 primaries. Though he did not unseat the incumbent Bush, his jeremiad-like address at the 1992 Republican National Convention in Houston resounded through American conservatism and national politics writ large. Buchanan claimed that a "cultural war" had engulfed the nation. A Democratic administration, he warned, would bring homosexuality, feminism, abortion on demand, godlessness, and a draft dodger (in the form of Bill Clinton, the Democratic nominee) into the heart of American government. Implying that the conservative revolution remained superficial and fragile, Buchanan's intemperance signaled something that close observers could have predicted: the arrival of a new and unyielding righteousness in mainstream American politics. For the second election cycle in a row, a candidate claiming to speak for absolute religious values and to command a constituency of religious followers had been ushered to the center ring of the nation's politic circus.[26]

That worldview was in evidence in the Southern Baptist Convention controversy of the late 1980s as well as in Buchanan's speech. It posited a never-ending "war" over American "values." In this war, because it was fought over moral absolutes rather than the content of a shared citizenship, any action or rhetoric was justified and any compromise was a betrayal. Even though many establishment Republicans found this worldview off-putting, Buchanan garnered just under three million Republican primary votes to just over nine million for Bush. More than his fellow cultural warrior Pat Robertson, Buchanan discovered that he had the power to influence conservative debate, even if he would not be president. The number of Americans who shared his worldview, or at least voted for it, was growing. Robertson's 5 percent had become Buchanan's 25 percent.[27]

However, many critics in the Republican camp blamed Bush's 1992 presidential loss on Buchanan and rushed to distance the party from the Religious Right's radicalism. After the 1992 election, Oregon Republican Party Chair Craig L. Berkman lashed out at its intransigence: "We have to get the party back from the mean-spirited, intolerant people who want to interject big government into people's personal lives." In that election cycle, antigay Measure 9 in Oregon and Measure 2 in Colorado revealed the power, as well as the limits, of the "culture war" political formula. In Oregon, the far-right Oregon Citizens Alliance (OCA) placed before voters a measure that would have defined homosexuality as "abnormal, wrong, unnatural, and perverse," while denying all protections to lesbian and gay people. Echoing Buchanan's speech just a few months before, Lon Mabon, head of the OCA, told his followers that "these are the first units of the cultural war meeting on a political battlefield." While Oregon's voters turned down Mabon's measure, the less rhetorically extreme Colorado measure passed. This law forbade local protections in housing and employment for lesbians and gay men, backed by supporters who claimed these were "special privileges." In the difference between the Oregon and Colorado measures, the right found its calibrated route to political success, even if the surprise Supreme Court decision in *Romer v. Evans* (1996) declared the Colorado measure unconstitutional.[28]

Colorado and Oregon were part of conservative religious activists' renewed attention to local organizing following the relative disappointment of the Reagan Revolution and the Moral Majority's overwhelming focus on Washington, D.C. In Oregon, despite the statewide defeat in 1992, the OCA won more than two dozen antigay measures at the municipal and county levels between 1992 and 1994 and established a strong presence throughout the state, except metropolitan Portland. In Oklahoma, conservative evangelicals helped Republicans sweep Democrats out of power in the 1994 elections; five of the state's seven congressional representatives (they enjoyed a 7–1 advantage over Democrats) had strong ties to the Religious Right. In South Carolina, a born-again Southern Baptist, with fervent support among the state's Pentecostal and charismatic activists, won the governorship. In Louisiana, conservative evangelicals controlled a third of the Republican Party's state committee, and in California Religious Right activists were victorious in eleven of thirteen targeted state assembly races. The Religious Right found local success in Texas, Alaska, Georgia, and Florida as well. In all, the Christian Coalition and other Religious Right and pro-family groups made 1994 the year of evangelical political resurgence.[29]

By that year, Republican Party strategists and opinion-makers had institutionalized the far right's rhetoric of cultural warfare. In 1992, owing to Buchanan's challenge of President Bush in the primaries and the increasing power of evangelical activists, the Republican Party platform had embraced a wholesale conservative family values ideology. "If I didn't know any better, I would assume the platform was written by the religious right," said Martin Mawyer, president of the Christian Action Network. However, in the wake of the party's presidential loss in 1992, strategists led by Newt Gingrich proposed the "Contract with America" for the 1994 congressional midterm elections, which was composed of conservative economic orthodoxy more than family values demands. Evangelical disappointment with the Republican promises of 1994 was palpable, however. "There are many of us who think that America's deepest problems are not economic in orientation, they are laden with the debate over values," said James A. Smith of the Southern Baptist Christian Life Commission. In the spring of 1995 Ralph Reed, director of the Christian Coalition from 1989 to 1997, as a response to Gingrich's choice of tactic, introduced his organization's own "Contract with the American Family" to "strengthen families and restore common sense values."[30]

Tactical adjustments from year to year or campaign to campaign, however, did little to change the basic conservative dynamic at work in these years. There is little doubt that many Republicans remained uncomfortable with the Religious Right. Nevertheless, a substantial portion of far-right family values conservatives believed they were fighting a cultural war. And that was enough to make a political difference. To many conservatives, their rhetoric and determination had risen justifiably. They had to match what they saw as the extreme demands of feminists, lesbians and gay men, and others on the liberal left. Their rhetoric and successful political tactics set the stage for a new political era. With liberals on the defensive, centrist Democrats in the 1990s grew more aggressive in their efforts to find a political defensible middle ground—a "vital center" for a new age—that could enable them to win elections and fend off the right's rage.

The surge of right-wing activism in the half decade following the Reagan presidency amplified the disagreements that the administration had endeavored to contain between 1981 and 1988. Pat Robertson's bid for the Republican presidential nomination in 1988 in this respect represented the closing of one era and the opening of another. On one side of that divide, the Christian and profamily right had spent a decade institution-building, forging the political capacity to join the Reagan coalition and shape its tone and agenda. Robertson's campaign, along with the far more fiery Operation Rescue protests in New York, Atlanta, and Wichita, were tacit admissions that for all of that work, the ordinary realities of political give-and-take had prevented movement conservatives from achieving their ultimate objectives. Developments during the decade regarding abortion and HIV/AIDS demonstrated that an increasing number of conservatives were determined to advance an ever narrower, indeed nearly absolutist, definition of family and sexual morality. In the singular logic of political movements, the right's defeats encouraged an internal narrative of victimization, which in turn amplified the call to action among the conservative grassroots.

What came to be called the culture war was therefore a struggle for the hearts and minds of conservatives, as much as or more than a battle cry against liberalism. Buchanan's 1992 jeremiad was directed at candidate Clinton, but his real audience was in the convention hall itself. Beyond the obvious fact that the twenty-first century canonization of Reagan on the right indulged in substantial revisionism, what can we learn about the Reagan presidency and its relationship to social movements from the days of rage? I would hazard two interrelated observations.

First, the critiques of government leveled by various factions of the right merged ideologically but diverged tactically. In other words, family values worked ideologically as an anti-statist doctrine. Its emphasis on heterosexual nuclear families in need of moral protection—rather than economic support—was one of the critical elements that gave twentieth-century conservatism its first real mass movement capacity (the other was the broad resistance to desegregation). But ideological alignment did not mean tactical or temperamental alignment. Reagan made heroic efforts to institutionalize the family values right in his administration in the president's second term, especially with key appointments, executive orders, and the creation of the Working Group on the Family. The right's attempt to remake government from the inside out made small gains (such as institutionalization of the child tax credit and the final defeat of the movement for government subsidized child care) but was also too achingly slow, and was obstructed by far too many compromises and defeats, to mollify a movement that still looked at formal politics from the outside in.

One might well argue that this is simply to reiterate an obvious truism: social movements, of whatever political persuasion, are by their nature allergic to the compromises of legislative politics, especially in a two-party, non-parliamentary system. But all social movements are not created equal. And this is the second point. *Inerrancy* was not an accidental term. The most aggressive and committed among movement conservative activists were fired by an unforgiving sense of moral absolutes. By the 1984 elections, pro-life and pro-choice activists had remade the two parties by purging them of their opponents: pro-choice Republicans largely disappeared as did most pro-life Democrats in a process that was not natural or inevitable but was doggedly pursued from the ground up in the election cycles between 1974 and 1982. Yet this very success ironically meant that over time the profamily right eroded its capacity to discipline Republican politicians—they were all, by the 1990s, already pro-life. Their only option was escalation.

Other conservative strategists plotted a less wrathful way forward. With great fanfare in 1987, Paul Weyrich and the Free Congress Foundation announced the publication of *Cultural Conservatism*. Written by Lind and a Catholic thinker named William Marshner, husband of the antifeminist activist Connie Marshner, *Cultural Conservatism* represented an attempt to correct what Weyrich called "certain shortcomings" of the religious and profamily right while still recognizing the limitations of what Reagan had achieved. The way forward, the book stressed, was a cultural renewal that would address the "moral vacuum" at the center of post-1960s American life. Weyrich, no political neophyte, sought a tactical middle ground. He criticized Reagan, writing that "nothing this president has done . . . could not be wiped away by a single Democratic president working with solid liberal majorities." But he also called on conservatives to contain their "hatred of government" in order to create a sustainable political coalition capable of producing lasting change.[31]

During the years of the Reagan presidency, the religious and profamily right claimed two massive accomplishments. First, they shifted the political debate about American citizenship away from rights toward government provision—what government ought to *provide*. Whether it was access to abortion and sex education or to research and potentially life-saving AIDS drugs, the right used family politics both to challenge women's and lesbian and gay rights and to oppose the taxpayer provisions and legislation (childcare or AIDS research, for example) that would render any such rights actual and meaningful. Second, they recast liberalism for large numbers of Americans as a moral threat rather than a lift up. In place of the post-1960s liberal left's expanded citizenship, capacious definition of family, and belief in government assistance, the right posited a moral family that required government protection. This shift in American politics was not attributable to one piece of legislation, once court decision, or one protest. Just as the left changed American politics in the 1960s and early 1970s through years of organizing, petition, and agitation, the religious and profamily right did something similar in the 1980s and 1990s.

And yet since Reagan's 1984 landslide reelection, the Republican presidential candidate has won the popular vote only two times—George H. W. Bush in 1988 and his son, George W. Bush, in 2004. That's two elections out of seven. Despite widespread political success at the state and local levels, movement conservatism has not consistently secured the presidency within its orbit. Explanations for Republicans' lack of success at winning the popular presidential vote since 1988 are varied and complex, of course. But any account certainly has to include an assessment of the challenges presidents and presidential candidates have faced in managing the New Right, one of the most important and volatile social movements in American history.

CHAPTER 5

There Will Be Oil

Presidents, Wildcat Religion, and the
Culture Wars of Pipeline Politics

DARREN DOCHUK

On a dull April day, at a nondescript place (a Holiday Inn coffee shop) George W. Bush submitted his life to God. Bush's momentous turn occurred in 1984 during an encounter with evangelist Arthur Blessitt, a peripatetic preacher known worldwide for dragging a twelve foot-tall, one-wheeled cross with him wherever he ministered. By 1984 he had lugged his crucifix thirty-six thousand miles in sixty countries on six continents. It was amid great fanfare then that the prophet arrived in Midland, Texas. Bush learned of the excitement from Jim Sale, a business acquaintance who served as chief organizer of Blessitt's visit. At Sale's urging, Bush met the minister at the local Holidome to talk about God. The minister wasted no time in asking his standard existential question: "If you died this moment, do you have the assurance you would go to heaven?" Bush blurted "no" and then succumbed to Blessitt's message. Holding hands, the two men prayed the sinner's prayer, and Bush left the hotel a changed man. Thrilled with the outcome, Blessitt wrote in his journal words evangelicals would remember for years: "A good and powerful day. Led Vice President Bush's son to Jesus today. George Bush Jr.!! This is great. Glory to God."[1]

Pundits too would soon trumpet these words as evidence of a president's remarkable faith. In the lead-up to the 2000 election conservative lobbyists touted Bush's conversion as a reason to vote Republican. Nimbly, they glanced over Blessitt's eccentricities to highlight other evidences of Bush's evangelical soul, for instance his 1985 encounter with a more respected preacher, Billy Graham. As Bush himself would retell it, it was under Graham's counsel at a gathering in Kennebunkport that his "rededication" to Christ became real: "He [Graham] led me to . . . a new walk where I would recommit my heart to Jesus Christ." Bush's team pointed to yet another illustration of their candidate's transformation. In 1986, while celebrating his fortieth birthday, Bush imbibed too much. The next day he decided he would quit drinking and turned to a men's bible study group for mentoring. During the next few years he continued to "mature" as a Christian: he gave up smoking (a last vestige of his "former lifestyle"), prayed regularly, and read devotional literature before going to bed. Inspired by Graham and pushed by alcoholism into a relationship with God, Bush thus approached Washington able, in his devotees' opinions, to echo Harry Truman's meditation: "I ask only to be a good and faithful servant of my Lord."[2]

Though spanning a spectrum of opinion, with some doubting the authenticity of Bush's faith and others refusing to question it, historians have cited Bush's redemptive narratives as evidence of God's presence in the White House. Reveling in this triumph of Christian witness, Religious Right chroniclers have heralded the Lord's providential design for drawing a back-slider back to faith and into the ultimate halls of power. Even when harboring some hesitancy about the depths of his daily Christian practice they have painted Bush as the "real deal in terms of his walk with Christ." Left-leaning scribes have seen Bush's spirituality as a ruse driven by opportunism, but a sign nonetheless of a skilled politician who could use theology to connect with his people. Between these extremes of hagiography and censure lies a third line of reasoning, which takes Bush's faith seriously though critically. If the 2001–2009 years saw American evangelicals reach the pinnacle of political influence, than we need to explain what millennial visions drove these citizens toward success, and how one man was able to steer them there. A good place to start, they suggest, is with the millennial visions of the man himself and the dramatic conversion experience that instilled these in his heart.[3]

Whatever their purview, Bush biographers have latched on to his faith as evidence of an exceptional authority, following a pattern evinced in older presidential histories. During the Watergate scandal, Arthur Schlesinger Jr. coined the unflattering term "imperial presidency" to describe the unassailable power of the presidency and legitimize (grudgingly) a "presidential synthesis" of history in which the supreme commander dictates policy, brokers deals with foreign nations, nurses the confidence of his people, and marks political time. Some of Schlesinger's contemporaries pointed out that the imperial presidency was also pastoral. Theodore White charged that "the Presidency hovers over the popular American imagination almost as a sacer- dotal office," to which Michael Novak added: "Every four years Americans elect . . . not only a king, [but] also a high priest and prophet." Our recent revolution in political history has challenged Schlesinger's outlook and re- sulted in nuanced depiction of governance in which contingency, challenged leadership, and untidy compromise are the norm. Even as younger political historians now seek to reintegrate the presidency in their texts, they reject the notion handed down by Schlesinger that the chief executive acts like a "free-floating leader" who shapes "the spirit of the era." But if the new po- litical history has effectively dismantled the imperial presidency, the priestly one spoken of by White and Novak still survives.[4]

Indeed, those relatively few historians who have foregrounded religion in their studies of the presidency have generally done so in ways that resonate with the spirit of the old presidential synthesis. The narrative arc, evidenced in tales about Bush's dramatic conversion, remains familiar. A shared style adds to the effect. Besides embracing the biographical approach by treating their subjects in stand-alone (often chapter-by-chapter) terms with faith cor- doned off as an isolated impulse, chroniclers tend to catalogue the theologies of the presidents without tracking them into the day-to-day muddles of real politics. When the relationship between belief and action is measured, it is usually done so within the limiting context of culture war issues (abortion, gay marriage, gender equality) that test the mettle of a president's moral code. What remains, therefore, is a rather superficial literature in which priestly presidents still act as free-floating agents who shape the spirit of their age.

To be fair, recent studies have made this simplistic reasoning less tenable. Though holding to many conventions, Gary Scott Smith's *Faith and the Presi- dency*, for instance, offers an intricate reading of the subject by measuring several presidents' religious beliefs alongside their political programs. Smith contends that even in an era of government expansion and secularization, "the influence of a president's faith . . . and the role of religion in shaping policies have become even more important." Making greater strides toward a fresh understanding have been scholars of foreign policy, no two more im- portant than William Inboden and Andrew Preston. Both demonstrate that sacred ideas have always influenced how the nation engages the world with sword and shield, interests of security and peace, in hand. Scholars of religion have also delivered more complex accounts of faith's striking dominance in Washington. Whereas some such as Randall Balmer have offered prescriptive accounts, which beg believers to keep God *out of* the White House, others like D. Michael Lindsay have focused on the descriptive by measuring how evangelicalism's elites have constructed an elaborate political apparatus with which all of the nation's leaders must contend. From out of Lindsay's account comes a sense that while the president may still be a priest of sorts, he is also a parishioner who is forced to abide by doctrines imposed on him by god-fearing powerbrokers that control the capital.[5]

Notable progress aside, the study of religion and presidential politics has yet to display the rigor demanded of it by the new political history and required of it to dismantle longstanding assumptions about the priestly presidency. Equipped with interdisciplinary methods and a breadth of concerns, practitioners of the new political history have explored a vast array of contexts in which a wide range of political actors work, making it easier to appreciate the environments that presidents inherit and wrestle with during and beyond their terms in office. Yet as impressive as this enterprise has been in revealing the many tangled economic and cultural, institutional and legislative milieus in which presidents operate, it has not sufficiently explicated the sacred environments that presidents inherit and inhabit. Much innovation is still required, in other words, before religion too can contribute to a fuller, textured recasting of presidential history. In their pursuit of this innovation, historians would do well to move beyond the stand-alone biographies, redemptive narratives, and testimonies of piety and probe instead the subtler moral geographies that give presidential politics life. It is in these more obscured and contested topographies of power, in which even seemingly mundane matters assume ultimate meaning, where the faith of a president assumes on-the-ground tangibility, and it is there that faith, politics, and the presidency reinforce each other in knottier but weightier ways.[6]

One of these illustrative topographies is the American oil patch, crude's extractive zones where wildcat capitalism, radical evangelicalism, and pipeline politics have long been fused in one quest for influence at the highest levels. This is, after all, the moral geography that created George W. Bush. Reconsider the nondescript space he inhabited around the moment of his conversion in 1984 and the hidden history of religion and presidential politics it opens up. Arthur Blessitt's appearance in Midland was no accident; sought out as someone who could heal a broken community, he came to West Texas to solve the spiritual needs of unemployed oilmen who were succumbing to seismic disruptions in their profession. Jim Sale, Bush's friend and a local oilman, was among those who welcomed Blessitt's ministry as the antidote to local woes. Bush, for his part, was ready to grab on to something spiritual, especially if it came packaged in the populist sensibilities that flourished around him while growing up in the tight-knit, church-centered life of 1950s Midland. By the mid-1980s he was facing extraordinary pressure that

came with life in a boom-bust vocation. With his oil company under heavy
debt and unable to draw his own salary, Bush struggled to stay afloat, at
home too, where the stresses of work corroded his marriage. Blessitt offered
Bush a blueprint for change, and evangelist Billy Graham helped map it out.
Together these counselors encouraged Bush to embrace a quintessentially
oil-patch faith, one that blended the enchantments of wildcat entrepreneurship with the promises of personal redemption, millennial expectation, and
the spiritual strength to survive.[7]

Survive he did, in splendid fashion. A short time after his mid-1980s crisis
Bush rode an upswing in Texas crude to levels of unprecedented corporate
success, which allowed him to chase success in another realm, this one political. During his climb into state and, later, national politics he stayed true to the
fuel and faith values of his heritage. Two of his earliest initiatives as president
reflected this indebtedness. First he "breathed life" into a "long-dormant
Republican initiative" to open up Alaska's Arctic National Wildlife Refuge
to oil drilling. Next he lobbied for a program that would allow Washington
to dole out money to churches that wanted to operate community-centered
social programs. Such was the conspicuous blend of petro-Protestant interests that would infuse other dimensions of his presidency, ranging from an
assertive, unilateral foreign policy in oil hotspots around the world to an eva-
sive environmental policy that would resist the Kyoto Protocol and similar
efforts to curtail gas emissions and global warming. Far from the conspiracy
of right-wing power some pundits hinted at, these actions by the Bush presidency were in fact natural byproducts of a man and a mission forged out of
the sacred topography of the West Texas oil patch.[8]

This is the backdrop to Bush's encounter with God in a Holidome, but
what might it tell us about a longer history of evangelical mobilization and
presidential politics? Bush's experience actually represents a pattern of religious politicking that is deeply rooted in modern American history yet is
scarcely accounted for by a scholarship that still tends to paint evangelicalism
as a marginal, idling political force prior to the culture wars over social issues
in the 1970s and the Reagan Revolution of 1980. But when we peek at the
oil patch, we find that evangelicalism has never stood quiet, nor has it fas-
tened its politics solely to the social. Since the 1930s, evangelicals there have
operated brazenly in the public sphere on behalf of their doctrines of personal salvation and stewardship, which place the onus of societal redemption
and management of God's creation on the shoulders of the sanctified saint.
Rejecting the coercive and, in their minds, satanic influences of overbearing,
secular entities that suppress the will of the saint—be they regulatory agencies, bureaucratic states, or major oil conglomerates—they have translated

their theological sentiment into political defense of the embattled independent oilman and hands-off precepts of wildcat capitalism. In accordance with this agenda, they have battled restrictive land-use policies and government oversight of the small petroleum producer as much as court and legislative rulings that seemingly undermine biblical moral codes, and they have consistently fought to preserve their "rule of capture"—their all-encompassing right to save souls, raise families, chase capital, and extract the bounties of "the Creator" in ways that affirm their earthly dominion. Hardly marginal, this politicking has always generated an effect at the top rungs of governance, including the presidency. Even when presidents (in contrast to Bush) have found themselves out of touch or at odds with oil patch evangelicalism, they have always had to contend with it as a formidable force, as three illustrative moments suggest.[9]

Consider, in the first place, the role that oil patch evangelicalism played in fueling anti-Roosevelt animus during the 1930s. Until recently it was common among historians to see the interwar period as the moment that evangelicals retreated into the shadows to reconstitute their subculture. Humiliated by the Scopes Trial and battered by the Depression, fundamentalist church folk, in this interpretation, had little inclination to engage the mainstream politics in any meaningful way. Yet this logic never held in the oil patches of the Southwest. Amid the unprecedented boom of the East Texas fields, which spanned the 1930s, many local Baptists and Pentecostals, having found oil quite literally underneath their churches, began interpreting their new petro-wealth as providential. Quoting the Old Testament, they pointed to Moses and his deathbed blessing of the children of Israel, Asher supreme among them. "Asher is most blessed of sons; let him be favored by his brothers, and let him dip his foot in oil." Having dipped their feet in oil, Texas Protestants now fashioned themselves as Israel's remnant and America's future.[10]

They did so in theological terms, but politics immediately mattered. The theologizing of oil was indeed widespread, extending beyond the pew onto the oil derricks that rapidly overtook local communities. Convinced that God had placed them in charge of this supernatural resource, oil patch evangelicals began to speak confidently of a new age in which their consecrated wealth could help them sanctify a nation. This sentiment was codified in new institutions. While pouring petrodollars into their struggling schools in order to shore up a defense against Darwinism and secularization, evangelicals also channeled funds into their local congregations in order to build bigger testaments to God's grace. Once saddled with poverty, churches such as Longview Church of Christ now spent fortunes to erect Gothic cathedrals as evidence of God's illustrious work. More important to evangelicalism's long-range fortunes were the nondenominational ministries that it began erecting. Youth ministries such as the Navigators, lay organizations such as the Christian Business Men's Committee International, and coordinating bodies like the National Association of Evangelicals (NAE) benefited directly from the booming economy of the Texas fields. They also drew leadership from a new class of entrepreneurs schooled in the cutthroat climate of the oil patch, whose only theological training (as they liked to say) "came from the school of hard knocks." Self-made men in the mold of Herbert J. Taylor, former manager of Sinclair Oil, became the face of the New Evangelicalism that emerged from World War II ready to reform America.[11]

They were also the face of a new political expression. Buoyed by their good fortune, convinced that it was of God, entrepreneurs of Taylor's kind began shaping an anti–New Deal revolt. With capitalism triumphant in their churches, they turned their attention to protecting what they cherished most: their stewardship over the land. Convinced that God had placed them in charge of their pools and compelled them to extract, speedily yet efficiently, for the advancement of His Kingdom, they championed the potentials of technology (these were no antimoderns), conservation ("subduing" was balanced with "tilling and keeping" the earth), and a Christian conscience as the way toward maximized gain. Above all else, they championed the right of individuals to approach nature in the same way they approached God: on their own terms. Fortified in the local parish, this spirit animated myriad independent oil associations that cropped up at this time to protect the interests of the wildcatter. Though complicated by the exigencies of oil's volatile economics, which demanded some regulatory oversight, the politics of these associations was straightforward: to defend against oil's major companies, stare down the specter of government regulation, and demand the right to drill when and where they wanted.[12]

A host of enemies emerged in this context, none more feared than Washington. In the rush to recover a longer history of American conservatism, scholars have rightly pointed to corporate anger with Franklin D. Roosevelt during the late 1930s as a catalyst for change, and a few have placed Protestant executives such as Taylor and Sunoco chief J. Howard Pew at the heart of the story. This fresh approach reveals much, but not all, about the brewing insurgency against the New Deal order, for the Taylors and Pews of the church community were more than corporate types angered by FDR's higher taxes and pro-labor initiative; they were wildcatters who rejected the encroachment of a regulatory state on their soil. Indeed, at the same time that they fueled a corporate anti–New Deal backlash and fashioned a New

Evangelicalism, both based in the Northeast, they also sponsored rebellion in the Southwest through involvement with the Independent Petroleum Association of America (IPAA) and peer agencies. In this capacity they came head to head with the Roosevelt administration's designs for order in the East Texas fields, which, in the hands of Interior Secretary Harold Ickes, seemed like plays for power. Besides detesting his legislative intrusions in their local fields, they also rejected his efforts to shore up federal authority over U.S. oil's expansion abroad by way of the Anglo-American Petroleum Agreement, which they saw as a joint effort by big government and big oil (major oil companies) to secure their hegemony. By the early 1940s, they thus spoke with an angry lilt when portraying Ickes—and by extension, the president—as antichrist.[13]

If the oil-fueled anti-Roosevelt mobilization of the late 1930s marks one example of how religion can be mapped on to a new presidential history, a second is the partisan maneuvering that followed during the late 1940s and early 1950s. By this point Texas wildcatters had entered the public's imagination as the personification of the American dream, excesses and all. This was a manufactured image, crafted in part by the Southwest's "Big Rich"—men such as H. L. Hunt, Sid Richardson, and H. R. Cullen—but also by rank-and-file producers who populated the IPAA and Texas Independent Producers and Royalty Association (TIPRO), the latter of which was known for its swashbuckling style. TIPRO's image-making was, in its own right, a political act, for wrapped up in this posturing were some core claims: that free market capitalism was in need of renewal; that independent oilmen were the purist capitalists, hence able to advance this doctrine on a global stage; and that it was finally time to stop liberalism from squelching this spirit.[14]

But their politicking also stretched into the machinations of presidential campaigning. Independent oilmen had been ignored by elites in both parties during the 1940 election, though Republican rejection hurt most. Agitated by Ickes's assertions of federal control, Cullen and his associates looked for but were denied support from GOP leader Wendell Willkie. Willkie did not simply ignore them, he mocked them: "The good Lord put all this oil in the ground, then someone comes along who hasn't been a success at doing anything else, and takes it out of the ground. The minute he does that, he considers himself an expert on everything from politics to petticoats." Willkie failed to respect their power, and Texas independents determined never again to let a presidential candidate get away with that sin. They found occasion to test this resolve in the controversy over the tidelands. Following Harry Truman's 1945 executive proclamation, which placed the federal government in charge of oil deposits off the Gulf Coast, Louisiana and Texas state legislators, spurred on by wildcatters, claimed jurisdiction over near-offshore waters.[15]

Texans especially were incensed. For a century they had believed that their republic held sole ownership of waters stretching three leagues (ten miles) into the Gulf. Truman's initiative thus insulted a history they deemed sacrosanct, but it meant more than this. In 1939 the Texas Legislature earmarked all revenues from the tidelands for public education. By the mid-1940s Texans saw monies from offshore leasing as a way to guarantee citizens their God-given right to higher learning. In challenging the status quo Truman not only triggered a storm in Texas's legislature, he also set one off in the state's local towns, where a mantra of fuel and family values reverberated on the street. The struggle intensified during the 1948 presidential election. Sensing that they could break the Democratic lock on Texas, national Republicans drafted a convention platform that included a pledge to restore states' "historic rights to the tides of submerged lands, tributary waters, lakes and streams" and nominated Thomas Dewey and Earl Warren to head the ticket. A Californian who sought protection of his own state's offshore privileges, Warren was a relentless campaigner who skillfully framed the tidelands as a family values issue that affected "the heritage of every schoolchild." For those in the Southwest who appreciated Warren's words but not yet his party, there was another way to voice dissent; by endorsing Strom Thurmond's States' Rights Party, which promised to keep Washington's hands away from the Southwest's crude. Texas oilmen liked what they heard and threw their money behind Thurmond's crusade. Just how much they supplied is unclear, but as Joseph Crespino notes, the "tittle-tattle about the tidelands represented the most significant opportunity to date for conservative economic forces in the region to consolidate an anti–New Deal constituency." Truman's stunning electoral win killed this opportunity but not that anger that had created it.[16]

Independent oil's charge for state control of the tidelands climaxed between 1950 and the election of 1952. Religion contributed to the high emotions. During this two-year stretch, H. L. Hunt and J. Howard Pew bombarded Christian anticommunist organizations with the message that Washington had overstepped its bounds. While Hunt's "Facts Forum" newsletter directed conservative political anger against Washington's "oil grab," Pew quietly endorsed grassroots organizations that monitored federal policy impact on independent oil. One of the most important was the Women's Investors Research Institute, which gave Pew the evidence needed to warn evangelicals of big government's assault on their land. Other Texas independents aided the cause of wildcat capitalism and Christianity by endorsing high-profile speakers such as Walter Hallanan. An oilman from West Virginia and chairman of the

1952 Republican National Convention, Hallanan delivered potent sermons that excoriated Truman's handling of oil. At one gathering in Sinton, Texas, operational headquarters for his Plymouth Oil Company, he followed his script when painting the oil industry as the "outstanding symbol of free, competitive enterprise" and the force that had lifted "America out of the darkness, lethargy and drudgery . . . into the light." He also made it clear that rank-and-file oil families were custodians of this remarkable resource, morally equipped to handle the burden, yet in need of awareness about the immediate threat of socialism, which had skulked its way into Washington. Lest they forget the profundity of their charge, Hallanan reminded his rapt listeners that the "crisis" they faced was not economic but spiritual and demanded a response from the heart: "As we face the morning sun of tomorrow, let us all re-dedicate and re-consecrate ourselves to the proposition that Socialism and Americanism will not mix any more than oil and water. Let us squarely face the fact that we are to have one or the other. Let us restore together that our Republic, founded in faith, conscience, compassion and law, shall continue in freedom, in dignity and in peace." Texas's firebrand preachers could not have translated fear into action with more poignancy or verve.[17]

That did not stop them from trying, however. In the lead-up to the 1952 election, evangelical clerics and lay leaders lent the tidelands crusade critical energy. Of the former, Billy Graham was key since his membership at Dallas's First Baptist Church and proximity to Texas's powerful oilmen placed him an optimum position. It was Graham in fact who, at Sid Richardson's urging, helped pressure Dwight Eisenhower to run for the presidency. When Richardson traveled to Paris to implore Eisenhower to guide the GOP, he carried two letters of support, one from Dallas oilman Clint Murchison and the other from Graham. Eisenhower's decision to run on the Republican ticket answered these pleas from the oil patch. Graham, Richardson, and their allies also worked well together during the campaign, and Eisenhower again made their effort count. While Richardson generously donated to the Republican's campaign, Graham worked evangelical circles to enlist other Christian leaders, men like Houston oil executive Earl Hankamer. Besides serving as chairman of Graham's 1952 Houston Evangelistic Crusade, Hankamer expended his energy helping Eisenhower gain momentum in the Lone Star State. Meanwhile, numerous other outspoken Texans followed Hankamer and Graham's lead, none more famous than J. Frank Norris, who fashioned himself as both entrepreneur and evangelist. In his Fort Worth church and on his radio program, the pastor beseeched his followers to kill the liberal leviathan that Roosevelt and Truman had been growing for years. Though broad in scope, with Cold War angst about communism front and center, Norris's proclamations leaned on the logic of the independent oil-man, which held that the nation's survival would only be guaranteed when its most innovative leaders had the chance to extract material abundance from the earth and put it to use for the furtherance of a Christian, capitalist America.[18]

Eisenhower answered the call of the Texas preachers and the petro-patriarchs. In May of 1952, with the Republican primaries still playing out, H. J. Porter, head of TIPRO and the Eisenhower-for-President Club of Texas, made public his candidate's promise to place the tidelands back in state hands. The pledge energized the Texas electorate, and the excitement only grew as the candidate campaigned through the state's oil patch com-munities. There, on each occasion, Eisenhower faced droves of voters who wanted him to vow that Washington would, under his presidency, keep its hands off their crude. Eisenhower duly obliged. Speaking like the Texas son his audiences envisioned him to be, Eisenhower championed the states' rights platform articulated by his southwestern friends. "Federal ownership in this case [Tidelands]," he declared, "is one that is calculated . . . toward centralized ownership and control, a trend which I have bitterly opposed." Like Walter Hallanan, Eisenhower folded the case of Texas oil into a larger narrative about the necessity for free Americans to draw strength from a God that had blessed them with abundant resources and responsibilities—and to strike out against socialism. Having internalized his message, which struck every chord in their oil-patch conscience, their moral geography, Texans spearheaded Eisenhower's final run to the White House. "We must be deeply grateful that the election went the way it did," Graham wrote Hankamer after their work was done. "If it had gone the other way, it could have meant disaster." "I thoroughly agree," Hankamer replied, before adding: "I think it would be most effective for you to write General Eisenhower a personal let-ter, assuring him that you and a large group of your friends are remembering him daily in prayer."[19]

The unabashed evangelical politicking for petroleum would continue into the late 1960s and 1970s, which supplies the third illustrative moment in our religious history of pipeline and presidential politics. Always looking for allies in Washington, regardless of their party affiliation, oil patch Christians spent the late 1950s and early 1960s sorting out their allegiances while continuing to build their national and international ministries. By 1964, this emerging evangelical bloc would throw its significant support behind Barry Goldwater, whose campaign would cause liberal critics to rail against extremists on the oil-funded right. In 1966, aided by his "kitchen cabinet" of oil executives, a few of whom were invested in evangelical causes, Ronald Reagan won the

California gubernatorial race, thus guaranteeing conservatives leverage in a place of influence. In the coming years, Richard Nixon would rely on this same system of support to win the South. As Kevin Phillips and Kirkpatrick Sale noted at the time, Nixon's victories reflected a power shift in national politics, a shift fueled in part by oil interests and a Sunbelt evangelical electorate. What they did not notice were the thick connections that now linked these two entities together behind a political cause. By 1972, Nixon's vision was, like that of Goldwater and Reagan, tightly attuned to the religious topography of the oil patch. Through his ties to Billy Graham and various Sunbelt-based ministries, whose aspirations for influence stretched nationally, Nixon gained direct access to an ascendant force that would eventually redefine the American political landscape.[20]

This ascendant force—the Religious Right—certainly grew out of concern with society's leftward turn on social issues like abortion and gender equality, hot-button concerns that are typically underscored in histories of the movement, but liberal drifts in energy and land use factored in too. The history of oil patch evangelicalism in fact points to the "specter of environmentalism" as one of the precipitating factors behind the Reagan Revolution. In the wake of the Wilderness Act of 1964 and subsequent steps toward Washington oversight of western lands, oppositional voices began protesting the "federal land grab" that seemed set on destroying personal freedoms on the frontier. With a rhetoric that echoed through the tidelands controversy, conservatives marshaled their communities to repeal the act and roll back a federal state that appeared determined to steal, not just regulate their resources. Such panic was almost as crucial in sparking the Reagan Revolution as the myriad culture war issues that inspired right-wing activists to take to the streets in protest of the Equal Rights Amendment and Roe v. Wade. Indeed, in some cases, concerns generated by oil and the culture wars blended into a formidable agenda for change. Just as Earl Warren had done in 1948, right-wing Reaganites in Texas and California drew no hard and fast distinction between these concerns; their fight to thwart government's advance on their land was equated with the fight to preserve their jurisdiction over the home. Autonomy and true Christian Americanism were, in their eyes at least, threatened virtues in both realms.[21]

Oil patch evangelicals, unsurprisingly, rushed to join the crusade against the new environmentalism. As they did in the tidelands battle, Texas pastors used their pulpits to rail against the liberal enemy and, by 1980, tout Ronald Reagan as the man who could secure their rights to their land and, by extension, their oil. At First Baptist Church in Dallas, Reverend W. A. Criswell continued to oversee a powerful congregation (with twenty-five thousand members, the largest in the country) that boasted two generations of Hunts and other wealthy oil families and that exhibited few inhibitions when endorsing politicians who saw things their way. First Baptist's petro-patriarchs would, with Criswell's help, offer Reagan critical support in the 1980 election. So too would Fort Worth pastor James Robison and his legion of right-wing Christian activists. Soon to be remembered for his August 1980 speech to a meeting of Baptist pastors in which he implored "God's people to come out of the closet" and take their country back from homosexuals, communists, and liberal politicians, Robison was also an aggressive spokesperson for oil patch economics and a close friend of several accomplished wildcatters, including T. Cullen Davis and Eddie Chiles. Robison would also make a name for himself at this same 1980 gathering by introducing Reagan to his Baptist peers as a man who shared their values.[22]

Such was the institutional support that oil patch churches lent Reagan conservatism, but this outpouring was more than the conspiracy of a few. Though dismissed by some pundits as a ploy by the Texas rich, the preachers and petro-patriarchs that counted on Reagan to protect their moral geography were merely the leading edge of a popular phenomenon. Indeed, even as rank-and-file citizens flocked to their churches to hear their ministers speak out against liberalism's nefarious designs on their families, they also frequented the new bible bookstores that dotted their suburban landscapes for a knowledge they could apply to their thinking on political matters of all kinds, including environmental topics. There they purchased books that walked them through the energy crisis and the environmental policies that Washington was enacting around nation. Not all were negative in tone. By the late 1970s, evangelicals were a diverse lot, open to a range of political expressions. A few among them—generally younger ones with links to an evangelical left—jettisoned their parents' economics-centered religion for an environmentally-friendly one in which the social justice teachings of the Bible were privileged over capitalism's profit motives.[23]

Even still, the average Christian book buyer in Dallas and Tulsa looked to more critical tomes for instruction on federal energy policies. Among the most popular producers of such literature was John Walvoord, American evangelicalism's authority on biblical prophecy, end-times beliefs, and current events. From his professorship at Dallas Theological Seminary, long a bastion of fundamentalist theology and petro-friendly politics, Walvoord spoke to a sprawling national audience by way of his pen. His 1970s text *Armageddon: Oil and the Middle East Crisis* reached millions of readers. Straddling a blurred line between hopeful interpretation of Middle Eastern turbulence as a sign of Christ's impending return and criticism of the U.S.

government for letting this chaos occur, Walvoord channeled a good deal of his end-times angst against environmentalists and their political advocates who had made America so dependent on non-Christian others. Were Americans able once again to tap freely the bountiful oil pools just off the Gulf Coast and in Alaska, underneath southwestern soil and in the shale deposits of Colorado and Wyoming, he asserted, they would realize anew peace and the natural order of things: refreshed confidence in Christian community, personal fulfillment, capitalist verve, and an advancing gospel. This was the millennial splendor promised by God and black gold, and it was time, in his mind, for politicians and presidents to take it seriously.[24]

As if to answer Walvoord's wishes, Reagan appeared ready in 1980 not only to take his conservative constituents' social values seriously but to honor their environmental ones too. Indeed, Reagan rewarded his evangelical supporters by assigning a couple of them to key administrative posts. One was C. Everett Koop, the Presbyterian layman who would be named surgeon general, a position that would thrust him into the middle of the abortion controversy, a tension historians have explored in great depth. The other was James Watt, a Pentecostal from Wyoming who shared Walvoord's premillennialist beliefs and deep suspicions of the regulatory state. As secretary of the interior, Watt would see to it that evangelicalism's longstanding fears of federal encroachment on land and resources would find clear policy outlets. And in the spirit of the Southwest's wildcatters who had begun their fight against the New Deal order by confronting an interior secretary of a different ilk, he would promise to restore custodianship of the oil patch to the people who had long worked it as theirs.[25]

With Reagan's election in 1980 came stark evidence that evangelical politics was no longer marginal to the presidency. We now know, of course, that evangelical quiescence between the 1930s and 1970s was always a fiction and that the lead-up to the Reagan Revolution was in fact a lengthy one. Slowly but deliberately, religious historians are beginning to track the story of evangelical politics beyond the hot-button social issues of the Reagan years into the thicker, tangled, longer-developing politics of labor and economy, foreign policy and civil rights, globalization and the post-industrial city. Moreover, in addition to monitoring the grassroots, these scholars have also begun to expose the institutional ties that have long linked evangelical citizens to powerful elites and the nation's halls of power. Such innovations in the field have led to far richer depictions of how, as Mark Rozell and Gleaves Whitney offer, "religious interests clearly occupy a seat at the table of presidential politics and policy." Should these trends continue, away from conventional renderings of the priestly president, we will be rewarded with increasingly textured histories that embed low *and* high politics in their deepest social contexts.[26]

By paying attention to the moral geographies that presidencies and presidents inhabit, we will also be compensated with histories that make it harder to differentiate between the political and religious. Refreshingly so. Recent innovations in religious history have made easy categorization of the sacred and secular a difficult task. Rather than accept secularization as fact, the innovators have looked to the ordinary and routine in American life to delineate the profane: Oprah Winfrey and Wal-Mart, Chick-fil-A and supermalls, the chicken sandwich; these and other artifacts of late modernity have been unpacked for their religious significance. The spirit behind this invention has something to offer study of religion and presidential history, for it is in the hazy middle of competing interests, daily human experience, political negotiation, and encounters with nature that take place on purportedly secular terrains where we see faith shaping the course of politics in subtle but critical ways.

This, certainly, is the lesson of the oil patch. Throughout U.S. history, the nation's oil patches—from 1860s Western Pennsylvania to 1980s West Texas—have nursed a radical evangelicalism that fuels and reinforces the proclivities of independent oil, and together these two have made pipeline politics a going concern, not just for politicians and CEOs but also for Christian citizens and their church, and the White House has felt the effects. As a sentiment for protest, oil patch evangelicalism has helped stir up revolt against some presidential administrations and support for others; through its elaborate system of ministries it has lent moral support for oil-friendly interests and impressed on its favored presidential candidates the wishes of the wildcatter; by way of its extensive networks it has helped coordinate lobbies and raised up voices that can be heard in Washington; as pedagogy, it has shaped the way millions of Christians think about energy, environment, climate change, and America's place in the world. The effect, moreover, is a lingering one. Whereas some would still have us believe that evangelicalism (religion in general) influences presidential politics only intermittently or in isolation around election time, unfolding developments on the newest oil patches of America suggest otherwise. There, amid seemingly all-consuming struggles to secure presidential blessing for new pipelines and the beleaguered independent oilman, the political mantra to "drill, baby, drill" is still voiced as a theological imperative.

CHAPTER 6

Ike's World

In Search of Ideology in the Eisenhower Presidency

WILLIAM I. HITCHCOCK

Ideology is generally thought to be a bad word. It is associated with closed-minded zealots, revolutionaries, and extremists. No one wishes to be thought an ideologue. But for the historian, ideology is a useful conceptual term. It is shorthand for a frequently articulated set of principles, shared beliefs, and aspirations that guide collective action toward a common end. Ideologies do important work: They explain the world, they answer questions, and they guide political action. In times of crisis, ideologies explain why conflict arises, who the enemy is, and what must be done to turn back impending catastrophe. By creating an "us" and a "them," by simplifying otherwise complex phenomena, ideologies generate support among constituents and sharpen the perception of looming threats. Perhaps most important, ideologies are utopian, promising better days tomorrow in exchange for adherence today.

Historians do not often label United States presidents "ideologues." The compromises that chief executives are obliged to strike tend to make rigid adherence to a particular doctrine counterproductive. Ideology can define objectives and generate electoral support but can also become a burden as the broad brushstrokes of political rhetoric yield to the pointillist artistry of governance. In the field of foreign and security policy, however, where the president has more leeway than in domestic policy to articulate and pursue broad strategic objectives, ideology may be more consequential in presidential decisionmaking. Many historians of American foreign relations think so: It is stipulated in most scholarship in the field that U.S. foreign policy has reflected and even been driven by ideology. The precise contours of that ideology—a belief in American exceptionalism, a commitment to defend distinct racial hierarchies, advocacy of the benevolence of the marketplace, and so on—continue to be debated. Their existence does not.[1]

But what does ideology do? How does it act on policymakers? Since the opening of the Soviet archives in the early 1990s, Cold War historians have been reasserting the importance of ideology in Soviet behavior, stressing that ideology worked alongside geopolitical interests to trigger and intensify the Cold War.[2] Did ideology play a similar role on the American side? An emerging consensus holds that it did. Melvyn P. Leffler has recently argued that, during the Cold War, ideology deeply influenced American presidents. Ideology, in Leffler's analysis, kept the Cold War going, even when opportunities for peace presented themselves. According to Leffler, ideology bound American leaders to the Cold War order and prevented them from considering alternative, if unknown, paths toward a peaceful settlement of U.S.-Soviet tensions. Ideology led key presidents to perpetuate a conflict that, had reason prevailed, could have ended much sooner. This means that ideology made leaders do bad things that a more reasonable person, one not beholden to the same ideology, would not have done. How did ideology do this? Leffler argues that the ideology of American (and Soviet) Cold War leaders "affected their construction of 'reality'—their perception of threats and opportunities in a turbulent world." The world they saw was in fact an intellectual construct, organized through ideological assumptions about war, peace, Communism, liberalism, and so on. Of course geopolitics mattered. However, American leaders evaluated geopolitics through an ideological framework; the policies that followed therefore reflected their ideological preconceptions. But ideology was a trap, Leffler believes: Cold War "leaders had trouble liberating themselves from these ideas and memories *even when they saw reason* to do so." That is, ideology compelled American Cold War leaders to embrace rivalry and competition even when they could rationally perceive the benefits of moderation and compromise.[3]

Another influential scholar of the Cold War, Odd Arne Westad, also places ideology at the heart of Cold War decisionmaking, though his reading of how ideology works is slightly different from Leffler's. Where Leffler sees ideology as a kind of straitjacket restricting presidents, Westad sees ideology as an elixir, a tantalizing concoction that fueled American leaders in their competition with the Soviet Union. In his account of the Cold War in the

Third World, Westad argues that American ideology exalted "the free market, anti-Communism, fear of state power, [and] faith in technology." These concepts were considered to be dynamic, transformative, and transferrable to the wider world. In particular, American leaders saw the market as the means best suited to advance American interests overseas, and this "wish to make the world safe for capitalism" would lead "cold war administrations to embark on extensive aid programs for the Third World from the mid-1950s." This ideological faith in the power of the market was expressed in the form of development aid, the millenarian dream that American know-how could bring about the modernization of the Third World and fulfill the American promise on the global scale. Westad believes that the Cold War's propulsive force derived not from the geopolitical or military struggle focused on Europe, but in the ideologically driven competition between the United States and the Soviet Union over political and social development in the Third World.[4] Inherent in his argument is an assumption that ideology was not a trap for U.S. leaders but a positive program of action that in the end served to radicalize the Cold War.

Despite their differences, these two leading scholars of the Cold War agree that ideology mattered in shaping the choices that American leaders made. American presidents, these two scholars conclude, operated in an ideological framework, and their policies hewed closely to ideological imperatives they had articulated. If they are right, it should be possible for presidential historians to identify those moments when ideology operated in the decisionmaking process.

The historian of the Eisenhower presidency would seem to be at a disadvantage in such a search. After all, an ideology presupposes a belief system and an ability to articulate that system; Dwight D. Eisenhower did not even declare his party affiliation until a few months before deciding to run for president. The idea that Eisenhower had a fixed intellectual worldview or system of beliefs would once have elicited howls and jeers in many circles, and although much revisionist scholarship has given us a portrait of Eisenhower as far more engaged in policy and far more politically adept than once thought, it was easy for Alan Brinkley to state unequivocally in a 1990 essay that "Eisenhower was not an ideologue."[5] Even those scholars who have plumbed the intellectual history of Eisenhower's policy choices have stressed his pragmatism. Robert Griffith, in an important 1982 article, credited Eisenhower with a coherent intellectual vision, arguing that Eisenhower aspired to establish a "corporate commonwealth"—a polity governed by consensus, corporatism, businesslike efficiency and the spirit of free-market individualism moderated by earnest civic-mindedness. But Griffith did not declare

Eisenhower to be driven by ideology and in any case had little to say about the ideas animating Eisenhower's foreign policy.[6] Policy historians, it seems, prefer to think of Eisenhower as a pragmatist, animated by instincts and ideas but not adhering to a fixed ideology. Cold War historians have by contrast suggested that Eisenhower did make choices that were governed by a coherent and powerful ideology. Who is right? This essay tries to bridge these two conceptions by showing that Eisenhower was a leader who both nourished a deeply felt ideological worldview and who could and did set aside ideology to pursue specific interests. Ike sought to be both a strategist and a tactician. Such flexibility would normally be an asset to a president, and Eisenhower did show that he was willing to sacrifice ideology if he could advance the national interest in doing so. Yet in one crucial arena of policymaking—his nuclear strategy—Eisenhower found that his usual finesse in pivoting between ideology and interests worked against him and led him to reinforce a nuclear strategy that had already failed to deliver.

It is probably stretching things too far to declare Eisenhower an ideologue, but he did think of himself as a man of ideas, and he brought to the White House a number of basic concepts that guided his policy choices. First among these was a certain reading of American history. Eisenhower believed that what he called "the American System"—a term he used frequently, though in a very different manner than Henry Clay—was a distinctive, historically evolved practice of self-government based on individual freedom, democracy, faith in God, and the dynamism of free markets.[7] Eisenhower liked to evoke "our American System," which he claimed was premised on a tacit bargain between citizen and state: Individual rights should always trump federal interests, but the citizen must grant to the state his loyalty and provide his labor and public service for the common good. The American System worked so well because it did not coerce: By defending individual rights, Eisenhower believed, American democracy allowed personal citizens to develop their own talents and aspirations. In the process of pursuing their individual interests, Americans become loyal defenders of their own freedoms, and emerge as devoted citizens of the Republic. The loyalty of the American citizen is not compelled but is generated by his or her desire to defend and advance the ideals of personal freedom. The result is, ideally, a community of individual interests, bound together by voluntarism, fired by competition, sustained by national loyalty, and refereed by a distant and benevolent state.

A second core belief for Eisenhower was that government had a natural, and dangerous, propensity to expand. The basic values of American life existed, he believed, under the constant threat of a smothering government.

The inherent character of the modern state is to control, direct, and interfere with individual freedoms. Worse, citizens too readily appeal to the state for redress from the hard knocks of real life, assuming that the state has an obligation to provide for them. This yearning for paternal care is a weakness to guard against, not only because it leads to a flabby, dependent citizenry but because it invites the state to expand its power into the lives of the people. He put it starkly in a speech in Galveston, Texas, in December 1949: "If all that Americans want is security, they can go to prison. They'll have enough to eat, a bed and a roof over their head. But if an American wants to preserve his dignity and his equality as a human being, he must not bow his neck to any dictatorial government."[8]

An ever-expanding state in turn becomes a sloppy steward of national resources, inclined toward profligacy, deficits, corruption, and malfeasance. Political leaders must work against the natural tendencies of states to expand, curtail the growth of bureaucracy, and strive to protect individual rights from state direction and control. Far from serving communal, class, or party interests, political leaders must support individual citizens in their ongoing struggle to defend personal freedom from state control. To a faculty colleague at Columbia in 1949—quite typical of his expressed views at the time—he wrote that "each increase in centralized bureaucratic control of our national life increases the danger of bankruptcy in spirit and enterprise as well as finance, and facilitates a potential dictator's seizure of power."[9]

A third core belief concerned the nature of the existential threat posed by international Communism. The threat was twofold: ideological (the appeal of Marxist ideas in a postcolonial world) and geopolitical (the massive state power of the Soviet Union and the potential power of Mao's China). These states and their allies sought to advance an ideology directly contrary to the principles of the American System. Communism demands the subversion of the individual to the state; encourages class consciousness and conflict rather than community; is dynamic, expansive, and attractive to the weak and the poor because it offers immediate change in social hierarchies and in the distribution of power; denies any role for spirituality and faith and is relentlessly materialistic; adapts to modern conditions, showing flexibility and a talent for innovation and survival. Facing such an ideology, the American System stood at a disadvantage because it was premised on a restricted state, balanced spending, and a focus on quality of life, while the Communists could devote unlimited resources to arms and to science and technology in the name of advancing revolution. Communism appeals because it is on the move; the American System by contrast seems sluggish because it seeks to conserve, to defend rights and privileges already granted. There was a paradox here that

Eisenhower understood: If they wanted to protect individual liberty and freedoms, Americans would have to work in common cause. If they wished to enjoy the fruits of peace, they must remain vigilant, sacrifice their own ease and comfort, and even accept the possibility of war.

Finally, Eisenhower had always been an internationalist, and he strongly believed that in order to survive, the United States must engage and shape the world, not withdraw from it. While such strategic assets as nuclear weapons and alliances were essential to secure the Free World, the United States must depend upon an expansive free-market global economy to sustain the Free World. The Free World was a sensitive organism: It required both American power but also careful cultivation. A combination of aid, trade, and modernization led by western technocrats would encourage mutual integration and support, thereby creating a unified and consensual Free World system that would be able to contend with the rigid, doctrinaire, and determined Soviet bloc.

The struggle for the survival of the American System, Eisenhower hypothesized, would take many decades. The goal was not short-term victory but long-term survival through the patient accumulation of strength, allies, and innovation to deter war and enhance global stability. In the long run, shifts inside the USSR might compel a new orientation of Soviet power away from conflict and toward cooperation. But that was uncertain. The threat was likely to endure, so the American System must create the sinews of power that could contend with the global Communist threat for many decades to come.

Eisenhower, then, adhered to a political conception of the American System that stressed individualism, economic freedom, and the globalization of democratic capitalism. He also embraced a strategic vision that called for security through preparedness, vigilance, deterrence, and credibility. This ideology was settled in his mind by January 1953. But did Eisenhower govern by reference to these fixed ideas? Not exactly: He proved quite willing to tack back and forth between ideological purpose and tactical advantage.

For example, Eisenhower sounded profoundly ideological in his early public statements. His cheerless inaugural address, for example, directed the nation's attention directly to the struggle against the Soviet Union. Eisenhower worked over the draft word by word for weeks before the inauguration.[10] "Forces of good and evil are massed and armed and opposed as rarely before in history," he began. Therefore, Eisenhower urged his listeners to think about bigger issues than their personal needs. "Great as are the preoccupations absorbing us at home, concerned as we are with matters that deeply affect our livelihood today and our vision of the future, each of these domestic problems is dwarfed by, and often even created by, this question that involves all humankind." And that question was: Can freedom survive? In the global struggle, Communists would resort to any means to secure their ends. They "know no god but force, no devotion but its use. They tutor men in treason. They feed upon the hunger of others. Whatever defies them, they torture, especially the truth." In case his listeners had lost track of the message, he repeated his thesis: "Freedom is pitted against slavery; lightness against the dark."

With such an uncompromising foe, compromise was impossible. The struggle would be long, and victory would be defined only on American terms. "We shall never try to placate an aggressor by the false and wicked bargain of trading honor for security. Americans, indeed all free men, remember that in the final choice a soldier's pack is not so heavy a burden as a prisoner's chains." Eisenhower preferred war with honor to peace with dishonor.

This speech was followed in just a few weeks by an even more bellicose address: Eisenhower's State of the Union message to Congress, in which he blamed the Russians for creating a "world of turmoil" and declared that America would not sit back in a "a posture of paralyzed tension." Instead, he would embark on a "new positive foreign policy," which appeared to mean seeking to liberate enslaved peoples across the world. "We shall never acquiesce," he said, "in the enslavement of any people in order to purchase fancied gain for ourselves." Repudiating his predecessors Roosevelt and Truman, he called on "Congress at a later date to join in an appropriate resolution making clear that this Government recognizes no kind of commitment contained in secret understandings of the past with foreign governments which permit this kind of enslavement." As if to make good on this promise, he announced a redeployment of the Seventh Fleet in the Formosa Straits that was meant to send a message to the Communist Chinese that America just might "unleash" Chiang Kai-shek's Nationalist forces upon Red China. This was a sop to the Republican right wing, and no one believed that Chiang was in a position to launch an attack, but this purposeful break from Truman's policy clearly marked Eisenhower's determination to expand war in Asia if necessary.[11]

Eisenhower's public firmness was matched in confidential musings about the possibility of war with the Soviet Union. In September 1953, while discussing a new report from his CIA director that the USSR now possessed the hydrogen bomb, Eisenhower gravely declared that "the hour of decision" may be at hand. "We should presently have to face the question," he said at a meeting of the NSC, "of whether or not we would have to throw everything at once against the enemy. The question could no longer be excluded."[12] As he put it to his national security adviser, Robert Cutler, "It almost seems as if we might have to think about that thing I've always regarded as so abhorrent."[13]

Amid these dark counsels of Armageddon, perhaps it is not surprising to find that the official policy of the administration, as it worked its way through the planning process, made nuclear weapons its centerpiece. The new national security team, after an elaborate and detailed review, issued its Basic National Security Policy in October 1953; the paper was known as NSC 162/2 and was quickly dubbed the "New Look." Eisenhower was a hands-on participant in its formulation, even in the line-editing, so we can assume that the policy reflected his ideas. The assumptions were simple: The Soviet Union was seeking to consolidate and expand its sphere of power and was seeking "eventual domination of the non-Communist world." Leadership changes or periodic uprisings in satellite states would not result in a change of the Soviet Union's basic purpose. The United States must in response develop a three-tiered approach to its security. First, while maintaining conventional military forces, it must develop an arsenal of nuclear weapons capable of "inflicting massive retaliatory damage by offensive striking power." Second, the United States must maintain a robust and expanding economy while carefully cutting excess spending. Third, the United States must enroll allied partners in the global security effort. As for pursuing peace or negotiation, this idea received very little attention in the document and was considered useful only as theater: Gestures toward peace would reassure America's allies of "our desire to reach such settlements." But "the prospects for acceptable negotiated settlements are not encouraging."

NSC 162/2 ended with a restatement of the basic premise: The United States should make clear to the Soviets and the Chinese "its intention to react with military force against any aggression by Soviet bloc armed forces. In the event of hostilities, the United States will consider nuclear weapons to be as available for use as other munitions." That was the essence of the new national security strategy.[14] Eisenhower somewhat breezily informed British Prime Minister Winston Churchill and Foreign Secretary Anthony Eden at a meeting in Bermuda in early December 1953 that "we have come to the conclusion that the atom bomb has to be treated as just another weapon in the arsenal."[15]

For all of this bellicosity, however, Eisenhower showed an ability to pivot away from such ideologically charged language almost at will. Eisenhower had settled on ending the Korean War even before he took office. He knew the war was militarily unwinnable; he wanted to ease the massive budget pressures it was creating; and he was willing to make a deal. The armistice he accepted may not have been an example of "the false and wicked bargain of trading honor for security" that he forswore in his inaugural address. But it came fairly close.[16] He also made a bold public peace offering to the Soviets in the wake of Stalin's death in early March 1953. In this case, his personal belief in the benefits of peace trumped his ideological desire for victory in the Cold War. Pacing about the Oval Office, he told speechwriter Emmet Hughes that in light of Stalin's demise, he wanted to make a genuine effort to open dialogue on arms control. "We are in an armaments race. Where will it lead us? At worst, to atomic warfare. At best, to robbing every people and nation on earth of the fruits of their own toil." He demanded of his speechwriter a bold proposal that contained "no double talk, no sophisticated political formulas, no slick propaganda devices. Let us spell it out, whatever we really offer."[17] To the NSC, he declared that "if we must live in a permanent state of mobilization, our whole democratic way of life would be destroyed in the process."[18]

Eisenhower's eagerness to make a peaceful overture to the Russians was "undulled by elaborate counsels of caution" from John Foster Dulles and the State Department.[19] Over the next four weeks, Eisenhower and Hughes hammered out an extraordinary text that Ike delivered on April 16 at the American Society of Newspaper Editors. In it, the president stressed the terrible waste of resources that the superpowers were committing to the arms race and painted a picture of a world that could be turned toward more productive pursuits. If the superpowers could agree on arms reductions and limitations, "this Government is ready to ask its people to join with all nations in devoting a substantial percentage of the savings achieved by disarmament to a fund for world aid and reconstruction. The purposes of this great work would be to help other peoples to develop the undeveloped areas of the world, to stimulate profitable and fair world trade, to assist all peoples to know the blessings of productive freedom." All that was needed, apparently, was goodwill and sincerity. "We are ready, in short, to dedicate our strength to serving the needs, rather than the fears, of the world."[20] Eisenhower followed this overture with a plan—very much his own idea—to promote the international control of atomic energy and use it for peaceful purposes by developing countries. The "Atoms for Peace" proposal, made by Eisenhower at the United Nations on December 8, 1953, laid out a grim catalogue of the capabilities of the rival superpowers and then offered a hopeful prospect of a common endeavor to share nuclear technology.[21]

The tensions between his sharply worded public statements about the evils of Communism and his simultaneous peace proposals are more apparent than real. Eisenhower stipulated that Communism was aggressive, evil, and soulless and must be met in all corners of the globe with steely resolve, and he also averred that peace and compromise were the best way to enhance American prosperity and globalize the American way of life. Eisenhower could call for massive increases in nuclear weapons and ponder a first strike on the Soviets and just as easily repeat his abhorrence of war, beseech the Russians for arms limitations, and clamor for the construction of more schools. Both strategic choices were part of a common intellectual and strategic cast of mind that emphasized preparedness, vigilance, and every reasonable effort to avoid war.

An ability to tack between broad principles and tactical necessity would seem to be advantageous in presidential leadership. Yet it led Eisenhower into some difficulty in one crucial area of policymaking: his nuclear and security strategy.[22] After promulgating NSC 162/2 in 1953, with its emphasis on massive nuclear deterrence, budget cuts for conventional weapons, and burden-sharing with allies, the administration built on it. This is quite evident in NSC 5501, which the NSC approved in January 1955. The basic thesis was that the U.S.-Soviet nuclear stalemate was going to endure, and that it was tolerable. It lent stability to international affairs. The Soviet Union was led by rational actors who could be deterred, so a robust nuclear deterrent was vital to America's security. Furthermore, the natural propensity of some of America's allies toward neutrality or separate deals with the Soviets could be blocked by a demonstration of America's continued resolve to defend them, a purpose that the nuclear deterrent would serve. The general consensus was that a direct Soviet attack on America was unlikely, but this only raised the stakes of any peripheral conflicts. Subversion of small neutral states had enormous significance and had to be halted by a robust plan for material and technological aid to such countries to forge a positive relationship with the United States. America's global security depended on winning converts, not merely holding the Soviets at bay. As a State Department memo put it in commenting on NSC 5501, "We shall have to attempt to replace the cement of fear with new means of cohesion."[23]

But America could not wage the Cold War merely through foreign aid. The keystone of the arch was the nuclear deterrent, and this must be massive, technologically advanced, and understood by all concerned to be an available tool in America's arsenal. American nuclear capabilities must remain well in advance of Soviet achievements: There could be no resting on laurels. Were America to be perceived as settling into a defensive posture, the result would be a rapid breakdown of the western alliance and "a somewhat more 'third force' orientation in the cold war." Without a constantly expanding nuclear arsenal, America could expect its Free World allies to consider breaking ranks.[24] The president gave voice to this line of thinking in a meeting of his National Security Council in late 1955. Considering the need to build a new class of ICBMs with a range of 1,500 miles, Eisenhower had no qualms: "We had simply got to achieve such missiles as promptly as possible, if only because of the enormous psychological and political significance of ballistic missiles." The president acknowledged their limited military value but stressed the "profound and overriding political and psychological importance of the U.S. achieving such a weapon."[25] This became something of a mantra for the administration. "If the United States," claimed Secretary of State John Foster Dulles, "were ever to get into a military posture inferior to that of the USSR, this country would suffer defeat without the occurrence of a war." With a larger arsenal of nuclear weapons, the Soviets could "checkmate" the United States, and "we would be obliged to give in." As a consequence, national security required constant expansion of "these terrible missiles. . . . We simply cannot afford to be inferior to the USSR."[26]

As it turned out, however, the New Look had a serious flaw. It had no answer for the security threats and challenges that were popping up in the developing world, threats and challenges that by the mid-1950s were far more active and explosive than the now fairly stable Great Power standoff. Securing the homeland by creating a massive nuclear deterrent was relatively easy; providing a road map for the Third World so that it could "meet the basic needs and aspirations of its peoples" was going to be much harder.[27]

The realization that the New Look was flawed slowly dawned on Eisenhower's military strategists. By late 1955, policy documents began to note "a change in character" in the East-West conflict: The Soviets, breaking out of Stalinist rigidity, were showing greater flexibility, creativity, and opportunism in the Cold War conflict. They were spending greater effort on South Asia and the Middle East and worrying less about divided and stalemated Europe. When the CIA produced its National Intelligence Estimate on "World Situation and Trends" in late 1955, it argued that the nuclear balance between East and West had actually opened up Soviet opportunities around the world: By making world war unlikely, the nuclear stalemate had led small, neutral countries to worry less about choosing sides and more about economic development. Inevitably, they were inclined to "accept Soviet offers of trade and aid and to normalize relations with the Bloc." Austria, Yugoslavia, Egypt, and other Arab states were all moving toward Moscow, not Washington.[28]

By early 1956, planners seemed to have agreed that "Soviet appeals to local aspirations, resentments and fears have been shrewdly combined to foster trends toward neutralism."[29] Eisenhower himself, considering how to handle this opportunistic threat, seemed open to new approaches. When presented with a "very dark picture" by the Joint Chiefs of Staff about America's inadequate commitment to develop its nuclear and military capabilities and about the failure of U.S. allies to develop their own military assets, Eisenhower pushed back. He said that it might be wiser and cheaper to encourage some states to remain neutral. In any case, he said, he was "inclined to have more faith now in economic aid to meet current problems than in military aid."[30] By June 1957, this view was reflected in national security documents: In NSC 5707/8, the administration outlined its intention to "place relatively more stress on promoting growth and development in the Free World" than on military rivalry with the Soviets.[31]

The double blows of the Sputnik launch in October 1957 and the Gaither Report of a month later widened these hidden fissures in the rock of the New Look. Alongside the alarm at Soviet advances in rocketry and the depression over Gaither's indictment of (allegedly) inadequate American preparations for nuclear war, administration officials suddenly had to confront the limitations of the "New Look" strategy on which they had bet so heavily. Both Dulles and Eisenhower seemed to hint at this in their reaction to the Gaither report. Dulles, once a great advocate for the New Look, seemed to be softening. If the United States spent terrific sums on preparing for a "military conflict that may never be waged," then it would lose the ability to wage the Cold War with more flexible assets like economic, military, and technological aid to allies and potential friends.[32] This view was echoed in the National Intelligence Estimate on "Soviet Capabilities and Policies" of November 12, 1957, which painted a picture of a dynamic, innovative Soviet Union, now under the leadership of Nikita Khrushchev and showing "flexibility and pragmatism" in international affairs. The Soviets seemed to have no interest in general war and instead were achieving "greater freedom of maneuver in local situations." The present world situation was "ripe" for the Soviets, as they had largely given up on purely military means to achieve their goals. Subversion, revolutionary ideology, and technological aid were now their chief weapons.[33] If this were so, what good would America's vast nuclear arsenal be in countering this onslaught? To put it another way, how could Eisenhower pivot from his grand strategy of massive deterrence to the tactical flexibility needed to engage the Third World?

This was just the question that now burst into the open within the administration. In a remarkably frank exchange in the National Security Council on March 20, 1958, General Robert Cutler, Eisenhower's national security adviser, expressed the seditious view that mutual deterrence tended to benefit the Russians: By making Great Power war unthinkable, it opened up the chance for the Soviets to "nibble their way into the fabric of the Free World by small aggressions." The CIA director, Allen Dulles, added an additional dimension to the argument: The real problem was not Soviet aggression as much as anticolonial nationalism in Indonesia, North Africa, and the Middle East. Nuclear arsenals were utterly useless in the face of such challenges precisely because these movements were not directed from Moscow. Both Eisenhower and John Foster Dulles disagreed with Cutler and Allen Dulles, but ten days later in a private conversation, the two men evidently had second thoughts, agreeing that—in Eisenhower's words—"our strategic concept did not adequately take account of the possibility of limited war." In short, Ike recognized that the New Look had shackled him to an inflexible grand strategy.[34]

What was the way out of this trap? The answer emerged on May 1, 1958, in one of the more remarkable National Security Council meetings of Eisenhower's presidency.[35] The discussion revealed just how much division there was within the government about national security policy. Should the United States continue to premise its security wholly on nuclear deterrence and massive nuclear response in the case of a Soviet attack on, say, Berlin, Western Europe, or South Korea? Or should it develop greater conventional forces to allow for smaller-scale, limited responses to regional conflicts short of nuclear war? The military men in the room spoke unabashedly for their own bureaucratic interests. The chief of staff of the Army, Maxwell Taylor, who was developing into a fierce critic of the New Look, called for great flexibility and a corresponding increase in conventional capabilities to respond globally to brush-fire conflicts. General Nathan Twining, the Air Force chief who was serving as chairman of the Joint Chiefs of Staff, disagreed: What was needed was continued emphasis on nuclear weapons and strategic bombers—under Air Force control. CIA director Allen Dulles then chimed in: The real threat to American interests was in "the newly developing areas of the world" such as Indonesia and Laos, where the United States was "suffering the hardest blows." That was where more money was needed.

It fell to Secretary John Foster Dulles to resolve these competing demands, which he artfully did by suggesting that everyone was right: What was needed was both a massive nuclear deterrent as well as "an adequate capability to deal with wars not directly involving the United States and the USSR." The defense budget "should not compel us to allocate so much of our resources to maintenance of the nuclear deterrent that we will weaken our capability for limited war." Nuclear weapons were crucial—the "New Look" thesis still held. But the United States needed a "supplementary strategy" to provide greater flexibility, and this required sums to be spent on conventional military forces as well as the arming of allies. The Defense

Department promptly agreed: The United States must have its cake and eat it, and NSC 5810/1, approved by Eisenhower after repeated parsing and editing, allowed for both. As the defense secretary noted, the stated U.S. policy was now to insure "adequate but not excessive capability to deter general war" through a nuclear arsenal as well as "adequate and flexible limited war capabilities."[36] Presto! The issue was solved, not by choosing between two difficult alternatives but by agreeing that everyone should get what they wanted. The New Look was rescued even as it was repudiated. Ideology and pragmatism could both be honored.

As policymaking, this was a poor performance. The baleful consequences of this non-solution have been noted by scholars over the years: Eisenhower, in the words of one, "wound up with the worst of both worlds: the high risks of strategic warfare and the high costs of limited conflict."[37] And those costs were exceptionally high. The numbers show that for all of Eisenhower's insisting on holding the line against defense spending, his unwillingness to choose between the New Look and what would become known later as "flexible response" left him unable to restrict in any meaningful way the federal dollars devoted to defense. Ike's defense budgets remained at almost wartime levels throughout his peacetime administration. In 1950, the United States had spent $13.7 billion on national defense. At the peak of the Korean War, this sum rose to $52.8 billion. It came down only slightly under Ike: for the seven years from 1954 to 1960 inclusive, U.S. defense spending averaged $45.8 billion a year and never fell below $42.5 billion in any year. Over the same period, Eisenhower's defense budget annually consumed on average a staggering 58.7 percent of federal expenditures. In the post-Korea Eisenhower years, when the Korean War spending boom was over, America's annual defense outlays represented roughly 10 percent of its GDP—double the peacetime figure from the Truman years.[38] For a president who has gone down in the popular mind as a budget hawk, a man who "slashed defense spending" according to his most recent biographer, this balance sheet is damning.[39]

This brief survey suggests that when historians invoke ideology to explain Eisenhower's policies, they need to account for the plasticity of this president's worldview. Certainly he developed an ideological language that reflected his ambitions for the country. He also proved willing to adapt and willing to pursue such obviously desirable objectives as peace in Korea or arms control despite ideological pressures for more aggressive policies. Melvyn Leffler has asserted that Eisenhower could not "liberate himself from his fears or transcend his ideological makeup."[40] That is not quite accurate, for as we have seen, Eisenhower could pivot from broad principle to tactical necessity with relative ease. Yet this flexibility, so useful in presidential decisionmaking, could also produce a kind of intellectual drift. As this essay has shown, ideology brought Eisenhower to embrace the New Look nuclear strategy as a way to contain the existential threat of global Communism, yet because of his deep belief in the principle of massive retaliation as deterrence, he was unwilling to abandon it even when it obviously had failed to provide a flexible and comprehensive strategy for dealing with global security challenges of the kind that were emerging across the Third World in the 1950s. Ike got stuck in the middle of the road, trying to be both an ideologue and a pragmatist, both a strategist and a tactician. At least in the arena of nuclear policy, Eisenhower was unable to square his desire for ideological consistency with his need, as a chief executive, to adapt and develop new approaches on the fly.

CHAPTER 7

Black Appointees, Political Legitimacy, and the American Presidency

N. D. B. CONNOLLY

In late August of 2005, Secretary of State Condoleezza Rice decided to take a vacation. After nine solid months of work-related travel, including trips to forty-six countries, Rice thought it was time for a holiday in New York City. She hoped to attend the U.S. Open, do some shopping with some friends, and maybe catch a Broadway show. She had also been following reports that a hurricane called Katrina had just hit coastal Louisiana, Mississippi, and Alabama.

Recognizing the seriousness of the news, Rice made a few phone calls. She first called State Department offices in New Orleans; she had to make sure her staffers had cleared out. She then called Michael Chertoff, secretary of homeland security, to see if there was anything she could do. Chertoff, in the midst of an obvious crisis, waved her off. His agency was on it. So, Rice went to see *Spamalot*, a musical comedy, and the next morning she browsed for shoes at a Ferragamo boutique on Manhattan's Fifth Avenue. When she returned to her hotel room, Rice had barely dropped her bags before she turned on the television and was confronted with horrific images. "The airwaves were filled with devastating pictures from New Orleans," she recalls, "and the faces of most of the people in distress were black. . . . I knew right away, I should never have left Washington."[1]

What exactly was the nation's chief foreign relations officer supposed to do during this profound *domestic* crisis? "I wasn't just the secretary of state with responsibility for foreign affairs; I was the highest-ranking black in the administration. . . . What had I been thinking?" After making emergency travel arrangements, Rice called President George W. Bush. "Mr. President," she remembers saying, "I'm coming back. I don't know how much I can do, but we clearly have a race problem." "Yeah," the president acknowledged. "Why don't you come on back?" According to Rice, the graveness of Bush's tone surprised even her. It was clear, though, that the president and his highest-ranking African American appointee had reached some kind of understanding, one mired in the country's sticky racial history. Possessing what many considered to be one of the country's most brilliant political minds, Rice returned to her post, and by her own account, her blackness had everything to do with it.[2]

How has blackness served and perhaps even preserved the American presidency? More precisely, how have black people, through presidential appointments, proved instrumental to the preservation of America's political center? With the election of President Barack Obama in 2008, observers across the United States and around the world considered how an African American in the White House might change the historical meaning and workings of America's highest elected office. Tens of millions of voters celebrated Obama's ascendancy to the presidency.[3] Countless others openly resisted it, calling Obama's legitimacy and, frequently, his very citizenship into question.[4] The relationship between black people, political legitimacy, and American presidents, however, is far older than Barack Obama. Since at least the 1930s, and some might argue even earlier, U.S. presidents have used black appointees to perform important political work, work that often proved necessary for securing the chief executive's symbolic power and governing authority. Black appointees have shielded their presidents from challenges on questions of civil rights. They have also used their visibility as high-level public servants to declare the greatness of American democracy on the world stage. Presidents, in turn, have looked to their black staffers to build new constituencies for winning elections, advancing public policy, and, at times, for staving off potential crises still unseen. Black appointees, for their part, have understood and embraced their own complex positions as protectors of the White House against attacks from without. They have also, whenever possible, worked to take advantage of their privileged access to power, sometimes securing important reforms from within. Many served out of a deep sense of duty, while, at the very same time, pursuing presidential favor for reasons of political pragmatism and naked careerism. Regardless of the various *motivations* African American appointees and their presidents brought to their working relationships in the White House, the *history* of these appointments can serve as a single narrative that has much to tell us about the workings of American democracy and the modern presidency itself.

This essay argues that, while political parties, presidents, and black appointees have had diverse agendas and at times conflicting understandings of executive power across time and relative to the color line, all have operated within a relatively consistent political script that has endured a great many historical changes and political circumstances. Over the long run of twentieth-century presidential politics, there have been two constants among many: the fact of a majority white electorate and the shifting rules of racial liberalism regulating that electorate. Within such a world, black appointees became both necessary and hazardous for those wishing to govern. Indeed, quite apart from whether the actual president is black, blackness, through presidential appointments, has mattered a great deal to the American presidency and to the perceived authority of those who hold the office.

Simply consider the dilemma facing Condoleezza Rice. In the wake of a human catastrophe on the scale of Hurricane Katrina—some 1,800 people dead, 400,000 displaced, and well over $100 billion in property damage—it perhaps seems cynical to suggest that White House officials and the president himself would think to showcase the administration's African American staffers just because those appointees were black.[5] Amid the clear humanitarian and financial calamities following Katrina, though, the White House's political troubles seemed equally undeniable. Media outlets as mainstream as NBC News and CNN pondered why it seemed that U.S. citizens, most of them black and poor, were being left dead or stranded on rooftops and in stadium bleachers.[6] There was also a broader historical context wherein Republican presidents had long endured charges of being tone-deaf to the age-old, sociological foundations of poverty and insensitive to black poverty in particular. George W. Bush, in 2000, had campaigned on a platform of "compassionate conservatism," which represented, in part, his attempt to build a "big tent" GOP that could welcome greater numbers of women and minorities.[7] Ninety percent of black voters and some two-thirds of Hispanics voted against Bush in his first presidential bid.[8] Widespread accounts of black disfranchisement in Florida, Ohio, and elsewhere further stained Bush's legitimacy and affirmed the modern GOP's ostensibly abysmal record on race. Still, and in part to prove his commitment to minorities, Bush, as president-elect, chose two African Americans (Rice and Colin Powell), two women (Rice and Karen Hughes), and a Latino (Alberto Gonzales) as his first four high-level cabinet appointments.[9] By August of 2005, it seemed to matter little. As the casualties mounted and images continued to pour in of people stranded and dying, it seemed that Katrina had washed away much of the president's effort on the race question.

So began Secretary Rice's role in the recovery. Immediately on reuniting with the president, she offered to visit displaced New Orleanians in Houston, in her words, to "show the flag for the administration." White House officials determined that her skills as the nation's chief diplomat were better served improving relations with Black America. She first brokered a meeting with the president of the NAACP, Bruce Gordon, and carefully avoided legitimizing others whom she pejoratively described as "self-described black leaders." The secretary then went on several television news programs and appeared in national newspapers to rehabilitate the president's reputation. She explicitly shot down the most serious charges—"George Bush doesn't care about black people"—and highlighted the president's record of black political appointments and support for historically black colleges.[10] Rice also met with survivors on the ground in her home state of Alabama, where she told hurricane victims gathered at a Sunday morning black church service, "The Lord is going to come on time—if we just wait." Mere days from boutique-hopping on Fifth Avenue, Rice now advised Americans to observe patience through their poverty. The timing, in its tragedy and irony, was not lost on the secretary. As she wrote years later, "I'm still mad at myself for only belatedly understanding my own role and responsibilities in the crisis."[11]

The responsibilities of black political appointees can be broad and demanding indeed. They extend beyond the hefty titles held and soaring oaths taken by black judges, staffers, or cabinet members. They also include expectations that, in their historical ties to white supremacy, only black appointees seem able to fulfill. Rice's disappointment at "only belatedly understanding my . . . role" says far less about any self-professed lapse in judgment than it says about the hold that America's racial history has over the country's institutions in general and the presidency in particular. From President Franklin Roosevelt's "Black Cabinet" to E. Frederic Murrow of the Eisenhower administration to Colin Powell and countless others, black presidential appointees, for decades, had been asked to do what Secretary Rice had done. They cautioned patience among the dispossessed. They warded off scandals generated by "the Negro problem." And they symbolized in their very person the egalitarian and meritocratic promise of the United States. It was a script that was written and rewritten through the events of Jim Crow, the Cold War, the civil rights revolution, and the eventual arrival of an apparently "color-blind" America. And as the curtain went up on Hurricane Katrina, it was a script that Secretary Rice had briefly though gravely forgot.

Setting the Rules

To understand the political script binding blackness to the American presidency, one must first consider mores of government employment going back to the late nineteenth century, a time when white supremacy clearly set the terms for black work in public service. In an age of mass black disenfranchisement, white Americans used lynching and intimidation to circumscribe black people's political power. African Americans with discernible white patrons or ties to business joined other working-class folk in trying to access the modicum of political power made available by federal jobs.[12] The most elite appointees, such as Judson Lyons, the register of the Treasury (1898–1906), or Blanche K. Bruce, recorder of deeds (1890–1893), secured their positions only though interwoven patronage networks that had either white politicians or Booker T. Washington at the top.[13]

Though never a federal appointee himself, Washington, founder and head of the Tuskegee Institute, played a central role in doling out government appointments and, consequently, in shaping American political culture. According to Booker T.'s longtime critic, W. E. B. DuBois, "Few political appointments of Negroes were made anywhere in the United States without his consent."[14] DuBois spoke with some authority on the matter, because, in 1900, he'd tried and failed to secure Washington's precious endorsement for a position as the superintendent of Negro schools in the nation's capital.[15] (The famous ideological conflict between Washington and DuBois may well have begun over Washington's denial of DuBois's request for a letter of recommendation). Washington's good word could reach all the way to the White House, especially by the time of the first Roosevelt administration. According to historian Eric Yellin, President Theodore Roosevelt "leaned exclusively on Washington for advice and [black] patronage recommendations."[16] Judson Lyons, a longtime beneficiary of Tuskegee's influence, actually lost his position in Treasury because, as the *Washington Bee* reported, "he has not danced while Mr. Washington played the fiddle."[17]

Booker T. Washington represented a kind of hopefulness and pragmatism that black moderates widely espoused and that white Americans preferred to see in "representative Negroes." His approach to white power would remain a strain within black politics long after his death in 1915. In cities across the country and for the next hundred years, in fact, black chambers of commerce, professional clubs, and veterans' organizations—incubators of pragmatic politics—served as the principal feeders for high-level government appointments.

Under Jim Crow, African Americans hoping to access administrative power had to (1) put white authority figures at ease about broad black discontent and (2) help white higher-ups govern under apartheid. And they had to do this while attempting to (3) build black voting constituencies that, while helping their presidents, might also fulfill their own aims of electing black candidates to Congress or at least influencing white officeholders to heed the demands of black voters.

During the 1930s, President Franklin Roosevelt managed the black electorate by appointing his Federal Council on Negro Affairs or, as some called it, his "Black Cabinet." Mary McLeod Bethune, William Hastie, Robert Clifton Weaver, and others stood among a handful of highly accomplished black educators, economists, and lawyers who advised the president and Eleanor Roosevelt on how best to respond to black poverty and tamp down black militancy, particularly radicalism of the communist variety. Beyond serving as advisers, the Black Cabinet, during the Great Depression, helped bring modest federal jobs out of Washington and into local communities. Thanks largely to their efforts in the late 1930s, many Southern cities, for the first time ever, saw African Americans managing government labor pools and heading brand-new public housing projects.[18]

More radical voices on the black left expressed concern that President Roosevelt's council of Negro advisers offered even greater incentives for the best and brightest African Americans to pursue more moderate and, thus, more conservative forms of political activity. George Streator, a black labor organizer and collaborator of DuBois's, dismissed "all [the] Negro intellectuals hoping to work . . . in some government job." "Will not these black bureaucrats," he wondered in 1935, "behave precisely as Britain's Nigerian chiefs and priests?"[19] Black political appointees, many militants believed, served as facilitators of capitalist exploitation and white indirect rule. Such arguments seemed hard to shake, as FDR, in the interest of preserving legislative support among Southern Democrats, consistently resisted calls from his Black Cabinet to advance an anti-lynching bill or to extend social security or labor organizing protections to agricultural workers and domestics, the principal jobs occupied by African Americans.[20]

Generally, Roosevelt's black advisers were tasked with selling the New Deal's housing and federal employment benefits to black people. And, in light of the GOP's ongoing neglect of African American voters during the 1920s, the efforts of Roosevelt's appointees greatly increased the number of black Democrats in cities and rural areas across America.[21] Fully seventy-five percent of African Americans voted for Franklin Roosevelt in the 1936 presidential election, a record at the time. In return, a few Black Cabinet members, such as William Hastie, were allowed to turn largely symbolic posts into high-level appointments, thus helping the president further govern a changing country.

Out in the Cold

For roughly thirty years, William Hastie had consistently been the highest-ranking black appointee in the U.S. government.[22] A Harvard graduate, he served as an assistant solicitor for the Department of the Interior under Harold Ickes before Roosevelt named him to a federal judgeship in the Virgin Islands in 1937. Hastie then served as a civilian aide to the secretary of war during World War II and later, under President Truman, gained the governorship of the Virgin Islands.[23] In his many roles, Hastie showed himself to be a disciplined political operative with a gift for jurisprudence under Jim Crow. He also did so while maintaining a principled objection to racial segregation, no mean feat in a government largely populated by unrepentant segregationists.[24] In 1942, for instance, Hastie resigned from his War Department post because his superiors had forced Tuskegee Airmen to serve in segregated squadrons.[25] His vocal opposition to Jim Crow, while increasingly common among black public servants by the early 1940s, would put him squarely in the crosshairs of Southern senators during his various confirmation hearings. At the very same time, though, Hastie's public statements against segregation made him a valuable appointee for presidents, like Roosevelt and, later, Harry Truman, looking to showcase their racial progressivism in the absence of more far-reaching civil rights legislation.

It's important to note that Jim Crow's political script received an important revision during the years of Hastie's ascension. Prior to World War II, American presidents could safely stake out segregationist positions with few political consequences. President Woodrow Wilson, for instance, was a known segregationist who enjoyed two-terms in office. He successfully argued that racial segregation in federal jobs made government more efficient. On Wilson's watch, the forced demotion of black federal appointees and the imposition of Jim Crow across Washington's bureaucracy would remove, in his words, "the friction, or rather the discontent and uneasiness which had prevailed in many . . . [government] departments."[26] Wilson publicly endorsed D. W. Griffith's 1915 film, *Birth of A Nation*, reputedly calling it "history written in lightning" and screening it at the White House. He also presided over the U.S. occupation of Haiti on the grounds that the Haitian people, like the depiction of Reconstruction-era Negroes in *Birth*, seemed unfit for self-governance.[27]

After the global battle against fascism in the 1930s and 1940s, Jim Crow's administrative mores had begun to bend, though not break. Such was, in part, the emerging world brought about by FDR's Black Cabinet. And within this evolving political context, Hastie and other African Americans who sought real institutional power—the power conveyed by presidents—had to help their commanders-in-chief rebuff increasingly vocal challenges on matters of civil rights. In 1949, for instance, President Truman nominated Hastie to be the first African American justice on the U.S. Court of Appeals, a quid pro quo, some believed, for Hastie having stumped for the president in opposition to criticisms leveled against Truman by Henry Wallace's Progressive Party.

Though Hastie remained committed to the principles of anti-racism, his relationship to the left remained complicated. Like many African Americans, Hastie had built alliances with socialists and communists during the 1930s. Those groups, after all, held the most progressive positions on civil rights at the time. By the mid- to late 1940s, though, liberal anticommunist organizations, such as the Americans for Democratic Action, and more established groups, including the NAACP, moved to seize the political high ground from the radical left. Foreshadowing, perhaps, the political tactics that crested under McCarthyism, black liberals like Hastie elected to oppose the Communist Party openly, to associate the White House's political enemies with communism, and to do both without sacrificing their progressive credentials on race. "I am convinced," Hastie maintained in 1950, "that the new Progressive Party is a political puppet securely tied to the Communist Party."[28]

As had happened during the era of Booker T, in other words, white governing interests between the 1930s and 1950s again used elite black appointees to help fashion a particular brand of racial centrism. Yet, instead of it being the party of Teddy Roosevelt in the Progressive Era, it was the Democratic Party of FDR and Harry Truman during the late New Deal and post–World War II eras. Crafting, in effect, modern liberalism, black appointees and similar operatives advanced the slow and steady marginalization of the Communist Party from American politics.[29]

Under Democratic presidents (once considered the bane of black voters), Hastie served as a symbol of what was possible in America. He toured black civic groups, college campuses, and churches exhibiting both soaring personal success and the benefits of placing "racial betterment ahead of personal considerations."[30] Here stood another important piece of the black operative's script—hope. During the Cold War, many ambitious African American pols, including the NAACP's Roy Wilkins and Walter White, proved quite adept at securing new levels of influence in the White House by attacking such "pessimistic" figures as Paul Robeson or the communist William Patterson.[31] Indeed, any African Americans who aspired to secure a future within the country's political mainstream could not, in the words of one 1940s black editor, "be 'heartless' enough to strike a pessimistic note to an audience of hopeful Negroes."[32] It seemed that the wartime and postwar politics of hope, as was true of earlier eras, required protecting liberalism from any credible critique that might diminish America's growing prominence on the global stage. It was a message—hope—that, some six decades later, presidential candidate Barack Obama would ride into the White House. Still, as Obama learned early and often during his candidacy and eventual presidency, dutifully pronouncing one's belief in America, no matter how lofty one's perch, often provided insufficient cover from racist attacks from the right.

Hastie's political career again proves illustrative here. At midcentury, the politics of Jim Crow and the Cold War made vocal integrationists, especially prominent ones like Hastie, vulnerable to red-baiting, regardless of their professed disdain for communism.[33] At Hastie's confirmation hearing in 1950, his first question, after providing his name, address, and education, included the now-familiar query: "Mr. Hastie, have you ever belonged to, or have you ever been associated with, any organization known as a communist organization?"[34] Following the question, the subsequent four-day marathon of interrogations sought to ensnare Hastie on perjury charges by catching him making even a single sympathetic statement about communists. Senators Pat McCarran (D-NV) and Forrest Donnell (R-MO) pressed Hastie on seemingly unpatriotic statements he once made about the federal government. They purported to have Hastie on record saying that "public officials who did not fight discrimination were a greater menace to national security than the radical groups now being tried for disloyalty."[35] He denied ever making such remarks. Hastie, again according to senators, also condemned the FBI for administrative overreach and for branding Americans engaged in interracial friendships as "subversives."[36] (This charge against the bureau later proved to be true.) Yet, there, too, Hastie denied ever making such statements. On one matter after another, it seemed that Judge Hastie had exhibited too much pessimism about American institutions and the race question.

Hastie's proposed 1949 appointment to the Court of Appeals also ran into opposition from a collection of African American lawyers, again making Hastie the center of Cold War racial intrigues. The attorneys accused the Truman White House of using Hastie as a token candidate meant to take the place of a more substantive black appointment. Instead of seeing Hastie appointed to the appellate court, a group of black lawyers in Philadelphia and Washington wanted to see Truman appoint Hastie to the federal bench in Washington, D.C. They noted that, in spite of Hastie's appointment in the Virgin Islands, an African American had never held a federal judgeship *inside* the United States. Many further claimed that the president, in concert with Democratic Party chair, James Finnegan, and Sen. Francis Myers (D-PA), hatched Hastie's appointment to trick black voters into believing that the Democrats were more progressive on the race question than they really were. Appointing Hastie to the appeals court, black observers remarked, would help Myers and the White House maintain black support in spite of doing next to nothing on civil rights. They warned that Truman seemed to be distracting attention away from the White House's "failure to pass any of the civil rights legislation which the President and the Democratic Party promised."[37] Putting Hastie on the bench in Philadelphia actually weakened his voice in critical civil rights cases, the *Pittsburgh Courier* observed. The paper then drew an even more damning conclusion about the Truman White House generally: "Negroes of the nation have been short-changed in these appointments. There is nothing to be elated about."[38] The Senate Judiciary Committee eventually confirmed Hastie—over one opposing vote from Sen. James Eastland (D-MS)—and he went on to serve on the appellate court for the next twenty-two years.[39]

In securing some of the country's most impressive presidential appointments over the course of his career, William Hastie seemed to have mastered the overlapping administrative cultures of American apartheid and anticommunism. This also meant, however, that, as Cold War liberalism evolved into civil rights liberalism, Hastie's professional fortunes remained anchored in shifting sand. Black appointees, like everyone else, could be swept off the scene by changing political tides, it seemed.

In 1962, a vacancy opened on the U.S. Supreme Court, and President John F. Kennedy, considering his legacy, flirted with the idea of appointing Hastie.[40] The most renowned black lawyers at the time, including Charles Hamilton Houston and Thurgood Marshall, all considered Hastie the finest legal mind among them. Said Marshall years later from his office in the U.S. Supreme Court, "Hastie should have been on this court way back. He's a great man. Much better than I am. Much better than I will ever be. Honest."[41] However, Bobby Kennedy, the attorney general and the president's closest adviser, encouraged his brother not to appoint Hastie based on conversations he'd had with sitting justices. Chief Justice Earl Warren, in the attorney general's words, remained "violently opposed to having Hastie on the Court." Citing Hastie's rumored impatience with leftists, Warren charged that the country's ranking black jurist was "not a liberal, and he'll be opposed to all the measures that we are interested in."[42] This opinion of Hastie echoed elsewhere on the Court, though it seemed mostly based on Hastie's personal relationships with jurists (such as his mentor Felix Frankfurter) who, in the context of the Cold War, had a record of defending states' rights. Justices, perhaps incorrectly, also characterized Hastie's own decisions on the appellate court as "conservative."[43] Being a staunch anticommunist had not kept Hastie, in 1950, from being suspected as a communist sympathizer. And a substantial record of opposing Jim Crow had not kept Hastie, in 1962, from being branded a political conservative.[44] Black centrism, clearly, had its own unique hazards.

Life on the Inside

As Hastie's lost Supreme Court appointment affirms, the White House could be a tangled mess of intrigues and egos twisted among a scattering of certainties and half-truths. Yet for African American appointees working *within* the White House, such intrigues were compounded by the unique responsibilities and challenges that simply accompanied "the Negro problem." The country's first African American White House aide, E. Frederic Morrow, first joined General Dwight Eisenhower's campaign staff in 1952 before gaining a position at the White House five years later. During the immediate postwar years, the GOP was not prepared to surrender black voters completely to the Democratic Party. At the time of Eisenhower's election, in fact, nearly a third of black voters still self-identified as Republicans.[45]

Of the dozens of black public servants that Eisenhower appointed to the United Nations, the Department of Labor, and elsewhere, Morrow became the highest paid and the most visible.[46] That also made him a target. Angry white citizens sent an avalanche of letters to the White House protesting Morrow's appointment. White male staffers threatened to quit, or took to calling Morrow "Ike's straw boss," reflecting his status as a kind of scarecrow authority figure.[47] White secretaries, refusing to be alone with him in his office to take dictation, would enter his office only in pairs, if they answered his calls at all. In a tattered office, ignored by secretarial staff, and the victim of an in-house isolation campaign, Morrow clung to hope: "It was the bottom of the stairs. But it was a challenge. Then and there, I renewed faith in myself."[48]

A lawyer trained at Rutgers and a one-time public affairs adviser at CBS, Morrow tried mightily to project his expertise, including experiences he had at the Department of Commerce. "I made it clear when I accepted this job that I would not be a special adviser on racial problems."[49] But, Morrow's title—administrative officer for special projects—was, in the words of one historian, a "purposely vague title referring to equally vague work."[50]

Regardless of his declarations to the contrary, Morrow served, in effect, as Eisenhower's racial Swiss Army Knife. He received awards from black organizations on the president's behalf and wrote speeches for the president to deliver to black audiences.[51] Such acts, as described in *Ebony* magazine, were designed "to better communications between Ike and Negroes and also to improve the image of the President."[52] Morrow also debriefed with President Eisenhower when racial incidents loomed. After a particularly striking gaffe where the president encouraged the Negro Publishers Association to cultivate "patience" among black people, Morrow warned the president and his staffers that "patience" was a dirty word, at least coming from a white leader. And when racist whites in a Delaware restaurant refused to serve Ghana's minister of finance, Komla Agbeli Gbedemah, in 1957, it fell to Morrow to broker an ameliorative breakfast meeting between the finance minister and Eisenhower. The inverse of Secretary of State Condoleezza Rice's experience during Hurricane Katrina, Morrow, as a domestic adviser, was repeatedly asked to be the administration's black face and political insurance against potentially rough foreign relations with Africa and the wider colored world.[53]

The U.S. Supreme Court's rulings in *Brown v. Board of Education* (1954–1955) and the Southern intransigence in response presented still more challenges to the White House's footing on the race question, further illustrating the many roles presidents expected black appointees to play. Specifically, Morrow tried to move both black and white politics into a more centrist position by encouraging Republican leadership to be more inclusive and discouraging African American leaders from organizing spectacles of black political power. In 1958, for instance, Morrow asked Jackie Robinson, whom he'd met at an NAACP dinner two years earlier, not to participate in a thousand-person anti-segregation march in Washington, D.C.[54] Marchers planned to bring a signed petition right to the doorstep of the White House. Morrow believed that, as pioneers in their respective professional areas, "Robinson and I have a rather close friendship." He therefore took the Dodgers star "into [his] confidence," warning him that marching on the president with an ultimatum, from the White House's perspective, would only embolden "the Communists."[55] Robinson went public with the warning. Within thirty-six hours, the black press had effectively branded Morrow a "traitor."[56] "I only tried to do a duty that I felt I owed to the president as well as to my race," he later wrote.[57] Eisenhower's growing unpopularity among black newspapermen and professionals made Morrow even more toxic. By 1959, the invitations to speak stopped coming as frequently. Morrow later admitted, "I didn't know if I would ride out the storm. The reaction was intense."[58]

Things were no easier for Morrow inside the White House. After a sweep of Republican losses in the 1958 midterm elections, Eisenhower blamed the black vote for not appreciating the White House's record on civil rights, which included ending President Woodrow Wilson's now forty-year-old practice of Jim Crowing federal facilities in the nation's capital. Eisenhower also sent the National Guard to force school desegregation in Little Rock, and passed the first civil rights act of the twentieth century (1957).[59] Morrow, ever hopeful, penned in his diary that the losses of 1958 might spur the White House to be even more forceful on civil rights. "I am glad it was a crushing . . . defeat," he confessed. "This should indicate, even to the most obtuse, that something must be done . . . if Republicans are to survive as a party."[60] Morrow then conveyed his private musings to top Republicans in a White House memo: "Negroes had a large hand in this Democratic victory and Republicans . . . made little or no effort to interest them."[61] Morrow's frankness did not generate the results he intended. According to one report, his candid assessment of Republicans' race problem, "created a furor in GOP ranks." And Eisenhower held fast to the idea that, as president, he had catered to the civil rights constituency only to have it abandon him. "Consequently," as described in *Ebony*, "there was a tapering off of activities in race relations at the executive level."[62]

In light of the frustrations Hastie and Murrow faced working "within the system," one should keep in mind that Democratic and Republican administrations did not just place heavy expectations on their black appointees; the people those appointees purportedly represented—black voters—placed expectations on the White House as well. As activists and everyday people pushed for racial justice across the country and in the South especially, African Americans and their allies looked to U.S. presidents to defend American citizens from racial violence. The present-day reputations the parties currently enjoy on matters of racial justice—Democrats as pro–civil rights and multicultural, Republicans as friends, first and foremost, to white voters—began solidifying in the 1960s. And, accurate or not, these reputations have largely been shaped by black White House aides. In no case was that truer than with arguably the most effective African American White House aide in U.S. history, Louis Martin.

Recruited by Sargent Shriver to assist on JFK's election campaign, Martin eventually served as a White House adviser to Presidents Kennedy, Johnson, and Carter.[63] He functioned, in many respects, as the unofficial liaison between the black freedom struggle and the White House. In 1960, Democrats, relative to Republicans, could still claim no substantive distinction on questions of civil rights. In that year's election between Kennedy and Richard

Nixon, in fact, Nixon was actually more popular in many corners of black America. Eisenhower's vice president carried the black vote in Atlanta, for instance.[64] At the same time, Kennedy, as both a candidate and in his first two years as president, remained far more committed to foreign affairs than to civil rights. In his efforts to maintain support among Southern congressmen, Kennedy's preferred approach to civil rights was to secure black votes by maintaining a Cold War race strategy of reaching out to African nations.[65]

Arguably, Louis Martin made the difference. He took the traditional role that black appointees had played—defending the White House from attacks on the left—and used it to influence presidents to take an unprecedented step toward improved racial equality. In February of 1963, Kennedy began actively pushing a civil rights agenda in response to grassroots direct action campaigns. But, in consultation with white staffers concerned with the administration's reelection, Kennedy's efforts remained focused only on voting, specifically on eliminating literacy tests. As part of a coordinated effort to bring about a "New Deal in Race Relations," Martin pushed the president to lean on Congress to include critical public accommodations language in whatever civil rights bill the White House backed. Martin, according to observers in the White House, secured what became, after Kennedy's assassination, the heart of the 1964 Civil Rights Act.[66] Martin also carefully arranged a landmark meeting between Kennedy and the organizers of the March on Washington for Jobs and Freedom in the summer of 1963. (Kennedy had initially resisted a meeting after march organizers denied the president's request to speak at the event.) Then, under President Lyndon Johnson, he arranged for the commander-in-chief to meet with the National Negro Press Association twice a year, more than any other president. He also helped pave the way, particularly during the Johnson years, for other high-level black appointments, including Andrew Brimmer (Federal Reserve) and Robert Weaver (Housing and Urban Development).[67] Martin had actually compiled a list of what he liked to call his "700 Super Blacks," educated and accomplished African Americans, whom he worked to have appointed at every level of the federal bureaucracy.[68] Beyond opening the door for a few in the most prominent positions, progress seemed slow, however. Only 2 percent of subcabinet-level positions under President Johnson were held by black Americans.[69]

Holding the Center

The passage of the Civil Rights and Voting Rights Acts promised to expand black power not just beyond direct action campaigns but also beyond the old politics of patronage. As in earlier eras, conflicts and negotiations between the black left and more centrist civil rights figures continued. This time, they revolved largely around contested definitions of "Black Power." As the historian Yohuru Williams has described, in spite of its many variations—black capitalism, black separatism, self-defense, cultural pride—"Black Power," as a phrase, seemed to invite white anxiety and, by extension, violent state repression.[70] Moreover, on questions concerning lingering features of white supremacy, one generation's progressives seemed to be another generation's obstructionists. In May 1969, William Hastie, by this point an appellate court judge of nearly twenty years, had joined a gathering of self-described black liberals, including Robert Weaver, Kenneth Clark, and John Hope Franklin at Haverford College. Their hope was to begin formulating a "pro-integrationist" challenge to what many perceived as dangerous racial separatism coming from Black Power activists. At the event, Hastie recounted an interaction he'd had with a college student following a lecture he'd given at Temple University's Law School. The student, as Hastie tells it, said to his honor, "'The trouble with you judges is that you are nothing but lackeys for the establishment.' And I said to him, 'Now, young man, you just stop right there. Let me get you straight. I am not a lackey for the establishment. I *am* the establishment!'"[71] For Hastie, that distinction had been hard-earned.

More pertinently, Hastie's retort actually reflected a very serious change occurring in American political culture. By the late 1960s and early 1970s, affirmative action programs, antidiscrimination enforcement in government employment, and steady economic growth had created an expanded black middle class. New divisions emerged between black professionals and their counterparts among America's working poor. And an entirely new collection of black elected officials—many of whom boasted a record of advancing civil rights at the local level—advocated for continued commitments to entrepreneurship in place of protest and radical race rhetoric.[72]

The White House capitalized on these developments. President Richard Nixon argued that capitalist strains of Black Power offered the best route for African Americans, and, by executive order in 1969, he showed his commitment to black commerce (and the lengths to which he would go to sever black voters from the Democratic Party) by establishing a National Advisory Council on Black Enterprise. "High on the list of priorities for the decade of the seventies," the council argued in its final report, "is the provision of a substantially increased stake in the American economy for members of minority groups. This will come about through expanded opportunities for ownership and economic resources."[73] At the very same time of these and similar recommendations, incidentally, assassination campaigns largely orchestrated by the FBI further ensured that charismatic, anticapitalist black leadership would not be around to challenge more moderate, corporate-minded African Americans seeking public service positions.[74]

By virtue of ideological shifts and state repression of the left, the 1970s seemed to promise unprecedented black unity and the possible creation, for the first time ever, of a national black platform. African Americans from a variety of political orientations began seeking what would come to be called "community control," a notion, among poorer black communities especially, that included taking over everything from local tax assessment powers to the distribution of government contracts to curriculum design in public schools.[75] Nixon's take on "community control" was dismantling large-scale urban redevelopment programs in favor of smaller community development block grants, federally funded and locally administered. However, Nixon's continued support of "Black Capitalism" could not paper over deep ideological fissures between moderates and radicals over whether American democracy was even capable of meeting black needs. Delegates at the 1972 National Black Political Convention in Gary, Indiana, conveyed what many believed to be a troubling continuity: "Here at Gary, let us never forget that while the times and the names of the parties have continually changed, one truth has faced us insistently, never changing: Both parties have betrayed us whenever their interests conflicted with ours (which is most of the time)." Their statement continued, in a pointed shot at the limitations of presidential politics, "If white 'liberalism' could have solved our problems, then Lincoln and Roosevelt and Kennedy would have done so."[76]

The strength of such antiestablishment sentiments notwithstanding, these ideas coexisted with William Hastie's "I *am* the establishment," driving black people—left and right—into political campaigns across the country.[77] In the turn to electoral politics—"Black Politics"—groups as diverse as the Mississippi Freedom Democratic Party, the Freedom Now Party, the Black Panther Party for Self Defense, and the Congressional Black Caucus could all be placed on a single political and historical spectrum.[78] And subsequent electoral victories meant that black presidential appointees would no longer be the only, or even the most important, operators in the American political mainstream. Between 1970 and 1975, the number of black elected officials in America more than doubled, from just under 1,500 to some 3,500 officeholders. Many of these politicians held state legislature seats and mayoral positions in cities such as Flint, Michigan, and Los Angeles, California. Not a few were the beneficiaries of white flight to Northern suburbs and across the Sunbelt South. Many African Americans, including senior black appointees in Washington, saw the arrival of more black office holders as a direct consequence of their efforts from the inside.

As segments of the black grassroots rode into office, presidents continued making black appointments, but administrations usually preferred to fish their candidates from the country's entrepreneurial and legal classes, mostly by utilizing emergent black professional networks. Presidents Nixon, Carter, and Reagan presided over the appointment of real estate developers from Nashville, minority business owners from Los Angeles, and law-and-order types from Savannah, Georgia. One could certainly find more black faces in high places. Yet, their politics, relative to the late 1960s, would not move the center to the left in any discernible way. President Carter became the most effective proponent of integrating African Americans into the federal bureaucracy during this period. Under Carter, subcabinet level black appointees increased to roughly 12 percent of all such appointees, up from 2 percent under Johnson and 5 percent under Nixon and Ford.[79]

A New Mainstream

The long history of black political appointees makes it possible to reframe what historians have called the "Rise of the Right" as more a story about the preservation of the center.[80] In her history of the U.S. Commission on Civil Rights, Mary Frances Berry describes how the regulatory enforcement of civil rights suffered a profound weakening through several rounds of presidential appointments under Presidents Ronald Reagan, George H. W. Bush, and George W. Bush. Herself a member of the commission between 1980 and 2004, Berry blames Republicans for making the commission an especially welcome home for right-wing ideologues of color who "stifled [the commission] from fully carrying out its mandate."[81] There's no debating the point that with conservative electoral successes came more conservative appointees of color.[82] However, when we consider the informal racial responsibilities of presidential appointees over the run of the twentieth century, we notice a certain political template: Advance the administration's agenda, fend off attacks from the left, become a symbol of the possibilities afforded hardworking Americans.

As the political center shifted during the 1970s and into the 1980s, the criteria for credible black appointees shifted only in degree, not in kind. Blacks still needed to be pro-business, and preferably Ivy League–educated. And after the red-blooded Americanism of the Reagan era, they also had to comply with a political discourse set in the narrowest of colorblind terms. In fact, black appointment under Democratic presidents, post-Reagan, brings the volatility of presidential race politics squarely into view.

In 1993, Harvard Law professor Lani Guinier had been President Bill Clinton's appointee to head the Civil Rights Division of the U.S. Justice

Department. Guinier had been a longtime friend of the Clintons since their days at Yale Law School. Her appointment fell apart, however, even before her confirmation hearings began. Conservative editorialists at *The Wall Street Journal* misrepresented her positions on voting rights and affirmative action. They smeared her as a black nationalist and "quota queen," drawing from that era's dominant caricature of poor black women—the "welfare queen." The *New York Times*, a presumed guardian of liberalism in the press, condemned Guinier's law review articles as "poorly written, provocative, and easy to caricature." The paper also claimed that Guinier, thinking only of her own ambitions, gave "right-wing snipers a broad target for charges of radicalism," implicating the White House and giving "moderate readers" cause for alarm. Under advisement from Democratic senators, including Carol Moseley-Braun (D-IL), Clinton cut her loose without so much as an opportunity for Guinier to defend herself in public.[83]

In 2008, the environmentalist Van Jones, an appointee under President Barack Obama, became a political sensation through his ability to articulate a "Green Collar Economy." Jones's vision of the sustainable economy, in one swoop, promised to solve racial inequality and restore the planet, all while working within acceptable free-market principles. Less than a year after the publication of his *New York Times* bestseller, Jones was appointed adviser to the White House's Council on Environmental Quality. Just a few weeks later he was gone, thanks to some inconvenient remarks he made about obstructionist Republican operatives being "assholes."[84] For good measure, GOP representatives highlighted his alleged association with Marxist organizers in California's Bay Area.

And then, of course, there's the story of the longtime civil rights activist Shirley Sherrod. At the first whiff that Sherrod, a black staffer in the U.S. Department of Agriculture, *might* have spouted black nationalist views and discriminated against white farmers, officials in the Obama White House immediately demanded and secured her resignation.[85] Sherrod, it was later learned, suffered a political hit-job by right-wing propagandists who reengineered her speech and posted it online after a little creative editing. In each of these cases—Guinier, Jones, and Sherrod—conservative political agents pounced on what seemed to be unacceptable politics, in Guinier and Sherrod's cases in particular, "black" politics. What remains just as crucial to attend to here, however, is the swiftness with which *Democratic* operatives—black and white—flushed these appointees from their respective or potential posts.

In the post-civil rights era, it seems the racial politics of resignation were just as important as the earlier politics of appointment. Black appointees continued to feel special pressures generated by a two-pronged continuity:

a majority white electorate and the racial expectations of that electorate. To ignore the robustness of white political power—embedded *within* liberalism and extant even in the 1990s and 2000s—makes swift dismissals like those suffered by Jones, Guinier, or Sherrod practically inexplicable, even, at times, to those being told to leave. As Sherrod, in her memoir, wonders in professed shame and confusion: "How can I explain to my children that I got fired by the first black president?"[86]

The explanation, in part, has its roots in history. Regardless of the perceived or projected color of the president, the ghost of Jim Crow's political cultural inspired operatives in the post–civil rights era to view black appointments as both fraught and necessary. For African American appointees, their efforts remained harder to realize because of lingering concerns about black anti-Americanism and disturbingly durable beliefs about black incompetence.

But history vexes the old "white" politics of racial exclusion as well. Today, no viable presidential administration can go without black political appointees, and not simply because the presence of black staffers serves as evidence of a racially sensitive White House. Black appointees—precisely *because of their blackness*—protect American liberalism *and* conservatism. They authorize the country's otherwise suspect proclamations about being a nation of laws and a perfectible democracy. Black appointees affirm the stories that Americans tell themselves about themselves. And through the conquered racism in their own biographies, they narrate the greatness of America in ways that only they can and in ways that presidents undoubtedly need. During the mid- to late 1950s, E. Frederic Morrow gave over three hundred speeches on behalf of the White House. He proudly began his 1960 GOP convention speech as he had so many others: "100 years ago . . . my grandfather was a slave."[87] Condoleezza Rice was known to tell audiences that she hadn't attended racially integrated schools until the tenth grade.[88] And few would dispute that Barack Obama's successful run to the White House actually began with proclamations given, as a senator, at the 2004 Democratic National Convention, fulfilling, in his own way, his role in the script. Before declaring the greatness of "One America," Obama pointed out that his father was a Kenyan goatherd and the son of a lowly domestic servant to British colonists. "Through hard work and perseverance," the young senator explained, "my father got a scholarship to study in a magical place—America." "In no other country on Earth," he told the entire world, "is my story even possible."[89]

With the arrival of the Obama era, some observers have suggested that African American political appointees remain even more expendable under a black president than under white ones. The dangers of guilt by association are greater, and when we consider the role African American appointees have historically served, black presidents likely don't need the same political cover on civil rights. (This certainly seemed true under the man Toni Morrison famously called the "first black president," Bill Clinton, and now under the second one, as it were.)

Still, if we consider the role that appointees must also play, then we can understand in many respects the moderate tack President Obama has taken relative to issues of mass incarceration, police brutality, chronic black under-employment, and a host of other issues. Patience in government responsiveness, faith in the affairs of state: these are themes that black political appointees have been delivering to African Americans for nearly one hundred years and probably longer. And these are the watchwords of an administration that continues to work within the confines of America's presidential pageant.

CHAPTER 8

Presidents and the Media

SUSAN J. DOUGLAS

Ever since George Washington's ambivalent attitudes toward (indeed, often passionate hatred of) the press, American presidents have had to calculate how to deal with the news media and, as communications technologies and outlets evolved and expanded, with the broader media overall. And they have had to confront how these powerful institutions can shape, at times irrevocably and fatally, presidential destiny. In turn, media institutions, executives, and practitioners have had to recalibrate their practices and routines in response to presidential media management strategies. Communications networks have always existed in the United States, and the nature of these networks—how they are organized, who controls them, what the means of information transmission are—has changed profoundly since the founding of the nation. Yet most presidents have confronted what were for them "new media," new media environments and constituents—audiences if you will—with changing reading and meaning-making competencies based on this evolving terrain.

The history of presidents and the media is a complex and contradictory story of love and hate, of presidential efforts to coopt, to censor and to control, to evade, and to manipulate and to defame. In turn, within the media themselves, journalistic routines and practices around political reporting in general and presidential coverage in particular have also evolved, from the highly partisan wars between federalist and anti-federalist papers of the late eighteenth and early nineteenth centuries to the rise of the norm of objectivity in the twentieth century and to a return, more recently, of a partisan media, particularly on cable TV, surrounded by a host of new media outlets that provide opportunities and pitfalls for presidents and presidential candidates. Presidents always face institutional constraints, including those imposed by media organizations, and in some cases their personalities and will—presidential agency, one might say—can vault over these but more often succumb to them.

With the rise and evolution of modern media since the late nineteenth century, there has been a struggle between the presidency and various media (and especially the news media) to shape and define the "common sense" about specific presidents as well as about the power of the office itself. This struggle involves, for presidential administrations, crafting effective messages; cultivating an appealing public, "front stage" persona for the president; and understanding the existing media landscape and the communications technologies that sustain it. But the press does not want to feel out of control either, does not want to feel that the president always has the upper hand. And for them, catching the president in a "backstage" mode, when he thinks the cameras aren't on, is also a major scoop and one that allows them to contest the common sense the administration seeks to construct.[1]

This essay analyzes this fraught relationship between the presidency and the media and reviews the rise of what we now take for granted as "the media presidency—a form of presidential leadership in which popular authority is derived from a president's ability to appeal to public opinion" through the mass media.[2] It focuses on key turning points in the evolution of the media landscape, those moments when new communications technologies, and the organizations that deploy them, disrupt the routines and practices presidents and their staffs had grown used to. And in this history, it's not that one communications technology displaced its predecessors, but rather that there has been an increased layering of and interaction between media forms, exerting ever growing and multiple demands, that presidents have had to navigate. This continued expansion of media outlets and institutions and the increasingly dominant role the media have come to play in presidential politics have in turn expanded and altered the structure of the presidency, with increasing staff, elaborated organizational structures, and ever-evolving strategies to deal with and manage the metastasizing media environment.

While it might be tempting to view various presidents as operating within a stable media environment—McKinley during the era of newspaper domination and "yellow journalism," or FDR during the "golden era" of radio—all presidents have confronted evolving and unpredictable media landscapes that contributed to the crucial institutional, technological, and cultural contexts within which they had to operate. And although many bemoan, today, the impact of highly partisan and thus divisive media outlets, there has always been partisanship in the press. But there has been a cyclical history to such partisan media, times when the relationship between the presidency and the press has been mutually respectful and times when it has been utterly antagonistic, and that too has shaped presidential fortunes and strategies.

Nonetheless, some periods of media transition have been less stable and more unpredictable than others. This was not some smooth, evolutionary process but an erratic and uneven one. The changes have involved not just technological innovation but also the expansion and eventual consolidation of media organizations and a steadily growing cadre of professionals—PR specialists, advertising gurus, media consultants, pollsters, and the like—who have played a central role in upheavals in the media environment. The twenty-five years leading up to World War I saw a revolution in advertising techniques, the rise of public relations, the emergence of film as a mass form, and the use of photography in newspapers and magazines, all of which led to a much richer media environment to navigate. The rapid diffusion of radio in the 1920s and early 1930s constituted another crucial moment of media transition when, despite the saturation of visual media in the country, Americans were thrown back into a culture of orality and aurality that presidents would need to confront. In the early 1950s, with the rapid diffusion of television, presidents had to figure out how to master this medium at the same time that another communications technology, public opinion polling, was becoming more sophisticated and prevalent. The 1970s and 1980s represent a relatively stable media environment, as the TV news conventions had become well established. When cable news emerged with the founding of CNN in the early 1980s and led to the rise of the twenty-four-hour news cycle, presidents had an entirely new clock and set of time pressures confronting them and their staffs, and this introduced yet another key media transition period in the late 1980s and 1990s. Finally, with the spread of internet use in the early twenty-first century and the associated explosive rise of social media, the first decade of the century constituted another dramatic transition moment in the media environment in which presidents had to govern.

Having said this, it is important to challenge the notion of communications "revolutions" and to debunk technological determinism.[3] Communications technologies are, after all, socially constructed through processes of struggle, negotiation, rejection, and subsequent new directions as inventors, companies, power brokers (like politicians), and everyday users interact and compete over what final form a medium, such as radio, will take. Thus, there is no predetermined or inevitable way for devices or media forms to evolve; rather, through this process some technical variants survive and flourish while others disappear. Nonetheless, one particular medium will have different consequences than another media because of its inherent properties: what we now see as its technological affordances.[4] For Ian Hutchby, who advanced this concept, each communications technology, because of its attributes and capabilities, "affords" or enables certain interactions and constrains others. Radio, for example, denies sight to its audience, so it enhances the importance of speaking and listening in communicative exchanges. What do certain communications technologies and certain media privilege and permit, given their inherent technological properties, that others don't, and what does that mean?

When thinking about the presidency and the media, then, it is essential to consider the affordances offered by certain media at certain times and how the president succeeded or failed in taking advantage of them. Some presidents—we think of Kennedy's or Reagan's use of television, for example—exploited these affordances brilliantly, while others fumbled quite badly. Presidencies have been shaped by and had to respond to these developments in both the hardware and the software, as it were, of media institutions and practices. Thus, while we need to consider the technological affordances of certain media and what features their corporate owners privileged, we also need to assess the media aptitude of presidencies.

These media aptitudes include appreciating—or having shrewd advisers who appreciate—how "new" media can give the president direct and less mediated access to the public. And they include appreciating how various media—radio, television, Facebook—require different presentational, rhetorical, and performative styles. Most successful presidents have indeed been "innovators in public communication, using new technology to create new politics."[5] And while most presidents hate the press, those who court members of the press, cater to their needs, disguise their disdain and resentment, even seem to like them, fare much better than those who fail to do all this.

While an overview of the presidency and the media could certainly begin with Washington's administration, we think of the modern media as taking form in the post–Civil War period, with the establishment, by the end of World War I, of major media institutions that presidents had to deal with and whose influence, indeed, they helped to enhance. At the beginning of the post–Civil War period, much about America's politics and media had been free-wheeling and anarchic, but by the early 1920s, bureaucratization had profoundly affected both institutions. And the pivotal administration here, however short-lived, was that of William McKinley.

At McKinley's inauguration in March 1897, according to Stephen Ponder, "no organized relationship existed" between the president and journalists; they focused primarily on Congress.[6] However, McKinley was no stranger to strategic communications—Mark Hanna, the wealthy industrialist who backed McKinley for president—staged what was at that time the most expensive presidential campaign in American history. And what was brilliant about it was the way in which Hanna anticipated the use of media networks to educate and persuade the electorate. While McKinley stayed in Ohio to conduct his famous "front porch" campaign, Hanna organized the distribution of nearly 200 million leaflets, tracts, and posters supporting McKinley and denouncing William Jennings Bryan, the populist candidate. He backed this up with armies of "spellbinders" who went around the country making pro-McKinley and anti-Bryan speeches and insisting that only McKinley would assure American prosperity. Hanna, then, in a pre-broadcasting period, established multiple yet highly centralized channels of communication to disseminate and reinforce the Republican message.

Once in office, McKinley, under the advice of his staff, established a more formalized relationship with journalists and the press. His first secretary (an antecedent to the chief of staff, a position not introduced until Eisenhower), John Addison Porter, was a newspaper proprietor, and he met with reporters twice a day to brief them on White House news. George Cortelyou, McKinley's assistant secretary, was a pivotal figure in the presidencies of both McKinley and Theodore Roosevelt; he arranged journalists' access to interviews and events, gave them new working space inside the Executive Mansion, encouraged them to accompany McKinley on speaking tours, and gave press briefings after Cabinet meetings.[7] Cortelyou also initiated the practice of collecting and monitoring newspaper clippings so that the president would know what was being said, pro and con, about him. And he began to develop a news summary of these clippings, especially as pressure mounted in 1898 to declare war on Spain.

This was one of the new media environments facing the presidency, defined by the rise of mass-circulation newspapers and magazines, nearly all of them supported by advertising; and the establishment of newspaper chains. Between 1870 and 1900, the number of daily newspapers had quadrupled, with combined newspaper circulation totaling more than 15 million by 1900. The number of magazines published rose from 700 in 1865 to 4,400 by 1890. Newspapers like the New York *Sun*, Joseph Pulitzer's *World*, and William Randolph Hearst's *Journal* had used exposés of governmental and corporate malfeasance to boost circulation; by the late 1890s, emboldened by their staggering circulation and by the success of various of their crusades, some, particularly those run by the jingoist Hearst, sought to affect foreign policy as well. This rise in the influence of the press corresponds to the diminishing influence of political parties, especially in the wake of muckraking exposes of political bosses and progressive reforms such as the recall, referendum, and initiative as well as the direct election of senators by the public instead of by their state legislatures.

Historians naturally disagree over the extent to which such papers and magazines could shape public opinion, particularly over how much of a role they played in the decision of the United States to declare war on Spain in 1898. But McKinley and his advisers had to pay increasing attention to campaigns like Hearst's, whose *Journal* began devoting more space to Cuba's rebellion against Spanish rule. The paper famously depicted three Cuban women being strip-searched by male Spanish authorities and declared that the explosion of the battleship *Maine* in the Havana harbor in February 1898 was "the work of an enemy." Many papers, indeed, fanned war fever until a "war psychosis" broke out.[8] In the wake of the *Maine* explosion, reporters increasingly flocked to the Executive Mansion to get McKinley's response to the crisis.

In this media environment, it was the newspapers, not the president, who were setting the agenda. Administrations therefore had to develop new forms of press management, and this was a crucial precedent. In April of 1898 McKinley and Congress declared war on Spain, and the administration sought to control the flow of information by setting up a "war room" with twenty telegraph lines. It also imposed censorship on military information and expanded the space available to journalists. Cortelyou developed the antecedent to the press release by providing reporters with occasional written statements about policies in advance and also provided them with increased opportunities to speak with the president. He also wanted reporters to cover more of McKinley's public appearances, so he arranged for many of them to accompany the president; in a stroke of genius, he had a stenographer record his remarks at each stop, got them immediately typed up, and then distributed them to the journalists. On McKinley's speaking tour in the spring of 1901, responding to the increased use of photography in newspaper and magazines, the press car on the train featured a sleeping compartment that had been turned into a darkroom.[9] By responding shrewdly to the increased agenda-setting power of the press by anticipating and then fulfilling their needs, Cortelyou took some of the first steps in shaping the media presidency. He established regular, routinized "channels" for passing information favorable to the president to the public through the press; he thus also played a central role in making the presidency "a beat."[10]

When McKinley was assassinated in September of 1901, an even more masterful manipulator of the media, Theodore Roosevelt, became president. In addition to his understanding of the importance of news management, Roosevelt had an almost instinctual appreciation of the role of publicity. This was hardly insignificant, given the times. In addition to the dominance of mass-circulation papers and magazines, an emerging persuasion culture, particularly in the form of advertising and the rise of public relations, was reshaping media practices and public values and opinions. Magazine and newspaper advertising and personality profiles in particular emphasized the centrality of character traits and appearance to individual success.[11]

In this new milieu of increasing and competing persuasive messages, which deployed a variety of tactics including fear, anxiety, visions of a more idealized future self, and the trope of the crucial "first impression," presidents could hardly be as remote as they had been prior to McKinley, and, moreover, they had to mesh with and exploit this new media environment. Roosevelt was brilliant at this. He retained Cortelyou and made managing the press one of his top priorities and also established regular, permanent quarters for reporters in the new West Wing of the White House.[12]

With a press that was increasingly highlighting the feature story and the personal attributes of famous people, Roosevelt sought to personalize the presidency as a way to get more favorable and sustained coverage. He met regularly with reporters and instituted his famous "shaving hour" press briefings as he sat in his barber's chair, the antecedent to the press conference. While these were off-the-record monologues (sometimes even rants), they established a powerful bond between the president and many reporters and helped set the stage for the stories to come. These reporters who met regularly with Roosevelt formed the beginnings of the White House press corps. Roosevelt worked successfully to redirect the focus of journalists' attention from Congress to the presidency and to redefine the real locus of power in Washington. He contributed significantly to using the media to personalize the presidency.

Ironically, it was President Woodrow Wilson, the academic and idealist known for his strong commitment to democratic values and processes, who brought information management—even manipulation—to its apogee in the federal government. He instituted regularly scheduled press conferences and made personal appearances to Congress to sell his agenda. He believed in a strong executive branch and in the use of the media to reinforce presidential power. At the same time, however, he loathed publicity, especially personal publicity about him and his family.[13] He discontinued the press conferences in 1915, frustrated by how his remarks were misreported or misconstrued.

By the time of the U.S. entry into World War I, Wilson had become even more disillusioned with the press, especially with its accuracy, and had contemplated establishing a presidential publicity bureau.

After the United States entered the war, that is exactly what Wilson did, creating the first ministry of information—and often, more accurately, propaganda—in the country's history. The Committee on Public Information, headed by Progressive journalist George Creel, censored news stories, strategized to drum up support for the war at home and abroad, and published a government newspaper, the *Official U.S. Bulletin*. "Administration activities must be dramatized and staged," wrote Creel, "and every energy exerted to arouse ardor and enthusiasm."[14] Millions of public relations handouts were given to the press, which did not have to print them, but they were typically the only source of information about the war.

Another innovation was the army, upward of seventy-five thousand strong, of "Four Minute Men," who delivered rapid-fire, pro-war, pro-administration speeches during the four minutes it took to change movie reels in the cinema, as well as on streetcars and ferries and in public parks, lumber camps, factories, and so forth. It's estimated that in eighteen months, they delivered over 7.5 million speeches to over 314 million people.[15] Like Mark Hanna twenty years earlier, Creel sought to establish in the pre-broadcasting era various extensive and overlapping communications networks that conveyed a consistent and relatively simultaneous political message to the American public. The government was also ruthless in its censorship practices, both of incoming and outgoing mail and of print material it deemed might interfere with the success of the war or incite disloyalty. With the opportunity that the war provided, Wilson, through George Creel, took advantage of every possible affordance of each of the various media then available to promote support for the war and for the president himself. The Wilson administration "laid the groundwork for a permanent relationship between the executive and the news media." Presidential use of the press, and the media more broadly, was now fully institutionalized.[16]

The 1920s witnessed the beginning of one of the most profound transformations in the relationship between the media and the presidency in the United States. Politicians could now address millions of voters simultaneously, presenting their opinions and appeals directly, without having to rely on surrogates or reporters. Yet radio, and later television, revealed much more about the person than print: inflection, tone and timbre of voice, fervor of delivery, and sincerity were all there for the listener to assess. With so much more revealed, so much more had to be controlled, and presidents now had to work as carefully on their public performances as they did on their political positions.[17] While Warren G. Harding, Calvin Coolidge, and Herbert Hoover were the first three presidents of the new radio age, none of them figured out how to exploit the medium the way that Franklin Roosevelt did. Indeed, you can't say Roosevelt's name without immediately thinking "fireside chats," so effective was FDR's command of the relatively new technology. Through radio Roosevelt sought to circumvent the gatekeepers of the dominant newspapers, many of whose publishers were Republican and opposed the New Deal; indeed, in both the 1936 and 1940 elections, two-thirds of the nation's newspapers editorially opposed Roosevelt's reelection. His use of the new medium was crucial to his political survival.

But also, as a communications medium that denied sight to its audience—especially important for Roosevelt, who was a paralytic and whose staff worked assiduously to minimize images of his disability from public view—radio allowed him to convey both enormous authority and empathy and to avoid the slightest suggestion of his disability. Roosevelt and his aides understood that radio was a very intimate medium that could make the listener feel like the speaker was speaking to him or her personally. He thus deliberately imagined his audience as a few people sitting around his fireplace with him; he did not use the stentorian political oratory of the stump but the intimate "I-you" mode of address that had become popular in mass-circulation magazines like *The Ladies Home Journal* that had come to address its readers as "you." He opened the chats with "My friends," and was careful to use simple, direct, informal language. While each chat indeed sounded relaxed and unrehearsed, each talk "was the result of extensive preparation, having gone through perhaps a dozen drafts."[18] Having discovered that a separation between his two front lower teeth produced a slight whistle on the air, he had a removable bridge made that eliminated the sound. Now that is paying attention to the affordances of a particular medium!

Roosevelt also officially established the position of White House press secretary, hiring former journalist Stephen Early to help institutionalize and formalize interactions with the press. As Roosevelt and his team sought to sell the New Deal and the expanded role of the federal government in economic affairs, Early felt that managing the press was crucial. He established twice-weekly press conferences, eliminated the requirement that journalists submit written questions in advance, and provided typed versions of quotations from Roosevelt for their use.[19]

Less known are Roosevelt's behind-the-scenes machinations with prominent journalists and regulators. Appreciating the influence and success of Walter Winchell, who hosted his highly popular *Jergens Journal* on Sunday nights, FDR invited him to meet in Washington in 1932 shortly after the election.[20] Winchell (whose column was, by the early 1940s, in 725 newspapers) became a die-hard fan. The Roosevelt administration fed Winchell news tips, inside information, and positive angles on FDR's policies, which Winchell happily reproduced. Once France and England declared war on Germany, Winchell, at the prodding of the White House, helped prepare the country for war. This was not insignificant because by late 1940, Winchell was tied with Bob Hope for the highest rated program on radio.

At the same time, the Roosevelt administration set its sights on Boake Carter, also a very successful news commentator on CBS. Carter hated Roosevelt and the New Deal, and by the late 1930s he had developed a national following. The Roosevelt administration became increasingly incensed by Carter's passionate isolationist (and pro-Nazi) stance on the air and his virulent attacks on New Deal initiatives. By 1937 the White House started putting pressure on William Paley, the head of CBS, to pull him off the air. In 1938, they suggested to Paley that it might be time for the government to investigate monopoly practices in the broadcasting industry; that August Paley yanked Carter off the air.[21]

Once America went to war in 1941, Roosevelt, like Wilson before him, established an agency to control the production and flow of government information—the Office of War Information (OWI). But the Roosevelt administration had a much more sophisticated and developed array of media with which to work: broadcast radio, film with sound, large-format photojournalism magazines like *Life*, as well as a more experienced advertising and PR industry. The OWI worked very closely with all of these media outlets, and this was the first time the government had interacted with so many mass-media channels to sell a war, and presidential and military leadership, to the country. The Roosevelt administration sought to exploit every media affordance at its disposal and dramatically enhanced and increased the structures within the White House to do so.

In the late 1940s and early 1950s, presidents were about to confront yet another profound transformation in their media environment, one that offered its own affordances and hazards. Now image—not just that forged through voice and words but through facial expressions, body language, eye movements, a face-to-face mode of address—was central to presidential success. And by now another communications technology, public opinion polling, having become more scientific and reliable, could be used in the service of presidential media leadership.

The first full-blown television presidency was Dwight Eisenhower's, and his use of the medium was anticipated in his presidential campaign. Aided by several advertising agencies, the Eisenhower campaign produced fast-paced documentaries and thirty-second spot commercials that addressed issues Gallup pollsters had identified as salient for the public. His "Eisenhower Answers America" TV spots presented a candidate who was frank, forthright, and in touch with people's concerns.[22] On the day before the election, 130 spots aired in New York City alone.[23] While multiple factors influenced the outcome of the election, the overwhelming success of Eisenhower's media strategy was not lost on future candidates or the burgeoning industry of political consultants.

Indeed, while it is conventional wisdom that John Kennedy was the first true television president, Craig Allen argues that this designation belongs to Eisenhower. This was not insignificant, as the percentage of Americans who owned TVs skyrocketed from 30 percent in 1952 to 90 percent by the end of his presidency. Eisenhower was the first president to have televised "fireside chats," and he also introduced the televised news conference in 1955 as a way to speak directly to the people. These were not broadcast live, however; his media-savvy press secretary James Hagerty edited the film prior to their broadcast.

Hagerty and Eisenhower were unhappy with the president's initial forays into television, so they turned to the movie and television actor and producer Robert Montgomery, who worked with and coached Eisenhower on how to present himself on television. He adjusted the lectern from which Eisenhower spoke to just the right height and made sure that the camera angle would convey eye-to-eye contact with the TV viewer; he persuaded Eisenhower to use a teleprompter.[24] Montgomery also urged Eisenhower to deliver his televised speeches standing, as this made him look more forceful.[25] Eisenhower established the first White House TV studio and introduced the "photo opportunity," which was then made available to the fledging TV news programs. This practice was one of the things that led to Daniel Boorstin's famous term from *The Image*, the "pseudo-event." Indeed, James Hagerty was the first press secretary to evoke the term *news management*, given his skill at staging appearances and announcements that would deflect or minimize criticism of the president or enhance his image.[26]

These were significant precedents to set in the presidential use of a powerful new medium, and Eisenhower's role in doing so was underappreciated until Allen's 1993 book *Eisenhower and the Mass Media: Peace, Prosperity, and Prime-Time TV*. Nonetheless, it was the match between this visual and aural medium and the election of a young, telegenic, and quick-witted president that cemented the new role that imagery would play in presidential politics and leadership. It has become conventional wisdom that those who listened to the Kennedy-Nixon debates on the radio felt that Nixon had won, while those who watched them on TV felt that Kennedy had won. This conclusion was based on a survey done by a Philadelphia-based market research firm that telephoned people the day after the first debate and asked them which candidate had won, and how they had followed the debate, on TV or radio. The widely reported survey results reinforced the belief that with this new visual medium physical appearance and deportment were now of paramount importance for presidents in the television age.[27]

Once in the White House, Kennedy proved to be an adroit media politician. This was crucial, as he had won—if he really did win—by the narrowest of margins. He initiated the live, televised press conference, a forum that conveyed his ability to be both authoritative and informal and that showed off his quick wit. Nonetheless, Kennedy, believing that newspapers and magazines were the most important influences on public opinion, sought to use his televised appearances to shape coverage in print media. After all, when Kennedy took office, the nightly television news was still only fifteen minutes long and consisted largely of rip and read stories. Kennedy also feared overexposure on television, so he limited his appearances. He also had a keen appreciation of the importance of cultivating print journalists. Indeed, some felt that Kennedy "held court" with certain journalists, and we now know that many knew about his womanizing and health problems but regarded reporting about his personal life as off-limits.[28]

The Kennedy administration also sought, in the name of containing Communism during the Cold War, to squash stories it felt undermined foreign policy and to plant favorable stories with friendly reporters. This media manipulation, especially about the Bay of Pigs and the Cuban Missile Crisis, was much more feasible without television news bureaus or cameras in foreign countries. When Johnson and then Nixon sought to follow the Kennedy media management model (which often included deception), they did so with TV news programs that were now a half-hour long and that had established foreign news bureaus around the world. The glare of increased television coverage, especially of the war in Vietnam, was one of the factors that led to Johnson's infamous "credibility gap."[29]

It was the riveting images from the civil rights movement, like those of children being attacked with fire hoses and police dogs as well as the nation-bonding role that television news played during and after the Kennedy assassination, that prompted the networks to expand their evening news shows and their news divisions. Presidents were now not just dealing with a visual medium, they were also dealing with media organizations of increased reach, sophistication, and confidence.

Known for one of the most famous campaign ads ever—the devastating "Daisy" commercial portraying Barry Goldwater as much too eager to drop a nuclear bomb—Johnson was nonetheless not a president known for effectively exploiting the media affordances of the time. And the increasing demonstrations against the war in Vietnam, Walter Cronkite's negative assessment of the war in February 1968, and the escalating student protests all gave rise to a more adversarial press in the late 1960s. In addition, Richard Nixon, who after having lost the race for governor of California in 1962 blamed the media for favoring his opponent, in 1968 decided to run for president. He and his advisers faced a press corps he had self-pityingly derided, one that was becoming more critical of the government and political figures.

Nixon sought to respond to this with a makeover selling himself as "the New Nixon," with the help of Roger Ailes, then the producer of *The Mike Douglas Show*. The revolution in advertising in the mid-1960s, as exemplified by the iconic Volkswagen campaign, brought a new self-reflexivity, along with ironic humor, less text, and stronger, more dramatic visuals to ad copy and aesthetics. Political advertising would have to fit into and take advantage of these approaches. Using various PR and advertising techniques, Nixon outspent Humphrey almost two to one on television and newspaper ads.[30] And he notoriously appeared on the irreverent show *Laugh-In* mouthing one of the show's famous tag lines, "Sock it to me?" to suggest that he had a sense of humor about himself. After the election, the journalist Joe McGinniss published his bestselling *The Selling of the President*, describing the sales and PR techniques deployed by Nixon's ad team. The book made journalists much more conscious of the role and impact of political advertising and PR techniques in presidential image-making.[31]

Despite his two successful presidential campaigns, Nixon hated the press, which became increasingly difficult for him to disguise. To seek to control the news, his administration established the Office of White House Communications to institutionalize the kinds of PR and news management he had used during the campaign and further manage the image of the presidency given the new centrality of television to presidential politics.[32] At the same time, he and Vice President Spiro Agnew chose a combative stance, attacking news organizations and even placing some reporters under surveillance. Given this and the growing oppositional social and political movements of the time, Nixon faced an increasingly hostile and suspicious press corps. The televised Watergate hearings, which gripped the nation, and often interrupted regularly scheduled programming, compelled him to resign.

By the 1970s, then, the news media—the network news, newspapers like *The New York Times* and *The Washington Post* that defied presidential authority, the creation of *60 Minutes*, the debut of NPR and *All Things Considered*—enjoyed considerable clout and had become highly suspicious of the government in general and presidents in particular. Coverage of the president became more adversarial. And the president had become the most newsworthy person in the country.[33] Thus, while this was a time of media stability—cable news would not start to disrupt this latest media formation until the 1980s—presidents who failed to grasp how this media environment was, once again, setting the agenda and definitions of success for presidents would find themselves struggling politically.

This was true for Gerald Ford, as he and his administration had minimal skills in dealing with television, fatal in the wake of Watergate. Nor did Jimmy Carter and his team have a noteworthy aptitude for dealing with television. Both men confronted relatively stable media environments, but with two salient new features: video technology, which accelerated the delivery of images to newsrooms and made possible "live coverage" from portable cameras, and geo-synchronous satellites, which instantly transmit video-taped news around the word. Image-based stories, especially of "back-stage" blunders—Gerald Ford stumbling, or those about Carter's idiosyncratic family, especially his brother Billy (who had used his brother's fame to launch "Billy Beer"), over time undermined the image of both men. And Carter's daring, even profound July 1979 "crisis of confidence" speech, quickly dubbed the "malaise speech" (a word he actually never used), in which he criticized American consumer culture, initially bolstered his approval rating by an impressive 11 percent. But it is remembered today as a disaster, because in its wake he asked for the resignations of his entire cabinet, which left the impression that his administration was falling apart.[34] Finally and fatally for Carter was the seizure of American hostages and the embassy in Tehran in 1979, which could now be covered on a daily basis via satellite. Wall-to-wall coverage of the crisis and ABC's "countdown" of how many days the hostages had been held, proved to be Carter's final undoing.

There would be no such failure to manage the press in the Reagan White House. A former movie actor and radio announcer, Reagan had ample training in how to address cameras and microphones; he was extremely adept at exploiting the affordances of television and radio. And his advisers, especially Michael Deaver, his deputy chief of staff, and David Gergen, the White House director of communications, were determined to shift what they saw as a balance of power in favor of the press and return that control to the presidency. They also benefited from operating in a time of media stability, just before cable news would come into its own. Deaver and Gergen, both understanding that the "care and feeding" of the press was crucial to such control, further institutionalized news management.[35] White House aides provided reporters with Reagan's itinerary every day, gave them summaries or full copies of his speeches or comments in advance, and adhered to the "message of the day." Thus, they did much of the journalists' work for them, making their jobs easier. They understood that sound bites for presidents were getting shorter and shorter and that imagery mattered, so they planned the photo opportunities in advance so that the imagery would be positive and reinforce the message. Reagan's aides used carefully orchestrated leaks to shape foreign policy and its coverage. As a result of all this, at least until the disaster of Iran-Contra, Reagan enjoyed, by all accounts, much better press coverage than he deserved, given the unpopularity of various of his policies.

Also significant for the future of the media and politics was the Reagan administration's elimination of the Fairness Doctrine, which had, since 1949, required broadcast stations to address all sides of public controversies. In 1987, Reagan's FCC chairman, Mark Fowler, announced that they would no longer enforce the Fairness Doctrine. Congress passed a bill reinstating it; Reagan vetoed the bill, and there has been no Fairness Doctrine since. Reagan paved the way for radio stations, for example, to feature back-to-back conservative talk show hosts, who quickly played a key role in making the media environment more partisan. The various deregulatory moves under Reagan's FCC also paved the way for increased media conglomeration.

It was another telegenic candidate, Bill Clinton, who initially charmed the press and also expanded the media venues he used to get elected. The 1992 campaign introduced new media anomalies, as third party candidate Ross Perot announced his candidacy on CNN's *Larry King Live* and used paid infomercials as his campaign weapon.[36] Clinton used the news media, particularly his and Hillary Clinton's appearance on *60 Minutes*, to blunt charges of infidelity (charges that were in fact accurate). Clinton went on MTV and famously answered a question about his preferred underwear and played the saxophone on Arsenio Hall's talk show. All of this personalized his appeal.

But Clinton and his team failed miserably at using the lessons taught by Reagan. One of their very first blunders was to take on the geography of the White House pressroom. This room is cramped, with reporters jammed in cheek by jowl; as one noted, "You can't make a call or type a sentence without your neighbors and competitors catching wind of your scoop." The pressroom is connected by a narrow hall to the White House briefing room. Before or after briefings, reporters could also go to the "upper press office" where the press secretary was. George Stephanopoulos banned this, infuriating reporters. Reporters also quickly came to resent what they saw as presidential disrespect and arrogance. Briefings were late, often by hours.

Appointments with reporters were cancelled. Clinton's team failed to return phone calls, and Clinton himself violated unspoken rules of seniority and hierarchy when calling on reporters during press conferences.[37] Despite his enormous personal skills as a communicator, his administration's unskilled media apparatus and his personal hatred of the press gave him one of the shortest presidential honeymoons in recent history.

But the Clinton White House also confronted another transition in the media environment: the emergence of the 24–7 news cycle established by the rise, first, of the CNN news channel and then the establishment of Fox News in 1996. The presidency was now subject to new time pressures: Reporters wanted more instant answers, and cable news channels were constantly looking for stories—and pundits—to fill the news hole. For a president who did not respect reporters and hated the press in general, this expansion in their need for news through the technology of cable TV was not a welcome development.

And finally for Clinton (and his successors) was the increased consolidation of the corporate media, with fewer entities owning more outlets and with an increased emphasis on the need for ratings and profits. News organizations closed many of their foreign bureaus, cut back on political and investigative reporting, and added much more "lifestyle" stories about crime and natural disasters and scandals.[38] This trend offered the perfect media environment for the Monica Lewinsky scandal, a story that we can be confident would never have gone public during the Kennedy administration.

George W. Bush was yet another president to undergo an image makeover during his run for the presidency, with photos of him clearing brush in a cowboy hat to emphasize his Texas ties and deemphasize his privileged roots in Connecticut. But Bush entered the White House under a cloud, having been put into office by a controversial Supreme Court decision. The initial coverage of his presidency emphasized how much he exercised every day and how little he seemed to be working.

But 9/11 changed all that and also inaugurated one of the most determined, disciplined, and, at least initially, highly successful propaganda campaigns by any recent president. Given the national trauma over the event and the desire to cohere as a nation, the majority of the country rallied behind the president, making his administration's task much easier, as media manipulation and control is much more possible to achieve during wartime or its equivalent. And many in the press, given the sense of national emergency, were, in retrospect, much too compliant in accepting administration information about the "war on terror."

Determined to pin the 9/11 terrorist attacks on Saddam Hussein, the administration, through its top officials, repeatedly accused Hussein of harboring "weapons of mass destruction," of having pursued the acquisition of nuclear weapons, and of having ties to Osama Bin Laden and Al-Qaeda. This repeated linking of Iraq to the 9/11 attacks—which was false—worked: In September of 2002, an NBC/*Wall Street Journal* poll found that 53 percent of Americans believed that members of Al-Qaeda were based in Iraq, and a CBS poll found that 51 percent believed Saddam Hussein was "personally involved" in 9/11.[39]

The Bush team adroitly mixed PR and propaganda techniques and brought in professionals to maximize the affordances of television: They hired Scott Sforza, a former ABC producer; Bob DeServi, a former NBC cameraman and a master at lighting; and Greg Jensen, former Fox News producer to help them stage events. For his TV address on the first anniversary of 9/11, the Bush administration rented three barges of giant Musco lights, the kind used to illuminate sports stadiums and rock concerts, sent them across New York harbor, and tied them to the base of the Statue of Liberty so that it could serve as a backdrop for Bush's speech from Ellis Island. For a speech at Mount Rushmore, the White House positioned the platform for TV cameras so that Bush's face would be aligned with the iconic presidential faces carved in stone.[40]

But the problem with the Bush team is that they became too cocky in what they thought they could achieve through media manipulation; they overreached. The turning point came with Bush's "top gun" landing on the USS *Abraham Lincoln* in May 2003 to announce the end of major combat in Iraq. Some later estimated that the event cost $1 million. Every aspect of the event was choreographed, especially the now-infamous "Mission Accomplished" banner placed like "a halo hovering over the president."[41] Bush himself arrived wearing an olive-green flight suit with a helmet tucked under his arm, having allegedly co-piloted a navy jet onto the ship's deck.

What presidents learn, often the hard way, is that when the gap between the PR message and actual events or the president's actual persona or policies grows too large, the PR staging can backfire. After the initial dazzle over the event, journalists noted that the mission had not been accomplished at all; U.S. troops were still in Iraq and indeed are still there to this day. Also revealed was that there was no need for Bush to fly in on a navy jet. You could see San Diego from the USS *Abraham Lincoln*; Bush could have come out on a motorboat or a helicopter. But because the Bush team wanted the image of Bush as a fighter pilot, the ship had to be repositioned to keep the TV cameras from picking up San Diego in the background.

While George Bush did achieve reelection in 2004, the gap between how he handled the catastrophe of Hurricane Katrina in 2005 and what television cameras were showing to the American people further undermined his credibility. The disaster illustrated that even under the most disciplined of media strategies, if the president doesn't get out ahead of the news and there is a gap between presidential performance and presidential imagery, the media will typically expose that.

By 2004, another medium was entering maturity and was being used by more and more Americans: the internet. In 2004, thirty-three million Americans had access to broadband coverage; by 2008 sixty-eight million did. By the time Barack Obama ran in 2008—a man, it was said, who could not be separated from his Blackberry—the explosion in the internet's reach, and the affordances of social media like Facebook and YouTube meant that presidents and presidential candidates were once again confronting an emerging, transitioning media environment while still also having to master traditional media, especially television.

The Obama campaign exploited these new media aggressively and brilliantly, to connect directly with potential voters and especially to fundraise. As David Plouffe, Obama's campaign manager, noted, given that their email list reached thirteen million people, "we had essentially created our own television network, only better, because we communicated directly with no filter to what would amount to about 20 percent of the total number of votes." With new media, candidates like Obama were benefiting from a new "two-step flow" where "online attention and online fundraising led to mainstream media attention."[42] In addition, the internet, with its user-generated content, made possible experiences that could not have happened in other media. Individuals spent "more than 14 million hours watching over 1800 Obama campaign-related videos on YouTube that garnered more than 50 million views." Will.i.am's "Yes We Can" YouTube video in support of Obama got over twenty million hits. And those who reported seeing campaign information on the internet were more likely to vote for Obama.[43]

Yet because the internet, email, and social media offer the greatest affordances yet for user-generated content, presidents and presidential candidates are vulnerable to rogue videos, blogs, emails, and the like that can support them or circulate highly damning accusations. The circulation of a sermon by Obama's former pastor Jeremiah Wright on YouTube stirred controversy about Obama's loyalty to the United States; a recording at an Obama fundraiser in which the candidate noted that some small-town dwellers "get bitter [and] cling to guns or religion" were cautionary examples of the uncontrollable nature of new and emerging media, even for the most media-savvy candidates and their advisers. President Obama also confronted a much more partisan media environment on television, with Fox News ceaselessly attacking him and MSNBC, with only slightly less vigor, attacking his opponents. With audiences for the nightly network news declining and the circulation of Fox News reports and criticisms repeated in other venues, rumors and unfounded charges against the president have gained, and retained, unusual salience.

The history of the presidency and the media, then, is one of changing and expanding media environments based on new communications technologies and their affordances, interacting with presidential administrations. Given these moments of stability and transition, each president has had to figure out how to create communications networks where none existed or to maximize or extend those that do. These efforts have transformed the office of the presidency since the 1890s, producing increasingly bureaucratized structures dedicated to dealing with, coopting, and circumventing the media. As administrations seek to respond to these changes through a repertoire of media management strategies, so too have journalists and the organizations they work for sought to respond in kind to regain their ability to shape political agendas. Those presidents who have had staff members who quickly grasped the affordances of existing media and exploited them, even stretched and expanded them, have had more successful presidencies than their less media-adept counterparts. Having a comfort with or an aptitude about how to use the dominant media of the time is also extremely important, as is managing one's "frontstage" and "backstage" performances. And using new media forms to try to reach voters directly and circumvent the media gatekeepers has also been important to successful presidents. Anticipating and fulfilling the needs of reporters without deceiving them is crucial to the eventual construction of a common understanding about a president.

It has been this interplay between grasping, quickly, the affordances of existing and emerging media and knowing what content and what performances they require and best support that has been key to presidents who have had to lead and govern through our constantly shifting media environments.

CHAPTER 9

The Making of the Celebrity Presidency

KATHRYN CRAMER BROWNELL

As the 1960 election heated up, the two presidential hopefuls relied on television production studios to present their qualifications to living room audiences across the country. With an early lead in the polls, Vice President Richard M. Nixon used his television advertisements to remind viewers of the prosperity of the previous eight years under his and President Dwight D. Eisenhower's watch. In an effort to dismiss the liberal critiques that he was a "Tricky Dick" who pandered to the party's right wing with anticommunist hysteria to win elections, Nixon carefully recast his image as a "moderate" Republican. As a contender for the presidency, he stressed his credentials and experience as vice president to assume the leadership of the country. During his television advertisements, Nixon appeared in an office setting and spoke directly to the camera in an effort to communicate to voters his credibility as a serious statesman with the experience and foresight to defeat communists abroad and generate economic strength at home.[1]

Television viewers across the country met a very different candidate from the Democratic Party. Designed by Jack Denove Production Company, John F. Kennedy's advertisements featured memorable scenes captured from the campaign, often highlighting the clamorous crowds that were greeting him in cities across the country. Other spots featured prominent entertainers, like the actor Henry Fonda and the singer and civil rights activist

Harry Belafonte, endorsing the popular candidate. Emulating a commercial for cereal, the Kennedy camp even featured a popular cartoon that simply repeated "Kennedy, Kennedy, Kennedy" to a catchy jingle that ended with an attractive picture of the senator and his family. Whereas Nixon turned to television to sell his leadership qualifications much like an applicant for a job, Kennedy used the medium to construct a fan base that he hoped would become a voter base in November. Purposefully promoting the presidential aspirant as a celebrity, the senator's campaign team relied on a "slick high octane publicity machine" to transform John Kennedy, or simply "Jack," into a popular media icon to gain political legitimacy.[2] Kennedy's electoral success against Nixon, slim though it was, ultimately validated a "showbiz" style of politics honed in California politics and Hollywood studios over the previous thirty years.[3]

Presidential scholars frequently point to the 1960 election as a "revolutionary" moment in which television transformed the electoral process and almost overnight created the modern "celebrity presidency."[4] And yet, these accounts tend to focus almost entirely on the television debates between the two presidential contenders. By excluding the broader context of media politics that preceded and surrounded the election campaign, this dominant narrative has reproduced what media scholars call "technological determinism." First articulated by Marshall McLuhan in 1964, the theory asserts that new technology, like television in the 1960 election, had preconfigured features that shaped how the medium would transform social, cultural, and political structures.[5] Media scholars have since expanded beyond McLuhan's assertion that the "medium is the message" through analyses of how individuals, cultural values, political decisions, and social structures shape the use and impact of a new technology.[6] Political scientists, historians, and other chroniclers of the 1960 election, however, have continued to subscribe to this assumption, particularly when explaining the twentieth-century rise of the modern "celebrity presidency."[7] The producer of the television debates, Don Hewitt, remembered the first debate as the moment when politicians looked at television and declared, "That's the only way to campaign." The evening, he recalled, was a "great night for John Kennedy, and the worst night that ever happened in American politics."[8]

Scholarship on the American presidency has reinforced this memory, pointing to Kennedy's election in 1960 as the triumph of "style" and image over "substance" and serious policy debates.[9] This narrative, however, over-romanticizes the existence of a "golden age" of American democracy before the encroachment of mass media made expensive advertisements and television necessary. Moreover, it also overlooks the long, contested evolution of a "showbiz" political style—an always controversial political strategy rooted in over forty years of negotiations between politicians and professional image makers. Kennedy's celebrity status was not instantaneous, inevitable, or pre-determined. Rather, Kennedy pursued an "extrapartisan" campaign that used Hollywood studio structures to transform him into a celebrity as a means of establishing his credibility among partisans.[10] This tactic proved novel and ultimately successful. And yet, it also generated immense criticism, especially as he took the oath of office and encountered the challenge of governance in the media age with a regionally and ideologically divided party.

On the campaign trail, Nixon had joined prominent politicians from both parties in a critique of Kennedy's attempts to pander for "cheap publicity."[11] But the memory of Kennedy's celebrity appeal loomed large for Nixon and his advisers and this specific interpretation of the 1960 election in turn created popular political perceptions of the power of television that have since shaped the American presidency.[12] Historians have pointed to the range of factors that gave Kennedy the small margin of victory in that bitterly fought race—from the role of organized labor to Mayor Richard Daley's patronage machine in Chicago to the Kennedy phone call to Coretta Scott King after the imprisonment of her husband Martin Luther King Jr. during a civil rights demonstration.[13] Yet Richard Nixon firmly believed that Kennedy's superior media image and his "slick high octane publicity machine" had given him the edge. As he sought to capture the presidency eight years later, Nixon hired a team of show business professionals who also reinforced this analysis of the 1960 election, constantly reminding him that his political defeats came because he neglected to prioritize showbiz politics in his campaign. The making of the celebrity presidency came not because television inherently changed the political process in a certain way. Rather, Kennedy's victory created a bipartisan political belief that constructing a celebrity image and building a well-oiled media exploitation machine could be more than a controversial sideshow or a distraction to American politics; it could become a source of political authority and serve as a path to the American presidency.

Since the advent of radio and the motion picture in the early twentieth century, advances in mass media technology have offered politicians opportunities to communicate to a growing and diversifying electorate. In a political world dominated by party bosses and newspaper editors, however, advertising men, movie executives, and radio personalities frequently emerged as political outsiders. During the 1920s, President Calvin Coolidge and his successor Herbert Hoover utilized Hollywood publicity at various points during their presidencies while also upholding a public image as conservative traditionalists.[14] Hoover, in particular, saw the usefulness of "merchandising" policies to gain interest group support, but he remained skeptical of efforts to use the silver screen to win votes.[15] The motion picture industry and its carefully honed publicity strategies stood firmly on the periphery of the national political process.

Direct presidential use of advertising or professional silver screen productions aroused controversy and frequently raised profound fears about the dangerous tools used by totalitarian governments like Adolf Hitler's Nazi Germany to control information and to manipulate the public through "black magic."[16] Throughout Franklin D. Roosevelt's administration, as he took to the airwaves and to movie theaters to promote the New Deal, the war effort, and most controversially, his reelection in 1944, critics constantly accused the popular president of using advances in communications technology to misguide the American people.[17] The postwar environment intensified these fears. The liberation of Nazi Germany reinforced concern over the insidious effects of mass persuasion. The burgeoning Cold War environment deepened suspicions that motion pictures and radio programs potentially contained subversive "propaganda" that could undermine American democracy.[18] In fact, anxiety over the use of professional entertainment to sell a political agenda and the place of celebrities in American politics underlined the highly publicized House Un-American Activities Committee (HUAC) hearings of communist infiltration of the motion picture industry in 1947.[19]

These volatile discussions about the opportunities and dangers of propaganda, in turn, shaped political attitudes and approaches toward the new technology of television.[20] As television ownership jumped from only 2.9 percent of households in 1948 to over 80 percent of families eight years later, advertising executives and Hollywood entertainers urged presidential candidates to embrace professionally designed television programming as a partisan tool.[21] In 1952, both candidates on the Republican ticket took advantage of the growth of the medium to communicate to the public. The new California senator and vice presidential hopeful, Richard Nixon, went on the air to disclose his entire tax history to ward off criticisms of campaign finance violations. As he ended the address with his famous promise to keep the family dog "Checkers," who came from a supporter in Texas, an outpouring of support came in from viewers across the country, solidifying his candidacy.[22] Likewise, the popular general-turned-Republican-candidate Dwight D. Eisenhower worked with advertisers and Hollywood studio executives through his Citizens for Eisenhower Committee to design effective television spot campaigns, such as the thirty-second "Eisenhower Answers

America" advertisements in which the former general would answer questions posed to him by seemingly ordinary citizens.[23]

The Citizens Committee, however, relied on more than just filmed television advertisements featuring Eisenhower. The organization also worked diligently to bring in top studio writers, film editors, and television directors to package the advertisements and oversee Eisenhower's performances.[24] These media experts offered insight into camera and lighting angles, effective story lines, and even market segmentation ideas. By buying the last five minutes of shows like *Robert Montgomery Presents*—a variety show hosted by a prominent celebrity supporter of Eisenhower's—the Citizens Committee emphasized how it should use Montgomery's variety show to "present a number of other actors and artists who are pro-Ike" and transition in the last five minutes into a more explicit Eisenhower endorsement.[25]

Madison Avenue and television executives joined Hollywood entertainers—many of whom worked for Roosevelt's campaigns but had become disgruntled with the Democratic Party under Truman—to turn the slogan "I Like Ike" into a well-rounded television production complete with catchy jingles and celebrity supporters to promote "Ike" as a personality and to encourage voters to cross party lines and cast a vote for the former general. When Eisenhower moved to 1600 Pennsylvania Avenue, many figures on his production team accompanied him. As the first television adviser to the president, Robert Montgomery advocated using the camera to enhance political discussions. Voters, the actor stressed, could better evaluate the ideas and stances of candidates or policies because "it is impossible for a candidate on television to get up before a vast audience and tell a series of untruths to 100 million people in this country and get away with it."[26]

As Eisenhower accepted the advice of political consultants and formally brought figures like Montgomery to build a television studio in the White House, he capitalized on a style of political communication and mobilization that had shaped California politics over the previous twenty years. At the same time, political scientists also recognized how the California political landscape, shaped by its combination of progressive reforms, suburban ethos, diverse demographics, and the powerful interests of the motion picture industry, held answers for understanding how national politicians and political parties could adjust to the technological, cultural, and spatial changes of the post–World War II period. In the 1950s a political scientist named Robert Pitchell sought to understand the "New Look" in American campaigns in which professionals "raise money, determine issues, write speeches, handle press releases, prepare advertising copy, program radio and television shows, and develop whatever publicity techniques are necessary for a given campaign." Pitchell argued that scholars needed to look to California, where this professionalized image-making, rooted in collaborations between political consultants and the entertainment industry, has "flourished in the past two decades."[27]

California, it seemed, offered the answers for political success in the television age, but the controversy that had surrounded the political use of radio and motion pictures also intensified with television. In both 1952 and 1956, the Democratic presidential challenger, Adlai Stevenson, had little patience and quite a bit of disdain for the rising political emphasis placed on television images, and he openly criticized the Republican use of political advertising. During his acceptance speech at the Democratic National Convention in 1956, Stevenson attacked the administration's use of men who "evidently believe that the minds of Americans can be manipulated by shows, slogans, and the arts of advertising."[28]

The Democratic Party did use radio and television to appeal to voters, but this remained a peripheral component of the campaign. With memories of the backlash against the New Deal fresh and a HUAC investigation of communist propaganda efforts still ensuing, the party focused on tried and true strategies for voter turnout: labor unions. The Democratic National Committee even went so far as to dismiss advice and free productions made by the Hollywood for Stevenson Committee designed to help the party combat the "deadliness of straight political speechifying" when recruiting supporters.[29] While Stevenson appreciated the support of entertainers as he toured California, during the national campaign he wanted to avoid "shows, slogans, and the arts of advertising."[30] Moreover, his personal desire to deliver long speeches made it difficult for the hired advertising agency to produce compelling spot advertisements. Stevenson saw television as potentially dangerous tool that manipulated the public and threatened to undermine democracy with public relations "spin," and he was not alone. Earlier that year, John Schneider's *Golden Kazoo* hit bookshelves with what the *New York Times* called a "somber and frightening" forecast of how Madison Avenue would soon control the electoral process.[31] With candidates sold to "the lowest common denominator," only playing "a bit part in a spectacular that will demonstrate a vote-winning point," Schneider's story presented a dystopian view of the democratic system under the control of advertisers.[32]

During the 1952 election, both parties focused on high voter turnout as a strategy to win.[33] With a majority of voters registered as Democrats and the support of labor in place, Stevenson's campaign unsuccessfully relied on the party's New Deal organizational structure. Eisenhower's campaign, on the other hand, focused on bringing "stay at home" voters to the polls.

As the prominent Princeton University political scientist Stanley Kelley Jr. observed that year, such a voter had "not shown himself susceptible to the leadership of the precinct worker, he was a consumer of the mass media."[34] Publicity men—trained in Hollywood studios and in Madison Avenue offices—assumed an authoritative position in this Eisenhower operation. As these media experts worked to translate the general's wartime popularity into political credibility via a "mass media blitz," they celebrated how the campaign "picked up where FDR left off in the establishment of contact with the public through mass communications media."[35] Once in office, Eisenhower began to build a Republican party that was modern not just in its message but also in its organization. Over the course of his administration, the president developed party-building "campaign schools," which taught Republicans lessons about "methods of reaching non-Republican voters" through television, radio, and the press.[36]

Eisenhower's approach to party-building reflected new political priorities suited for the television era. The reliance on the "ad man," explained Kelley, did not undermine traditional political institutions but rather took over from "the big city boss with new campaign techniques to mold the mind of the voter."[37] Rather than building a bloc of voters committed to one party through the strings of patronage, the public relations man "fights his battles in the mind of the voter." However, the resulting party and campaign structure did require a presidential contender to assume a "position in the spotlight" to garner national attention and credibility during the electoral battle. Eisenhower's popularity from World War II allowed him to assume this leadership position in the Republican Party, but, as Kelley observed in 1956, this required "a systematic large-scale, privately sponsored publicity build-up."[38] The era of the political consultant made "star quality" and a personal "Hollywood Dream Machine" an essential component of politics. In doing so, it opened up new paths for political hopefuls to assert their authority in a political culture that increasingly valued media attention.

With his eye on the Democratic nomination, John Kennedy incorporated lessons learned from the Hollywood studios his father ran and he visited as a young adult to create "Jack Kennedy fans" on the campaign trail.[39] According to one newspaper account of his Wisconsin primary battle, "Senator Kennedy, supported by a slick high octane machine, is a celebrity to folks here. His supporters compared him to a movie star. He spent as much time signing autographs as he did shaking hands. Often he was almost mobbed by autograph seekers."[40] Unlike Eisenhower and Roosevelt before him, Kennedy did not just rely on Hollywood personalities to produce positive television or radio spot advertisements, sell a particular political ideology, or teach him the "tricks of the trade" to help his celluloid image. Kennedy used his personal fascination with Hollywood stars and his father's professional connections in the studios to make him a celebrity in his own right to gain authority in a party dominated by labor union leaders and powerful party men like Senate Majority Leader Lyndon Johnson or Chicago Mayor Richard Daley. Kennedy's embrace of Hollywood exploitation strategies not only expanded the reach of his political message, as it had with Roosevelt and Eisenhower, it also allowed Kennedy to make himself a viable political candidate from the beginning. The success of this new media-driven political strategy ultimately made primary campaigns, television, emotional appeals, and strong financial backing necessary to garner national political attention from an electorate that grew and diversified during the 1960s.

John Kennedy's media campaign, from the primary to the general election, mirrored the style and organization of campaigns that had flourished over the previous twenty years in California state politics. The Kennedy family had deep roots in the Hollywood studio system, which made the entire Kennedy camp aware of the importance of staging effective performances and exploiting media opportunities. During the 1920s, his father, Joseph ran three production studios on the West Coast, and similar to other studio executives like Louis B. Mayer and Jack Warner, he actively crafted public personas for his employees, using the Hollywood media exploitation strategies—frequently called the "Hollywood Dream Machine"—to turn obscure actors into stars seemingly overnight. Even as Joseph Kennedy sold his studio interests at an enormous profit before the stock market crash, he continued to keep an eye on the industry, subscribing to trade papers and even traveling out to studio lots for vacations with his son.[41] Through these trips, John Kennedy gained personal experience in Hollywood studios and cultivated relationships with actors and actresses, from Olivia de Havilland to his brother-in-law Peter Lawford and friend Frank Sinatra, all of whom taught him lessons in communication that would prove increasingly valuable as television and advertising took hold of American politics in the 1950s.[42]

As he hit the primary trail in the winter of 1960, John Kennedy, with the help of his father and brother, Robert, used this expertise to generate excitement, votes, and credibility. The campaign team hired Jack Denove Productions to film Kennedy's speeches and voter interactions. The production company later edited the footage to create effective television advertisements that brought the live excitement of campaign events to the living rooms of viewers across the country. This tactic enhanced the celebrity status of the presidential hopeful as voters watched him on television for several days before he traveled to small towns and crowded cities. In the Wisconsin primary, fifty-two television spots lasting twenty seconds played across the electoral battlefield, with paid newspaper and radio announcements to publicize what new Kennedy spots would soon be on television.[43] As Kennedy arrived at local city halls with Frank Sinatra's personalized "High Hopes" playing from the loud speakers, fans screamed with excitement and overwhelmed him with requests for autographs.

Primary, Robert Drew's documentary of the Wisconsin race, highlighted the different responses of Wisconsin voters to Kennedy and his opponent Hubert Humphrey. The Minnesota senator waged a more traditional campaign of hand-shaking and direct appeals to farmers and workers based on his policy credentials. In contrast to Hubert Humphrey, who spoke to small, scattered crowds with jokes about his Polish roots and coffee habits, Drew showed Kennedy, with his supporting cast including his wife "Jackie" and brother "Bobby," entering an overcrowded, loud, and jubilant hall where every participant joyously sang about the senator's "high in the sky, apple pie hopes," lyrics they learned from Sinatra.[44] Drew jumped from scenes of Humphrey handing out cards with information about his campaign to ones of girls sprinting down the street in hopes of simply touching the senator from Massachusetts. Called the "Battle of Contrasts" by the *New York Times*, the Wisconsin primary pitted a traditional Democratic campaign beholden to farm and labor interests against the politics of celebrity.[45]

As the Kennedy crowds swelled, however, the ire and suspicion of liberals within the party also started to manifest in both public and private denunciations of the senator's tactics and the new style of politics that relied on ever-escalating mass media expenses. The "matriarch" of the Democratic Party and the guardian of its New Deal liberalism, Eleanor Roosevelt, openly criticized the political achievements of the "charming young man" who lacked experience and political independence because "his father has been spending oodles of money all over the country and probably has a paid representative in every state by now."[46] Hubert Humphrey also used Kennedy's celebrity style as a way to attack his opponent, frequently referring to him as "Jack who has jack."[47] After outspending the Minnesota senator by a factor of four in primary races, John Kennedy traveled to the Democratic National Convention armed with victories that he hoped would convince the party bosses to support his candidacy.[48] With only sixteen races open to presidential hopefuls, Kennedy's primary triumphs did not secure his nomination alone. He faced intense competitions from more senior and powerful party figures, like Lyndon Johnson, and the liberal grassroots base that launched a last-minute "Draft Stevenson" effort. Though he had pursued an effective primary campaign, Kennedy's success at the convention still depended on the ability to trade dollars for political support from state leaders and back-room negotiations with party officials like Johnson, who agreed to accept a position on the ticket as the vice president.[49] Kennedy, the handsome and telegenic star of the Democratic Party, won the nomination, but it proved a hard-fought, controversial decision.

Having watched the primary race and the Democratic convention unfold, Richard Nixon picked up his attacks on Kennedy where Roosevelt and Humphrey left off. Throughout the campaign he charged his opponent with inexperience and an overreliance on "cheap publicity" that was undignified in the pursuit of the presidency. Since the 1952 election, Eisenhower had come to understand the importance of artfully crafted political productions and had built the Citizens for Eisenhower committee into a well-funded publicity team. Nixon, however, overlooked the importance of this mobilization, and in many ways, his media strategy proved reminiscent of his 1952 "Checkers Speech." But in 1960, the man previously deemed "savvy" on television suddenly became "flatfooted."[50] With little experience within Eisenhower's prime-time presidential operation, Nixon approached television like Humphrey, Roosevelt, and Stevenson. He saw the camera as a way to gain public trust and overcome criticisms that he was a manipulative and "tricky" candidate. He even renamed his small advertising agency "Campaign Associates" and moved its office to Vanderbilt Street, a lesser known street in New York City only a block from famous "Madison Avenue," in an effort to disguise their activities.[51] The vice president also declined Eisenhower's offer to have Robert Montgomery advise him on his television appearances. Television, to Nixon in 1960, emerged as a way to have a conversation with the people and to show his mastery of the issues and experience. It stood as a means to an end, not the primary focus itself.

The famous television debates, which have dominated discussions of the 1960 election, stood not so much as a turning point in the election but rather as a barometer of the two candidates' different attitudes toward the medium. As funds ran low, Kennedy's campaign focused less on constructing pricey advertisements and more on creating media events during which Kennedy himself would appear as a guest on news shows or with his opponent in debates. Kennedy took the advice of CBS President Sig Michelson, who urged Kennedy to take advantage of the potential in "day-to-day news coverage" and not just rely on "paid advertisements."[52] As their research consistently showed higher approval ratings and viewer interest for the senator than for his Republican challenger, the Kennedy team continued to saturate news shows like *Meet the Press, Face the Nation, Person to Person, Presidential Countdown,* and even the more entertainment-based *Jack Paar Show* with Kennedy interviews.[53] The director of the presidential debates program, Don Hewitt, later recalled that Nixon and Kennedy approached the television program very differently. Considering it "just another campaign appearance," Nixon showed up looking "like death warmed over," while Kennedy arrived to the studio well practiced in the importance of news events in the broader media strategy of the campaign.[54]

As over seventy million viewers tuned into the debates, the event, claimed Don Hewitt, changed the American political process by making it "hostage to money." But the television debates did not themselves create the relationship linking television, money, and politics. Rather, they created a popular belief that a "showbiz" political style could determine political success.[55] In the aftermath of the election, the *New York Times* observed, "Hollywood—even the Republican part of it—was congratulating itself today on having won a presidential election. . . . From a bipartisan standpoint, opinion was unanimous that it was the dramatics of television toward which Hollywood has a justly proprietary attitude that had yielded Senator Kennedy's decisive margin."[56] Nixon, too, believed this analysis, and this perception became his reality.[57] Two years later, after suffering defeat to Democrat Pat Brown for the California governorship, Nixon held what he called his "last press conference," where he bitterly blamed the press for his political failures over the previous two years.[58] This loss confirmed to Nixon that the media culture had shifted and that political success depended not on being the best person for the job, but creating a public image through the mass media that convinced voters of the merits of a policy or a candidate.

During the mid-1960s, Nixon remained out of the public eye but stayed very aware of the possibilities of reasserting his candidacy in the 1968 election, and determined to develop a new media strategy that would appeal to the hearts of the American voters in ways that movie stars and newly crafted political celebrities had. He scrutinized the appeal of the actor-turned-governor, Ronald Reagan, noting that for Reagan, "image is the reality."[59] Nixon's research noted that the governor was not a "political fraud" but rather a "suburban politician who communicates the message his audience, largely in the South, largely immigrant in origin and parentage, wants to hear."[60] Along with unveiling to Nixon the "right ingredients for a mass lower class appeal" that could restructure the Republican Party, Reagan's political success in California revealed a "political style that is well suited to an age of mass media," because the governor had a "way of stating the issues that is unfailing newsworthy, if not new."[61] Trained in the Hollywood studio system, Reagan, observed Nixon, knew how to use emotional, entertaining, media-driven performances to appeal to "the heart" of diverse audiences.[62]

Studying how Reagan won the race he had lost, Nixon understood that to achieve his political goals, he had to construct a strategy that prioritized the mass media, and in particular television, in ways that he had previously neglected to do. And to do this, he followed in Kennedy's footsteps and began to build a production team that would also reassert his political potential and credibility for the presidency by taking to the primary trail and turning himself into a celebrity. His colleague in New York City, Leonard (Len) Garment reaffirmed Nixon's analysis of the 1960 election. "Today's candidate," Garment told Nixon, "must learn to grapple, to cope, and to conquer television—refine and project a 'saleable' television image—in order to become attractive to the electorate."[63] William Gavin, a schoolteacher from Pennsylvania well versed in recently crafted scholarly theories from the new field of "media studies," reminded the potential candidate of Marshall McLuhan's recently advanced theory that the "medium is the message"; with this in mind, he told Nixon he just needed the proper television strategy to win.[64] As he signed on to Nixon's campaign team, Gavin urged Nixon to go on the offensive with television and "revolutionize" the medium and, in the process, American politics.[65] Harry Treleaven, an advertising man who had recently crafted George H. W. Bush's successful congressional campaign in Texas, also joined Ray Price, the former editorial writer for the *New York Herald Tribune*, Frank Shakespeare, a television executive at CBS, and Roger Ailes, the successful producer of *The Mike Douglas Show*, to prove to Nixon that television was "not a gimmick" but rather a way to attain political power.[66]

With the Republican primaries on the horizon, Richard Nixon had gathered a talented group of advertising and television men with the production and sales knowledge that far surpassed what Eisenhower, Kennedy, or the sitting president, Lyndon Johnson, had previously organized. Like Kennedy in 1960, Richard Nixon and not the party's national committee had assembled the media team because Nixon needed to show his electability through primary contests. Therefore, he gathered consultants dedicated to him, not the GOP. But while Kennedy used his carefully constructed popularity to assert his political legitimacy in the party, Nixon used a meticulously crafted image to assuage party leaders that his public image was not that of a "loser" or "Tricky Dick." Nixon had credibility within the party; he needed to show that he had popularity among the public as well.

Determined to conquer the "new politics of media campaigning," Nixon constructed a "well-oiled publicity machine" and embraced the cheap publicity for which he had previously condemned his opponent.[67] Far from appropriating television simply to speak directly to viewers through an office setting, Nixon's team used powerful images of the Vietnam War and rioting in the streets with dramatic music to show the problems of liberal leadership and the need for "Nixon Now." To connect to suburban audiences, the candidate appeared on the hit show *Rowan & Martin's Laugh-In* to declare, famously, "Sock it to me?" as other celebrities regularly had. Scholars frequently point to Nixon's appearance on the number one television show as simply a publicity stunt or an interesting anecdote from the campaign. But Nixon's appearance on *Laugh-In* revealed how Nixon had prioritized television and popular entertainment to connect with what his team called the "new voter attitudes" of the "television generation."[68] Like Kennedy before him, he turned to entertainment in an effort to make the candidate a constant part of the media environment and assert his image of a likeable, popular personality to gain political success.

Richard Nixon's media comeback during the 1968 campaign was so stunning that reporter Joe McGinniss turned it into a bestselling exposé. *The Selling of the President* told the story of how artfully crafted media messages and professional entertainment philosophies turned the loser of the 1960 presidential election into the winner of the highest office in the land.[69] Nixon's presidential victory—driven by a very specific interpretation of Kennedy's use of television and celebrity appeal in the 1960 election—certified the political power of publicity strategies rooted in Hollywood studios that had slowly, and controversially, entered American politics over the previous forty years. Moreover, while Kennedy faced frequent criticisms for his celebrity connections and style once in office, Nixon further entrenched show business strategies within his administration and the organizational structures of the Republican Party. Just as studio executives in the motion picture industry had built up stars and maintained their popularity through the "Hollywood Dream Machine," so too did Nixon's advisers constantly work to create and monitor media messages and public opinion surrounding the new president.[70] Two years into the Nixon administration, the well-oiled publicity team assumed the official name the "Committee to Re-Elect the President." While today that group is better known for their clandestine behavior exposed in the Watergate scandal, the committee first and foremost sought to control media messages and construct positive publicity about the president. Under Nixon, the construction of the president as a "celebrity" through a "slick high octane publicity machine" became not just a campaign strategy but a permanent function of the American presidency.

PART III

The Presidency and Political Structure

This portion of the volume focuses on the political structures that presidents must engage; it begins, therefore, with an essay that considers the bedrock of any polity—the way in which civil society itself is organized.

While the inner workings of the National Manufacturers Association, not to mention the Dansk Arbejdsgiversforeningen, may seem far removed from the determinants of presidential authority, Cathie Jo Martin's historical comparison of the United States and Denmark in the early twentieth century demonstrates that the degree of coordination among key organizations in civil society forms an essential variable in an executive's ability to govern effectively.

Martin homes in on the very feature that Tocqueville relished in America, its proliferation of associations, as an important impediment to presidential power. This pluralist landscape, devoid of peak organizations that aggregate interests within civil society, robs presidents of the ability to make and implement policy in a collaborative, de-politicized fashion. Such peak organizations in Denmark, Martin argues, obtained buy-in not only within sectors but also across the kind of regional and occupational dividing lines that are so common in the United States. Ironically, for a nation that supposedly hates excessive governance, industrial and unemployment policy in the United States was hashed out in Congress, in contrast to Denmark, where the same types of organizations implemented such policies in civil society, further contributing to broad citizen embrace of their resolution. Martin's perspective points to a burgeoning literature in American Political Development that considers the ways in which the state interacts with civil society and the implications of such structures for political outcomes. Greater awareness of these deeply embedded relationships goes a long way toward illuminating the limits on any president's agency.

In an earlier essay, Will Hitchcock grappled with the constraints and opportunities that a president's ideology presented, investigating the case of Dwight D. Eisenhower. In this section, Dan Galvin revisits Eisenhower's presidency. Galvin explores when and how presidents invest time and political resources in order to reshape the very political landscape that they operate in. Current scholarship suggests that any efforts to bend the structures that limit presidential action, especially given the president's limited time, are foolhardy. Yet Galvin shows that Eisenhower rolled up his sleeves and tried to remake the Republican Party rather than relying on readily available extra-party organizations to promote his agenda and reelection. He did so in order to ensure the long-term success of his program and to secure his legacy. Galvin directs attention to an important element of presidential impact—one that is often neglected in the rush to issue "scorecards" on presidential performance. Rather than measuring presidents by their dexterity in circumventing the many constraints that they face, scholars should take stock of how presidents "disrupt" the landscape that they inherit, how those revised structures shape future political outcomes, and perhaps most importantly, why presidents would invest resources in these efforts. In short, why do presidents take the long view at all? That long view, Galvin argues, might well be a president's most enduring contribution, as its legacy determines the constraints under which future presidents will operate.

By the middle third of the twentieth century, the structure of knowledge, in the form of applied expertise, had become an important part of the landscape in which presidents operated. From Franklin D. Roosevelt's Brain Trust to John F. Kennedy's bold initiative to land a man on the moon, effective mobilization of professional agendas, insights, and techniques had become crucial to the national security and economic well-being of the nation. Michael Bernstein chronicles the role of presidents in guiding the political economy built upon a consensus among Keynesian economists, fueled by a commitment to robust military spending abroad, linked to mildly redistributive social spending at home, and embodied in a mixed economy. This Cold War Keynesian bargain enjoyed bipartisan support for thirty years after World War II. Presidents from Truman through Nixon enjoyed an extraordinary degree of control over the nation's economic affairs as long as the growth promised by the advocates for this approach to fiscal management was realized. Bernstein then turns to the dissolution of this regime and the emergence of a supply side alternative. The following essay underscores the hubris of those who mistook expertise for the source of the thirty-year reign of presidential macroeconomic management. Specific historical conditions, not the power of economists, explain why a delicately balanced set of tradeoffs prevailed until the mid-1970s—primarily the Cold War and America's unique economic position after World War II. Bernstein's analysis suggests that while presidents must indeed master the structures of knowledge that frame their administrations, the influence of experts is in turn highly dependent on underlying political and geopolitical circumstances.

In the final essay of his section, Gareth Davies uses natural disasters as a window into some of the major trends that have influenced the ongoing struggle between presidents (in their role as agents of political and policy agendas) and the social, cultural, and political constraints that limit presidential discretion. Before the mid-1960s it was unusual for presidents to respond in a personal fashion to disasters, no matter what their scope, because disasters were seen as acts of god or nature that were simply beyond the responsibility of the national government. Public expectations changed as the capacity of the national government grew from the New Deal to the Great Society, shifting the sole responsibility for action from subnational units of government and voluntary agencies like the Red Cross, to partnerships with federal bureaucracies. Davies argues that the ongoing, indeed expected, intervention of the White House after 1970 reflects three key developments. Eviscerating the "legitimation" barrier was the first: In the wake of the Great Society (and with America's expanded global military role) no task lay beyond the legitimate responsibility of the federal government. Second, in a society increasingly infused with electronic media, the line between presidential campaigning and governance eroded. Demonstrating compassion and bold leadership through tactical interventions after disasters provided a relatively low-cost way to use the power of the presidency to further one's political fortunes. Ironically, doing more only heightened expectations and demands for action. In the cynical post-Vietnam and post-Watergate environment, a suddenly inquisitive press corps that claimed to speak for rights denied to citizens simply demanded presidential consolation and federal cash for victims of what would have been considered misfortune just a few decades earlier. By charting this line from Calvin Coolidge's response to flooding on the Mississippi through George W. Bush's response to Katrina, Davies underscores the power of social change—an entitled citizenry, for instance—and evolving political structures—the dramatic shift from local to national responsibility. He also points to the ways in which presidential agency can permanently alter the landscape for his successors, as was the case with Lyndon Johnson's response to Hurricane Betsy.

CHAPTER 10

Stand by Me

*Coalitions and Presidential Power
from a Cross-National Perspective*

CATHIE JO MARTIN

American presidents are essentially fall guys, and it is not surprising that they so often let us down. Compared with most of our north European allies, we ask so much of our presidents but give them so little support from civil society. Tocqueville, of course, saw things differently. To his nineteenth-century eyes, strong communal organizations in the United States compensated for the absence of a powerful national executive bureaucracy. Yet from a cross-national perspective, American parties and industrial relations organizations are very weakly organized, and this weakness hinders presidents in their quests to forge policy.

This chapter uses a European lens to reflect on how executives rely on civil society to wield political power and how crucial differences in parties and labor market groups aid or hinder political leadership. Although the popular press depicts Europe as the land of "big government," policymaking processes in many countries are delegated to the "social partners." Both employers and workers are unified in powerful peak associations that meet in collective bargaining negotiations or in committees convened by ministries to make political deals. Those who have to live with the rules do the heavy lifting, and this politics of ownership often makes for high levels of support for executive policy reforms. In contrast, American business and labor interests are weakly organized, and policy outcomes reflect piecemeal concessions to varied interests. Most American policymaking happens through Congress, where politicians in the two major parties have little reason to cooperate, which tends to make negotiations hyper-politicized. The high noon brinksmanship between Democrats and Republicans is fundamentally at odds with the quieter mechanisms for policymaking seen in northern Europe.

The chapter explores historical episodes when political leaders in the United States and Denmark sought to mobilize business organizations around policy goals. American presidents and Danish prime ministers had similar ambitions for economic coordination in the 1890s, American liberal political ideology notwithstanding. Presidents, like Danish prime ministers, periodically turned to associationalism or coalition-building as a mechanism for organizing and coordinating key groups of economic actors.[1] In the 1890s, candidate William McKinley nurtured the development of the National Association of Manufacturers (NAM) to foster industrial development and to secure the Republican nomination at the same time as Niels Andersen, leader of the Danish Right Party, created the Confederation of Danish Employers (DA). In the 1920s, Herbert Hoover turned to major industrial associations at the same time as the Danish government reached out to the DA and the corresponding peak union to combat unemployment and to enhance industrial productivity. Yet whereas Danish prime ministers were able to get what they wanted from their social partners, American presidents were unable to build much enduring support among business and labor.

These diverse cross-national experiences offer normative lessons. First, we should encourage the development of responsible associations for organizing the political interests of business and labor in the arena of economic policymaking. Governments elsewhere have benefitted from giving the social partners formal authority in long-term political planning but demanding responsible action in return. Second, we should rely more on task forces and other processes of governance that build broad political agreement among experts and stakeholders *before* reforms are subject to legislative consideration. We should seek mechanisms such as a penalty default to ensure that legislators pay attention to these expert task forces. These reforms should help executive leaders advance public policies that expand the collective pie rather than simply redistribute resources and that build toward longer-term ambitions rather than shorter-term expediencies. Third, although an ambitious endeavor, significant reform of party politics could augment presidential leadership capabilities: Parties were central to the initial organization of the key industrial relations partners, and they could undoubtedly aid in the transformation of civil society today.

Social Institutions and Presidential Leadership

The separation of powers is a popular scapegoat for presidential failures and, indeed, prime ministers—with closer connections to their legislative bodies than presidents—have an easier time obtaining partisan majorities. Yet significant legislative action has also occurred under conditions of divided government.[2] Moreover, coalition governments—the norm in many European countries—require party negotiations yet produce policy compromises.

Thus, in thinking about presidential capacities for policy reforms, it behooves us to look also at the scaffolding of civil society, set by the structures of political party competition and industrial relations organizations. First, proportional multi-party systems inspire a politics of compromise that differs significantly from the politics of conflict found in two-party, majoritarian systems. In proportional representation (PR) systems, parties represent clear constituencies, have programmatic agendas that command more enduring constituent support, spend less money appealing to the median voter, and must cooperate to form coalition governments. In majoritarian systems, parties compete for the median voter and have few incentives for cooperation; therefore, the out-party often works to thwart presidential power.[3] PR party systems are more likely than majoritarian systems to foster consideration of collective concerns, and executives are more likely to build broad support for their policy reforms.[4]

Second, executive capacities to build policy coalitions depend on whether key economic actors or social classes are organized into broad cohesive groups or remain fragmented and antagonistic. Many north European countries have highly centralized, unitary peak associations for employers and workers. These groups nurture collective positions among their members, engage in significant nonmarket coordination with workers through collective bargaining, and form (binding) policies with labor and the state in tripartite committees set up by the relevant ministries.[5] Thus, Nordic employers belong to industry groups that are organized into one big association at the top. These big-tent groups have legal rights to self-regulation (together with labor unions) and constantly contemplate what works best in the long term rather than how a strategy will affect one's bottom line in the more immediate future. In this stand-by-me world, individual firms have cover to do the right thing for the long run because other companies are also committed. In sharp contrast, American employers have very weak business groups to help them meet collective political goals, and employers have a hard time focusing on the big picture. Firms vie for political power with campaign finance contributions, but the United States lacks a unitary umbrella association to reconcile conflicting business interests or to restrain demands on Congress. This produces significant infighting within both business and labor over matters of public policy and a relative lack of cooperation between the labor market partners or with government.[6]

Countries also vary in the degree to which policymaking transpires in highly politicized legislative channels or in less visible private channels of policymaking organized by industrial relations institutions. Corporatist countries give industrial relations institutions and nonlegislative tripartite negotiations a prominent role in policymaking, and this paradoxically depoliticizes the policymaking process. Iterative interactions among negotiators, particularly when engaged in longstanding processes of cooperation, help participants to take the longer view and to grasp one another's perspectives.[7] Closed-door protection from media glare and lobbyist pressures allows private-sector negotiators to trade public posturing for private deliberation. Outcomes in these countries are more universalistic and less subject to capture by narrow private interests, more enduring and less transitory, more pragmatic and less symbolic. In contrast, the United States does everything through Congress; as the system lacks strong collective associations, individualistic interests lobby for sectarian concerns, a process that often produces horse trades instead of broader policy initiatives. Our presidents may enjoy greater jurisdictional control over policymaking, but European executives may have more substantive influence on policy through the tripartite processes that build a shared conception of political problems among diverse stakeholders.[8]

The following pages reflect on a period beginning in the 1890s in which governmental leaders in the United States and Denmark sought to introduce greater coordination into the workings of the macroeconomy. Executives from conservative parties and their business allies in many countries (opposed by agricultural interests) sought industrial development policies to compete in emerging global markets and to control labor. The economic initiatives and coalition efforts of the respective political leaders were surprisingly similar during this early period, but the outcomes were very different. The American presidents failed to obtain support from core interest groups to achieve their macroeconomic goals, whereas labor market institutions supported Danish macroeconomic initiatives. American two-party competition worked against these cooperative ambitions, but Danish multi-party competition created incentives for political leaders to organize strong employers' organizations, and this left a legacy of enduring support for executive leadership.

Presidential Leadership and Industrial Relations in the United States

In the United States, presidential hopeful William McKinley helped to create the National Association of Manufacturing as a national peak employers' association to build industrial power and to advance the Republican Party's electoral and policy agendas. Party competition was organized along regional lines, and industrialists were concentrated in the northeastern Republican stronghold, but industrialists in other regions lacked an ideological partisan home, as the Democratic Party held positions consistent with their dominant agricultural constituencies. The McKinley campaign organized NAM in part to make electoral appeals to these other manufacturers and to gain the Republican nomination at the convention (where votes from Democratic states mattered greatly in the contest for the nominee). NAM's creators also sought business support for its industrial policy agenda.[9]

NAM's initial policy positions reflected a vision of industrial cooperation that resembled positions of contemporaneous European employers. NAM's manifesto stressed industrial development objectives, such as the extension of domestic and foreign markets, reciprocal tariffs, the Nicaragua Canal, the expansion of a merchant marine, and the expansion of waterways. NAM identified industrial cooperation among agents in business, labor, and the state as necessary to economic development. Although far from neutral on the balance of class power, NAM's leaders before 1903 viewed stable, cooperative labor relations as essential to firms' export ambitions. NAM envisioned becoming the peak association for sectoral industry groups with a proto-corporatist organizational structure and sought a privileged role in shaping public policy. The association sought legislation to obtain a federal act of incorporation or a national charter and lobbied for the creation of a new Cabinet-level Department of Commerce (finally established in 1903) to act as a clearing house for technical expertise, to rationalize business-oriented regulation, and to represent business in the new vision of coordination.[10]

The structure of party politics worked against the realization of NAM's corporatist aspirations, as Democratic congressmen from the South and the West defeated these proposals, fearing northeastern dominance. Losing the campaign to become a proto-corporatist representative of business, NAM rapidly lost members at the end of the century and subsequently developed an anti-labor focus in 1903. This critical juncture signaled a setback for coordination in the American political economy and strengthened the liberal impulse among U.S. employers.

The impulse for high levels of industrial coordination again grew significantly during the First World War, and executives across the world faced significant postwar challenges related to economic growth, unemployment, labor radicalism, and reconstruction (even in neutral Denmark and the United States, territorially unscathed by war). Political leaders in many countries sought expanded unemployment protections and industrial cooperation for productivity, efficiency, and labor peace. Yet party and industrial relations systems involved social partners in economic policymaking quite differently, and this powerfully influenced political leaders' capacities to achieve economic ends.

The U.S. Secretary of Commerce, Herbert Hoover, had a very modern—even Keynesian—view of the problem of structural unemployment and its solutions: automatic macroeconomic stabilization policy, unemployment protections, workforce development, and public works. Hoover, deeply inspired by European ideas during his involvement in postwar reconstruction, promoted macroeconomic interventions to fight unemployment; for example, his presidency of the Federated American Engineering Societies produced a report on "Waste in Industry" with recommendations for unemployment and labor relations.[11]

On joining President Harding's cabinet as secretary of commerce, Hoover persuaded his boss to establish a President's Conference on Unemployment in 1921 to study and make recommendations about unemployment, Hoover's foundational ideas are reflected in this conference report. The conference's Committee on Unemployment Statistics argued for "employment indices based on a regular monthly comparison of the number of employees and their earnings as shown by payrolls of identical establishments." The Committee on Public Works, coming to the conclusion that jobs in public works programs were infinitely better than relief, called for congressional legislation to offer loans to the Reclamation Service to expand public works.[12] The guiding principles of the conference anticipated Keynesian structural analyses of macroeconomic dynamics; as the report observed about the business cycle, "Any permanent policy on unemployment must be based in part on a study of the business cycle, since the unemployed are mainly men who have been laid off because their employers cannot make profits. Social costs of cyclical unemployment must be weighed in terms of direct loss of production from idleness of men and plant in periods of depression."[13]

Hoover also appointed a committee to write a report on "Business Cycles and Unemployment," and support from this endeavor came from an A-team assortment of interests across the economic spectrum. Orchestrated by the National Bureau of Economic Research, the committee was funded by the

Carnegie Foundation, the U.S. Chamber of Commerce, the Federated American Engineering Societies, the U.S. Chamber of Commerce, the Russell Sage Foundation, and the American Federation of Labor, among others.[14]

Hoover sought industrial coordination to implement macroeconomic stabilization solutions to structural unemployment, with what historian Ellis Hawley calls "associational politics," aimed at achieving higher levels of productivity, efficiency, and labor peace. Hoover himself coined the phrase "governance by committee"; this reflects the European roots of his inspiration, a corporatist system of consensual self-regulation that he greatly preferred to politicized policymaking. The libertarian Rothbard denigrated Hoover's interest in corporatism as a forerunner of fascism.[15] Hoover's associational state would function through cooperating committees and expert councils, and he viewed the Commerce Department as directing associational activity toward postwar reconstruction. Hoover pushed for an expansion and reorganization of the Commerce Department to include the Bureau of Mines, the Patent Office, and a bureau of transportation.[16] As the leader of Second Industrial Conference in 1919 and 1920, Hoover also advocated a model of representation by business and labor on mediation boards, although these were never given powers of self-regulation and could only act in an advisory capacity.[17]

Hoover's ideas were aired in Congress and also drew considerable support initially from some employers and union representatives. Senator William Kenyon of Iowa, a Republican, introduced legislation in Congress to implement the recommendations of the President's Conference on Unemployment. The legislation asked heads of executive departments to identify and prepare engineering plans for public works projects so that they might immediately begin when the funds became available. The Department of Commerce was to begin collecting monthly statistics on business conditions so that public officials could take preventive measures against unemployment or delay public works to head off inflation during economic booms. *The American Contractor* strongly endorsed the legislation as "an important forward step in nation's economic, industrial and financial life." Joseph Defrees, president of the U.S. Chamber of Commerce, testified ardently in favor of legislation to expand the government's collection of economic and labor market statistics and to establish a national budget.[18]

But partisan politics and interest group incapacities stood in the way of success. The parties were split on policies for industrial coordination, with the Democrats and their agricultural constituents reluctant to endorse political arrangements that would foster growing industrial power. Southern Democrats rallied against the bill (along with western Republican Senators). Senator Harrison, a Democrat from Mississippi, sought to kill the bill by greatly limiting its scope (removing river and harbor, flood control, and irrigation projects from its jurisdiction.) Some senators feared that presidential fine-tuning would make economic life more unstable. Legislators from agricultural states also blamed the president Hoover for giving limited support to the southwestern farm program, to which they responded with an opposition to industrial development measures. Moreover, the Treasury and other executive department leaders resisted the turf-building ambitions of Hoover and the Commerce Department as encroachments on their jurisdictions.[19]

The unemployment legislation also suffered from the institutional weaknesses of the societal groups to provide real support and to engage in self-governance. Hoover's structures of voluntary associationalism never really gave the social partners much power or responsibility, and the mechanisms for policymaking largely enabled industry insiders to secure private gains rather than to make social and economic investments for the public good.[20] Pluralist organization encourages intra-group divisions, and employers remained divided over Hoover's vision of the path to economic recovery. Bankers resisted the unemployment conference's criticism that high interest rates on loans and commissions were standing in the way of building operations. The Chamber of Commerce supported Harding and Hoover, but NAM had preferred cutting unemployment through tariff protection to reduce foreign imports. NAM claimed that three-fourths of its members supported the American Valuation plan, which would value goods according to U.S. prices rather than home prices and would prevent cheap foreign imports from flooding U.S. markets.[21] NAM's *American Industries* editorialized: "If the hardships of unemployment and its attendant evils are to be removed it is essential that there shall be a prompt return to a policy of protection for American labor on the farm, in the mine, and in the factory; and to make such protection effective under the new and altogether unprecedented economic conditions now prevailing in competing countries."[22]

Hoover's efforts to organize civil society were resurrected in FDR's strategy for advancing economic policy during the New Deal, most prominently displayed in his mobilization of support for the ill-fated National Recovery Act. Although President Hoover responded to the Great Depression in 1929 with little of the enthusiasm for economic coordination that he had demonstrated as secretary of commerce, Roosevelt returned to a model of coordinated capitalism (albeit with less volunteerism and with greater formal constraints) as an avenue for economic recovery. The National Recovery Act set up codes of fair competition in each industry and sought to bring enlightened business managers into associations. Employers (together with labor in some sectors) were to negotiate rules of the game, develop collective wages to stave off industrial instability, and, presumably, help to attain Democratic goals. The legislation was welcomed by many large employers as a way to prevent cutthroat wage competition (using government to force "sweat-shops" to pay minimum wage) and to advance industrial self-regulation. The legislation was also motivated by concerns over social justice and the desire to extend to small employers the trade advantages of their larger brethren; indeed, for historian Donald Brand, the NRA exhibited the capacities of public sector leaders to press employers into service for the state. Secretary of Labor Frances Perkins explained that "if the ten per cent of business men who are willing to exploit labor can be controlled . . . I feel that the others can be depended upon to fix fair standards of hours and wages."[23]

Yet the NRA produced codes replete with anticompetitive price-raising provisions and few safeguards for consumers; consequently, the model of collectivist business planning increasingly came under attack by labor and consumers. Sectors with strong labor unions urging compliance with the codes were more successful in achieving regulatory objectives than industries relying only on self-regulation by industrial associations, largely because the employers' organizations were unable to articulate broad collective interests. As associational politics fell out of favor, employers also drew away from the social and macroeconomic policies—deficit financing, public works, and social protections—commonly accepted by collectivist capitalists in other countries and likely to stimulate demand-led recovery. The Chamber of Commerce and the National Association of Manufacturers both ultimately renounced the NRA, and the Supreme Court struck down the legislation in 1935; the measure's attack from supporters on both the left and the right muted the public outcry to the court's action. Whereas the National Recovery Act was a failure, Roosevelt also used an associational strategy to mobilize strategic interests in more successful New Deal ventures such as the Agricultural Adjustment Act, which brought a vast network of farmers into a nexus of state-society relations.[24]

Executive Leadership and Industrial Relations in Denmark

Baron Tage Reedtz-Thott became council president of Denmark in 1894 at a time when his Right Party (Højre) was fearful of the growing threat of democratization and the Social Democratic Party. The Danish system of partisan representation included three main parties: the Right Party (in control of the executive branch for the latter part of the nineteenth century) had been supported by most manufacturers, many aristocrats, and a number of urban workers; the Liberals were dominated by agricultural interests; and the rising Social Democrats claimed an increasing share of the workers. The Right Party was losing its grip in the 1890s, and the moderate parliamentary faction led by Reedtz-Thott (including most urban industrialists) initially sought a center-right voting coalition with the centrist Liberal Party against the left. This move was bitterly opposed by the more conservative wing of the party, which included most aristocrats. Although himself a baron, Reedtz-Thott was influenced by the Danish pastor and social philosopher N. F. S. Grundtvig, father of the folk high school movement and a proponent of mass education and social harmony. Under Reedtz-Thott's leadership, the moderate wings of the Right and Liberal parties negotiated on education, social, tax, economic, and defense initiatives. But the Right Party lost many parliamentary seats through the voting coalition, and a crucial finance measure was voted down 1895. At this point, the center-right alliance ceased, the conservative wing of the Right Party gained the upper hand, and centrists feared that a farmer-worker alliance would gain control of government.[25]

The macrocorporatist system of industrial relations, which organized business and labor engagement at a very high level, was born of this struggle for party control. After the failure of the center-right alliance, the moderate Right politicians moved to another strategy to stave off democratization, namely to transfer policymaking power to a private system of industrial relations, thinking that employers might wield greater power by negotiating privately with labor than by confronting workers and farmers in parliamentary channels. A new peak employers' federation (the precursor to Dansk Arbejdsgiversforeningen, or DA) was formed by Right Party legislator (and later the parties' major spokesman within parliament) Niels Andersen, who was also a leading railroad and defense construction entrepreneur. When he stepped down as chairman of the DA in 1911, Andersen mused, "It is almost more important to have a good employers' association than a good government."[26]

The Right Party's desires to sustain political control and to limit social democratic reforms were paralleled in the employers' association's ambitions to achieve self-regulation in public policy and to secure industrial peace without ceding excessive power to labor. DA had significant input into the Industrial Injuries Insurance Act of 1898, both by securing a means for employers to opt out of the public plan and by ensuring that the public plan would be controlled by organized business and labor through the establishment of a workmen's compensation board. The organizers of DA used this legislation to bring in members from the handicrafts and trade sectors, thus extending its reach beyond industry, and argued that joining DA would "prevent the negative economic effects of a law that requires employers to pay support for work accidents. . . . But this concern, as contemplated, will also be able to create the foundation for another Collaboration between the trades and association with common interests."[27]

The employers' association, seeking to control industrial conflict, also actively lobbied workers to form a parallel encompassing labor union. The fundamental outlines of the well-known Danish Model of industrial relations were consolidated in 1899 with the well-known September Compromise, which constituted the first general agreement between DA and the peak labor organization, LO (Landsorganisation). The Right Party and employers escalated what began as a minimal strike to advance a national system of collective bargaining. The employers could have decimated the union movement, but instead it sought the significant expansion of a system of industrial self-regulation.[28]

In the wake of the First World War, Denmark adopted an approach to unemployment that was quite similar to Hoover's vision and did so with enormous support from interests across the economic spectrum. National legislation to combat unemployment began in 1907, when the parliament passed a voluntary private unemployment plan with some state subsidies to replace the existing incoherent patchwork of private and local public programs. The unemployment program was expanded as part of emergency legislation in August 1914, and separately, a law creating an early national labor exchange was passed in 1913. The unemployment program and labor exchange were joined together in a modern comprehensive unemployment protection in 1921, and the multi-tiered, corporatist forums of the social partners were given control over the administration of the unemployment system. The social partners played an important role in the institutionalization of unemployment protections, and the corporatist structure of business and labor representation combined with the dynamics of partisan coalition-building contributed to the capacities of political leaders to pass this cornerstone of the capitalist welfare state.

An unemployment commission was set up in 1903 to propose legislation and to resolve the conflicting goals of and political positions on unemployment protections. Before 1900, organized labor supported unemployment funds as a mechanism for expanding its own power, but many worried that the coverage of marginal workers with voluntary funds might prompt the desertion of skilled workers from the system. Therefore, unions sought state support to augment or rationalize this uneven patchwork system. The Right Party and employers also supported unemployment insurance but ardently rejected any plan that would shift the balance of labor market power to unions.[29]

A law in 1907 adopted the totality of the commission's report and passed unanimously with the support of all political parties, although the Social Democrats and the Right Party were particularly strong supporters, since unemployment would benefit rural agricultural workers less than urban industrial ones. Participants agreed that unemployment was unavoidable at this stage of capitalist development, that excessive social assistance would be morally degrading, and that a voluntary plan was preferable to public assistance; on this last point, business wanted to contain the development of a social right, labor wanted to maintain control over the funds, and rich sectors wanted to avoid pooling funds with poor ones. Although the Social Democrats sought to vest unions with direct control of the insurance measures, the Right Party insisted that separate insurance funds be created. These funds would not compete for members or be offered to those who had neglected their work, engaged in misconduct, refused available jobs, or engaged in a strike. Employers allowed special organizations with union connections to administer the funds, because business wanted to avoid paying into the plans. In subsequent legislation, employers and the Right Party successfully pushed for the separation of the unemployment insurance and social assistance streams as well as for corporatist board control over the assistance program. But ultimately, the separation of social assistance and unemployment insurance (for workers who had paid into the program) was viewed by the right as an ill-conceived notion, as the social assistance portion grew in size and even a subsequent subsidy to municipalities did not prevent the drag on local economies. Therefore, the right and business began to advocate a rationalization of the many threads of unemployment policy.[30]

Like the United States, Denmark adopted many policies for social and economic coordination at the onset of the war; for example, the Justice and Commerce ministries were accorded significant powers to manage exports and currency controls. But also like the United States, peaceful industrial relations and support for cooperation declined precipitously with the end of conflict. Syndicalism—a direct attack on the prevailing coordinated industrial relations system and major peak associations—gained ground during the war and drove labor market conflict over the eight-hour day and the English week (ending at noon on Saturday). After 1916, the unofficial strike rate exploded, peaking in 1919 and 1920, then again in 1925. Some employers paralleled the syndicalist drive for deregulation of industrial relations with cries for a resurrection of free-market capitalism.[31]

Centralized coordination was a middle-way strategy that had the political utility of supporting politically-centrist business and labor actors and their political allies against attacks from both the right and the left; consequently, the DA and LO continued to argue for cooperative policies in setting the new postwar terms for the peaceful economy. For example, a body called the Joint Council of Trades, developed in 1917, included business and labor members representing the encompassing groups in industry, commerce, trade, and shipping; the forum sustained high levels of cooperation in the Danish economy. The collective bargaining round between LO and DA also reduced working hours.[32]

The centrist social partners were victorious in the arena of unemployment insurance when the tensions between wartime control and postwar deregulation were resolved by expanding and institutionalizing the jurisdiction of the private social partners. The 1921 Unemployment Act reorganized the various modes of unemployment compensation (insurance, general assistance, and public works) into a single comprehensive law, introduced a central unemployment fund for extraordinary unemployment coverage with employer contributions, and created an Unemployment Council composed of labor and employer representatives to oversee the management of the funds. The new central fund was given the authority to choose several interventions to curb unemployment for those made jobless by exceptional circumstances: doling out benefits to the indigent to augment local governments' efforts, offering public works employment, and increasing educational interventions to reduce longer-term skills gaps. Most importantly, the 1921 reform completed the construction of new corporatist institutions to monitor the local labor exchanges, to run the Central Unemployment Fund, and to plan national works projects.[33]

Employers were particularly eager in the 1921 plan to strengthen their role in the oversight of special funds for extraordinary unemployment. The main thrust of the 1921 act was not to change the worker-run unemployment insurance funds that govern normal unemployment but to deal with the extraordinary unemployment; to this end, the government created funds for state support during crises and restricted support so that workers would have incentives to find other employment. An emergency relief oversight committee was set up in Copenhagen and in each county, composed of three representatives from DA, three from LO, one from the agricultural society, and one from the small holding society.[34] The various parties also supported or opposed aspects of reform related to distribution of the tax burden and control. The ruling Liberal Party sought employers' contributions to unemployment pools, in a never-ending game of trying to shift taxes and duties from wealthy farmers to industrialists. Unions and the closely related unemployment funds strongly resisted the imposition of employer contributions because they did not want business representation on the corporatist boards. The Conservative Party (a successor to the old Right Party) joined the Liberal Party in securing greater business influence on the evolving corporatist framework, and employers were considered to be a major victor in the legislation.[35]

These early episodes of economic policymaking created legacies for subsequent attempts by Danish prime ministers to respond to economic and social problems. The industrial system of self-regulation worked to unify business and labor positions on policy problems and solutions; therefore, political executives could call on their social partners to aid in building consensus for new policy initiatives. Parliament often passed without significant alteration expert task force recommendations, and these prelegislative deals at once cemented the allegiance of core groups and restricted the use of legislation to buy the unnecessary support of marginal actors. Moreover, the structure of the industrial relations system pulled positions to the left over the long term: The establishment of control by social partners over unemployment insurance over time contributed to high unionization rates because workers had a material incentive to join unions for access to unemployment insurance funds. Unemployment insurance legislation in the early twentieth century created a crucial legacy for the subsequent evolution of labor power.

Conclusion

In our efforts to recast presidential history, it is important to note the structural constraints on executive power from a comparative perspective. American presidents have a particularly difficult time constructing coalitions in support of their economic policies, and this greatly delimits the range and success of presidential socioeconomic goals compared with those of executives elsewhere. The institutions that convene key economic groups to reflect on policy initiatives—parties and industrial relations institutions—influence the capacity of executives to govern. Strong national private systems of policymaking in countries with macrocorporatist labor market institutions depoliticize policy, because encompassing business and labor associations resolve zero-sum conflicts within their constituencies even before the groups bring their issues to the negotiating table or to legislative venues. The delegation of power to social partners makes societal groups much more committed to policies, because they feel a sense of ownership over the policies, and highly organized labor market institutions are associated with higher levels of equality and less capture by narrow sectarian interests. Many Americans perceive the U.S. government as less intrusive and interventionist than the purported "Big Brother" socialist countries of Europe, yet policymaking is much more politicized in the United States.

These observations contribute to the broader paradoxes of the American state from a comparative perspective. The United States is perceived as the paragon of market efficiency, but government has duplication of effort and inefficiencies, and the U.S. system of interest representation contributes to these problems. Viewed as having a small laissez-faire state, the United States does more through government than its Scandinavian counterparts, where self-regulation is the norm. Although broad social groups play a bigger role vis-à-vis legislators in negotiating public policy in Europe, policy outcomes in these countries are less subject to capture by private interests. American legislators create policies for political contingency that are often unrealistic and difficult to implement, whereas European policy compromises produced by the social partners are often more universalistic and less targeted to specific interests, more enduring and less transitory, more pragmatic and less symbolic. Untenable is the conception—dating from Tocqueville—that strong American communities compensate for the absence of a powerful national bureaucracy; instead, weak societal organizations contribute to the enervation of government and to equality.

CHAPTER 11

Taking the Long View

Presidents in a System Stacked against Them

DANIEL J. GALVIN

Most political scientists studying the presidency share Richard Neustadt's well-known premise that modern presidents work within a political system that is stacked against them.[1] Though they may enter office with grand ambitions and lofty promises of change—and face sky-high expectations that they will deliver—their time in office is limited, their resources are few, and their structural constraints are many. Durably alter the political landscape? Subdue the forces that rule Washington and create lasting change? Unlikely. Presidents make do with the tools they have, and some do better than others, but most find themselves tinkering "at the margins."[2]

Presidents are thus advised (by practitioners) and expected (by scholars) to calibrate their horizons and adjust their goals accordingly. Strategize backward from four years out: Score some quick wins, build up chits with key players, act unilaterally to rack up accomplishments. Do not waste time bargaining with intractable opponents or enter games the president cannot win. Rather than take the long view and attempt to reconfigure their structural constraints, presidents are expected to maximize their immediate benefit, given existing constraints.

Presidents are thus treated as myopic, instrumental actors whose behavior is unlikely to have much, if any, lasting effect on the political environment in which they operate. Inherited institutional, organizational, and political arrangements are obstacles that must be worked around—they are not, themselves, objects of contestation. "There is little evidence that presidents can restructure the political landscape and pave the way for change," explains presidency scholar George C. Edwards III. "Although not prisoners of their environment, they are likely to be highly constrained by it."[3]

Even scholars of rational choice institutionalism, who ventured into presidency studies heralding a clean break from the Neustadtian tradition, built those same premises—*presidential myopia* and *fixed constraints*—into the fabric of their assumptions.[4] In his seminal 1985 essay, for example, Terry Moe wrote that every president faces the same set of "severe" constraints, including constitutional checks and balances, institutional complexity and inertia, pervasive knowledge problems, and serious time pressures (two terms, at most, and a ticking clock).[5] In consequence, Moe wrote:

> The administration must be nimble and constantly on the move or it will be overwhelmed by the increasing odds against its success. These pressures drive out grand designs and long-term plans; they also drive out thoughtful, careful analysis. But the pressures themselves arise from the realities of politics, and the president ignores them at his peril: if he wants to be successful, he usually has no choice but to think in the short term and to demand supporting institutions that respond quickly and appropriately to his political needs.[6]

Subsequent work in the rational choice tradition followed up on these insights by designing game-theoretic models in which presidents seek to maximize their leverage and outmaneuver their opponents within fixed constraints but have little, if any, concern for the future or even for their potential to affect the next strategic game. The dependent variable of interest remains how much the president can squeeze out of a system that is fundamentally stacked against him within a short time frame. Thus, rather than treat *presidential myopia* and *fixed constraints* as hypotheses to be subjected to empirical scrutiny, they became unquestioned premises upon which increasingly sophisticated analyses were built.

The alternative possibility, that presidents might, at least under certain conditions, take the long view and seek to alter in a durable way those features of their political environment they find most frustrating, is precluded by the very terms of the analysis. Yet it is hardly a stretch to think that presidents might see it that way, that when confronted with formidable obstacles, their goals might expand to include not only maximizing their benefit *given* those obstacles but also razing or reconfiguring those obstacles so as to put themselves, their allies, and their successors in a more advantageous position in the future.

There are a few studies that proceed along these lines, enough to suggest that presidents are not always confined to working within the confines of the political universe as they find it but may, in fact, have the capacity to alter structural features of their environment. This research, typically associated with the study of American Political Development (APD), conceptualizes the presidency as a "blunt, disruptive force" that always shakes up the basic contours of American politics.[7] Presidents are viewed as agents of systemic change who have contributed to many important developments in American political history. They have been state builders and institutional innovators;[8] coalition shufflers and social movement collaborators;[9] and agents of constitutional reconstruction.[10] Whether by design or by accident—intentionally or just willy-nilly—presidential action is shown to be consistently formative for American politics.[11]

These studies suggest an exciting new research agenda for presidency studies, one that shifts analytical emphasis away from presidential scorecards and strategic games and toward the effects that presidents have on the environment in which they operate. Yet for all the progress that has been made in conceptualizing presidents as agents of change, we still know far too little about the conditions under which presidents will be more or less likely to try to reshape their political confines in a *purposeful* way. Though the presidency may be a "battering ram," surely not all presidents are equally disruptive, and surely not all try—at least, not to the same extent.[12] What, then, explains the variation? Under what conditions will presidents be most inclined to take forward action to transform the structures surrounding them?

Getting traction on this question is important, for if scholarship in the APD tradition is to draw sharper contrasts or to identify greater synergies with scholarship in the rational choice and behavioralist traditions, it needs to have more to say about *purposive* presidential action and variation in presidential decisionmaking processes. Moreover, if presidents' purposive efforts can be linked more clearly to specific historical developments, we may gain new insights into the contributions presidents have made, and continue to make, to the changing shape of American politics.

This chapter seeks to take a step in this direction. It begins with a theoretical proposition, tests it on a "least-likely case," and then discusses its broader scholarly and substantive significance. The proposition, in brief, is that presidents will be most likely to think long-term and take forward action to reshape their structural confines when they perceive their historical legacy to be in jeopardy. Such concerns may arise under several different circumstances, but they should *regularly* arise, I argue, when the president finds his political party to be at a significant competitive disadvantage vis-à-vis the opposition party. Under such conditions, the president faces a short-term as well as a long-term problem: not only does his party lack the majorities to help him secure legislative accomplishments in the present, but the president lacks a reliable political vehicle that can promote his political purposes and serve as a testament to his presidency in the future. His party's competitive weakness will be seen as an impediment to the fulfillment of his grand ambitions, an obstacle to his achieving historical greatness. Rather than simply accept it as a given and work around it, the president will be motivated to try to change it. He will try to strengthen his party, rebrand it, and rebuild it into a political force that can help him achieve his objectives, both now and in the future.

To test this proposition, I examine the "least-likely" case of President Dwight D. Eisenhower.[13] Eisenhower was an unlikely party-builder if ever there was one. Recruited by both parties, Ike was widely seen as a statesman who rose above party. But in the context of the Republican Party's evident electoral weaknesses and uncertain future electoral prospects, Eisenhower became concerned that his "middle way" brand of politics would fade into history once he left office. Rather than downgrade his ambitions and simply make the best of the situation he inherited, Eisenhower tried to redress his party's deficiencies and alter its future trajectory. Reviewing several moves Eisenhower made in this direction, I suggest that even this president—one who truly needed no party—faced strong contextual incentives to take the long view and try to reshape the most frustrating features of his structural environment. Though Eisenhower ultimately failed to produce a consensus around his vision of "Modern Republicanism," his party-building efforts had important long-term effects on the GOP. In the final section of the essay, I consider the substantive and scholarly implications of this unlikely case.

The "Least-Likely" Case of President Dwight D. Eisenhower

Dwight D. Eisenhower was elected in 1952 with 55 percent of the popular vote and 83 percent of the electoral votes. His newly adopted party, however, lagged far behind. A mere 34 percent of the American public identified with the GOP in 1952, and Eisenhower received a higher share of the vote than the Republican congressional candidate in 79 percent of all districts. While his coattails brought new Republican majorities to Congress, they were slim majorities—a one-seat edge in the Senate and an eight-seat edge in the House—and they disappeared in the 1954 midterm elections when Eisenhower was not on the ticket. Thus, despite his personal popularity, the Republican Party was still at a significant competitive disadvantage vis-à-vis the Democratic Party, and Eisenhower knew it.[14]

Eisenhower's campaign manager recorded that "Ike's goal" was not just to win in 1952 but also to "build as we go" and to "reinstitute the GOP as majority party."[15] Why try to help grow his newly adopted party? As a trusted adviser wrote during Eisenhower's first year, despite the president's "remarkably high level of popularity with the people," he had no guarantee that his political purposes—variously called the "middle way" or "Modern Republicanism"—could survive beyond his time in office. Strengthening the Republican Party was therefore seen as "an insurance for the future public support of the Administration's programs and policies."[16] Eisenhower agreed with this assessment and became determined to revitalize party structures and broaden its appeal.[17]

A review of the scholarly literature on Eisenhower's presidency would lead one to believe that Eisenhower did no such thing. According to the received wisdom, Eisenhower was uninterested in party politics and disengaged from the Republican Party. Despite a wave of revisionist scholarship showing him to be a more active and engaged leader than his contemporaries thought, scholars still tend to view him as a president "above party."[18]

Analysts often point out that Eisenhower had little *need* for the Republican Party. The argument is that he must have "recognized that his own popularity was so much greater than his party's that he could only damage his position by too strong an association with it."[19] What's more, Ike always had an "out": The Citizens for Eisenhower groups who ran his 1952 campaign offered a reliable extrapartisan vehicle for building political support throughout his presidency, if he chose to nurture it.[20]

Yet Eisenhower did work to build the Republican Party. While many of his efforts were not publicly known, Eisenhower worked tirelessly behind the scenes to help grow the GOP and expand its reach. After twenty years of Democratic dominance, Eisenhower knew that his adopted party had a long way to go, notwithstanding its slim (and brief) congressional majorities in the 53rd Congress. If his presidency was to be anything more than an interregnum between periods of Democratic dominance—if he was to have anything more than a fleeting impact on the course of American political development—he believed that the GOP would need to be recast in his image and its organizational capacities significantly strengthened. Under the banner of Modern Republicanism, Eisenhower hoped to lead his party out of the wilderness, equip it to compete with the Democrats, and enable it to perpetuate his political vision long after he had left the White House.

Perhaps the reason Eisenhower's party-building efforts have been lost to history has to do with the methodological approach that is typically used. Scholars often begin with an observed outcome of interest and then trace backward the factors that were important in producing it. A popular synoptic history of the Republican Party, for example, overlooks Eisenhower's party building because he is said to have "largely failed to make any impression on the GOP."[21] This claim would surely have surprised Eisenhower's conservative adversaries in the 1950s who decried Ike's *harmful* effect on the party and pointed to congressional Republican losses in 1954, 1956, and 1958. But because Eisenhower failed to remake his party in his image, it is not terribly surprising that his party-building efforts have received scant attention. But a president's success at achieving his particular goals and his political and historical significance are two very different things. Though Eisenhower ultimately failed to produce a new consensus around Modern Republicanism, his efforts proved to be of real consequence for the Republican Party's long-term development.

Citizens for Eisenhower and the Republican Party

With his party so much less popular than he and so often out of step with his "middle way" philosophy, the question remains: Why did Eisenhower not simply ignore the GOP and turn to Citizens for Eisenhower groups to help build his political support? Those groups, which were deeply committed to helping Eisenhower advance his goals, could perform most of the electoral and policy-publicity roles that the Republican Party might otherwise undertake but would more reliably follow his lead. Going this route certainly would have been easier than trying to reconstruct a large and cumbersome party apparatus.

The reason Eisenhower opted instead to work to revitalize and rebrand the formal Republican Party organization was that he saw the Citizens groups as *ephemeral* and the Republican Party as *durable*. Whereas the Citizens groups would fade once he left the scene, a reconstituted Republican Party could persevere over the long run, perpetuating his policy commitments and personal brand of politics well into the future. Thus, he bypassed the otherwise attractive alternative of building up his personal networks of support and made the conscious (though often difficult) decision to rebuild the organizational foundations of his party and confront its ideological divisions. He consistently exhorted Citizens activists and other young up-and-comers to join the Republican Party and to try to change it from the inside.

His efforts began in earnest in 1954, when polls began to show Democrats increasingly likely to retake control of Congress in the midterm elections. Eisenhower worried that such an outcome might give the "extreme right wing" an opportunity to "recaptur[e] the leadership of the party." And "if the Right Wing really recaptures the Republican Party, there simply isn't going to be any Republican influence in this country within a matter of a few brief years," he wrote. The party would surely split, and "a new Party will be inevitable."[22] Concerned, Eisenhower traveled more than ten thousand miles and made nearly forty speeches on behalf of Republican candidates in the final weeks of the campaign, despite his wavering health.[23] Importantly, he also began urging former Citizens supporters to set aside their antipathy for the formalities of party and go to work "electing a Republican majority to the Congress."[24]

When Republicans lost control of both houses of Congress and their minorities at the state level deepened as well, Eisenhower became even more determined to transform his party. He wrote: "The Republican Party must be completely reformed and revitalized . . . the Republican Party must be known as a progressive organization or it is sunk."[25] As he laid out a political strategy for the remainder of his first term, Eisenhower made party transformation a top priority:

> If there is one thing that I am going to try to do during the next two years, I have just one purpose, outside the job of keeping this world at peace, and that is to build up a strong progressive Republican Party in this country. . . . If the right wing wants a fight, they're going to get it. If they want to leave the Republican Party and form a third party, that's their business, but before I end up, either this Republican Party will reflect progressivism or I won't be with them anymore.[26]

The best way to remake the GOP into a "progressive" party—one that would presumably appeal to a majority of the electorate—was, he concluded, to bring Citizens leaders and activists into the party fold.

Eisenhower thus began a concerted effort to persuade the Citizens to join the ranks of the party organization officially. To Paul Hoffman, a friend and former Citizens leader, Eisenhower indicated that he intended to reshape the Republican Party not through a "revolution" but "more surely by the evolution of *infiltrating the organization* with people who thoroughly believe in the President's political philosophy."[27] This transformation of the formal party apparatus would be helped enormously by "volunteers" such as Hoffman and his fellow Citizens, Ike said, whose "heroic efforts" would surely "obtain results." Sherman Adams, writing at Eisenhower's urging, encouraged Citizens activists to "devote all the time and effort they have to contribute" to this party-changing campaign.[28]

Eisenhower also launched several organizational innovations within the party to help move things forward. For example, he directed Adams to create a new "Civilian Committee" to serve in an advisory role to the Republican National Committee and the White House. The RNC would act as an official entry point into Republican Party politics for Eisenhower's many friends in the business community, most of whom were active in the Citizens groups but not in the Republican Party proper. In their new capacity as "Civilian advisers" to the RNC, Ike wanted these men to survey "local and national issues in each state" and recruit "fine young men and women both for party work and for candidates."[29] Eisenhower also directed Adams to form an adjunct Finance Committee to draw on their connections in the business community. Rather than establish the group as a wholly separate entity operating at the expense of the party apparatus, the Finance Committee was established for the explicit purpose of raising funds for Republican Party operations.[30] Eisenhower also wanted former Citizens leaders to be embedded within the RNC leadership structure. "For help in the work of the National Committee," Ike wrote, "I would like to see [RNC Chairman] Len Hall . . . secure as his two principal deputies people like Walter Williams and Mary Lord," the two co-chairmen of Citizens for Eisenhower.[31] Williams and Lord soon assumed top positions inside the RNC.[32]

In the winter and spring of 1955, Eisenhower pushed his political advisers to "develop a program which would show the country that the Republican National Committee was sincerely endeavoring to bring Citizens for Eisenhower and other supporters of the President into Party organization."[33] To achieve "the President's desire to see that Citizens become new working Republicans," Citizens leaders and party leaders began to hash out the details of "merging" the two entities at the state and national levels.[34] By May, plans were set to bring Clancy Adamy, a thirty-eight-year-old former Citizens leader into the RNC as an assistant to the chairman and director of a new "Division for the Enrollment of New Republicans" within the RNC.[35] The new division would emphasize the recruitment of "younger members of communities," Hall announced.[36] The stated objective was "to expand the base of the Republican Party by encouraging former Citizens for Eisenhower workers to come into the party framework."[37]

Taken together, the new party committees and the Division for the Enrollment of New Republicans were part of a broader plan to "dramatize the open-door policy, i.e., that there is room for every American in the political activities carried on by the Republican Party."[38] Along with other organizational efforts, these programs aimed to implement Eisenhower's "overall plan for the changing of the Republican Party from a minority to a majority party."[39] By establishing a new formal division within the RNC framework and dedicating it to Citizens recruitment and youth outreach, Eisenhower institutionalized his efforts to grow the Republican Party and swell its ranks with his own supporters.

Eisenhower also used less formal methods. Many young businessmen were attracted to Eisenhower personally and to his "middle way" approach but were turned off by conservative Republicans in Congress. So Eisenhower frequently encouraged his friends in the business community to give young Republicans a chance to speak in public and to search their personal networks for quality young candidates to run for office as Republicans in order to plant the seeds for the party's future. In December 1953, Eisenhower asked one prominent businessman to "take advantage of every opportunity to put in a word, in any locality, in favor of virile, forward-looking, energetic, Republican candidates as opposed to the 'party-hack' type."[40] He also sent his own lists of men who might speak at partisan events: "To my mind they should ask for the 'comers' . . . meaning the kind I have just named. If they can't place such a person in the primary slot, at least they should get their secondary speaker from this group and he would, on the average, steal the show."[41] Though he met with mixed success, Eisenhower consistently sought to infuse the Republican Party with the "fire and energy" of young people. He continually directed his party chairmen to place these types of men "in critical positions" in the party, to involve them in new activities, and let them "start a cult of optimism and work" to carry the party forward. Integrating new networks of young, energetic, moderate Republicans into the party apparatus, Ike thought, would provide the "necessary horse power" for progress.[42]

Citizen leaders repeatedly sought Eisenhower's advice and support for their plans to build and sustain their network of extrapartisan groups, both for the 1956 reelection campaign and beyond. But Eisenhower consistently declined their overtures and urged them to join the Republican Party instead. In 1956, he directed that all reelection campaign activities be run through the RNC. On a few occasions, however, Eisenhower was tempted to strengthen the Citizens groups and leave the Republican Party behind. But he always revised his thoughts and encouraged Citizens to redirect their efforts to strengthening and "revitalizing" the Republican Party. After the second round of midterm GOP defeats in 1958, for example, Eisenhower was clearly struggling with the issue. Two Citizens leaders in California asked him for advice about what their organization ought to do in the future. In an original draft reply, which he never sent, Eisenhower revealed that he seriously considered giving the two leaders his explicit approval for their extrapartisan activities. His unsent draft read: "I would hope that your present organization might not only be kept alive, but strengthened. . . . As

the titale [*sic*] implies, 'Citizens for Eisenhower-Nixon' are not formally incorporated into any party. They choose to cast their votes, and, to win other
votes, for candidates of their own choice, rather than any party label." He
considered encouraging the Citizens leaders to maintain their independence:
"Citizens can build for itself a permanent organization of real strength that is
in sympathy with the regular Republican Party but is also able to attract In-
dependsn [*sic*] and like-minded Democrats."[43] But in the draft he ultimately
sent, instead of sending words of encouragement, Ike asked the Citizens
leaders to devote their energies to helping him rebuild the GOP. He knew
that they would not disband their organization, but he asked them to "suggest to your people that they work with the regular Republican Party in an
effort to reinvigorate and rebuild it."[44] The final draft reduced a meandering
six-page draft to a short three-paragraph note. Eisenhower had weighed his
options and elected to focus on building the Republican Party over other
alternatives.

Rebranding the Republican Party

Given the Republican Party's glaring electoral weaknesses during the 1950s,
it is not surprising that Eisenhower expressed great frustration with the party
throughout his two terms in office. Indeed, even during that brief moment
of unified Republican control, Eisenhower found Republican congressional
leaders to be so out of step with his "middle way" approach that he considered leaving the party and starting a new one from scratch. After Eisenhower
nominated moderate California Republican governor Earl Warren to the
Supreme Court, for example, he anticipated resistance from congressional
leaders. Such resistance, he wrote, might cause him to abandon the GOP
once and for all. On the basis of Warren's eminent qualifications, Eisenhower
wrote, his "confirmation should be immediate and overwhelming. If the Republicans as a body should try to repudiate him, I shall leave the Republican
Party and try to organize an intelligent group of Independents, no matter
how small."[45] Though Ike never pursued the idea, Adams explained that he
did weigh the pluses and minuses of such a strategy:

> Eisenhower's thoughts about a new political party . . . were confined to
> a few thinking-aloud sessions with me in the privacy of his office. . . .
> He was well aware of the dangerous confusion that might come from
> breaking up the two-party system. He recalled, too, how the third parties
> launched by Theodore Roosevelt and the elder Robert M. La Follette
> became one-man ventures rather than popular movements. Eisenhower

decided to go on hoping that the Republican Party could be changed by younger blood into a broader and more effective political force.[46]

When Citizens leader Lucius Clay pushed Eisenhower to make a decisive break with his party, Eisenhower argued that a reconstituted Republican Party offered a source of longevity for his political purposes that a thoroughly personalized party would not. He recorded in his diary: "Admittedly it was probably easier to personalize such an effort and therefore to use my name as an adjective in describing it ["Eisenhower Republicanism"]. But I pointed out that if we focused the whole effort on me as an individual then it would follow that in the event of my disability or death, the whole effort would collapse. This, I pointed out, was absurd. The idea is far bigger than any one individual."[47]

Eisenhower preferred the label "Modern Republicanism" to other alternatives but was not fully committed to that appellation. He also entertained "'Republicanism of the 20th Century' or '20th Century Republicanism,' or any other appropriate designation," and he told one friend that he considered using "Party of justice for all the people," but it was not "quite catchy or short enough, but it does indicate what I think should be our basic 'selling' effort."[48] Eisenhower never quite settled on a title with which he was entirely comfortable.

Nevertheless, Eisenhower's many supporters embraced Modern Republicanism, and by the end of 1956, Paul Hoffman estimated that "forty-two new state chairmen of the Republican Party are new, solid, Eisenhower men. Eighty-five of the 146 members of the National Committee of 1952 have been replaced by new faces. In state after state, the young men and women we first brought into politics through the Citizens for Eisenhower movement have begun to occupy commanding posts in the regular structure."[49] Eisenhower had successfully cleaned house and stocked the regular party apparatus with loyal followers. "The way we did it," RNC Chairman Meade Alcorn explained, "was to ask them [RNC members] to do a lot of things that they hadn't been asked to do before, and when they either didn't do them or said that they were not in a position to do them, it ultimately brought about the resignations or retirements of quite a few of them. And as a consequence, we got the average age on the National Committee rather dramatically reduced."[50]

The forward march of Modern Republicanism within the party structure produced a backlash in other corners of the party, however. By labeling and differentiating his philosophy, Eisenhower put on the defensive those who did not identify as such. Conservative Republicans argued that Eisenhower had only "contributed" to the party's "chaos" by "abjuring all theory, and personalizing his leadership of the party to the point of blurring beyond distinct recognition the principles on which Republicanism rests."[51] Instead of providing a set of ideas around which Republicans of all stripes could rally, Eisenhower's rebranding effort created resentments and hardened ideological divisions within the party.

As his second term began, Eisenhower was determined to push his efforts to new heights. As the first constitutionally mandated lame-duck president, his time was short, and yet he wrote, "I still have a job of re-forming and re-vamping the Republican Party."[52] If the party was to be remade into a majority party that could promote his brand of politics after he left office, Eisenhower believed, two things were necessary. First, the party would need to "adopt and live by" his Modern Republican philosophy, and second, "it must organize itself far better than it has in the past, particularly at the precinct, district and county levels. We have had a Party that I am afraid wanted to have too many generals and too few fighting men."[53] Building an organizational foundation for sustained party activity at the local level was essential:

> I firmly believe that to have a strong basis for the Modern Republicanism that will best represent the interests of all the people, the Party must build upward from the precinct, to the district, to the county and to the state level. Only on such a firm foundation can there be a permanent change. If people will work together, at all levels, the job can be done.[54]

In 1957, Eisenhower worked with Alcorn to hold a series of regional conferences for precisely these purposes. In addition to subcommittees dedicated to improving the party's organizational capacities, the regional conferences had focused discussions on "Republican Goals."[55] Held in April 1957, the conferences were followed up with parallel state conferences, county conferences, and a national wrap-up conference in June. Alcorn was responsible for coordinating the massive organizational undertaking, but it was all done under Eisenhower's watchful eye. "As a matter of fact," Alcorn told the RNC Executive Committee, "It was upon his insistence that the idea of carrying these conferences down to the county levels was put in . . . he said: 'This has my complete approval if you will go down to the county level and make them do the same thing there.'"[56]

Although Alcorn said he believed there was "a common denominator of belief running throughout the thinking of all Republicans," he still feared a rupture within the party. It would be a "catastrophe," Alcorn said, if "we let the discussion get to the point where we say, 'Well, there is one group over here and another group over here, and we have two parties within one.' . . . I hope it never happens."[57] But Alcorn and Eisenhower unwittingly brought the "catastrophe" on themselves. Operationally, the regional conferences were an unqualified success; held in all six regions of the United States, they brought together party leaders and members who, in many cases, had never before sat down together to discuss their problems and share their goals and ideas.[58] But they did not build the consensus Eisenhower had hoped. Instead of unifying the party in support of the administration, the conferences provided an opportunity for opponents to come together, hone their message, and challenge the president to embrace their more conservative positions. They vented their shared dissatisfaction with Eisenhower's budget proposal, farm policy, and other legislative initiatives. Newspapers reported the dissension with headlines such as "Party Heads Tell Alcorn of Unrest," "Alcorn Asks for Criticism and He Gets It," "Midwest GOP Snubs Eisenhower Plea," and "GOP Rift 'Approved.'" The *Washington Post* noted that the conferences evidenced the "obvious resistance" of local party leaders to the administration's moderation and encouraged the further organization of the opposition. The conferences brought "strong criticism" of Eisenhower's budget, "strong opposition" to federal school aid and grants-in-aid to the states, and "hostility" to farm-benefit limits.[59]

Senator Barry Goldwater's public break with the administration in early 1957 did not help matters; on the floor of the Senate, Goldwater assailed Eisenhower's failure to produce a balanced budget and declared that the president had perpetrated a "betrayal of the people's trust" by submitting a $71.8 billion budget. He reminded his audience of Eisenhower's pledge to cut spending, lower taxes, reduce the debt, and balance the budget. "It is curious," Goldwater said, "that the Administration's departure from its pledges to the American people should occur during what I believe will be the rather brief tenure of this splinterized concept of Republican philosophy."[60] Old-guard Republicans and McCarthyites praised Goldwater for "not hesitat[ing] to stand up for his beliefs."[61] The grassroots conservative discontent evident in the regional conferences, coupled with Goldwater's emergence as the "most articulate spokesman" for the conservative ideology, created the impression that "the prospects of conservatives capturing power are brighter today than at any time since 1952," wrote L. Brent Bozell in *National Review.*[62]

Alcorn tried to make the best of the situation at the wrap-up conference in Washington: "We asked you folks to let your hair down, and you were just wonderful. . . . You talked frankly. You told us what was the matter with us. . . . Out of that criticism and that self-examination ought to come a more united and stronger party."[63] But the regional conferences were clearly a consensus-building failure. They exposed the deep philosophical divisions in the party and left Eisenhower and Alcorn "in the position of trying to equate party division with party strength—a job that calls for more than an ordinary amount of political rationalization."[64] Though Eisenhower had successfully implemented a large party-building program to develop and articulate consensus party principles, by the end of the regional conferences the GOP was more divided than before.

Yet Eisenhower kept at it, even after Republicans lost twelve senate seats and forty-eight House seats in the 1958 elections. His efforts multiplied and became more urgent in the final years of his term. Among other initiatives, he formed a "Committee on Program and Progress" to articulate progressive Republican ideas for the 1960s; launched and then continually expanded "Operation Dixie," a major Republican Party effort to build party organizations in the South; and helped to fortify the party's organizational capacities through new grassroots organizing initiatives, several new fundraising programs, and an intensive, nationwide campaign training workshop.[65] At the RNC meeting in early 1959, he tried to rally the troops:

> I deeply regret that some people look upon our party as a kind of hibernating elephant who wakes with a mighty trumpet blast at election time and then rests calmly until the next campaign. Political activity must be a matter of unremitting effort. It must go on 365 days a year. . . . Immediately we must give the millions of Americans who look to the Republican Party for progressive leadership a clear understanding of our long-range objectives. . . . This demands constant attention to organization, to cooperation at all levels, to assuring that candidates are capable, vigorous, personable and dedicated; that finances are secured on a continuing and satisfactory basis; and that every Republican and every friend of Republicanism keep everlastingly at the job of recruiting for the party.[66]

At the same meeting, Goldwater made his own suggestion for how to rebuild the party after the devastation of 1958: "Let the Party quit copying the New Deal." Goldwater challenged Eisenhower to explain exactly what the GOP stood for.[67] Representative Richard Simpson, the chairman of the Republican Congressional Campaign Committee, called on Ike to "give us a statement of principles for which we can stand."[68]

Conservative Republicans used Eisenhower's party reinvigoration efforts to mobilize their supporters and develop a sharper conservative alternative of their own. In a direct response to the vague report issued by Eisenhower's "Committee on Program and Progress" announcing the party's goals for the next decade, conservative House Republicans delivered a series of speeches entitled "Meeting the Challenges of the Sixties"—an imitation of the Committee's theme—and introduced it into the *Congressional Record*. Their goal was to "clarify the differences in party responses to the challenges of the 1960s."[69] Goldwater and Bozell's *The Conscience of a Conservative* was published in April 1960 and quickly became a bestselling title; the articulation of conservative ideas had taken off, partly as a reaction against Eisenhower's rebranding efforts.

The ensuing years witnessed the blossoming of conservative organizations that were motivated by the chance, at long last, to repudiate Modern Republicanism and nominate an authentically conservative presidential candidate who would be *unlike* Ike. Conservative Republicans rejected Nixon, whose overtures to Nelson Rockefeller and Henry Cabot Lodge for the vice presidential nomination seemed to demonstrate his inability to dissociate from the "New Deal imitators." After the 1960 election, Goldwater proclaimed that Nixon had lost to John F. Kennedy because he was "not Republican enough."[70] Conservatives marshaled their troops, consolidated their support, took control of the demoralized party structure, and nominated Goldwater as the party's nominee for president in 1964.

Conclusion

Over the course of Dwight Eisenhower's eight years in office, his party's competitive standing went from bad to worse. This posed a serious threat to his legacy: Without a strong majority to sustain and perpetuate his commitments into the future, his "Modern Republican" or "middle way" philosophy was susceptible to vanishing upon his exit from the national political scene. It also made Eisenhower worry (correctly) that his party's electoral woes would create an opening for right-wing forces to capture the party and push it in a more conservative direction, thus relegating Eisenhower and his personal brand of politics to the dustbin of history. Those potentialities created a powerful incentive for Eisenhower to take action. Rather than accept his structural constraints as fixed, Eisenhower became determined to *change* them by rebuilding and rebranding his party. He stacked his party structure with "Citizens for Eisenhower" activists; elevated young, moderate businessmen to positions of political prominence; replaced holdover national committeemen with self-identified Modern Republicans; sought to build a consensus around the "middle way"; and launched numerous initiatives to repair the party's organizational machinery.

At the structural level of the party, Eisenhower's party-building efforts were an unqualified success. His initiatives enhanced the party's capacities by strengthening its fundraising systems, candidate recruitment processes, publicity programs, activist enrollment efforts, and campaign operations. In the ensuing three decades, those investments gradually multiplied and expanded the party's organizational capacities, enabling it to provide a wider range of services for its candidates and officeholders.[71] Eisenhower's consensus-building initiatives, however, were unqualified failures. Rather than forge party-wide agreement around his favored center-right policy prescriptions, his efforts spurred conservatives to articulate a sharper alternative to both New Deal liberalism and what they called Eisenhower's "me-tooism."[72] Forced to play the role of the foil to the growing conservative movement, Eisenhower unwittingly contributed to his party's rightward drift. Indeed, it seems safe to conclude that had Eisenhower not undertaken his numerous party building and rebranding initiatives, conservatives would not have been as determined to rush the party structure when they did or in the way they did. Eisenhower's efforts may therefore be seen as a necessary condition for the *timing* and *form* of the party's right turn in the late 1950s and 1960s.[73] In other words, though Eisenhower failed to achieve his substantive objectives, his party-building efforts had important downstream consequences: They helped to alter the Republican Party's trajectory and contributed to the emergence of sharper ideological cleavages and new axes of contention in American politics.

Standard measures of "presidential success" (legislative scorecards, the proximity of policy outcomes to the president's ideal point, appraisals of presidential "skill") completely miss out on these important effects. Yet if we are to develop a fuller and more accurate picture of Eisenhower (or any president) and his place in history, we must not only compare his aims to his outcomes and appraise his behavior, we must also consider his historical and political significance—that is, his impact on things like his party's trajectory and the course of American political development more broadly. The usual standards of evaluation, in other words, are in need of modification and refinement.

The Eisenhower presidency offers a hard test of the theoretical proposition outlined above. If our expectations hold in this unlikely setting, there is reason to think they may hold in more likely settings as well. A political novice, Eisenhower was an unlikely party builder; yet he waded into the thicket of partisan politics and sought to rebuild his party's structure, reshape its ideas, and renovate its membership and leadership. Purposeful, forward-looking action of this sort, I have argued, is likely to occur when presidents perceive their historical legacy to be at risk. Rather than simply work with or around the political structure as they find it, presidents so situated are likely to try to reshape their political constraints. Party-building is one way in which they may do it.

This paper examines only one case. As such, it can confirm the plausibility of the theoretical proposition and recommend further investigation, but that is all it can do. Further tests are needed against a wider range of cases. For example, as I have discussed elsewhere, *every* Republican president in the modern period pursued strikingly similar party-building efforts as Eisenhower, while every Democratic president exhibited precisely the opposite behaviors.[74] More empirical work is needed, however, if we are to move beyond the taken-for-granted assumptions of *presidential myopia* and *fixed constraints* that motivate most of the political science literature on the presidency.

In what other circumstances might presidents take the long view and purposefully attempt to alter their structural confines? Which structural constraints do they choose to confront? Which resources do they bring to bear on their transformative projects? What downstream consequences do their actions have? Some good candidates for further study might include the federal bureaucracy, the law, and the media, but the list surely does not end there. Examining the dynamics at play in different settings should enhance our understanding of the incentives and constraints presidents face in different contexts. It should also enable us to treat with more confidence presidents as formative actors in American political development who not only ride, but also seek to steer, the course of history.

CHAPTER 12

American Presidential Authority and Economic Expertise since World War II

MICHAEL A. BERNSTEIN

Victory in World War II and the subsequent prosecution of the Cold War involved the forging of a unique link between international objectives and domestic policy goals in the United States. This altogether unprecedented agenda served to transform the nature of the American presidency and its relationship with professional social scientists, especially with economists. Maintaining large military deployments around the world and pursuing an aggressive strategy of containment against Soviet and Chinese interests posed significant political, economic, and operational challenges for the federal government. The resultant bipartisan pursuit of relatively enormous amounts of peacetime public spending was the essential economic ingredient not only of the military success of the Cold War but also of the rise of the mixed economy of the post–World War II era.

On the one side, massive allocations of public resources to military-industrial procurement and force deployments played a key role in driving the Soviet economy (and military) into oblivion. On the other, Cold War spending became the central political practice supporting an increasingly active commitment by Washington to economic and social programs at home that fostered employment growth and business-cycle stabilization. The pursuit of this remarkable strategy of linking imperial dominion to domestic growth powerfully framed a new relationship between the Office of the President and the professional policy sciences. What powerfully linked the American presidency with a historically unprecedented activism in the social sciences was first and foremost political in nature. The Cold War era was in large measure defined by a broad level of agreement between the two major political parties—a virtual consensus that tied government spending on overseas initiatives (diplomatic, economic, and military) to domestic countercyclical policies focused on high employment and robust growth in the gross domestic product (GDP). Underlying this circumstance was, of course, the blurring of party differences wrought by the beginnings of the Cold War itself—along with the marginalization of the right by the 1940s victory of the Allied Powers over fascism and the 1950s suppression of the left by the unrelenting momentum of McCarthyism.

Even so, a unique engagement of presidential authority with economic expertise, which accomplished so much in the 1960s and 1970s, proved immensely fragile in the face of the political and economic turmoil of the 1980s. The consequences of that ironic turn of events manifest themselves to this day—both in the actions of a professional community increasingly separated from the public sphere in which it once played such a dramatic role and in the growing inability of American presidents to explain, motivate, and implement economic and social policy of genuine coherence and impact. It is in the narrative of the history of national economic policy and the American presidency that this reality is so strikingly revealed.

It was the economy's performance in the last quarter of 1965 that forecast the end of both the nation's unprecedented postwar affluence and the unique contexts in which fiscal interventionism had seemed so straightforward. During those three months, GDP increased by the largest amount in history; the danger signs were to be found in the behavior of the price level. Within a year, the rate of inflation rose to almost 3 percent, increased to just under 4 percent by the second half of 1967, and accelerated toward 4.5 percent by the middle of 1968. Rising prices not only damaged the economy's vitality but also eroded the ability of the executive branch to manage macroeconomic performance through timely intervention. Through the 1970s and 1980s, this harsh political economic reality was made vivid.

On its face, the proximate cause of the inflationary spiral that unhinged the balanced the growth of the 1960s was the escalating fiscal burden of the Vietnam War. Excessively stimulated by a military mobilization that occurred at precisely the time that major domestic spending initiatives were also beginning, the national economy of the 1960s strained to operate efficiently at its capacity ceiling. And the failure to finance the Vietnam War through appropriate tax policies led directly to the increasing federal deficits of the late 1960s. Yet military expenditures were not solely responsible for the continued fiscal imbalance that spanned the 1970s. Indeed, of the $86 billion by which federal spending rose from 1969 through 1973, almost $78 billion were allocated to "transfer payments" such as Social Security, Medicare, housing assistance, and educational subsidies.

The rapid rise in world oil prices that began in October 1973 served to derange completely the economic mechanisms that had been the foundation of the "mixed private-public" economic policymaking of the postwar era and also, relatedly, of an unprecedented degree of presidential activism in economic affairs. The "Great Society" programs and military spending became easy targets in a process of political retrenchment that would ultimately span the remainder of the century and beyond. As the economic logic of fiscal activism was dismantled by events, the entire political terrain on which economic policy and presidential actions were directed toward economic outcomes was decisively transformed. After the 1970s, no American president would have the opportunity to intervene in and manage macroeconomic performance in the dramatic fashion that had emerged right after World War II.

It was of course not simply the undisciplined financing of war that had placed the government's economic policy initiatives in such frustrating and disturbing straits. Domestic initiatives had also brought pressure to bear on the Treasury that further bedeviled the efforts of experts to keep the economy on a balanced and measured course. In his determination to erect "a social consciousness in concrete," President Lyndon Johnson was entirely unreceptive to policy proposals that, to his mind, ran the risk of depleting the fund for his Great Society programs. Despite his apparent awareness of the need for a tax increase as early as 1966, for example, the president worried that placing a surcharge bill before the Congress would simply provide social conservatives the ammunition they needed to dismantle the structures of reform. Indeed, in that year, rather than embrace the increasing anxieties of his chief economic advisers, Johnson instead secured a $290 million increase in the budget for the Office of Economic Opportunity (OEO), the primary institutional venue for the prosecution of his "War on Poverty." Even though he understood that the "fiscal situation is abominable," he was absolutely committed to preserving the domestic liberalism that was the defining characteristic of his presidency.[1]

Conservatives were more than willing, therefore, to blame the nation's enduring fiscal problems in the wake of the Vietnam era on the Great Society programs themselves. That the war had destabilized federal finance from the start and, more to the point, that conservatives had refused to underwrite the war adequately unless domestic spending programs were drastically cut was conveniently forgotten. In point of fact, transfer disbursements were just that—the reallocation of tax receipts from one set of citizens to another.

Using Vietnam as a political weapon against the president, conservatives in the Congress succeeded in separating such transfer commitments from their tax base. Political expediency aside, this revolt against New Deal liberalism became especially potent precisely because the logic of Keynesianism—that the intertemporal flexibility of public finance could both stimulate growth and ultimately requite its debts—was subverted at its source.[2]

Ironically enough, while the careful judgments and prognostications of the highest-ranking economists in the Council of Economic Advisors (CEA), the Bureau of the Budget, and the Treasury were ignored, the technical skills of other professionals were used to further the dimensions of Johnson's social programs. Having witnessed, for example, the successful implementation of the Planning, Programming, and Budgeting System (PPBS) at the Pentagon, the president insisted that similar methods be employed at OEO and other domestic agencies. Political and military considerations might interfere with the utilization of an unalloyed expertise when it came to worrying about growth rates and inflation; at the more middling federal echelons, by contrast, state-of-the-art professional methods were welcome and encouraged. If the economy could not be "fine-tuned" by its most visible advisers, nonetheless the constituent parts of the executive branch bureaucracy could be as well managed as contemporary professional practice might allow.[3]

Wishful thinking cannot of course last forever; the imperatives of arithmetic ultimately forced the president's hand, his fear that a request for a tax surcharge would encourage the right wing in Congress to demand domestic spending cuts in exchange notwithstanding. It was not a Republican opponent but rather the Democratic chair of the House Ways and Means Committee, Wilbur Mills of Arkansas, who made Johnson's anxious expectation a reality. By the fall of 1967, Mills succeeded in bottling up in his committee the proposed 10 percent tax increase that the White House had reluctantly been forced to send to the Hill. The wrangling over spending cuts as political payment for the tax increase continued for months; the surtax itself did not go into effect until almost a year later. By that point, the inflationary momentum of the economy had reached a magnitude well beyond the corrective potential of what had become a rather timid gesture toward fiscal rectitude.[4]

Although subsequent events, the rapid rise in world oil prices that began in October 1973 most prominent among them, would make the inflation of the late 1960s seem quite modest in retrospect, the ineffectiveness of the 1968 income tax surcharge marked the beginning of the most unstable economic performance witnessed in the United States since the Great Depression. Inflation, which accelerated throughout the late 1960s and 1970s, was now easily (if inaccurately) viewed as the direct result of fiscal intervention-ism and "big government." Military miscalculation and dissembling; political grandstanding; Cold War ideology taken to an extreme that was as unprec-edented as it was undebated; a Congress denied the opportunity to consider a formal declaration of war; and (perhaps most importantly) the determination of Washington conservatives to hold effective economic policy hostage to an anti–Great Society agenda accompanied by an equal determination by liber-als to refuse the ransom demand—all these essential ingredients of the "fiscal fiasco" were resolutely forgotten.

By 1970, as a consequence, the entire analytical framework most Ameri-can economists and presidents used to think about policy matters had thus dramatically changed. The postwar expansion that had left the national economy globally dominant was fast proving itself at an end—nowhere more strikingly than in the nation's factories. Early in the 1950s, American manufacturing had generated levels of output roughly four times that of its nearest competitors; investment in the industrial sector had been greater than in the rest of the world, total employment virtually twice as large as that of Britain and even greater with reference to Japan. In 1969, national employ-ment in manufacturing began to shrink from a bit over fourteen million workers to just under twelve million by 1986. Rates of growth in output similarly trended downward; by 1980 the United States was producing less than 30 percent of the world's manufactured goods, a share much reduced from the 40 percent levels achieved in the early 1960s. A comparable dete-rioration took place in the American share of world manufacturing exports. From the time Johnson assumed the presidency to the celebration of the nation's bicentennial, the proportion fell by a fifth.

Coupled with the inflationary environment created by the Vietnam War, changes in the world oil market in the early 1970s further weakened the American economy and eviscerated most of the prosperity bequeathed by the New Frontier and the Great Society. A poorly performing economy further weakened presidential authority in macroeconomic policymaking. When on October 17, 1973, the Organization of the Petroleum Exporting Countries (OPEC) announced its intention to cut production by 5 per-cent per month for the next two years, worldwide energy prices took off. Crude prices immediately rose by two-thirds; in January 1974 they doubled. Not surprisingly, as a result, average annual inflation rates for the national economy throughout the 1970s stood at roughly 9 percent. For the decade 1972–1982, it is estimated that the increase in the American cost of living rose by approximately 133 percent. Poor crop yields in 1971 and 1972 due to drought conditions in the nation's agricultural regions only made the inflationary spiral worse. As the costs of production accelerated upward, the national unemployment rate also began to rise; from almost 5 percent in 1973, it increased to a bit over 8 percent of the labor force two years later. By 1982 that rate rose toward 10 percent. For the 1970s, the decennial average was just below 7 percent. Within a very short time, the American economy now exhibited the worst of both worlds—high inflation and high unemployment. Professional economists and the presidents they had served had every reason to be perplexed.[5]

The OPEC price shock, while different in form and etiology, had many of the same consequences as the 1929 New York stock market debacle. Real incomes fell dramatically. The values of bank, private, and corporate investment portfolios were seriously imperiled. With consumer and investor confidence dealt a serious blow, aggregate investment declined as firms became less confident about the future and households postponed major expenditures. Profit margins shrank as the costs of production rose. Capacity utilization and employment consequently declined as well. The cumulative oil price increases of the 1970s also had a devastating impact on the national balance of international payments—a $40 billion deficit in fuel imports alone emerged by decade's end. Macroeconomic growth rates deteriorated. This combination of apparent stagnation and high inflation gave rise to a new entry in the manual of economic pathology—"stagflation." With this novel malady defined, economists and pundits alike also devised a new diagnostic—the "misery index," a sum of the rates of inflation and unemployment. Throughout most of the 1970s that index hovered around the 20 percent range; its disconcerting message helped lay the foundations for a major transformation in American economic policy and in the economic role of American presidents for decades to come.[6]

As the macroeconomic volatility of the 1970s worsened, the intellectual foundation of economic policy similarly shifted and with it the interventionist policy options available to the nation's presidents. The academic consensus that appeared to have framed federal government intervention in the national economy had been an essential ingredient of the sway and influence that postwar presidents had enjoyed in policy debates. As that apparent foundation of agreement was undermined by the impact of real events, the authority of the chief executive was accordingly reduced. With the demise of the Bretton Woods system of fixed exchange rates and with the perceived disappearance of a determinate quantitative relationship tying high unemployment rates to lower inflation, confidence in the Keynesian revolution in economic thought also diminished. Whatever ingredients might have existed for a consensus among policy analysts dissolved. Spending by the government was increasingly excoriated, although countercyclical action was now condemned not so much for its alleged inflationary bias as for its possibly negative impacts on the incentives for risk-bearing and productive behavior in the marketplace. As noted by one astute observer of the American economic profession, himself a vigorous and accomplished champion of Keynesian methodology, by 1980 it was very difficult indeed "to find an American academic macroeconomist under the age of 40 who professed to be a Keynesian." Thus was accomplished "an astonishing intellectual turnabout in less than a decade."[7]

To be sure, the end of a Keynesian consensus, such as had existed among American economists at the time, was not solely a scholarly enterprise. After all, acceptance of interventionist fiscal policy in the early 1960s had been linked with the emergence of a majority political coalition supportive of both increased defense spending and the implementation of redistributive measures linked with civil rights reform. As that bipartisan association was for a variety of political and social reasons undermined, the commitment to Keynesianism waned as well. Yoked to a reaction against redistribution and federalism was thus a vigorous and cogent revival of old-fashioned policy thinking. Classical monetary theory, so inspired by the work of Milton Friedman, reemerged as a powerful and legitimate counterpart to the wisdom and learning of what had been the New Economics of the 1960s.

If rapid inflation subverted the political foundations of a successful Keynesianism and of activist presidents, it also directly challenged the intellectual authority of the New Economics by demonstrating the inability of spending policy to halt the rise in the cost of living. Indeed, throughout much of the 1970s and 1980s, Keynesian theorists could propose little in the way of anti-inflation measures other than what some have called "fiscalism in reverse"—the reduction of public expenditures as a whole. This allowed for a monetarist proposal for the elimination of countercyclical spending and the imposition of fixed (and preannounced) policy targets for key monetary variables (most importantly the rate of growth in the money supply itself) to take center stage in Washington. Keynes's General Theory of economic processes was thus relegated to the status of a specific argument concerning the Great Depression; it was hardly applicable, in the mind of a new generation of specialists, to an altogether novel situation in which high inflation, high unemployment, and low growth rates all prevailed at the same time. In place of Keynes's apparently outmoded message, late-twentieth-century American economists sought to erect an altogether new paradigm.[8]

Once the battle ensign of a supremely confident social science community enlisted in the service of the state, Keynesianism by the late 1960s served as a gravestone for the dashed expectations of activist presidents and of the New Economists. With the blueprint for economic statecraft in tatters, investigators turned their attention to the reconstruction of first principles. If even the increasingly apparent failure of fiscal interventionism had little to do with analytical errors and far more to do with political manipulation, it was necessary nonetheless to rescue economics from the nonscientific discourse of partisan debate and refashion the rigor and reliability that had made the field one of the great academic success stories of the century. It was in this context that a "new classical macroeconomics" came to dominate the professional literature. This "new macroeconomics" proposed an emphasis on expectations formation as the key to understanding economic mechanisms rather than the fallacy of composition that Keynes himself had believed to be the essential axiom of modern social theory.[9] And it served to undermine the very idea of macroeconomic management that had transformed the presidency in the wake of the New Deal.

So eager were mainstream economists to disassociate themselves from the purported inadequacies of Keynesian theory that, in very large numbers, they uncritically embraced a simple, some critics would ultimately say tautological, assumption—the "rational expectations" hypothesis. Central to this proposition was the idea that market actors would behave in conformity with a "rational" assessment of all available information. If this were true, all economic outcomes—prices, wages, interest rates—were necessarily the result of the sum total of individual actions that were themselves premised on a cogent and self-seeking prediction of possible market results. In other words, market movements (whether in individual sectors or for the economy as a whole) obtained as a result of individual behaviors guided by informed calculation. Economic performance was thus the result of the rationally generated expectations of individuals; to be otherwise, such individual behaviors could not be rational. The circularity of the argument garnered less comment than the seemingly powerful analytical tools it could provide in the pursuit of a new scientific macroeconomics.[10]

The recasting of the theoretical bearing and public influence of American economists in the years after the Vietnam War did not, of course, take place in a vacuum. Independent of the technical skirmishes that punctuated the pages of leading journals and inflamed the proceedings of many conferences, the controversies in which the profession's mainstream now found itself caught up drew much of their brio from political contests transacted on a much larger stage. High unemployment and rapid inflation, owing to the material insecurity and deprivation they caused, served as accelerants for a political blaze that would ultimately consume much of the social initiatives of the New Frontier and the Great Society. A backlash against civil rights reform magnified by the fear and anger that emerged from the urban insurrections of the late 1960s and that only hardened as the coalition for change grew to include immigration and homosexual rights activists; counterattacks upon a resurgent feminism; intergenerational strife that had for several years pitted young against old and that ultimately portrayed the student movements of the 1960s as the worst manifestation of an undisciplined, hedonistic, and coddled youth duped by the New Left; and the growing wariness of both the corporate world and much of organized labor regarding the goals of environmental protection—all of these were essential ingredients in a rightward shift in the national political spectrum that proved as decisive a force in the transformation of American economic policy practice as any scholarly argument.

If a late-twentieth-century American politics of reaction and resentment rested on foundations that far transcended matters of economic doctrine and practice, conservative rhetoric successfully cast government as the patron of liberal reform that had overstepped its bounds. An immensely powerful link could then be drawn between economic instability, on the one side, and statist interventionism, on the other. An adroit if disingenuous tactic was this, for it played on substantial middle-class anxieties about tax burdens while at the same time avoiding any honest reckoning with the proximate causes of a volatile price level and a slack labor market. Resolutely ignored were the predominantly exogenous sources of the era's persistent inflation, and the attendant unemployment it fostered —for instance, runaway Pentagon spending during the Vietnam War, poor crop yields in the wake of an extraordinary period of drought, and the manipulation of the world oil market by a powerful and determined cartel. Conservative rhetoric could nonetheless frame the economic turmoil of the times as a direct outgrowth of an overgrown and irresponsible public sector. When coupled with the cynicism and outrage cultivated by the scandals that surrounded Washington after Republican Party operatives broke into the Democratic National Committee's Watergate offices in the spring of 1972—events that led two years later to President Richard Nixon's forced resignation under threat of impeachment—the avenging contentions became virtually irresistible.[11] And thus the ability of American presidents to manage the national macroeconomy was lost.

Misery loves company. By the mid-1970s, conservative politicians desperate to reverse the high tide of federal interventionism epitomized by the New Frontier and the Great Society, middle-class Americans increasingly hard-pressed by deteriorating incomes and rising taxes, and an array of constituencies determined to strike back at the liberal reforms of the preceding two decades found common cause in economic reaction. Two specific developments during 1978, each rooted in what were perceived to be the past failures of public policy, signaled the beginning of a return to economic practices that predated the New Deal. One was a popular movement, termed a "taxpayers' revolt," to limit government spending and tax revenues by statute. While the ultimate goal of this mobilization, the ratification of a constitutional amendment requiring balanced federal budgets, remains unrealized to this day, certain notable successes at the state and local level gave its leaders heart. Almost certainly the most influential of these triumphs was the 1978 passage of a statewide proposition in California that limited property tax assessments. As momentum gained at the local level, national leaders jumped on the bandwagon of economy in government in order to push further proposals that would inflexibly limit federal employment and spending.[12]

The second development resulted from the battering of the dollar in foreign exchange markets that emerged after Richard Nixon left office. Holders of dollars worldwide sold them in large amounts throughout the late 1970s because they feared that American economic policies would continue to cause "stagflation," weak capital formation, and limited real economic growth. In response, the Federal Reserve Board moved to support the dollar through monetary stringency, and President Jimmy Carter promulgated a wide-ranging program that included voluntary guidelines for wage and price increases, further measures to support the dollar's international value, and a renewed pledge to hold down government employment and spending in order to reduce large federal deficits. All of these initiatives expressed a growing belief among some national leaders and many voters that government policies requiring significant spending, deficit financing, and money creation (to ease the interest rate pressures that deficits would otherwise create) were more a cause of economic instability than a cure.[13]

Ronald Reagan's stunning landslide victory over Jimmy Carter in the 1980 presidential election formally signaled the transition from Keynes-style demand management in Washington to the allegedly new, yet in fact strikingly old, strategies of "supply-side economics." Believing that the fundamental source of the problems facing the contemporary American economy had to do with supply problems rather than demand fluctuations, the supply-side theorists focused their policy proposals on the means by which macroeconomic supply conditions might be improved. Increasing the output of goods and services, it was presumed, would alleviate the twin problems of stagnation and inflation that had troubled the economy since the late 1960s.

Supply-side theory drew attention to what were believed to be the distortions created by high levels of government spending, high taxation of income, and extensive governmental regulation of economic affairs. Excessive income taxation, it was argued, stifled productive effort, for example, by discouraging overtime work. It robbed individuals of the fruits of enterprise and risk-bearing. Finally, it distorted economic decisionmaking so as to slow growth and create the very fiscal pressures that had contributed to the problems of "stagflation" in the first instance. The solution would involve a radical reduction in taxes, a systematic shrinking of government spending programs and thus federal agency budgets, and the elimination of costly regulatory measures.

In February 1981, the new Reagan administration presented its "Program for Economic Recovery" to the Congress. Inspired by the arguments of supply-side economists, the proposal called for the control of federal spending, the reduction or elimination of a wide variety of social entitlement and redistributive plans that had their roots in the politics of the New Frontier and the Great Society, and the aggressive reduction of tax rates on incomes. In particular, it called for 10 percent annual reductions in marginal income tax rates for three years beginning in the summer of 1981. Along with this economic platform, the president's program also provided for the implementation of investment incentives for private business (by means of accelerated depreciation schedules), for the streamlining or elimination of a host of regulatory codes, and for monetary stringency. The hope, along with the expectation that such measures would stimulate growth through investment, jobs creation, and greater labor productivity, was that the federal budget might be balanced within three years; the associated savings on interest payments and a decrease of the loanable funds shortages caused by the massive government presence in the nation's capital markets would be the most immediate benefits of the new policies.

By August, the Economic Recovery Tax Act became law, implementing, in the form of income tax reduction, a major component of the supply-side protocol. Over the next three years, major cuts were also made in such federal programs as unemployment insurance, food stamps, Aid to Families with Dependent Children, Medicaid, student loans, retirement benefits, grants for mass transportation, and benefits to import-affected industries. Paralleling these transformations in fiscal policy was a strict anti-inflationary monetary posture. The results were mixed. On the one side, inflation was strikingly reduced. From 9 percent in 1981, the annual rate of increase in the price level fell to 3.5 percent by the end of Reagan's first presidential term. Unemployment, after rising to 9.7 percent in 1982, fell to 7.5 percent in 1984–85 and to

5 percent by the end of 1988. Yet consistent with their belief that an "inflation threshold" existed, Reagan administration officials did not seek to press job idleness below the 1988 mark. In this, what came to be known as "Reaganomics" sharply distinguished itself from the Keynesian-style full-employment commitments of both its Democratic and Republican predecessors.

During the 1980 presidential campaign, Ronald Reagan had asked members of the American electorate if they were better off (then) than they had been four years earlier. For a vast majority, this had been a most persuasive rhetorical quip, given that the rates of inflation and unemployment had remained so high throughout the Carter presidency itself. The passionate response that Reagan's interrogatory evoked expressed itself almost entirely in an anti-statist fashion; in the highly charged political environment of the 1980 campaign, tax reduction became not an instrument of countercyclical policy tooled by a professional expertise but rather a symbol of relief for a populace hard-pressed by economic instability itself. Far from being a measured response to unemployment and excess capacity, as had been the case with the "Kennedy round" of tax cuts in the early 1960s, the downward revision of the revenue schedules undertaken in 1981 was a crude sop in an election year. No doubt Keynes himself would have been appalled at this opportunistic manipulation of what he had believed to be one of the finer achievements of a "general theory" of economics. That the Reagan tax cuts were disproportionately favorable to the wealthiest segments of society and thus at variance with the redistributive objectives of Keynesian practice was simply another manifestation of their distorted intent.[14]

At the same time that the first round of Reagan tax cuts was implemented, the largest peacetime increase of American armed forces and weapons systems began. Indeed, the stimulatory impacts of so unrestrained an indulgence in federal spending prompted many supply-side advocates to claim (erroneously) that the tax-cut strategy had done its job. So dramatic was President Reagan's military buildup, a strategy epitomized by his determination to create a six-hundred-ship navy, that by the end of the 1980s the national economy allocated close to $300 billion annually to the Pentagon—an increase of approximately 120 percent for the decade as a whole. The fiscal consequences of defense spending in the 1980s were such that the purported budgetary benefits of supply-side economics could never be measured. During the first Reagan term, the annual federal deficit grew from 2.7 percent to 5.2 percent of GDP. If fiscal balance had been the central promise of the new departures in policy practice undertaken in 1981, the federal ledger by 1983 had become an indelible record of failure. By 1989, the total national debt stood at some $2 trillion; in this regard, Ronald

Reagan stood unchallenged as one of the most profligate peacetime spenders in the history of the republic.[15]

Perhaps it was fitting that supply-side theory had painted itself into the corner of federal deficits, much as the New Economics had done. Indeed, the entire idea of peacetime military expansion after World War II had been sold in part to the Congress and local public officials on the basis of all the resources and funding that would flow their way. Military bases brought jobs to local communities and profits to local businesses. Defense spending in general created better-paying jobs that provided higher purchasing power for the other products of domestic industry. Compensatory demand management, in fact, had counted in its bag of tools the potentially stabilizing influence of Pentagon procurement (not to mention of other public goods disbursements) in the face of the business cycle. Seven successive post–New Deal presidential administrations had also embraced that logic. The exigencies of the Cold War had combined with the domestic politics of the "mixed economy" to forge that kind of bipartisan commitment to public spending. Why should Reaganomics have been any different?

Yet it was, in ways that were quite profound. Keynesian-style demand management had always grounded itself on the assumption that budget deficits incurred in bad times would be redeemed with higher tax receipts in the boom. Moreover, as a surging economy approached its capacity ceiling, the reimposition of higher tax rates would be justified as an instrument of further stability. In stark contrast, Reaganomics made no such claim upon the future. Tax reduction as a political strategy, especially when coupled with increased spending on federal operations such as defense, carried no guarantees of subsequent restoration. Quite the contrary. To the extent that revenue cuts became fixed by a kind of political inertia and insofar as the tax base itself had been more or less permanently eroded by reductions in tax rates themselves, the very tools of Keynesian fiscal policy were blunted. Thus it was, in an exquisite historical irony, that Ronald Reagan's immediate successors in the White House—George H. W. Bush and William Clinton—faced the sheer impossibility of implementing countercyclical fiscal measures even if they had wished to do so. In this sense, although the Reagan administration practiced a kind of accidental Keynesianism in its dramatic expansion of military spending while at the same time reducing federal taxes, supply-side economics did unambiguously achieve one particular policy objective: It made the future use of Keynesian spending policies entirely problematic, if not impossible.

Warnings about the absolute magnitude of the national debt, deployed as justifications for anti-Keynesian policy initiatives, had been well-worn canards. Often accused of simply espousing a reckless overspending agenda that would lead to permanent indebtedness, Keynesian analysts could not repeat often enough their view that just as taxes should be cut in recession, they should be raised in robust expansion. They were similarly ignored when they pointed out that timely growth stimulation today would yield higher incomes and wealth tomorrow from which greater tax receipts could be earned at lower proportionate cost. Suggestions that it was not the size of the national debt but the share of the domestic product it represented that was the crucial policy variable also fell on deaf ears.

So thorough had been the disgrace of Keynesianism that the most rigorous appeals to common sense and evidence in defense of the New Economics, not to mention the indications of the failures of Reaganomics, came to nothing. Even thoughtful liberal Democratic allies in the Congress, enacting on an individual basis what ultimately happened to the economic principles that animated their party as a whole, mouthed the rhetoric of supply-side theory. Nine months before Ronald Reagan's first election to the presidency, Senator William Proxmire of Wisconsin took the New Economists to task for positions that could "not be justified either politically or economically." Furious that federal shortfalls had not ultimately been made good by surpluses, he told Arthur Okun that "neither the President, the Congress, nor the public can accept the consensus of the professional economists that a deficit is justified in almost every year." In Proxmire's view, "to maintain its credibility," the profession had to "do better than that." Okun's retort, that "elected officials" had to "do better than climbing on bandwagons of uninformed public opinion," was a clear indication of a professional community's growing ineffectuality.[16] It was also a powerful acknowledgment of the serious erosion that had taken place with regard to presidential authority over economic affairs.

Cutting the tax lifeline of federal economic policy practice during the 1980s was as effective a conservative strategy of political retrenchment as it was manipulative of public sentiment. In place of the Keynesian argument that more equitably distributed incomes and wealth, effected by the tax system itself, would generate higher aggregate consumption and thus more robust economic growth, the "new classical" economists posed a simpler view of the market system. Tax cuts, which would necessarily place proportionately more discretionary income in the hands of the wealthiest portions of the population, would, they claimed, encourage investment, which in turn would enhance employment. Thus would the benefits of fiscal austerity "trickle down" through the income distribution. That greater tax savings for the rich would stimulate investment was a proposition that directly contravened Keynes's claim that it was investment, through its impact on employment and production (and thus incomes), that ultimately caused rises in savings. Overall, taxes could thus be condemned as the mortal enemy of the incentives to work and to invest. Lost from view was the Keynesian rejoinder that judicious tax policy, through the enhancement of consumption and investment it would procure, could guarantee the profits of enterprise and thereby the prosperity of the whole.[17]

One phrase perhaps best summarizes the origins, consequences, and legacies of the contemporary economic policy environment that now confronts every American president: tax cuts. The passion for tax cuts as a kind of "holy grail" of a "new classical" economics has been so intense that even the major political parties, since the end of Ronald Reagan's second presidential term, find little about which to disagree on that score. All that has been left is political posturing for targeted constituencies. For the Republicans this has meant emphasizing the usefulness of tax reduction for upper-income groups and the broadening of the argument to include proposals for reductions in the prevailing levy on capital gains; for the Democrats the riposte has been to focus on what has beguilingly been labeled "middle class tax relief." Both parties have flirted with radical suggestions to eliminate the entire structure of income taxation itself—usually toying with half-baked ideas concerning the implementation of a single (or "flat") rate income tax or a national sales (or "value added") tax. With genuine justification, an observer new to the scene might conclude that John Maynard Keynes (not to mention his like-minded colleagues and students) had never published a word.[18]

Like most nostrums, tax reduction policies have created more problems than they have solved. Federal spending, whether engrossed by military initiatives such as those undertaken during the Reagan presidency or propelled by transfer-payment programs long on the books, rose in both absolute terms and on a per-capita basis throughout the 1980s and early 1990s. A rising national debt then only made more obvious the failures (and the failings) of supply-side economics and its attendant pieties. It is hardly surprising, therefore, that conservatives consistently focused their attention on disbursements themselves. Within this context thus arose a recurring offensive against economic statecraft itself, the continuation of an attack originally launched by the Reagan tax cuts—the proposal for a balanced budget amendment to the United States Constitution.[19]

A hardy perennial in the garden of conservative economic ideas, the balanced budget amendment became decidedly fashionable in 1985, when the National Governors Association passed a resolution urging its adoption. Ever since, it has been the catalyst for a great deal of campaign posturing and a consistent addition to the list of bills pending before each Congress. While it has consistently failed to achieve passage, it remains a talisman of the right—appropriately so given that it would, by statute, eliminate the essential instrument of Keynesian fiscal policy (not to mention of interventionist foreign policy) from use by the Treasury, a kind of final nail in the Keynesian coffin. No wonder, then, that it has been and remains an object of great admiration among conservatives and equally loathsome to liberals.[20]

For fairly obvious political reasons, critics of Keynesian-style spending techniques have always focused their attacks on absolute levels of indebtedness. Large numbers, especially those rendered in red, are impressive instruments of persuasion. Yet as any banker knows, let alone economic specialists, debt burden may only be meaningfully evaluated with reference to the ultimate ability to pay. In this context, the national debt, representing a claim on the wealth and income streams of future generations, necessarily has to be measured with reference to the GDP itself.

As a share of annual income, debt reveals its true lading. By this measure, American public finance, while obviously deranged in the wake of the Vietnam era, had since the early 1980s shown tangible improvement well into the 1990s—not surprisingly, as the ratio of annual deficits to the GDP had steadily fallen from a high of 6.3 percent in 1983 to 1.4 percent in 1996. Looking at the debt as a whole, in 1995 the national shortfall stood at $3.6 trillion, just over 50 percent of a $7 trillion GDP. With the repeated implementation of tax cut strategies since the 1990s and with massive increases in public spending associated with both domestic programs such as Medicare and Social Security and military operations in two theaters of war since 2001, the national debt, currently estimated to be a bit less than $16 trillion, stands at about 103 percent of GDP. Even so, this compares favorably with a debt/GDP proportion of over 100 percent at the end of World War II—interestingly enough, the beginning of a period of growth and expansion in the national economy that was historically unprecedented. In this context, the central target variable would link any rate of growth in the debt to the rate of growth of the macroeconomy—a notion altogether obscured in the public debates surrounding fiscal policies during the past three decades.

The sheer obtuseness of the public discussions concerning government finance in the late 1980s and early 1990s prompted a number of professional economists to act. In January of 1997, the late James Tobin (then professor emeritus at Yale University and a Nobel laureate) led an effort to petition Congress on the matter. Calling the proposed balanced budget amendment "unsound and unnecessary," the document was ultimately signed by

1,200 colleagues, eleven of them Nobel Memorial Prize winners. At the end of that month, it was presented on Capitol Hill. Above and beyond the misunderstandings the petition sought to expose, it also expressed the conviction that "the Constitution is not the place to put specific economic policy." Reaction to this professional foray into the realm of public debate was inconsequential. The signatories of the "Economists' Statement Opposing the Balanced Budget Amendment" found themselves prophets with neither honor nor influence.

Yet the debate over the national debt contained an important if fairly unwelcome lesson for economists who coveted a place in public affairs and for elected officials, such as presidents, who wished to rely on them. Instruments of economic policy, most especially those having to do with government finance, were clearly first and foremost political creations. No public outcry, for example, shook Washington in the autumn of 1945 when the financial obligations incurred in the wake of four years of international conflict assumed dimensions that, in the short run, altogether dwarfed the productive capacity of the nation's markets. A remarkable degree of political solidarity concerning war aims had prevented it. Similarly, throughout the 1980s and 1990s, it was politics rather than economics that not only framed policy outcomes but, more to the point, also set the terms of public debate. If economists found themselves demoralized and confused by the indifference that met their arguments and prognostications, they might have been forgiven their lament. Theirs was a discipline, the product of a century of intellectual and social evolution, that fostered in its practitioners the notion that they could decisively separate ideology from analysis. It also encouraged in several American presidents, at least until the Vietnam era, the idea that social science could serve the government with unassailable authority. In a supreme irony, the result was that, in matters of national policy, economic expertise was ultimately thoroughly undermined and presidential authority decisively compromised.

In point of fact, the transformation of the nation's political landscape in the wake of the Vietnam era had subverted the very foundations of the liberalism that had made sense out of a "New Economics" and that had transformed the American presidency into a supremely powerful institution the Founders would have hardly recognized. An emphasis on political economic issues that had framed the high tide of activist government since the New Deal had provided a community of professionals and a new Democratic Party coalition with the means to achieve a variety of ends. But as soon as social issues concerning opportunity and equality occupied center stage, most vividly in the formulation of a "War on Poverty," American liberalism ran headlong into the abiding national puzzle of race and ethnicity. A backlash was the inevitable result, one that shifted a dynamic emphasis on productivity and plenty during the 1950s and 1960s to a static refrain concerning the costs and benefits, the winners and losers in market outcomes during the 1980s and 1990s. So dependent had the promise of liberalism been on sustained growth as a vehicle of redistributive betterment and justice that the first signs of macroeconomic instability robbed it of its voice and its authority. Indeed, by the last years of the century, the New Deal order was dead, as were the hopes and achievements of the New Economics and the vision of an enduring activist presidency.[21]

Whatever misgivings some may have had about the trend and impact of national economic policy in the early 1990s were only faintly heard. By mid-decade, a dramatic boom began in American stock and allied financial markets that continued, in almost uninterrupted fashion, until the terrorist attacks of September 2001. The presumption that the run-up would last forever infected the sensibilities of Americans from all walks of life. In 1995 alone, more than a hundred billion dollars was invested in the stock market—and investment in speculative capital simply increased from there. Many working people placed their entire retirement nest eggs into 401(k) plans and Investment Retirement Accounts. "Day trading," a highly volatile enterprise in which tens of thousands of dollars could be lost in scarcely any time at all, became a fad. With the proliferation of virtual, electronic marketplaces, many individuals tried their hands at such gambling—often without the time, training, and financial security to underwrite their excessive risk-taking. Meanwhile, electronic commerce took off, with spectacular run-ups in the stock values of firms that existed solely "online," many of which had never executed a genuine transaction nor met a formal delivery date for their output. By the early months of 2001, the Dow Jones Industrial Average had broken 10,000—a previously un-imagined plateau.

Economic booms never last forever, and that which had defined the American economy's prospects from the 1990s to the turn of the twenty-first century was no different. By the early summer months of 2001, warning signs emerged on virtually every market horizon. Energy prices accelerated upward; stock-market values softened, as profit-seekers cashed in on the high values generated in the boom; manufacturing output slowed; and layoffs began to rise. Then, with the September 11 attacks in New York City, western Pennsylvania, and Washington, D.C., the upper turning-point was clearly reached.

In the midst of the economic slide after 9/11, it became increasingly obvious that the national economy, working in a dramatically unregulated and "tax-revenue-poor" environment in which the federal government's capacity for countercyclical management had been decisively curtailed, had become quite fragile indeed. Strikingly enough, the very timidity of the fiscal spending proposals brought before the Congress to deal with the downturn provided ample testimony to this fact. Even the most aggressive pump-priming bills, debated on Capitol Hill, embraced spending targets that approximated a mere 1 to 2 percent of GDP. The fragile nature of the national infrastructure, in the face of the terrorist attacks, was also demonstrated by the inability of the Federal Aviation Administration to make rapid adjustments to the disarray occasioned in airline operations by the attacks themselves, and they were highlighted even further by the chaotic response of an enervated public health apparatus in the face of a series of horrifying, yet unexplained contaminations of the national postal system by letters laced with anthrax.

As if the recession after 9/11 and related economic dislocations were not enough, by early 2002 yet another dramatic incident further evidenced the fragility of the national marketplace. Enron Corporation, one of the largest firms in the country, with major interests in energy trading and distribution networks, filed for bankruptcy early in January of the new year. As liquidation proceedings documented, it rapidly became clear that the company had run up its stock values through a wide array of manipulations, falsified accounting records, and outright deceit. The accounting giant Arthur Andersen became implicated in the debacle when it was revealed that its auditors not only participated in the subterfuge but also began systematic shredding of documents when it became clear that the end was near.

The dismantling of Keynesian-style fiscal management (the policy hallmark of the Cold War era) and the deregulation of the nation's marketplaces, which began during the high tide of the Reagan presidency, had an enduring impact on the ability of the government both to maintain cyclical stability in the face of economic shocks and to sustain the regulatory vigilance and control of financial and other related practices. As a consequence, especially after the September 11 attacks, the federal government found itself incapable of taking matters decisively in hand.

Making war against Iraq, strangely enough, only further interfered with Washington's ability to manage the nation's economic affairs. The conservative constituency brought to power in the closely contested (and deeply controversial) 2000 presidential election had insisted on pursuing a conservative agenda in domestic affairs that conflicted directly with the fiscal realities of unilateral ambitions abroad. Throughout most of the Cold War era, successive presidential administrations (drawn from both major political parties) had yoked high levels of public spending for military and diplomatic initiatives overseas with measured countercyclical policies directed toward balanced and fair economic growth at home. Yet the very "victory" in the Cold War with the Soviet Union severed this link between an active role in the world and socioeconomic progress at home. While the aggressive foreign policy ambitions remained, the progressive domestic agenda did not.

In many respects, the collapse of the Cold War coalition that brought conservatives determined to confront Soviet influence in the wider world together with liberals focused on social needs at home was the direct result of the "success" of the Cold War itself. Liberals themselves, ironically enough, contributed to this remarkable script of political economic deconstruction. Eager to criticize the errors of American foreign policy in the wake of the debacle of the Vietnam War, the left nonetheless neglected to explore, in a thorough and rigorous fashion, the close economic and political linkages of military-industrial spending, anticommunist containment strategy, and social welfare initiatives that had defined the "New Deal Order" since the end of World War II. As a result, the primary mechanisms of fiscal and monetary control that had fostered the progressive social agendas of the Cold War era and the presidential powers that went with them—these were ripe pickings for a conservative insurgency determined to destroy the vestiges of the New Deal while remaining committed to the anticommunist containment goals of the past.

To be sure, after the end of major military operations in Iraq, there have emerged some rather crude examples of the ways in which a new conservative coalition seeks to tie foreign policy to domestic concerns. The award of reconstruction contracts to individual corporations, most of which had as their primary retainers major leaders in the American government (most notably and notoriously, former vice president Dick Cheney), gave concrete testimony to the derangement of the Cold War–era consensus regarding public spending strategies and anticommunist containment. The prospect of over a half a billion dollars mesmerized the Bechtel Corporation as it executed a contract to rebuild Iraqi infrastructure for which it never had to bid; similarly, Vice President Cheney's former employer, the Halliburton Corporation, earned as much as seven billion dollars to restore Iraqi oil fields to full production. These singular examples of political economic corruption stood in sharp contrast to Cold War projects like the Marshall Plan that had sought to benefit an entire national economy in the project of postwar reconstruction in Western Europe.

Needless to say, the postwar reconstruction of Iraq took place on a world stage markedly different from that of 1948. Over a half-century ago, the U.S. economy stood alone, among the major industrialized nations, as the source of manufacturing output and skilled labor. By the end of the 1990s, by comparison, U.S. policy was no longer oriented toward containing (a now nonexistent) communist influence but rather toward limiting the influence of foreign capital in its competition with American wealth in world markets. When, in May of 2003, WorldCom Corporation, one of the disgraced entities in the accounting scandals that had plagued the American economy since 2000, won a contract to build Iraq's first cell phone network, the effort was born as much of a determination to bring the money for the project home to a U.S. firm as it was to exclude prime foreign competitors from reaping any benefits at all. Part of the legislation passed in the Congress to frame the disbursement of public monies for postwar reconstruction in Iraq tried to require that any new telecommunications networks utilize technological standards developed by American, rather than European, firms.

A profound disjunction between American foreign policy and domestic management of economic needs placed the presidential administrations of both George W. Bush and Barack Obama in the grips of a profound dilemma. While they pursued their foreign strategies, tied as they were to exceedingly conservative fiscal and monetary policies at home, these administrations struggled to articulate a coherent economic agenda. Unemployment persisted in certain troubled sectors, capital markets were roiled by scandals and mismanagement, and the international value of the dollar steadily weakened as global financial markets became increasingly concerned about insipid economic performance and unstable credit markets in the United States as a whole. Earlier Cold War presidents had consistently found ways to stimulate economic growth and employment at home while containing Soviet and Chinese influence overseas. Born of decades of tax-cutting and deregulation, the impasse Bush and Obama ultimately faced was so deeply ingrained in American political practice that even the Great Slump of 2008 would not resolve it.

Far from providing the foundations of a bipartisan alliance sustaining the kinds of economic stabilization policies characteristic of the Cold War era, the contemporary "War on Terror" has served merely to undercut any meaningful commitment to countercyclical government spending. The Obama administration, even in the midst of a reelection campaign, was seriously undermined in the face of the weakest national economic performance since the Great Depression of the 1930s. While the 2009 American Recovery and Reinvestment Act was touted as inspired public policy deployed in pursuit of economic recovery, it actually represented precisely the kind of inadequate fiscal response to recession long condemned by economists in the post–World War II period. Indeed, not only was President Obama left unable to implement a meaningful and truly effective "stimulus package," the very failure of economic policy during his first term has now become the foundation of an ongoing claim by conservatives that economic intervention is neither warranted nor necessary.

The vantage point of approximately a half-century of investigation nonetheless leaves a variety of unanswered questions concerning policy activism and the American presidency. Most prominent among these would be the extent to which bipartisan consensus was simply the product of unique economic circumstances occasioned by the nation's victory in World War II. Or, conversely, was the quite special political collaboration on Cold War economic policy the primary fuel for robust economic growth in the first place? Precise answers to these queries is virtually impossible given the counterfactual premises with which they begin. But it remains necessary to disaggregate carefully specific historical circumstances from ideological proclivities that may have fostered, among major political actors of the day, a relatively strong willingness to compromise.

Weaned on the special material, social, and political conditions of the Cold War and American global hegemony, a succession of American presidents and generations of economists mistook historical specificity and contingency for general principles of public policy. Today, lacking the crucial political and international ingredients that had once made public spending and compensatory demand management both possible and uniquely effective, political leaders and economic analysts find themselves largely incapable of articulating new policy agendas. Indeed, political dialogue and "debate" are simply captured by amateurs, pundits, and candidates whose proposals are largely devoid of empirical validation and logical coherence.

One of Keynes's most celebrated students, Joan Robinson, argued in 1975 that mainstream economics had more applicability in a planned or wartime economy than in a decentralized market setting. That paradoxical characterization is particularly poignant today.[22] The immediate postwar decades afforded American presidents and their economic advisers an altogether unique and contingent set of circumstances that allowed for the rapid and effective deployment of countercyclical policies. With the elimination of those circumstances and with the emergence of an altogether different array of political and international constraints, contemporary American economists and the elected officials they serve, most importantly the president of the United States, have been deprived of the tools and opportunity to pursue full-employment growth and economic stability. In a peacetime, globally interdependent economy structured to foster the accumulation of private wealth in decentralized market settings, the sway of the American president in the material affairs of the nation has been dramatically reduced.

CHAPTER 13

The Changing Presidential Politics of Disaster

From Coolidge to Nixon

GARETH DAVIES

When tragedy strikes in the contemporary United States, Americans look to their president for leadership and balm. In July of 2012, Barack Obama twice flew out to Colorado in the aftermath of a disaster—first, when wildfires devastated the area around Colorado Springs and then after the shooting of a dozen moviegoers in Aurora. His predecessor, George W. Bush, made similar visits after the shootings at Virginia Tech in 2007, while just weeks later he was ministering to the people of Greensburg, Kansas, after a tornado. Visiting victims of the latter disaster, Bush explained that he brought with him "the prayers and concerns of the people of this country," that he might "lift people's spirits as best as I possibly can and to hopefully touch somebody's soul by representing our country, and to let people know that while there was a dark day in the past, there's brighter days ahead."[1]

In responding to such disasters, a lot can be at stake; indeed, the presidencies of all three of Obama's three immediate predecessors, and perhaps his too, were in some measure made or unmade by their response to a sudden, unanticipated catastrophe. In 1992, George H. W. Bush's prospects of reelection declined with his purportedly inadequate response to Hurricane Andrew. Conversely, Clinton's eloquent speech at the memorial ceremony for victims of the Oklahoma City bombing of 1995 helped him to bounce back from crushing midterm losses six months earlier. The presidency of George

W. Bush was both made and partially unmade by his response to disaster: by his commanding response to the 9/11 terrorist attacks, in the first case; by his weak response to Hurricane Katrina, in the second. And following his re-election in 2012, some pundits attributed Obama's victory to his empathetic response to Hurricane Sandy.[2]

If the role of "consoler-in-chief" is not entirely new, it is only recently that it has assumed its present-day proportions.[3] When Hurricane Audrey tore into the Louisiana cost in 1957, it was a vastly greater disaster than the Kansas tornado of 2007: Some five hundred people were killed, rather than eleven. But Dwight Eisenhower did not visit the scene, and there was no pressure for him to do so. Neither Eisenhower nor his political opponents seem to have felt that the grief generated by traumas such as these was any-thing but an essentially private matter. The president was not expected to channel the nation's emotions, nor to minister to the collective grief of its victims. When he held a press conference four days after Audrey, no one asked him about it.[4]

In this essay, I inquire when these new expectations of presidential leader-ship arose and in response to which stimuli. Focusing in particular on natural disasters, I suggest that it was during the presidencies of Lyndon Johnson and Richard Nixon that the decisive change took place. Before the Great Society, presidents did not routinely play a leading role when a natural disaster struck, despite the great expansion in government and in the presidency that oc-curred in response to the successive grand disasters of the Great Depression, World War II, and the Cold War during the middle third of the twentieth century. After the Great Society, it was taken for granted that the White House would play such a role.

This is not to say that there was no federal politics of disaster before the 1960s. To the contrary, Washington had been regularly involved in respond-ing to floods, hurricanes, and earthquakes since Reconstruction. Before the 1960s, though, this was usually a matter for Congress or for the executive bu-reaucracy, rather than for the White House. During the late nineteenth and early twentieth centuries, the U.S. Army or the Coast Guard might help to evacuate flood survivors, the Army Corps of Engineers would repair levees, and the Public Health Service sometimes provided medical support. Dur-ing the New Deal era, civilian agencies for the first time provided a larger role: The Small Business Administration offered emergency loans, the U.S. Department of Agriculture furnished crop insurance, the Internal Revenue Service permitted victims to make disaster-related deductions, the Bureau of Public Roads rebuilt highways, and the Department of the Interior repaired federal buildings.

Such aid was always "political" in the sense that who got what was often determined by the degree of influence wielded by particular legislators and governors. But this was not a form of politics that normally involved the White House in any substantial way; rather, this sort of business was contracted between members of Congress and executive agencies. Presidential expressions of concern were routine, but the chief executive was not expected to visit the scene, to emote, or to coordinate the relief activities of his administration. On those rare occasions where presidents *did* get involved, it was not because they believed it to be an inescapable part of their job but because the particular disaster gave them an opportunity to advance some broader public policy agenda. We will briefly consider these exceptions before inquiring why presidential involvement in disaster became a more routine occurrence during the 1960s and 1970s.

Coolidge and the 1927 Mississippi Flood

When the Mississippi River broke its banks in the spring of 1927, the extent of the disaster struck contemporaries as unique.[5] This was an understandable reaction, given the high death toll (over four hundred), the duration of the emergency (it took four months for the waters to subside), and the vast amount of economic disruption that the flood caused. It was not so very different in scale, however, from the vast flood that had inundated the Ohio Valley in 1913. New since then, though, was the communications world in which the disaster unfolded: This was the first great disaster to capture the headlines since the spread of radio, moving pictures, and reliable aviation. The cumulative impact of these new technologies was to make disasters far more immediate and vivid than they had been before, even to Americans living thousands of miles from the scene of the catastrophe. This in turn placed new pressure on politicians to respond to emergencies, even in the broadly conservative political culture of Coolidge's America.

In an atmosphere of crisis, politicians from the Mississippi Valley urged Coolidge to visit the scene of the disaster, to talk about it in a radio broadcast, and to summon Congress for a special session.[6] Why should this be, given the broader pattern of presidential detachment from disaster politics? Paradoxically, the pressure for a presidential response would probably have been less pronounced had the American state been more substantial in 1927 in ways that allowed for a regularized, bureaucratic response. As it was, strong demands for collective action were received by a still-modest American state whose administrative capacity to alleviate suffering was very limited, especially when Congress was out of session. Serendipitously, many of the Mississippi River's most deadly "spring rises" during the previous half-century had taken place in even-numbered years, when Congress was in session, and legislators had been able to give the Army and the Army Corps of Engineers the authority and funds that they needed in order to swing into action.[7] In this particular case, though, the lame-duck session of the outgoing 69th Congress had recently ended, and the new 70th Congress was not due to convene for another nine months.

Yet with newspaper reporters flying directly over the scene of the disaster and phoning their stories in, with millions of Americans watching dramatic footage of the flood on their Saturday morning visits to the movies, with newspapers now able to reproduce photographs of the suffering, and with popular entertainers such as Will Rogers broadcasting heartfelt pleas for voluntary donations over the radio, the pressure for national action was substantial. What is more, the presidencies of Theodore Roosevelt and Woodrow Wilson had established recent precedents for muscular White House leadership, while World War I had demonstrated the capacity of a president to organize vast governmental forces in an emergency. Coolidge found himself in a tricky position.

The president's response was canny—he deputed his activist commerce secretary, Herbert Hoover, to coordinate the national response to the 1927 flood. It was a shrewd move for two reasons. First, Hoover had an unparalleled reputation for handling humanitarian emergencies (Belgian food aid during World War I, famine relief in Russia in 1919, dealing with the postwar spike in U.S. unemployment). Second, he was a member of the central committee of the American Red Cross. In summoning Hoover to arms in *that* capacity, Coolidge was able to signal governmental concern without undermining traditions of voluntarism and charitable giving that he held dear. What's more, it worked: under Hoover's energetic stewardship, the Red Cross undertook a massive and efficient evacuation and relief operation, one that was widely trumpeted as illustrating alternatively the practical and moral superiority of private giving (Coolidge's view) or the boundless promise of modern, New Era cooperation (the Hoover line).

Disaster Politics and the Depression

During the presidencies of Herbert Hoover and Franklin Roosevelt, the federal government's role in attempting to relieve human need increased dramatically in response to the protracted emergency of the Great Depression. How did this affect the politics surrounding natural disasters—the drought that afflicted large swaths of Appalachia during 1930 and 1931, for example, or the Category 5 hurricane that crashed into the Florida Keys in 1935, or the floods that ravaged New England and the Ohio River Valley in 1936 and the Mississippi River Valley the following year? As one might imagine, the effect was substantial; indeed, the New Deal era marks the point at which the idea of a leading federal role in responding to disaster acquired a taken-for-granted character.[8] In part, that reflected the development of broad new ideas about governmental responsibility. But it owed more to new state capacity: With Congress in session for longer and a panoply of new federal agencies and workers on hand when disaster struck, Washington could make a more substantial contribution than before.

But if governmental action in response to disaster became increasingly ubiquitous as the 1930s ran on, presidential involvement remained sporadic. Herbert Hoover flung himself enthusiastically into the effort to combat the drought that spread across large swaths of the southeastern United States at the beginning of the decade but took no substantial action when a series of deadly tornadoes killed over three hundred people in the same area two years later.[9] Franklin Roosevelt stayed largely aloof from the catastrophic Labor Day hurricane of 1935 but played a conspicuous role after the following year's floods. What explains this pattern of intermittent involvement, which was characteristic not simply of the 1930s but of the middle third of the twentieth century more generally? How could disasters become routinely a matter for federal action without (as is now the case) routinely involving presidential leadership?

In part, it was precisely that "routine" character of federal assistance that sometimes vitiated the need for presidential leadership. In this new large-government world, it did not always require much federal initiative to crank the necessary administrative machinery into motion.[10] And for all that the rise of the presidency was one of the most signal features of governmental growth during these years, there was as yet little expectation that the president would minister personally to the emotional needs of his stricken people, when disaster struck.[11] Rather, on those rare occasions when presidents chose to get involved with disaster politics, they had a very particular reason for doing so. Hoover's activist response to the 1930–31 drought, for example, was motivated by his desire to illustrate the power of federalism and voluntarism to alleviate even large-scale hardship and to head off pressure for government relief.[12] When FDR took a personal interest in the terrible flooding that swept the northeastern United States in March 1936, the context was his desire to fend off attacks on his embattled Works Progress Administration and to dramatize his general election-year claim that government was now the servant of ordinary Americans and not just the rich.[13] And when Harry

S. Truman toured the flood-hit Missouri and Columbia rivers a decade or so later, his purpose was to illustrate the case for extending the principle of the Tennessee Valley Authority to those river systems. In the case of all three presidents, their terms featured plenty of other large disasters that elicited very little White House involvement, if any, and in no case did inaction trigger extensive criticism.

Disasters had now become a job for government, but this was a bureaucratic rather than a presidential task. That characteristic was reinforced in 1950 when Congress approved the Federal Disaster Act (PL 81-875), an effort to replace the nation's hitherto *ad hoc* response to disaster with a more systematic approach, based on inter-agency coordination. True, the president had to declare a state of disaster to exist before the federal machinery could crank into action, but thereafter the White House was usually out of the picture: Disasters were a matter for civil servants.

Why should that be? Partly, it reflected the fact that comparatively little money was at stake, by later standards: As late as 1953, the Red Cross spent more than the federal government on disaster relief, as did state and local civil defense authorities; when two major hurricanes hit the northeast in 1955, Washington picked up only 6 percent of the tab.[14] Also, and related, governors were less likely to request federal assistance than in later years: Eisenhower was asked to make fewer than twenty disaster declarations per year, compared to the ninety requests that crossed George W. Bush's desk a half-century later.[15] Finally, newspaper accounts and political discussion of midcentury disasters were generally restrained—disasters did not become political *causes célèbres*. From a present-day perspective, the lack of acrimony or points-scoring is astonishing. When a journalist interrupted a press conference that was largely about the Korean War to invite Truman's comment on a serious drought in Texas at a 1951 press conference, he inquired: "What can I do? I can't make it rain." His audience laughed, and the conversation moved on.[16]

Great Society Presidential Disaster Politics

During the 1960s, the politics of disaster, like so much else in American government, were transformed. Average annual spending on disaster during the Johnson presidency topped $270 million, nearly six times as much as during the Eisenhower administration, in inflation-adjusted dollars.[17] And whereas Washington had covered only 6.2 percent of total damages in response to the two northeastern hurricanes of 1955 and 12.8 percent after floods in 1964, when Hurricane Agnes hit Pennsylvania in 1972, that figure had shot up to 48.3 percent.[18]

In part, that pattern was attributable to an unusual cluster of disasters during 1964 and 1965: First, 200 Indianans were killed by tornadoes; then, drought and deadly wild fires hit California, followed by flooding in the Pacific Northwest; then, the most powerful earthquake in U.S. history hit Alaska; and, finally, New Orleans was hit by Hurricane Betsy—still its deadliest post–World War II storm save for Katrina. Such a concentration of catastrophes, spread over a broad geographical area, naturally increases the number of political leaders for whom disasters are politically salient: Something similar had preceded the 1950 Federal Disaster Act, and another cluster between 1989 and 1993 would be followed by a further spike in federal spending. In a larger sense, the increase reflected the political zeitgeist of the Great Society, with its underlying assumption that it was fundamentally the job of Washington to fix *any* serious problem in American society. As the Johnson administration was responding to these disasters, it was also driving through Congress the Civil Rights Act, the Voting Rights Act, the so-called war on poverty, the Elementary and Secondary Education Act, Medicare, the Clean Air Act, water pollution control, and wilderness legislation. In such an environment, it would have been surprising had the federal role in responding to natural disaster not decisively increased.

What did Johnson contribute to this pattern, though, and how did his approach to disaster politics change what Americans expected of their president, when catastrophe struck? When Richard Nixon received brickbats for his handling of Hurricanes Camille and Agnes, when George H. W. Bush was criticized during the aftermath of Hurricane Andrew, and when George W. Bush was assailed for his response to Katrina, to what extent were they the victims of new expectations of White House leadership that had been planted during the 1960s? Certainly, one can make the circumstantial case: Whereas before LBJ, it was rare for a president to be criticized for poor disaster management, presidents since Johnson have periodically come under attack, even when saying and doing far more than pre–Great Society occupants of the White House would ever have contemplated.

If one were looking to identify a single point of departure in Johnson's presidency, it would unquestionably be Hurricane Betsy. When it slammed into the Gulf Coast, the death toll of eighty-one was comparatively light, but large parts of New Orleans were engulfed by flood water, resulting in immense property damage—this was the first hurricane to cause a billion dollars' worth of damage.[19] The most heavily flooded parts, St. Bernard's Parish and the Lower Ninth Ward, were the same low-lying districts whose inhabitants would suffer most grievously when Katrina struck four decades later. And, as in 2005, thousands of mostly poor New Orleans residents who had not evacuated their homes before the storm huddled in unlit, sweltering refugee centers without water or electric power.

Johnson's response was unprecedented.[20] When Senator Russell Long of Louisiana phoned the president with a vivid personal account of the damage to his house and urged him to visit, Johnson abandoned his schedule, corralled the heads of the Office of Emergency Planning (OEP) and four other agencies, and they all hotfooted it straight down to New Orleans, touching down there five hours after Long's call. At the still-windswept Lakefront Airport, he described as "measureless" the "human suffering and physical damage" that he had glimpsed from the plane, explaining that "I am here because I want to see with my own eyes what the unhappy alliance of wind and water have done to this land and its good people."[21] Then Johnson strode into a darkened, unventilated refugee center, shouting out an encouraging message, his face illuminated by a flashlight. "I'm your president," he told his audience, "and I'm here to help." Learning that the refugees had nothing to drink, he urged the mayor to contact the local bottling plants. And on his departure from New Orleans, he assured a small audience of journalists and local officials that all "red tape" would be cut.

The visit appears to have had a powerful effect on Johnson. In her diary, his wife Lady Bird recounts his having returned from New Orleans after midnight, "looking exhausted but talking of nothing but the hurricane damage." In between late-night phone calls to federal departments (asking "whether food was being flown in and if enough medicine and cots were available"), Johnson told Lady Bird of "the man who rushed up to him and cried, 'I've lost my baby!'" She confided to her diary that "Lyndon's face contorted just as the man's had, as though he were about to cry. He said it was horrible."[22] Three days later, he was still preoccupied by what he had seen, phoning his deputy head of emergency planning, Bob Phillips, to insist again that "red tape" not stand in the way of relief:

> [I]n times of distress, it's necessary that all the members of the family get together and lay aside any individual problems they have or any personal grievances and try to take care of the sick mother, and we've got a sick mother on our hands. And as I said the other night when I was there, we've got to cut out all the red tape. . . . The people who've lost their homes . . . are not going to be very interested in any individual differences between federal or state or local agencies. So I hope that all the government people can put their shoulders to the wheel without regard to hours. . . . Bring to these people the kind of assistance they need in this emergency, worthy of a great government

and a great country. . . . If you have any problems, well, let me know about them.[23]

Why did Johnson react to Hurricane Betsy in this way, and what consequences flowed from his reaction? Doubtless, his actions owed much to his larger-than-life, empathetic personality and to the proprietorial approach he took to the management of "his" government: how many other presidents would have personally phoned the number-two man at OEP or sought middle-of-the-night information from federal agencies about food shipments to New Orleans? But they were triggered in the first instance by the power of Louisiana's congressional delegation: Russell Long had recently become Senate Majority Whip, Congressman Hale Boggs held the same position in the House, Senator Allen Ellender was second in seniority on the Appropriations Committee, and congressmen Edward Hébert and Otto Passman were influential members of the House. When Long phoned to tell him about the hurricane, LBJ was initially disinclined to visit the scene of the disaster: He was sick (about to have his gall bladder removed), and his friend Buford Ellington, head of OEP, did not think the trip warranted. But Johnson owed a lot to Long and Boggs, both strong allies who had taken substantial political risks on his behalf.[24] And he would need their support again, if the extraordinary momentum of the Great Society were to be sustained.

The impact of LBJ's response on the subsequent presidential politics of disaster is hard to assess. Forty years later, after the devastation of Katrina, some commentators tried to place the disaster into historical perspective by making unflattering comparisons between Bush and Johnson.[25] And when he came to write his memoirs, Bush himself followed their lead, wishing that he had provided the same kind of proactive and empathetic leadership.[26] But Johnson's actions in 1965 did not receive very much attention at the time, perhaps because reporters saw him as practicing "retail politics" rather than "wholesale politics": His trip to New Orleans and his visit to the refugee center were spontaneous acts aimed at victims of Betsy and their political representatives, rather than being stage-managed and designed to project empathy and command to a broader audience. Katrina received extended treatment in Bush's memoir, but LBJ did not refer to Betsy once—indeed, Lady Bird's published diary is the only memoir of the Johnson administration to do so. It was Katrina itself that caused a spotlight to be thrown on these now-distant events and to lead commentators to take an interest in recently released LBJ phone tapes that brought his reactions to Betsy vividly to life.[27]

So it is probably not the case that Johnson's response to Hurricane Betsy significantly affected the expectations that Americans in general had of presidential disaster leadership. In two other respects, however, he may have helped to establish a significant precedent, the trigger being not his visit to New Orleans but the strong support that he gave to the "Betsy Bill" that the Louisiana congressional delegation cooked up a few weeks later, during the frenetic closing days of the 89th Congress's first session. It is unlikely that this pork-laden measure would have passed absent LBJ's backing, even with the formidable backing of Long, Ellender, and Boggs. That it did so was significant. First, it allocated federal dollars for the relief of individual disaster victims for the first time (previously, this was understood to be a task for subnational governments and the Red Cross). Second, it approved a massive, federally funded hurricane-defense system for New Orleans (similarly, such barriers had normally been funded by local governments in the past). As is so often the case with American government, it did not take long for these major departures in policy to acquire a taken-for-granted character.

Beyond the Great Society

If Johnson's response to Hurricane Betsy contributed to a portentous increase in federal disaster spending, then it was in the immediate *aftermath* of the Great Society that new expectations of presidential leadership took root: By the end of Richard Nixon's first term, they were far more embedded than at the time of Betsy. Johnson and Nixon are less central to this story than is the broader transformation in American politics that political scientists have in mind when they identify the "permanent campaign" mindset; the "rhetorical," "personal," or "plebiscitary" presidency; or the technique of "going public" as being characteristic of contemporary politics, or when they refer to the period since the 1960s as the American "Second Republic."[28] There is no opportunity here for an extended examination of this epochal shifting of political gears, but the presidential politics of disaster do provide a nice illustration of one of its central features, namely the erosion of the usual distinction between governing and campaigning.

That distinction had never been complete, of course; throughout the twentieth century, elected officials had sought to enhance their popularity with key constituencies on an ongoing basis, and not just at election time.[29] Nevertheless, campaign politics and governing politics had generally been somewhat distinct enterprises until the late 1960s: on the campaign trail, one sought popularity, while in governing one deliberated about public policy and nurtured institutional relationships.[30] Presidential disaster politics during the middle decades of the twentieth century had reflected considerations of governance: Normally, the lead was taken by the relevant agencies, and the

White House, having little to add, stayed out of the picture; occasionally, though, the president intervened because doing so provided an opportunity to advance his broader public policy agenda (Truman selling his public power agenda, LBJ nurturing alliances on Capitol Hill). Now, the White House got involved in disaster politics much more frequently than before, yet its involvement simultaneously became more trivial in character—more about campaigning than about governing. To illustrate the new pattern, let us briefly consider Richard Nixon's response to two very different events: a comparatively low-profile drought that afflicted Texan ranchers during the middle of his first term, and a high-profile hurricane that struck the mid-Atlantic states in 1972, just as his campaign for reelection was cranking into high gear.

Disaster Politics Meets the Permanent Campaign

Nixon learned of the drought in April 1971 when he received a phone call from former Texas governor John Connally, a close confidant whom the president greatly admired.[31] A week earlier, Connally had been urging Nixon to seize opportunities to display decisive, manly leadership; now, he was suggesting that the drought could well be one such opportunity. With emergency planning head George "Abe" Lincoln also on the line, Connally told them that what his farmers needed was hay. He implored them: "Don't wait too damn long where everybody else gets the credit for it," and "don't be too niggardly." Rather than wait for a state request, Connally insisted, Nixon should just "go on and do it" on the grounds that "you're gonna get credit only to the extent that you do it voluntarily. Don't wait so long that they think they made you do it."

Nixon responded with alacrity to Connally's advice, remarking: "You can't screw around. You're absolutely right. You've got to . . . show that [you] care . . . right now!" Learning of problems with federal hay distribution during an earlier Texas drought, Nixon responded: "Oh Christ. We don't care about that. Just do something. . . . Better to get in a hassle doing something than to get in a hassle for doing nothing." A day later, in conversation with H. R. Haldeman, his chief of staff, Nixon was steamed up about his agriculture secretary's deliberative approach: Rather than giving farmers hay, he was just "farting around," worrying about the cost. "See what I mean?" he exclaimed. "We talk in terms of statistics," but "there isn't a God-damn word of warmth."

On assuming the presidency two years earlier, Nixon had sought to devolve all small and routine matters to his departments and agencies, leaving him free to focus on the really important issues. It is unlikely that he had hay provision to farmers in mind, so why was a comparatively minor drought commanding his attention now? Rather than seeking to advance his larger *public policy* agenda, as his predecessors had occasionally done in calling attention to natural disasters, Nixon's objective seems to have been purely personal—to project an image of decisive leadership and compassion, in a politically important Southern state that had denied him its electoral votes in 1968. In none of the taped conversations does he disclose any concern for the drought's victims or curiosity about the different ways that their plight might be alleviated. Neither is he worrying about the budgetary implications of generous disaster relief (this despite his broader preoccupation with fighting inflation). Instead, his sole concern is that the administration be seen to take decisive action in *some* form—one has the impression that almost *any* form would do, so long as it communicated a helpful message about Nixon's leadership.

This episode, trivial in itself, provides an early illustration of the progressive de-institutionalization of American politics during the post–Great Society era and of the emergence of a new politics based to an increasing extent on individual personality, public relations, sharp differentiation from one's political opponents, and a constant search for the approbation of key voting blocs (often through symbolic appeals rather than substantial programs). All presidents after Eisenhower practiced this new politics to some extent (think of Kennedy's use of television and Johnson's obsession with polling), and it was increasingly characteristic of congressional politics too. Still, it was peculiarly fateful that the burgeoning of these trends should have coincided so closely with Richard Nixon's ascension to the presidency, for here was someone who had been a precocious practitioner of image politics and the permanent campaign since the very earliest days of his career, when they were still in their infancy.[32]

When the first hurricane of the 1972 season, which was given the name of Agnes, reached the United States in late June, it soon lost force, but in its wake Atlantic states from Virginia to New York suffered torrential rainfall that left over one hundred dead. The worst effects of the storm were felt in the valley of Pennsylvania's Susquehanna River, especially in the state capital of Harrisburg and—the hardest hit of all—Wilkes-Barre. Of the 350,000 residents of Luzerne County who were forced to evacuate their homes and businesses, many were unable to return even once the waters had subsided, for their property was utterly destroyed. As well as needing shelter, many of these people faced severe financial difficulty—those with substantial mortgages, for example, or businesspeople whose premises, inventories, and fittings had been ruined.

But if this was a substantial disaster, its political context was more singular than the level of damage or the loss of life: The Susquehanna had flooded many times in its history, as of course had many other American rivers, and all the problems that newspapers were reporting following Agnes were familiar ones. But this was the biggest flood to have struck the United States since the great expansion in the expectations of government that had taken place during the 1960s, and it came, moreover, at a time when White House preoccupation with campaign politics was at a fever pitch, just four months ahead of the presidential election and a week after the Watergate break-in. How did these two contextual factors affect the political response to the disaster?

In policy terms, the Nixon administration's initial response was threefold: The White House asked Congress to appropriate a hundred million dollars in relief and reconstruction funds; OEP established fifty "command centers" throughout the disaster area; and the Department of Housing and Urban Development promised the homeless free trailers for up to eighteen months.[33] By historical standards, these were substantial responses, broadly congruent with the sort of federal response that had come to seem normal during the Johnson administration. Also like LBJ, Nixon interrupted his schedule to make a swift visit to the scene of the disaster. That, though, is where the similarities end, and three aspects of the administration response to Agnes in particular help illustrate the broader shift in American government, and its impact on the presidency, that had taken place since the mid 1960s.

The first has to do with Nixon's motivation in visiting Harrisburg: Taped conversations reveal that it was occasioned solely by a belief that it would generate helpful visual images—which indeed it did, at first, in the form of front-page newspaper photographs displaying Nixon looking steadfast, holding the hand of a small African American girl.[34] The second, though, concerns the sharp deterioration in the political mood that set in very shortly thereafter, beginning with Democratic governor Milton Shapp's strongly worded denunciation of White House unconcern, continuing with a series of poignant newspaper stories that conveyed in stark, emotive terms the human need that government policies were failing to meet.[35] Nothing like this had befallen LBJ after Betsy, nor Eisenhower after Audrey. Since then, though, a transformation had taken place in news reporting that accentuated the negative, assumed public figures to be knaves and scoundrels, and thereby both mirrored and reinforced the sharp collapse in esteem that politicians and political institutions had sustained over the previous half-decade.

In such an environment, and in the febrile context of an election year, Nixon perhaps had little choice but to take whatever political steps might insulate him from further damage, however inimical those steps might be to the administration's overall agenda (the New Federalism, for example, or the theme of economy in government) or to good public policy. In terms of the latter, experts in academia and at OEP were increasingly worrying that the relief approach to disaster created moral hazard, that is, that they encouraged disaster victims to rebuild in locations that were chronically subject to disaster on the assumption that Uncle Sam would pick up the tag.[36] Those experts favored an approach to disaster that emphasized community resilience rather than relief. In the politically charged aftermath of a modern disaster, though, according to the new logic of the permanent campaign, elected officials had few incentives to follow that approach, which was certain to prompt new charges of fecklessness or callous unconcern.

So what *did* Nixon do? First, Vice President Spiro Agnew was sent to New York and Pennsylvania to liaise with state and local government officials and to discover what they most needed from Washington. When one mayor angrily demanded "big grants, period," for those who had suffered property damage, the conservative Agnew airily indicated his strong sympathy for the idea.[37] Next, OEP director Lincoln invited local officials to visit the White House for a briefing session. (Where did this kind of direct interaction between Washington and local governments leave the states, inquired Carl Bernstein, an obscure writer on the *Washington Post*'s Metro section?)[38] Third, the Internal Revenue Service announced more generous tax writeoffs for disaster victims.[39] Finally, in a radio address from San Clemente, California, Nixon melodramatically labeled Agnes "the worst natural disaster in the whole of America's history," and demanded $1.7 billion in additional relief funds, the "largest single amount ever allocated to recovery efforts in this country." "Conscience commands it," he added grandly, and "humanity impels it."[40] (In making this request, Nixon was outflanking the Democratic Congress, which had not yet thought to offer so large a sum.)

In political terms, though, neither Nixon's rhetoric nor the additional federal dollars succeeded in quelling criticism of the White House, partly because Nixon's political enemies had an interest in fanning the flames, no matter what he did, and partly because of the great logistical difficulties that faced HUD as it sought to redeem its promise to supply trailer homes to the homeless. At the time of Hurricane Audrey, a decade and a half earlier, seemingly much greater federal failings had gone largely unremarked upon or had been swiftly forgiven.[41] And more recently, journalistic coverage of

Betsy's ravages had been underpinned by the assumption that human society was sometimes utterly powerless in the face of Mother Nature. Now, though, the inability of HUD to requisition and ship all the trailer homes that were needed, and immediately, generated a torrent of criticism. In those places where the homes *had* arrived, meanwhile, reporters assiduously documented complaints of their inadequacy.

Reading some of this criticism in his Sunday papers, Nixon cranked up his damage-limitation effort still more, curtly ordering HUD Secretary George Romney to visit Wilkes-Barre immediately and to sort out the problems of the thirty thousand people who had recently lost their homes.[42] But that visit only increased the administration's predicament, for when Romney protested that the government was doing far more than had ever been done after a flood, he was assailed by what one reporter described as a group of "25 screaming women." Giving as good as he got, Romney retorted that the power of government was not unlimited, but his audience was unimpressed: One demanded, "Where's my trailer?"; another complained about the amount spent on foreign aid; a third asked, "Why can't we get our house rebuilt?" Meanwhile, Governor Shapp suggested that an administration that was really serious about helping disaster victims would pay off the mortgages of everyone who had lost their homes.[43] Back in Washington, Romney told Nixon he had had enough and wanted to leave the administration. Perhaps reflecting on his recent experience, he wished to dedicate the next stage in his career to encouraging a renewed sense of personal responsibility in the nation.[44]

From that low point in the administration's post-Agnes propaganda offensive, things rapidly improved, following the deployment of Frank Carlucci to Wilkes-Barre.[45] As well as being a young and ambitious official at the Office of Management and Budget, Carlucci was a native of the city, and he deftly repaired the political damage wrought by the trailers episode. Now, newspaper coverage featured mostly positive accounts of his efforts on behalf of the people of Wilkes-Barre, sometimes including photographs of the sign outside his office, which read "Frank Carlucci—President's Personal Representative." In a testament to Carlucci's political success, Nixon made a return trip to the city in early September. When a federal volunteer told him of the next day's planned picnic for flood victims, Nixon turned to Carlucci and ordered him to "provide anything they need to make the picnic a success."[46] If newspaper coverage of his previous visit to the flood area had reproduced solemn images of the president, this time the *Times* and the *Post* showed him beaming, next to a similarly delighted-looking newlywed couple.

Conclusion

Already by the 1930s, the idea that the federal government had some role to play when disaster struck was well established, but only rarely did the White House get involved. When the president chose to get involved, the purpose was generally to advance his broader public policy agenda: Hoover in 1930, making the case for New Era voluntarism; FDR in 1936, illustrating the New Deal's broadened conception of governmental protection. That remained the case throughout the middle third of the twentieth century: When Lyndon Johnson visited New Orleans after Betsy, he too was motivated by broad public policy considerations—to enact the Great Society, LBJ needed the goodwill of Russell Long and Hale Boggs.

What of Richard Nixon's response to Hurricane Agnes, seven years later? On the one hand, it was a very engaged and hands-on response: Where LBJ had lent his support to the Betsy Bill and lobbied federal administrators in general terms, Nixon and his aides choreographed the federal response from the White House from the moment that HUD started to receive adverse publicity. But, on the other hand, Nixon's interest in Hurricane Agnes was also strikingly limited: What was disastrous about it, from his point of view, was less its human toll than the way that it threatened to imperil his reelection. At no point in the numerous taped conversations relating to the disaster did Nixon or his aides exhibit any concern with the substance of disaster policy as opposed to its politics.

In one sense, the explanation for the president's approach seems too obvious to warrant analysis: This was an election year, and Nixon was—in LBJ's words—a "chronic campaigner," someone who had viewed politics in intensely personal and combative terms throughout his career.[47] All of this is true, and yet to leave matters there would be to ignore the deeper forces at work. In a larger sense, Nixon's response to Agnes was shaped by the confluence of two forces in American political life that powerfully reshaped the presidency during the 1960s and 1970s: a broadened conception of the responsibilities of the federal government, which had been gathering momentum over the previous four decades, and a newly critical political and journalistic milieu. If expectations of government were already high by 1965, when Betsy struck, then political and media reactions to the disaster were still generally uncritical. Seven years later, it is not in truth obvious that the federal approach to Agnes was unusually deficient or worse than the Johnson administration's response to Betsy, but examples of unmet human need were now highlighted by reporters and politicians to a greater extent than before. Absent this new reporting culture, and the disputatious, untrusting political environment within which it emerged, it is highly improbable that Nixon would have responded so forcefully to the disaster.

In this new environment, with Americans demanding more from presidents than before but trusting them less, natural disasters presented a particular challenge, for it would be hard to identify a policy area where—at least in the case of a major catastrophe—a greater gulf separated the new expectations from the president's actual ability to help. That disequilibrium appeared for the first time in relation to Hurricane Agnes, then reached new heights during the administration of George H. W. Bush, when his response to Hurricane Andrew came under withering assault. And it reached its zenith with the firestorm that engulfed George W. Bush following Hurricane Katrina, which might reasonably be conceived as the apotheosis of the combination of changes in American political culture during the post–Great Society era that have been the subject of this essay.

CONCLUSION

The Perils and Prospects of Presidential History

BRUCE J. SCHULMAN

InsideJobs.com, the popular career advice website, includes "presidential historian" among the jobs it profiles; it even lists a salary range and suggests the required personal characteristics (you should be "levelheaded," holding "your emotions in check, even in tough situations"). A "Presidential Historian," the site explains, "is the person who knows the childhood of George Washington, the political views of Thomas Jefferson, and the height of Abraham Lincoln's hat."[1] That remains a familiar description, one that does a fair degree of justice to the bestselling authors whose faces pop up when you enter the term into a search engine, and it goes a long way toward explaining why presidential history occupies a kind of scholarly no man's land. Despite the unrivaled impact of the presidency in modern American life and the widespread popular interest in the office and its occupants, studies of the presidency, as Brian Balogh notes in the introduction to this volume, have long remained outside the mainstream of American historical scholarship, little influencing and little influenced by the field's central concerns, debates, and approaches.

The contributors to this book hope to redress that neglect, to jump-start a new generation of scholarship about the presidency that capitalizes on key insights of leading scholars, many of whom have not concentrated on the presidency. Pathbreaking work in subdisciplines ranging from cultural to social history has created new frameworks that can inform and enrich work on the presidency. It has already begun to do so; a number of senior scholars have ventured into presidential history after making a name for themselves in fields as disparate as intellectual and social history. This book seeks to galvanize interest in the presidency and extend it from presidential historians and political scientists to a broader range of historians, including those just embarking on their careers. By pointing to the rich opportunities for a conversation about political history that features the history of presidents and some of the most fruitful trends in historical scholarship over the past generation and by engaging some of the leading social scientists who concentrate on the presidency, we hope to foster a new generation of scholars to pursue of variety of analytical approaches to the American presidency. This particular initiative comes at a time that political history, in general, is experiencing a renewal and at a historical moment when the influence of the contemporary presidency has made a deep impression on the current generation of scholars. In short, this is a propitious time for historians of all stripes to "bring the president back in."

In the article that opens this anthology, Stephen Skowronek usefully distinguishes between the history of the presidency—understood as studies of the institution—and the history of presidents. The field and its reputation among professional historians and the reading public alike has been shaped, however, by the work of so-called presidential historians—a genre that resembles Skowronek's history of the presidents but fits comfortably into neither category of scholarship. "Presidential Historian" denotes a particular species—someone with a ready supply of anecdotes about the personal peculiarities, heroic qualities, and epic villainy of the forty-three men who have held the nation's highest office. While they engage in serious scholarship, the enterprise of "presidential historians" remains essentially biographical. Even broader works like Michael Beschloss's *Presidential Courage* and Doris Kearns Goodwin's *Team of Rivals* focus on illuminating the character of distinctive individuals. And, of course, "presidential historians" have readers and viewers—lots of them.

To be sure, academic historians of the presidency possess a ready store of telling presidential anecdotes (they have read the documents, listened to the tapes, reviewed the transcripts). But they operate under a different set of constraints (or, to spin it positively, they are armed with a different set of skills): training that prompts them to embed the richly anecdotal day-to-day chronicles of each presidency into broader contexts and analytic categories. The presidency interests them primarily because it at once embodies and shapes the broader processes around it: the structures and instability of the international economy, the reigning intellectual paradigms (and the challenges to them), the nature of the political parties, the capacities and preferences of bureaucracies, the federal system, the operations of Congress and the courts, the ebb and flow of religious enthusiasm, and shifts in sex roles and gendered political behavior. In particular, forty years of social and cultural history in the academy have reshaped the questions historians of the presidency ask and the issues they think important. It's not so much that the scholars whose work this volume assembles would never write a book about "presidential courage" or the relationship between a chief executive and his top advisers, but they would define the terms differently and pursue the inquiry with different objectives.

A few key issues animate this gap between popular "presidential history" and "serious historical scholarship" (and, to some extent, also frame tensions between historians of the presidency and political scientists). Without evoking nostalgia for a bygone era when giants like Richard Hofstadter, Daniel Boorstin, Allen Nevins, and Arthur Schlesinger strode the earth and a mass public actually read the work of professors, this divide matters; it has implications for how the principal historical narratives of the presidency have been shaped and for the potential to revise those received narratives based on the insights of cultural, social, and political history scholarship. The first point of conflict centers around what several contributors to this volume portray as the divide between agency and structure: the wide divergence in approach between, at one extreme, political scientists who almost wholly emphasize the structural constraints on the presidency and almost wholly neglect the agency of particular presidents and, at the other extreme, popular presidential biographers who stress the character, background, and personality of their subjects to the exclusion of structural factors. Between these two extremes lies a vast middle ground, to be sure—indeed, those extremes cannot capture the ways in which any historian embodies both tendencies at once in nuanced ways—but a debate about the relative importance of structure and agency remains central to the tensions between "presidential history" and the academic study of the institution.[2]

Historians of the presidency, Skowronek argued, had developed an obsession with biography, a genre that necessarily exaggerated the impact of individual presidents' characters and political skills.[3] In 2006, Ron Brownstein, Washington correspondent for the *Los Angeles Times*, interrogated the astonishing popularity of presidential biographies by interviewing authors Doris Kearns Goodwin, Robert Dallek, Sean Wilentz, Alan Brinkley, Richard Reeves, and Arthur Schlesinger as well as political insiders like former president Bill Clinton and Bush administration political strategist Karl Rove. While the assembled biographers offered a spirited defense of the trade they practice, they largely accepted the critique of academics like Skowronek. Dallek, for his part, has frequently described the major contribution of his work as demonstrating the crucial importance of the man who occupies the White House: The results of national elections affect the political landscape, rather than merely reflecting it.

Yet even some popular presidential biographers insisted that their work did not sentimentally over-stress the agency of their protagonists to the neglect of the larger social, economic, and institutional structures in which they operated. Brownstein even suggested that academic scholarship had subtly reshaped popular studies of the presidents. Like "a river seeping through cracks in old walls," Brownstein wrote, "the bottom-up school of history has changed the way modern writers treat presidents." To be sure, Brownstein offered rather thin evidence for this conclusion, citing only Goodwin's emphasis on the roles played by the wives and children of politicians.[4]

In fact, Brownstein's conclusion papered over a lingering divide within the historical discipline, one that long relegated the presidency to the margins of American historical scholarship even as it won a wide popular readership. That development highlights a second major tension that has tended to banish the presidency from "serious history": Recent scholarship reveals a continuing dispute between champions of cultural and social history who find presidential history hopelessly retrograde and those who make a case for its scholarly virtues. This dispute at once reflects a fissure within the discipline and a set of political judgments about the ideological work that historical scholarship ought to perform. For example, Joseph Ellis, professor of history at Mount Holyoke, assails the dominant position of cultural and social history in American universities and the corresponding devaluation of biography. "Any aspiring graduate student in history," Ellis wrote, "who expresses an interest in, say, Thomas Jefferson and his first term as president, rather than the Creole population that Jefferson appropriated for the United States in the Louisiana Purchase, has inadvertently committed professional suicide."[5] For Ellis, the profession privileges certain subfields because the preponderance of work in those fields reinforces a particular, ideologically charged critique of American democracy.

Well, without conceding the privileged position of studies of dispossessed groups within the historical academy, Allen Kulikoff, an eminent social historian of early America, has essentially reinforced Ellis's argument. Bemoaning the seeming inability of academic historians to reshape "the master narrative" that characterizes popular understanding of American history, Kulikoff, in a 2005 article tellingly titled, "The Founding Fathers: Best Sellers! TV Stars! Punctual Plumbers!" mocked heroic depictions of the founders like that of Ellis, contrasting them against work that, in his words, challenges "deeply-held beliefs about the heroism of the founders and the democracy they established, replacing it with skepticism, and with attention to women, slaves, Indians, and the poor." Not content to dominate the faculty lounges and leave the master narrative to popular authors, Kulikoff suggested that social and cultural historians might appropriate for themselves the genre of presidential history, using it as a Trojan horse to sneak their favored subject matter and their critical perspective on American democracy past unwary readers.[6]

But even that concession alarmed some academics. Writing in the official organ of the American Historical Association, the president of that body, Barbara Weinstein, dismissed the argument that academic historians had lost cultural authority by adopting the challenging subject matter and more complex methodologies of social and cultural history. She also vigorously denounced nostalgia for a bygone age when men were men, American historians crafted dramatic narratives of the great deeds of generals and presidents, and professors filled the bestseller lists. Characterizing that imaginary golden age as an era "when almost all major historians (not to mention politicians) were white males" who could presume to speak with a "natural authority," Weinstein labeled the "oracular statements" that past giants like Arthur Schlesinger favored as "inappropriate, even a bit absurd." Contemporary academics live in a disenchanted world: In Weinstein's mind, half a century of rigorous cultural and social history had laid bare the reckless oversimplifications and loaded ideological assumptions that undergirded the grand proclamations of popular presidential historians.[7]

Moreover, unlike Kulikoff, Weinstein insisted that the current generation of historians had actually reshaped the master narrative, exerting a profound impact on how the public viewed the nation's history. An entire scholarly movement had fundamentally altered Americans' perceptions of women, gays, African Americans, workers, and other historical actors.[8] Along with studies of broad cultural movements and *mentalités*, serious histories of the bottom-up variety constructed alternate versions of U.S. history, ones that undermined the triumphalism, the emphasis on heroic individuals, and the American exceptionalism of presidential history. Like tectonic plates, Weinstein suggested, historical accounts of presidents and their administrations float alongside social and cultural history, occasionally colliding but remaining separate continents.

At the same time, a fault line also emerged in the historical study of the presidency itself. If biographers like Ellis view something like a study of Jefferson's first term as an antidote to a historiography too steeped in trendy jargon and the struggles of the dispossessed, and cultural historians like Weinstein see that work as a rearguard action in service of a conservative political philosophy, a small cohort of scholars, including Sean Wilentz and David Greenberg, have pursued what we might call a third way. Not surprisingly, these historians tend to be crossover artists: They appear frequently in the public prints, publish with trade presses, and, in many cases, have backgrounds in journalism. But at the same time, they not only maintain strong academic credentials but also intervene regularly and forcefully in professional arguments.

In *The New Republic*, Wilentz offered this approach a historical pedigree. Denouncing the popular history of such figures as Ken Burns and David McCullough, Wilentz attributed their appeal to a backlash against the "remorseless reexamination" of America's past that academic historians undertook between the 1950s and the 1980s. While popular history had long been a staple of American letters, Wilentz asserted that the genre diverged onto two rival tracks during the early postwar period. Bernard DeVoto embodied the path Wilentz favored—the journalist-turned-historian who believed that historical writing should demonstrate literary style and a love of facts, while also advancing strong arguments. A number of professors followed in DeVoto's footsteps—a motley group of historians united only by their common commitment to treating history as "a battleground of contesting views about American life and development" rather than a "panoramic backward gaze." Instead of confirming "received myths and platitudes about America," this history meant to "rattle its readers."[9]

That kind of popular history, according to Wilentz, became roadkill before the steamroller of *American Heritage* magazine—an approach that transformed history into "passive nostalgic spectacle." Wilentz described David McCullough as "the most accomplished current practitioner of this style" but fingered Ken Burns as his public enemy number one, calling his Civil War documentary "crushingly sentimental and vacuous."[10] Although Wilentz never offered an explicit remedy to what he portrayed as the decline of popular history, he implied that historians should emulate DeVoto rather than McCullough. Laying out an agenda for his fellow academics, Wilentz suggested that bolder arguments and sharper prose (so long as form is used to reveal meaning) would dry up the market for the pabulum offered by popular historians.[11]

What then might this approach, this "Third Way," reveal about the potential—and not merely the multiple discontents—of "presidential history"? Our assumptions here—assumptions animating the rationale for this volume—are that we want writers and readers of popular presidential history, a genre that has been and will continue to feature biography, to take academic concerns seriously—that the next biographers of Carter and Reagan, for instance, will read the work of Robert Self, Alice O'Connor, Susan Douglas, and the other participants in this anthology. We also hope that professional historians renew the history of the presidency and make the institution central to their debates about American economic and cultural as well as political life. Recent scholarship in U.S. cultural history has gone political too. The dalliance of the 1990s (think of Alice Kessler-Harris's essay in the 1997 edition of the AHA's *The New American History*, in which she wrote that social history had "lost its way" because of its "disconnection from politics") has become a genuine affair. It's not just that future biographers of Reagan will read the work of cultural and intellectual historians; it's that those historians have also found Reagan (to choose just one example) a subject worthy of their attention.

To advance that agenda, the contributors to this volume believe that it is time to erase the top-down/bottom-up divide. To be sure, the skirmishes between social and political history during the 1970s and 1980s continue to cast a long shadow. When I taught at UCLA in the early 1990s, the department offered two rival U.S. survey courses—the history of the American people and the history of the United States—as if you could have one without the other! But one huge benefit of the professional turn toward cultural history has been the explosion of that false distinction and a new emphasis on the reciprocal interactions between different kinds of political and social actors. The presidency offers a key locus for these interactions. For example, neither bottom-up nor top-down models define contributor Robert Self's recent book, *All in the Family*; in Self's pages, archival sources housed at presidential libraries and the institutional structure of the executive branch undergird his history of "family values." The Reagan administration, for example, sits amid rather than above a wide range of social and political actors, both within and outside the government. It channels and delimits the energies of social and economic forces but is also buffeted and constrained by them. Self's book offers a promising model of how academic historians might approach the presidency.[12]

Second, while studies of the presidency will undoubtedly continue to focus on the lives and administrations of individual chief executives, they can and should rely less on the tools of traditional heroic biography—techniques that stress the subject's distinctive attributes and rip him (or, someday, her) out of the fibers and wrappings of history. Instead, they might engage more directly with the concerns and methods of "microhistory." While this genre, sometimes called "New Narrative History," often focuses on the lives of notable individuals, it seeks to embed subjects within their contexts, to illuminate broader structures rather than to obscure them. Biography, to quote one comparison of the two approaches, assumes "the singularity and significance of an individual's contribution to history." On the other hand, "however singular a person's life may be," microhistory finds the "value of examining" it in "how it serves as an allegory for the culture as a whole."[13]

For example, David Greenberg uses the presidency of Calvin Coolidge to frame arguments about both the development of American conservatism, challenging the normal periodization that locates the origins of the modern conservative movement in the post–World War II period, and the relationship between the state and the media. Greenberg's study of Coolidge thus intervenes forcefully in broader discussions of the transition from a politics of parties to a mass-mediated politics of interests. These books and others like them represent ways that so-called presidential historians might construct literary narratives that focus on the outsized inhabitants of the White House while still incorporating the insights of a generation of cultural and political historians.

The task will not prove as easy as we have made it sound: Even the way the United States stores its records in separate presidential libraries points researchers toward stories of individual presidents and administrations rather than making presidents, the shifts and continuities and dialogue among them, and their relationships to broader historical forces central to the enterprise of "presidential history." Recasting that history remains something of an errand into the wilderness, but as this book makes abundantly clear, rarely before have the conditions for running it seemed so promising.

NOTES

Introduction

1. The author thanks Stefanie Abbott, Ed Ayers, Kathleen Berggren, Ira Katznelson, Mel Leffler, Evan McCormick, Michael McGandy, Bruce Schulman, and two anonymous readers for their assistance with this introduction. He also thanks the Miller Center for its enduring support of this project and more broadly for its commitment to understanding politics from an historical perspective.

2. See Brian Balogh, "State of the State among Historians," *Social Science History* 27, no. 3 (2003): 455–63.

3. See Brian Balogh, "Reorganizing the Organizational Synthesis: Federal-Professional Relations in Modern America," *Studies in American Political Development* 5, no. 1 (Spring 1991): 119–72.

4. Julian E. Zelizer, "Clio's Lost Tribe: Policy History Since 1978," *Journal of Policy History* 12, no. 3 (2000): 369–94.

5. See Michael J. Hogan, *The Marshall Plan: America, Britain, and the Reconstruction of Western Europe, 1947–1952* (New York: Cambridge University Press, 1987). See also Edward Berkowitz, "The First Social Security Crisis," in *Social Security After Fifty*, ed. Berkowitz (New York: Greenwood Press, 1987); Edward Berkowitz, *Mr. Social Security: The Life of Wilbur J. Cohen* (Lawrence: University Press of Kansas, 1995); Martha Derthick, *Policymaking for Social Security* (Washington D.C.: Brookings Institution Press, 1979).

6. Karen Orren and Stephen Skowronek, *The Search for American Political Development* (New York: Cambridge University Press, 2004).

7. Stephen Skowronek, *Building a New American State* (New York: Cambridge University Press, 1982).

8. Skowronek, *Search for American Political Development*.

9. See John Morton Blum's early work, especially *The Republican Roosevelt* (Cambridge: Harvard University Press, 1954) and *Woodrow Wilson and the Politics of Morality* (Boston: Little, Brown, 1956); John Milton Cooper, *The Warrior and the Priest: Woodrow Wilson and Theodore Roosevelt* (Cambridge: Belknap Press of Harvard University Press, 1983); and Arthur Schlesinger's three-volume history on "the Age of Roosevelt": *The Crisis of the Old Order, 1919–1933* (Boston: Houghton Mifflin, 1957), *The Coming of the New Deal, 1934–1935* (Boston: Houghton Mifflin, 1958), and *The Politics of Upheaval, 1935–1936* (Boston: Houghton Mifflin, 1960).

10. It is no surprise that this book was in the field that used to be known as "diplomatic history," in which presidents have had a disproportionate degree of influence in the twentieth century. It is Fred Logevall's *Choosing War: The Last Chance for Peace and Escalation of War in Vietnam*, in which Lyndon Johnson's policies play a major role. In December 2012, Evan D. McCormick, a PhD candi-

date in history at the University of Virginia, reviewed the first books of all the twentieth-century U.S. historians currently teaching who were hired since 1993. McCormick looked at the top sixteen programs rated by the most recent rankings according to *U.S. News* (2009). There are sixteen schools because there was a three-way tie for 14th. The next three schools, not on this list, are Brown, NYU, and UT-Austin.

11. Balogh, "State of the State."

12. Ibid.

13. The turn from "diplomatic history" to studies of "America and the World" has taken various forms. For an example of the focus on ideology in decision making, see Michael H. Hunt, *Ideology and U.S. Foreign Policy* (New Haven: Yale University Press, 1987); for an example of a focus on the role of gender in power relations, see Kristin Hoganson, *Fighting for American Manhood: How Gender Politics Provoked the Spanish-American and Philippine-American Wars* (New Haven: Yale University Press, 1998); for an example of an international treatment of domestic racial issues, see Mary L. Dudziak, *Cold War Civil Rights: Race and the Image of American Democracy* (Princeton: Princeton University Press, 2000); for an example of a transnational approach to U.S. foreign policy issues, see Elizabeth Borgwardt, *A New Deal for the World: America's Vision for Human Rights* (Boston: Belknap Press of Harvard University Press, 2005) and Nick Cullather, *The Hungry World: America's Cold War Battle against Poverty in Asia* (Cambridge: Harvard University Press, 2010).

14. Michael Willrich, *City of Courts: Socializing Justice in Progressive Era Chicago* (New York: Cambridge University Press, 2003) and *Pox: An American History* (New York: Penguin, 2011). See Barbara Young Welke, *Recasting American Liberty: Gender, Race, Law, and the Railroad Revolution, 1865–1920* (New York: Cambridge University Press, 2001) and Risa Lauren Goluboff, *The Lost Promise of Civil Rights* (Cambridge: Harvard University Press, 2007).

15. James G. Wilson, *The Triumph of Improvisation: Gorbachev's Adaptability, Reagan's Engagement, and the End of the Cold War* (New York: Cornell University Press, 2014).

16. For examples, see Frank Costigliola, *Roosevelt's Lost Alliances: How Personal Politics Helped Start the Cold War* (Princeton: Princeton University Press, 2012); Bruce Schulman, *Lyndon B. Johnson and American Liberalism* (New York: St. Martin's, 2007); Thomas J. Sugrue, *Not Even Past: Barack Obama and the Burden of Race* (Princeton: Princeton University Press, 2010); David Greenberg, *Calvin Coolidge* (New York: Times Books, 2007) and *Nixon's Shadow: The History of an Image* (New York: W.W. Norton, 2003); James T. Kloppenberg, *Reading Obama: Dreams, Hope, and the American Political Tradition* (Princeton: Princeton University Press, 2011); Daniel T. Rodgers, *Age of Fracture* (Cambridge: Belknap Press of Harvard University Press, 2011); Sean Wilentz, *The Age of Reagan: A History, 1974–2008* (New York: Harper, 2008); Julian E. Zelizer, *Jimmy Carter* (New York: Times Books, 2010) and *The Presidency of George W. Bush: A First Historical Assessment* (Princeton: Princeton University Press, 2010), among others.

17. For examples, see Michael R. Beschloss, *Presidential Courage: Brave Leaders and How They Changed America, 1789–1989* (New York: Simon & Schuster, 2007); David G. McCullough, *John Adams* (New York: Simon & Schuster, 2001); and Doris Kearns Goodwin, *Team of Rivals: The Political Genius of Abraham Lincoln* (New York: Simon & Schuster, 2005).

1. The Unsettled State of Presidential History

1. See Harvey C. Mansfield Jr., *Taming the Prince: The Ambivalence of Modern Executive Power* (New York: Free Press, 1989); Forrest McDonald, *The American Presidency: An Intellectual History* (Lawrence: University Press of Kansas, 1994); Eric Nelson, "Patriot Royalism: The Stuart Monarchy in American Political Thought, 1769–75," *William and Mary Quarterly* 68 (2011): 533–72; John W. Compton and Karen Orren, "Political Theory in Institutional Context: The Case of Patriot Royalism," *American Political Thought*, forthcoming.

2. Charles C. Thach Jr., *The Creation of the Presidency, 1775–1789: A Study in Constitutional History* (Baltimore: Johns Hopkins University Press, 1923), 1, 124.

3. See Andrew Rudalevige, *The New Imperial Presidency: Renewing Presidential Power after Watergate* (Ann Arbor: University of Michigan Press, 2006).

4. Woodrow Wilson, *Congressional Government* (Boston: Houghton Mifflin, 1885); James MacGregor Burns, *Presidential Government: The Crucible of Leadership* (Boston: Houghton Mifflin, 1965).

5. Wilson, *Congressional Government*.

6. Harold J. Laski, *The American Presidency: An Interpretation* (London: George Allen and Unwin, 1940), 169–70.

7. Richard Neustadt, *Presidential Power: The Politics of Leadership* (New York: Wiley, 1960).

8. Henry Jones Ford, *The Rise and Growth of American Politics: A Sketch of Constitutional Development* (New York: Macmillan Company, 1898), 279.

9. Theodore Roosevelt, *An Autobiography* (New York: Charles Scribner's Sons, 1913), 372–80.

10. Woodrow Wilson, *Constitutional Government in the United States* (New York: Columbia University Press, 1908).

11. Ibid., 70.

12. Walter Lippmann, *Public Opinion* (New York: Harcourt, Brace and Company, 1922), 288; Neustadt, *Presidential Power*.

13. Herbert Croly, *The Promise of American Life*, ed. Arthur M. Schlesinger Jr. (Cambridge: Harvard University Press, 1965), 278; Herbert Croly, *Progressive Democracy* (Transaction, 1988), 145–48.

14. Franklin Pierce, *Federal Usurpation* (New York: D. Appleton and Company, 1908); Andrea Katz, "The Progressive Presidency and the Shaping of the Modern Executive," paper presented at the annual meeting for the American Political Science Association, Seattle, Washington, September 1–4, 2011.

15. Ford, *Rise and Growth*, 56.

16. Ibid., 292–93.

17. See Arthur M. Schlesinger Jr., *The Age of Jackson* (Boston: Little, Brown, 1945).

18. See more recently Bruce Ackerman, *We The People: Foundations* (Cambridge: Harvard University Press, 1991); Bruce Ackerman, *Failure of the Founding Fathers: Jefferson, Marshall, and the Rise of Presidential Democracy* (Cambridge: Harvard University Press, 2005). On ambivalence in the Progressive critique of party see, Eldon Eisenach, "Progressive Conundrum: Federal Constitution, National State, and Popular Sovereignty" in *The Progressives' Century: Democratic Reform, Constitutional*

Government and the Modern American State, ed. Stephen, Skowronek, Stephen Engel, and Bruce Ackerman (New Haven: Yale University Press, forthcoming 2016).

19. Wilson, *Constitutional Government*, 68.

20. Croly, *Promise of American Life*.

21. Woodrow Wilson, *Essential Writings and Speeches of the Scholar-President*, ed. Mario R. DiNunzio (New York: New York University Press, 2006), 103.

22. Sidney M. Milkis and Daniel J. Tichenor, "'Direct Democracy' and Social Justice: The Progressive Party Campaign of 1912," *Studies in American Political Development* 8 (1994): 282–340.

23. M. J. C. Vile, *Constitutionalism and the Separation of Powers*, 2d ed. (Indianapolis: Liberty Fund, 1998), 289–300.

24. James M. Landis, *The Administrative Process* (New Haven: Yale University Press, 1938), 47.

25. On the "parastate" see Eldon J. Eisenach, *The Lost Promise of Progressivism* (Lawrence: University Press of Kansas, 1994). On the Progressive theory of administration, see Blake Emerson, "Administration in the 'Land of the Future,'" a paper presented at the University of Texas Law Conference, October, 13, 2014.

26. Charles E. Merriam, *New Aspects of Politics*, 3d ed. (Chicago: University of Chicago Press, 1970), 246–83.

27. See Willmoore Kendall, "The Two Majorities," *Midwest Journal of Political Science* 4 (1960): 317–45; Alfred De Grazia, *Republic in Crisis: Congress against the Executive Force* (New York: Federal Legal Publications, 1965); James Burnham, *Congress and the American Tradition* (Chicago: H. Regnery Co., 1959); Patrick G. Lynch, "Protecting Individual Rights through a Federal System: James Buchanan's View of Federalism," *Publius* 34 (2004): 153–68.

28. Edward Corwin, *The President: Office and Powers* (New York: New York University Press, 1940); Clinton Rossiter, *Constitutional Dictatorship* (Princeton: Princeton University Press, 1948).

29. Arthur M. Schlesinger Jr., *Journals, 1952–2000* (New York: Penguin Press, 2007), 260.

30. Arthur M. Schlesinger Jr., *The Imperial Presidency* (Boston: Houghton Mifflin, 1973).

31. Theodore Lowi, *Personal President: Power Invested, Promise Unfulfilled* (Ithaca, NY: Cornell University Press, 1985).

32. Theodore Lowi, *The End of Liberalism: Ideology, Policy, and the Crisis of Public Authority* (New York: Norton, 1969).

33. See James W. Ceaser, *Presidential Selection: Theory and Development* (Princeton: Princeton University Press, 1979); Jeffrey Tulis, *The Rhetorical Presidency* (Princeton: Princeton University Press, 1987); Charles R. Kesler, "Woodrow Wilson and the Statesmanship of Progress," in *Natural Right and Political Right: Essays in Honor of Harry V. Jaffa*, ed. Thomas B. Silver and Peter W. Schramm (Durham, NC: Carolina Academic Press, 1984); Ronald J. Pestritto, *Woodrow Wilson and the Roots of Modern Liberalism* (Lanham, MD: Rowman and Littlefield, 2005); Terry Bimes and Stephen Skowronek, "Woodrow Wilson's Critique of Popular Leadership: Reassessing the Modern-Traditional Divide in Presidential History," in *Speaking to the People: The Rhetorical Presidency in Historical Perspective*, ed. Richard J. Ellis (Amherst: University of Massachusetts Press, 1998).

34. Tulis, *Rhetorical Presidency*.

35. Ibid., 46.

36. Terry M. Moe, "The Politicized Presidency," in *The New Direction of American Politics*, ed. John E. Chubb and Paul E. Peterson (Washington, DC: Brookings Institution, 1985), 235–73.

37. See Richard Nathan, *The Plot That Failed: Nixon and the Administrative Presidency* (New York: Wiley, 1975); James L. Sundquist, *The Decline and Resurgence of Congress* (Washington, DC: Brookings Institution, 1981); Paul C. Light, *Thickening Government: Federal Hierarchy and the Diffusion of Accountability* (Washington, DC: Brookings Institution, 1995); Benjamin Ginsberg and Martin Shefter, *Politics by Other Means* (New York: Norton, 2002).

38. Sidney M. Milkis, *The President and the Parties: The Transformation of the American Party System since the New Deal* (New York: Oxford University Press, 1993).

39. Samuel Kernell, *Going Public: New Strategies of Presidential Leadership* (Washington, DC: CQ Press, 1986)

40. George C. Edwards III, *At the Margins: Presidential Leadership of Congress* (New Haven: Yale University Press, 1983); George C. Edwards III, *On Deaf Ears: The Limits of the Bully Pulpit* (New Haven: Yale University Press, 2003); William G. Howell, *Power without Persuasion: The Politics of Direct Presidential Action* (Princeton: Princeton University Press, 2003); B. Dan Wood, *The Myth of Presidential Representation* (New York: Cambridge University Press, 2009)

41. Fred I. Greenstein, "Change and Continuity in the Modern Presidency," in *The New American Political System*, ed. Anthony King (Washington, DC: American Enterprise Institute, 1978), 45–87.

42. David K. Nichols, *The Myth of the Modern Presidency* (University Park: Pennsylvania State University Press, 1994).

43. Ibid., 5.

44. John T. Woolley, "Drawing Lines or Defining Variables? Studying Big Changes in the American Presidency," paper presented at the annual meeting for the American Political Science Association, Washington, DC, September 1–4, 2005, p. 20.

45. Wilfred E. Binkley, *President and Congress* (New York: Vintage Books, 1962).

46. Richard J. Ellis and Stephen Kirk, "Presidential Mandates in the Nineteenth Century: Conceptual Change and Institutional Development," *Studies in American Political Development* 9 (1995): 117–86.

47. Victoria A. Farrar-Myers, *Scripted for Change: The Institutionalization of the American Presidency* (College State: Texas A&M University Press, 2007).

48. Peri E. Arnold, *Remaking the Presidency: Roosevelt, Taft, and Wilson, 1901–1916* (Lawrence: University Press of Kansas, 2011).

49. Daniel Galvin and Colleen J. Shogan, "Presidential Politicization and Centralization across the Modern-Traditional Divide," *Polity* 36 (2004): 477–504.

50. Mel Laracey, *Presidents and the People: The Partisan Story of Going Public* (College Station: Texas A&M University Press, 2002).

51. Jeffrey Tulis, "Reflections on the Rhetorical Presidency in American Political Development," in *Speaking to the People: The Rhetorical Presidency in Historical Perspective*, ed. Richard J. Ellis, 211–33.

52. Steven G. Calabresi and Kevin H. Rhodes, "The Structural Constitution: Unitary Executive, Plural Judiciary," *Harvard Law Review* 105 (1992): 1153–1216.

53. Steven G. Calabresi and Christopher S. Yoo, *The Unitary Executive: Presidential Power from Washington to Bush* (New Haven: Yale University Press, 2008).

54. Ibid., 17.

55. See Terry Eastland, *Energy in the Executive: The Case for the Strong Presidency* (New York: Free Press, 1992); Hadley Arkes, "On the Moral Standing of the President as an Interpreter of the Constitution: Some Reflections on Our Current 'Crises,'" *PS* 20 (1987): 637–42.

56. *Morrison v. Olson*, 487 U.S. 654 (1988) and *Humphrey's Executor v. Federal Trade Commission*, 295 U.S. 202 (1935).

57. Calabresi and Yoo, *Unitary Executive*, 8.

58. John Yoo, *The Powers of War and Peace: The Constitution and Foreign Affairs after 9/11* (Chicago: University of Chicago Press, 2005), 30–54.

59. Ibid., 88–140.

60. Alexander Hamilton, "Pacificus No. 1 (June 29, 1793)," reprinted in *Classics of American Political and Constitutional Thought*, ed. Scott J. Hamond, Kevin R. Hardwick, and Howard L. Lubert (Indianapolis: Hackett, 2007), 633–40.

61. James Madison, "Helvidius, No. 1 (August 24, 1793)," in *Classics of American Political and Constitutional Thought*, ed. Hamond, Hardwick, and Lubert, 640–41.

62. Jeremy D. Bailey, "The New Unitary Executive and Democratic Theory: The Problem of Alexander Hamilton," *American Political Science Review* 102 (2008): 453–65.

63. Louis Fisher, *Presidential War Power*, 2d ed. (Lawrence: University of Kansas Press, 2004), 14–15.

64. Ibid., 237.

65. Eric A. Posner and Adrian Vermuele, *The Executive Unbound: After the Madisonian Republic* (New York: Oxford University Press, 2011).

66. Bruce Ackerman, *The Decline and Fall of the American Republic* (Cambridge: Harvard University Press, 2010).

2. Personal Dynamics and Presidential Transition

1. Lord Moran, *Churchill at War 1940–45* (New York: Carroll & Graf, 2002), 326.

2. Reminiscences of Marquis Childs (1959), Columbia Center for Oral History Collection, 109–10.

3. William E. Pemberton, *Harry S. Truman: Fair Dealer and Cold Warrior* (Boston: Twayne, 1989), 6.

4. Robert H. Ferrell, ed., *Off the Record: The Private Papers of Harry S. Truman* (New York: Harper & Row, 1980), 359.

5. Robert H. Ferrell, ed., *Dear Bess* (New York: W. W. Norton, 1983), 285.

6. Ibid., 516.

7. John M. Blum, ed., *The Price of Vision: The Diary of Henry A. Wallace* (Boston: Houghton Mifflin, 1973), 451.

8. Geoffrey C. Ward, ed., *Closest Companion* (Boston: Houghton Mifflin, 1995), 253.

9. Ibid., 423, emphasis in original.

10. Ferrell, ed., *Off the Record*, 35, emphasis in original.

11. Joseph E. Davies, "Discussion of Vatican with Molotov," May 28, 1943, box 13, Joseph E. Davies papers, Library of Congress, Washington, D.C.

12. Joseph P. Lash diary, January 1, 1942, box 31, Joseph P. Lash papers, Franklin D. Roosevelt Library, Hyde Park, N.Y.

13. Record of meetings between Foreign Secretary Anthony Eden and M. Joseph Stalin, December 16–20, 1941, PREM3/394/3, National Archives, United Kingdom (hereafter NA UK).

14. Lt. Miles, "The President at Home," December 20, 1943, F. O. 371/38516, NA UK.

15. Ibid.

16. Ibid.

17. Department of State, *Foreign Relations of the United States: The Conferences at Cairo and Tehran 1943* (Washington, DC: Government Printing Office, 1961), 594.

18. William C. Bullitt, "Memorandum of Conversation with Otto von Habsburg," January 16, 1944, box 73, William C. Bullitt papers, Sterling Library, Yale University, New Haven, Conn. Von Habsburg talked with Bullitt immediately after seeing FDR.

19. Arthur M. Schlesinger Jr., Seminar, May 31, 1967, box 869, W. Averell Harriman papers, Library of Congress, Washington, D.C.

20. "Notes of Stalin's Speech during a Reception at the Kremlin on June 23, 1944 to Celebrate . . . the Polish Provisional Government of National Unity," Cold War International History Project Stalin Document Reader, Woodrow Wilson Center, Washington, DC (1999), 21.

21. "Record of General de Gaulle's Meeting with Marshal Stalin, December 2, 1944," ibid., 88.

22. "Conversation between General de Gaulle and Marshal Stalin, December 6, 1944," ibid., 96, emphasis in original.

23. Schlesinger seminar, May 31, 1967, box 869, Harriman papers.

24. *Press Conferences of Franklin D. Roosevelt*, December 19, 1944, 24: 266–70; December 22, 1944, 24: 276–78.

25. *Press Conferences of Roosevelt*, February 23, 1945, 25: 72–73.

26. Walter Lippmann, "The President at Home Again," *Daily Boston Globe*, March 3, 1945, 4.

27. "Address of the President to the Joint Session of the Congress, March 1, 1945," box 86, Master Speech File, FDRL. On the drafting of the speech, see undated memorandum by Samuel I. Rosenman, "Yalta Speech," box 18, Samuel I. Rosenman papers, FDRL; Rosenman, *Working with Roosevelt* (New York: Harper & Brothers, 1952), 526–30.

28. Marquis Childs, "Report of a Conversation with President Roosevelt on Friday, April 7, 1944," box 4, Marquis Childs papers, Wisconsin Historical Society, Madison, Wisc.

29. Clark Kerr to Christopher Warner, June 21, 1945, F. O. 371/47862, NA UK.

30. Elie Abel, interview with Rudy Abramson, September 17, 1981 (in private possession).

31. Richard Helms, interview with Abramson [1980s] (in private possession).

32. *Foreign Relations of the United States 1945* (Washington, DC: Government Printing Office, 1967), 5: 232.

33. Ibid.

34. Pemberton, *Harry S. Truman*, 44.

3. Narrator-in-Chief

1. Steve Kraske, "Long Line Forms Overnight to Get Tickets for Obama's Osawatomie Visit," *Kansas City Star*, December 4, 2011. Available at www.kansascity.com/2011/12/03/3299812/president-to-speak-on-economy.html.

2. Theodore Roosevelt, "The New Nationalism," speech, Osawatomie, Kans., August 31, 1910.

3. A transcript of the speech can be found at www.nytimes.com/2008/03/27/us/politics/27text-obama.html.

4. Steve Benen, "Obama Identifies the 'Defining Issue of Our Time,'" *Washington Monthly*, available at www.washingtonmonthly.com/political-animal/2011_12/obama_identifies_the_defining033948.php; "Obama in Osawatomie," *New York Times*, December 6, 2011, available at www.nytimes.com/2011/12/07/opinion/president-obama-in-osawatomie.html; Tea Party Express, "A Response to President Obama's Osawatomie, KS Speech," available at www.teapartyexpress.org/355/a-response-to-president-obamas-osawatomie-ks-speech; "Glenn Beck's Reaction to President Obama's 'Income Inequality' Speech," available at http://www.youtube.com/watch?v=f4u78b6o-rM&feature=youtube_gdata_player.

5. Campbell Robertson, "For Obama, a 'Moment' Speech at a Time of Great Obstacles to Change," *New York Times*, September 8, 2011.

6. "Obama Reflects on His Biggest Mistake as President," *CBS News*, July 12, 2012, available at www.cbsnews.com/8301-503544_162-57471351-503544/obama-reflects-on-his-biggest-mistake-as-president/.

7. Democracy Corps Memo (Stan Greenberg, James Carville, Erica Seifert), "Shifting the Economic Narrative," June 11, 2012.

8. Ronald Brownstein, "Obama's Economic Narrative Gap," *National Journal*, April 17, 2012. Brownstein cited the work of presidential scholar Stephen Skowronek to conclude that Obama had too soon abandoned "the authority to repudiate" his predecessor. Skowronek, *Presidential Leadership in Political Time: Reprise and Reappraisal* (Lawrence: University Press of Kansas, 2008).

9. Frank Rich, "Why Has He Fallen Short?" *New York Review of Books*, August 10, 2010, available at www.nybooks.com/articles/archives/2010/aug/19/why-has-he-fallen-short/; Christina D. Romer, "Not My Father's Recession: The Extraordinary Challenges and Policy Responses of the First Twenty Months of the Obama Administration," speech at the National Press Club, Washington, D.C., September 1, 2010.

10. See, for example, the discussion of Obama's presidency in *Democracy*, issue no. 16 (Spring 2010), available at www.democracyjournal.org/16/6749.php.

11. Panic narratives of the nineteenth century have been discussed extensively in the historical literature. See, for example, Ann Fabian, "Speculation on Distress: The Popular Discourse of the Panics of 1837 and 1857," *Yale Journal of Criticism* 3, no. 1 (1989): 127–42; Jessica Lepler, "Pictures of Panic: Constructing Hard Times in Words and Images," *Common-Place* 10, no. 3 (April 2010); Scott Nelson, *A Nation*

of Deadbeats: An Uncommon History of America's Financial Disasters (New York: Knopf, 2012).

12. James P. Pfiffner and Roger H. Davidson, *Understanding the Presidency* (New York: Pearson, 2013), 165–68; Samuel Kernell, *Going Public: New Strategies of Presidential Leadership*, 4th ed. (Washington, DC: CQ Press, 2007).

13. These quotes are from speeches collected in TR's *The Roosevelt Policy* (New York: Current Literature Publication Company, 1908), 642, 648–49.

14. For a thorough discussion of President Carter's "crisis of confidence" (a.k.a. "malaise") speech, see Kevin Mattson, *"What the Heck Are You Up To, Mr. President?": Jimmy Carter, America's "Malaise," and the Speech That Should Have Changed the Country* (New York: Bloomsbury, 2009).

15. Franklin D. Roosevelt, "First Inaugural Address," Washington, D.C., March 4, 1933, reprinted in *Nothing to Fear: The Selected Addresses of Franklin Delano Roosevelt, 1932–1945*, ed. B. D. Zevin (London: Hodder and Stoughton, 1947), 12–17.

16. Roosevelt, "Fireside Chat on the Banking Crisis," in *Nothing to Fear*, ed. Zevin, 21.

17. Harry L. Hopkins, foreword to *Nothing to Fear*, ed. Zevin, vii.

18. Franklin D. Roosevelt, "Acceptance Speech for the Renomination for the Presidency, Philadelphia, PA June 27, 1936," http://www.presidency.ucsb.edu/ws/?pid=15314.

19. Franklin D. Roosevelt, "Fireside Chat on Economic Conditions," April 14, 1938, in *Nothing to Fear*, ed. Zevin, 142–43.

20. Cara A. Finnegan, *Picturing Poverty: Print Culture and FSA Photographs* (Washington, DC: Smithsonian, 2003); Hallie Flanagan, *Arena: The Story of the Federal Theatre* (New York: Limelight, 1985); Jerrold Hirsch, *Portrait of America: A Cultural History of the Federal Writers' Project* (Chapel Hill: University of North Carolina Press, 2003).

21. James T. Sparrow, *Warfare State: World War II and the Age of Big Government* (New York: Oxford University Press, 2011).

22. Suzanne Mettler, *The Submerged State: How Invisible Government Policies Undermine American Democracy* (Chicago: University of Chicago Press, 2011).

23. Ronald Reagan, "Inaugural Address," January 20, 1981. This and other Reagan speeches and public remarks cited in this chapter can be found at www.presidency.ucsb.edu/index_docs.php.

24. See, for example, Reagan's reversal of FDR's logic in arguing that political and economic freedoms should go hand in hand: "We protect the freedom of expression of the author, as we should, but what of the freedom of expression of the entrepreneur, whose pen and paper are capital and profits, whose book may be a new invention or small business? What of the creators of our economic life, whose contributions may not only delight the mind but improve the condition of man by feeding the poor with new gains, bringing hope to the sick with new cures, vanishing ignorance with wondrous new information technologies?" Reagan, "Remarks on Signing the Tax Reform Act of 1986," October 22, 1986.

25. Reagan, "Inaugural Address," January 21, 1985.

26. Ibid.; Daniel T. Rodgers, *Age of Fracture* (Cambridge: Harvard University Press, 2011), ch. 1.

27. Reagan, "Remarks on Signing the Tax Reform Act of 1986."

28. Amos Kiewe and Davis W. Houck, *A Shining City on a Hill: Ronald Reagan's Economic Rhetoric, 1951–1989* (Westport, CT: Praeger, 1991), 136–44; Kernell, *Going Public*, 148–82.

29. Reagan, "Remarks on Signing the Economic Recovery Tax Act of 1981 and the Omnibus Budget Reconciliation Act of 1981," August 13, 1981.

30. George C. Edwards, *On Deaf Ears: The Limits of the Bully Pulpit* (New Haven: Yale University Press, 2003).

31. Sidney Blumenthal, *The Permanent Campaign: Inside the World of Elite Political Operatives* (Boston: Beacon Press, 1980).

32. Franklin D. Roosevelt, "First Inaugural Address."

33. B. Dan Wood, *The Politics of Economic Leadership: The Causes and Consequences of Presidential Rhetoric* (Princeton: Princeton University Press, 2007); Michael A. Bernstein, *A Perilous Progress: Economists and Public Purpose in Twentieth-Century America* (Princeton: Princeton University Press, 2001).

34. William J. Barber, *Design within Disorder: Franklin D. Roosevelt, the Economists, and the Shaping of American Economic Policy, 1933–1945* (New York: Cambridge University Press, 1996).

35. Alan Brinkley, *The End of Reform: New Deal Liberalism in Recession and War* (New York: Knopf, 1995), 232–35.

36. Keynes pithily summarized his own analysis of the recession in a remarkably pointed letter to FDR of February 1, 1938, available at www.fdrlibrary.marist.edu/aboutfdr/pdfs/smFDR-Keynes_1938.pdf.

37. Bernstein, *Perilous Progress*, 115–40.

38. Kiron K. Skinner, Annelise Anderson, and Martin Anderson, eds., *Reagan, In His Own Hand* (New York: Simon and Schuster, 2001).

39. James K. Galbraith, *Created Unequal: The Crisis in American Pay* (New York: Free Press, 1998), 171–82.

40. Bernstein, *Perilous Progress*, 188–91; Rodgers, *Age of Fracture*, 50–55.

41. Reagan, "Remarks on Signing the Economic Recovery Tax Act of 1981 and the Omnibus Budget Reconciliation Act of 1981."

42. Brinkley, *End of Reform*, 48–64; Meg Jacobs, *Pocketbook Politics: Economic Citizenship in Twentieth-Century America* (Princeton: Princeton University Press, 2005); Edwin Amenta, *When Movements Matter: The Townsend Plan and the Rise of Social Security* (Princeton: Princeton University Press, 2006).

43. Alice O'Connor, "Financing the Counterrevolution," in *Rightward Bound: Making America Conservative in the 1970s*, ed. Bruce J. Schulman and Julian Zelizer (Harvard University Press, 2008), 148–68.

44. Robert Kuttner, *Obama's Challenge: America's Economic Crisis and the Power of a Transformative Presidency* (New York: Chelsea Green, 2008).

45. Alice O'Connor, "The End of Capitalism as We've Known It, and the Beginning of Reform," *Labor: Studies in Working-Class History of the Americas* 8, no. 4 (Winter 2011).

46. Shailagh Murray, "Obama's Reagan Comparison Sparks Debate," *Washington Post*, January 17, 2008, available at http://voices.washingtonpost.com/44/2008/01/obamas-reagan-comparison-spark-1.html.

47. Dan Pfeiffer, "You're Going to Want to Watch This Speech," *The White House Blog*, July 21, 2013, available at www.whitehouse.gov/blog/2013/07/20/youre-going-want-watch-speech.

48. "Full Transcript of the Mitt Romney Secret Video," *Mother Jones*, September 19, 2012, available at www.motherjones.com/politics/2012/09/full-tran script-mitt-romney-secret-video.

49. M. Stephen Weatherford, "The Wages of Competence: Obama, the Economy, and the 2010 Midterm Elections," *Presidential Studies Quarterly* 42, no. 1 (March 2012): 8–39; Thomas E. Mann and Norman J. Ornstein, *It's Even Worse Than It Looks: How the American Constitutional System Collided with the Politics of Extremism* (New York: Basic Books, 2012).

50. Jacob Hacker and Paul Pierson, *Winner-Take-All Politics: How Washington Made the Rich Richer—and Turned Its Back on the Middle Class* (New York: Simon and Schuster, 2010).

51. John Cassidy, *How Markets Fail: The Logic of Economic Calamities* (New York: Farrar Straus and Giroux, 2010).

52. Benedict Carey, "Academic Dream Team Helped Obama's Effort," *New York Times*, November 12, 2012, available at www.nytimes.com/2012/11/13/health/ dream-team-of-behavioral-scientists-advised-obama-campaign.html.

4. The Reagan Devolution

1. "The Republican Debate at the Reagan Library," *New York Times*, September 7, 2011, available at www.nytimes.com/2011/09/08/us/politics/08republican-debate text.html.

2. Lind quoted in Free Congress Research and Education Foundation, December 1, 1987, Box 54, National Association of Evangelicals Records, Wheaton College Manuscripts and Special Collections, Wheaton, Illinois (hereafter NAE).

3. For a useful summary of how Reagan governed, see Meg Jacobs and Julian E. Zelizer, *Conservatives in Power: The Reagan Years, 1981–1989: A Brief History with Documents* (Boston: Bedford/St. Martin's, 2010).

4. Richard Viguerie, "An Open Letter to Vice President George Bush," *Conservative Digest*, September 1984, 46–47.

5. Daniel Tichenor, "The President, Social Movements, and Contentious Change: Lessons from the Women's Suffrage and Labor Movements," *Presidential Studies Quarterly* 29, no. 1 (March 1999): 14–25; Stephen Skowronek, *The Politics Presidents Make: Leadership from John Adams to George Bush* (Cambridge: Harvard University Press, 1993), 9–10.

6. Rowland Evans and Robert Novak, *The Reagan Revolution* (New York: E. P. Dutton, 1981).

7. Charles Colson, "So Much for Our 'Great Awakening,'" *Christianity Today*, May 13, 1988, 72.

8. Cal Thomas to Morton Blackwell, March 30, 1982, Morton Blackwell to Cal Thomas, April 6, 1982, Blackwell Files, Box OA 9079, Ronald Reagan Presidential Archives (hereafter RR); "Reagan Stirs the Broadcasters with an Evangelical Speech," *Christianity Today*, March 2, 1984, 39–40.

9. Paul Weyrich, "Conservatism's Future: Pat Robertson," *Conservative Digest*, August 1985, 13; Weyrich, "How the Republicans Lost Senate Control," *Conservative Digest*, January 1987, 49–56; David Aikman, "Washington Scorecard: Evangelical Wins and Losses During the Reagan Years," *Christianity Today*, October 21, 1988, 22–23; Fred Barnes, "No Legacy," *New Republic*, July 4, 1988, 11–14; Colson, "So

Much for Our 'Great Awakening'"; John B. Judis, "Pop-Con Politics," *New Republic*, September 3, 1984, 18–21.

10. *Chicago Tribune*, September 9, 10, and 11, 1979; May 14, 1980, 10, C1; October 12, 1980, B10; November 30, 1984, B1. Scheidler eventually published what became the movement's "manual," *Closed: 99 Ways to Stop Abortion* (Westchester, IL: Crossways Books, 1985).

11. "Pro-Life Political Reporter," August 1981; *Moral Majority Report*, March 25, 1982, Box OA9079, Blackwell Files, RR.

12. *New York Times*, December 24, 1988, 8; "Can the Pro-Life Movement Survive?" *Christianity Today*, January 15, 1988, 36–38.

13. Andrew R. Flint and Joy Porter, "Jimmy Carter: The Re-emergence of Faith-Based Politics and the Abortion Rights Issue," *Presidential Studies Quarterly* 35, no. 1 (March 2005): 28–51.

14. "Anti-Abortion Terrorism in the United States: Case Histories" and "Attacks on Abortion Facilities, 1984–1985," folder 14, box 95, National Organization for Women Records, Schlesinger, Library, Radcliffe Institute for Advanced Study, Harvard University (hereafter NOW).

15. Terry quoted in Faye Ginsburg, "Rescuing the Nation: Operation Rescue and the Rise of Anti-Abortion Militance," in *Abortion Wars: A Half Century of Struggle, 1950–2000*, ed. Rickie Solinger (Berkeley: University of California Press, 1998), 227; Randall Terry, *Operation Rescue* (Springdale, PA: Whittaker House, 1988), 156, 195; Robert A. Van Dyk, "Challenging Choice: Abortion Clinic Blockades and the Dynamics of Collective Action," PhD dissertation, University of Washington, 1995, 132–50.

16. Bill J. Leonard, *God's Last and Only Hope: The Fragmentation of the Southern Baptist Convention* (Grand Rapids, MI: William B. Eerdman's Company, 1990); Nancy Tatom Ammerman, *Baptist Battles: Social Change and Religious Conflict in the Southern Baptist Convention* (New Brunswick, NJ: Rutgers University Press, 1990); Barry Hankins, *Uneasy in Babylon: Southern Baptist Conservatives and American Culture* (Tuscaloosa: University of Alabama Press, 2002).

17. *Los Angeles Times*, June 12, 1981, A7; William W. Finlator oral history, Southern Oral History Program, no. 4007, 17; McBeth, quoted in Rob James, *The Takeover in the Southern Baptist Convention: A Brief History* (Decatur, GA: SBC Today, 1989), 21; Simmons quoted in Hankins, *Uneasy in Babylon*, 177; Harold Lindsell, *The Battle for the Bible* (Grand Rapids, MI: Zondervan, 1976); Lindsell, *The Bible in the Balance* (Grand Rapids, MI: Zondervan, 1979).

18. Criswell quoted in the *New York Times*, June 20, 1988, A16.

19. "Why Is Pat Robertson Considering a Race for the Oval Office?" *Christianity Today*, January 17, 1986, 34; Nancy Tatom Ammerman, *Baptist Battles: Social Change and Religious Conflict in the Southern Baptist Convention* (New Brunswick, NJ: Rutgers University Press, 1990), 184; Oran B. Smith, *The Rise of Baptist Republicanism* (New York: New York University Press, 1997), 106–15, 140–52.

20. Paul Weyrich, "Conservatism's Future: Pat Robertson" and Richard Viguerie, "Pat Who?" *Conservative Digest*, August/September 1985, 13, 38; "The Answer to America's Problems," *Conservative Digest*, August/September 1985, 5–6; Robertson quoted on NBC Evening News, February 16, 1988, Record No. 560735, Vanderbilt

Television News Archive, Vanderbilt University (hereafter VTN); *Conservative Digest*, January 1988, 5–14, March 1988, 27–32; letter to George H. W. Bush from Ad Hoc Coalition of Evangelical Leaders, August 8, 1988, Box 48, NAE; press releases and press clippings about the 1988 campaign, Box 65, NAE; *Conservative Digest*, August/ September 1985, 13.

21. Barnes, "No Legacy"; letter to Reagan from Nellie J. Gray, March for Life President, April 3, 1987, Juanita Duggan Files, Box OA 17961, RR.

22. *The Family: Preserving America's Future, A Report to the President from the White House Working Group on the Family* (Washington, DC: Domestic Policy Council, 1986), 4, 58–59.

23. Sidney Blumenthal, "Reaganism on Fast Forward," *New Republic*, September 3, 1984, 14–17.

24. Untitled document on pro-life strategy, OA 9081, Morton Blackwell files, RR; Smith, "Pro-Life"; "Abortion, 1981–1982: Public Opinion," Dee Jepsen Files, Box OA 10773, RR; CBS *Evening News*, November 13, 1978, record no. 255466, VTN; "Call to Action for Reproductive Rights," September 14, 1979, "Reproductive Rights Alerts," and untitled NOW memo on human life amendment, folder 14, box 95, NOW; "April 'Must Do' Activities to Stop HLA/HLB," March 20, 1981, folder 14, box 96, NOW.

25. Letter to Patricia Ireland from Eleanor Holmes Norton, April 9, 1992, and Norton speech before Congress, April 7, 1992, folder 20, box 93, NOW.

26. *Time*, December 3, 1984.

27. Morris P. Fiorina with Samuel J. Abrams and Jeremy C. Pope, *Culture War? The Myth of a Polarized America* (New York: Pearson, 2006); *Los Angeles Times*, May 18, 1995, 10; James Davison Hunter and Alan Wolfe, *Is There a Culture War? A Dialogue on Values and American Public Life* (Washington, DC: Brookings Institution Press, 2006); Rhys H. Williams, ed., *Cultural Wars in American Politics: Critical Reviews of a Popular Myth* (New York: Aldine de Gruyter, 1997).

28. *Washington Post*, September 27, 1992, A21 and November 2, 1992, A7; *New York Times*, August 16 and November 14, 1992, 1, 6; *Dallas Morning News*, 1 November 1992, 28A; *National NOW Times*, August 1995. The anti-gay measure failed to receive enough signatures to make the ballot in ten states in 1994. See *Los Angeles Times*, July 12, 1994.

29. Mark J. Rozell and Clyde Wilcox, *God at the Grassroots: The Christian Right in the 1994 Elections* (Lanham, MD: Rowman and Littlefield, 1995); *Washington Post*, August 16, 1992, C4; "Evangelicals Evaluate Contract with America," *Baptist Press*, March 9, 1995, 1–6.

30. *Washington Post*, August 16, 1992, C4; "Evangelicals Evaluate Contract with America," *Baptist Press*, March 9, 1995, 1–6; *Contract with the American Family* (Nashville: Moorings, 1995).

31. Statements of Paul Weyrich and William Marshner, Free Congress Research and Education Foundation, December 1, 1987, box 54, NAE; Jerry Falwell, "A Pragmatic Proposal," *Fundamentalist Journal*, March 1983, 8; *New York Times*, November 30, 1987, B12; *Conservative Digest*, October 1987, 17–22, and May/June 1988, 57–68; Charles Colson, "How Prolife Protest Has Backfired," *Christianity Today*, December 15, 1989, 72.

5. There Will Be Oil

1. For Blessitt's take on this encounter, see Blessitt, "The Day I Prayed with George W. Bush to Receive Jesus!" *The Official Website of Arthur Blessitt*, available at www.blessitt.com/Inspiration_Witness/PrayingWithGeorgeWBush/Praying_With_Bush_Page1.html, accessed July 30, 2013. See also David Aikman, *A Man of Faith: The Spiritual Journey of George W. Bush* (Nashville: W Publishing Group, 2004), 42, 70–71; Alan Cooperman, "Openly Religious, to a Point: Bush Leaves the Specifics of His Faith to Speculation," *Washington Post*, September 16, 2004, A1.

2. George W. Bush, *A Charge to Keep* (New York: William Morrow, 1999): 18–19, 136, 206; Tony Carnes, "A Presidential Hopeful's Progress," *Christianity Today*, October 2, 2000, 62–64; Howard Fineman et al., "Bush and God: How Faith Changed His Life and Shapes His Presidency," *Newsweek*, March 10, 2003, 25; Aikman, *Man of Faith*, 45, 75–76.

3. Charles Marsh, *Wayward Christian Soldiers: Freeing the Gospel from Political Captivity* (New York: Oxford University Press, 2007), 21, 58–59. For generous readings of Bush and evangelicalism, see Paul Kengor, *God and George W. Bush: A Spiritual Life* (New York: Harper, 2004) and Stephen Mansfield, *The Faith of George W. Bush: Bush's Spiritual Journey and How It Shapes His Administration* (New York: Tarcher, 2003). More critical but comprehensive readings include Amy Sullivan, "Why W. Doesn't Go to Church," *New Republic*, October 11, 2004; and Marsh, *Wayward Christian Soldiers*.

4. Julian E. Zelizer, *Governing America: The Revival of Political* History (Princeton: Princeton University Press, 2012), 4, 11–13. Theodore H. White, *The Making of the President 1960* (New York: Atheneum Publishers, 1961), 64; Michael Novak, *Choosing Our King: Powerful Symbols in Presidential Politics* (New York: Macmillan, 1974), 3. See also Stephen Skowronek, *Presidential Leadership in Political Time: Reprise and Reappraisal* (Lawrence: University Press of Kansas, 2011), 3.

5. Gary Scott Smith, *Faith and the Presidency: From George Washington to George W. Bush* (New York: Oxford University Press, 2006), vii, 10–12. William Inboden, *Religion and American Foreign Policy, 1945–1960: The Soul of Containment* (New York: Cambridge University Press, 2008); Andrew Preston, *Sword of the Spirit, Shield of Faith: Religion in American War and Diplomacy* (New York: Knopf, 2012). Randall Balmer, *God in the White House: A History* (New York: HarperOne, 2008); D. Michael Lindsay, *Faith in the Halls of Power: How Evangelicals Joined the American Elite* (New York: Oxford University Press, 2007), 16. Other balanced overviews of religion and the presidency include Mark J. Rozell and Cleaves Whitney, eds., *Religion and the American Presidency* (New York: Palgrave Macmillan, 2007) and David L. Holmes, *The Faiths of the Postwar Presidents: From Truman to Obama* (Athens: University of Georgia Press, 2012).

6. Zelizer, *Governing America*, 4, 23. On lived religion and moral geographies, see R. Marie Griffith and Melani McAlister, "Introduction: Is the Public Square Still Naked?" in *Religion and Politics in the Contemporary United States*, ed. Marie Griffith and Melani McAlister, Special Issue of *American Quarterly* (Baltimore: Johns Hopkins University Press, 2008), 6.

7. Carnes, "Presidential Hopeful's Progress"; Smith, *Faith and the Presidency*, 367–68.

8. Alan Brinkley and Davis Dyer, eds., *The American Presidency* (Boston and New York: Houghton Mifflin Company, 2004), 536–37.

9. For a thorough history of the Religious Right, see Daniel K. Williams, *God's Own Party: The Making of the Christian Right* (New York: Oxford University Press, 2010).

10. Gene Cooper, "Ranger Raids Continued in New Oil Field," *Dallas Morning News*, March 4, 1931. On evangelical conceptions of Roosevelt as antichrist, see Matthew Avery Sutton, "Was FDR the Antichrist? The Birth of Fundamentalist Antiliberalism in a Global Age," *Journal of American History* 98 (2012): 1052–74.

11. Cooper, "Ranger Raids Continued." Paul H. Heidebrecht, *God's Man in the Marketplace: The Story of Herbert J. Taylor* (Downers Grove, IL: InterVarsity Press, 1990), 62–63, 119–20. See also Darren Dochuk, "Moving Mountains: The Business of Evangelicalism and Extraction in a Liberal Age," in *What's Good for Business: Business and American Politics since World War II*, ed. Kim Phillips-Fein and Julian E. Zelizer (New York: Oxford University Press, 2012): 72–90.

12. L. Shannon Jung, "The Recovery of Land: Agribusiness and Creation-Centered Stewardship," in *Religion and the Life of the Nation: American Recoveries*, ed. Rowland A. Sherrill (Urbana and Chicago: University of Illinois Press, 1990), 118–19.

13. Lawrence Goodwyn, *Texas Oil, American Dreams: A Study of the Texas Independent Producers and Royalty Owners* Association (Austin: Texas State Historical Association, 1996), 49–52, 58–60, 233.

14. Goodwyn, *Texas Oil, American Dreams*, 86–89; Roger M. Olien and Diana Davids Hinton, *Wildcatters: Texas Independent Oilmen* (College Station: Texas A&M University Press, 2007), 93–95, 111.

15. Roger M. Olien and Diana Davids Olien, *Oil and Ideology: The Cultural Creation of the American Petroleum Industry* (Chapel Hill: University of North Carolina Press, 2000), 204.

16. Lindsy Escoe Pack, "The Political Aspects of the Texas Tidelands Controversy," PhD dissertation, Texas A&M University, 1979, iii; Drew Pearson, "Ike Eisenhower and Texas Oil," *Dallas Morning News*, May 9, 1952; Joseph Crespino, *Strom Thurmond's America* (New York: Hill and Wang, 2012), 79.

17. Bryan Burrough, *The Big Rich: The Rise and Fall of the Greatest Texas Oil Fortunes* (New York: Penguin, 2009), 212. Reports of Women Investors Research Institute in folder 13, box 3, Bruce Alger Papers, Dallas Public Library. "Address of Walter S. Hallanan, Sinton, Texas, April 6, 1950," in Oil & Gas—Clippings & Publications, 1950 folder, Governor Allan Shivers Papers, Texas State Archives, Austin, Texas.

18. Nancy Gibbs and Michael Duffy, *The Preacher and the Presidents: Billy Graham in the White House* (New York: Center Street, 2007), 31–34; Drew Pearson, "Ike Eisenhower and Texas Oil" and "Cullen Raps Ike's Right on Amendment," *Dallas Morning News*, February 20, 1954; "Hugh Roy Cullen, Philanthropist and Oil Operator, Dies," *Dallas Morning News*, July 5, 1957; "'Oil Town' Story of Two-Fisted Sinner," *Houston Press*, June 2, 1952; George Fuermann, "Post Card," *Houston Press*, April 1, 1952.

19. "H. J. Porter, Key Republican in Texas in 50's Is Dead at 90," *New York Times*, December 10, 1986; "Closer Than Ever," *Time*, May 5, 1952; "Ike Is Wooing

Dixie with Tidelands Oil," *New York Post*, April 26, 1952; Billy Graham to Earl C. Hankamer, November 10, 1952; Earl C. Hankamer to Billy Graham, November 12, 1952; Billy Graham to Earl C. Hankamer, December 14, 1953, folder 1, Earl Hankamer Papers, Billy Graham Archives, Wheaton College, Illinois.

20. On Sunbelt evangelical Republican ascent, see Darren Dochuk, *From Bible Belt to Sunbelt: Plain-Folk Religion, Grassroots Politics, and the Rise of Evangelical Conservatism* (New York: Norton, 2011).

21. James Morton Turner, "'The Specter of Environmentalism': Wilderness, Environmental Politics, and the Evolution of the New Right," *Journal of American History* 96 (June 2009): 132.

22. Helen Parmley, "Reagan Reaps Bible, Cap," *Dallas Morning News*, August 23, 1980; "'Here's Life' Receives $60.4 Million in Pledges," *Dallas Morning News*, May 22, 1979; Helen Parmley, "Robison Case Gets Attention of Racehorse," *Dallas Morning News*, March 15, 1979.

23. See Robert H. Nelson, *The New Holy Wars: Economic Religion Vs. Environmental Religion in Contemporary America* (University Park: Pennsylvania State University Press, 2010). On the evangelical left, see David Swartz, *Moral Minority: The Evangelical Left in an Age of Conservatism* (Philadelphia: University of Pennsylvania Press, 2012).

24. John F. Walvoord, *Armageddon: Oil and the Middle East Crisis*, rev. ed. (Grand Rapids, Michigan: Zondervan, 1974), 46–47.

25. Lindsay, *Faith in the Halls of Power*, 19; Turner, "'Specter of Environmentalism,'" 134; Nelson, *New Holy Wars*, xviii–xix.

26. Rozell and Whitney, *Religion and the American Presidency*, 8.

6. Ike's World

1. The centrality of ideology in American foreign relations is a founding assumption of revisionism, going back to William A. Williams. Later work in this vein has sometimes conflated the terms *culture* and *ideology*, as in Michael Hunt, *Ideology and U.S. Foreign Policy* (New Haven: Yale University Press, 1987), or John Dower, *War without Mercy* (New York: Pantheon, 1986)—two books that treat American perceptions of Asian peoples.

2. An early example is Vlad Zubok and Constantine Pleshakov, *Inside the Kremlin's Cold War: From Stalin to Khrushchev* (Cambridge: Harvard, 1997). For a discussion of the debate, see Mark Kramer, "Ideology and the Cold War," *Review of International Studies* (1999): 25, 539–76. For a cry of frustration over the effort to use ideas (and culture) to explain foreign relations, see Robert Buzzanco, "Where's the Beef? Culture without Power in the Study of U.S. Foreign Relations," *Diplomatic History* 24, no. 4 (2000): 623–32.

3. Melvyn P. Leffler, *For the Soul of Mankind: The United States, the Soviet Union, and the Cold War* (New York: Hill and Wang, 2007), 8, emphasis added.

4. Odd Arne Westad, *The Global Cold War: Third World Interventions and the Making of Our Times* (New York: Cambridge University Press, 2005), 9, 31, 396.

5. Alan Brinkley, "A President for Certain Seasons," *Wilson Quarterly* 14, no. 2 (Spring 1990): 116.

6. Robert Griffith, "Dwight D. Eisenhower and the Corporate Commonwealth," *American Historical Review* 87, no. 1 (February 1982): 87–122.

7. It is a term that appears throughout his public speeches and private letters. For an especially robust statement about the "American System," see "Remarks to the 63rd Continental Congress of the National Society of the Daughters of the American Revolution," April 22, 1954, *The American Presidency Project*, available at www.presidency.ucsb.edu/ws/?pid=10216.

8. "Eisenhower Links Security to Prison," *New York Times*, December 9, 1949.

9. *Papers of Dwight D. Eisenhower, Columbia: vol. X*, letter to Professor Benjamin Wood, May 6, 1949, 570–72.

10. Emmet John Hughes, *Ordeal of Power: A Political Memoir of the Eisenhower Years* (New York: Atheneum, 1963), 53–57.

11. "Annual Message to the Congress on the State of the Union, February 2nd, 1953," available at www.eisenhower.archives.gov/all_about_ike/speeches/1953_state_of_the_union.pdf.

12. 163rd Meeting of the NSC, September 24, 1953, Ann Whitman File, NSC series, box 4, Dwight D. Eisenhower Library, Abilene, KS.

13. Robert Cutler Memorandum for C. D. Jackson, September 3, 1953. White House Central Files, Confidential File, reproduced in Nancy Young, ed., *Documentary History of the Eisenhower Presidency*, vol. 3 (Bethesda, MD: LexisNexis, 2006), 311.

14. NSC 162/2, October 30, 1953. The document is available at www.fas.org/irp/offdocs/nsc-hst/nsc-162-2.pdf. For a detailed analysis of its origins, see Robert R. Bowie and Richard H. Immerman, *Waging Peace: How Eisenhower Shaped an Enduring Cold War Strategy* (New York: Oxford University Press, 1998).

15. Memorandum of Conversation, December 5, 1953, Bermuda Conference, reproduced in Young, ed., *Documentary History of the Eisenhower Presidency*, 3: 468.

16. For Congressional Republican criticisms of the armistice, see Julian Zelizer, *Arsenal of Democracy* (New York: Basic, 2010), 122. China sought the armistice because of domestic politics, not atomic brinkmanship. See Chen Jian, *Mao's China and the Cold War* (Chapel Hill: University of North Carolina Press, 2000).

17. Hughes, *Ordeal of Power*, 103.

18. Memorandum of Discussion, NSC, March 25, 1953, *Foreign Relations of the United States* (hereafter *FRUS*), *1952–1954*, vol. 2, part 1 (Washington, DC: U.S. Department of State), 258–62.

19. Hughes, *Ordeal of Power*, 106.

20. "The Chance for Peace," delivered to the American Society of Newspaper Editors, April 16, 1953, available at www.presidency.ucsb.edu/ws/index.php?pid=9819.

21. Available at http://voicesofdemocracy.umd.edu/eisenhower-atoms-for-peace-speech-text/.

22. The key starting point for this subject is Campbell Craig, *Destroying the Village: Eisenhower and Thermonuclear War* (New York: Columbia University Press, 1998).

23. *FRUS, 1955–1957*, vol. 19, "Department of State General Comments on NSC 5501," October 3, 1955, 125.

24. Policy Planning Staff document from State Department, *FRUS 1955–1957*, vol. 19, undated but written in November 1955, 154–61.

25. NSC meeting, December 1, 1955, *FRUS 1955–1957*, vol. 19, 168–69.

26. NSC Meeting, January 11, 1957, *FRUS 1955–1957*, vol. 19, 407–8.

27. Administrations officials realized this as early as 1955. See "Basic National Security Policy," NSC 5501, January 7, 1955, *FRUS 1955–1957*, vol. 19, 34.

28. CIA, National Intelligence Estimate, "World Situation and Trends," November 1, 1955, *FRUS 1955–1957*, vol. 19, 133–34.

29. "Basic National Security Policy," NSC 5602, February 13, 1956, *FRUS 1955–1957*, vol. 19, 194.

30. Memorandum of Conversation, Eisenhower, Radford, et al., March 13, 1956, *FRUS 1955–1957*, vol. 19, 239, 241.

31. NSC 5707/8, June 3, 1957, *FRUS 1955–1957*, vol. 19, 513.

32. NSC meeting, November 7, 1957, *FRUS 1955–1957*, vol. 19, 634.

33. NIE 11-4-57, November 12, 1957, *FRUS 1955–1957*, vol. 19, 665–72. This view was also restated in the NIE 100-58, "Estimate of the World Situation," February 26, 1958.

34. NSC meeting, March 20, 1958, *FRUS 1958–1960*, vol. 3, 51–56; memorandum of conversation, Eisenhower and Dulles, April 1, 1958, *FRUS 1958–1960*, vol. 3, 57.

35. Minutes in *FRUS 1958–1960*, vol. 3, 79–97.

36. The quoted text is from a document presented by Defense Secretary Neil McElroy to the NSC meeting of July 24, 1958, *FRUS 1958–1960*, vol. 3, 129.

37. H. W. Brands, "The Age of Vulnerability: Eisenhower and the National Security State," *American Historical Review* 94, no. 4 (October 1989): 963–89. See also David Alan Rosenberg, "The Origins of Overkill: Nuclear Weapons and American Strategy, 1945–1960," *International Security* 7, no. 4 (Spring 1983): 3–71.

38. *Budget of the United States, 2009, Historical Tables*: (GPO, 2008), available at www.whitehouse.gov/sites/default/files/omb/budget/fy2009/pdf/hist.pdf.

39. Jean Edward Smith, *Eisenhower in War and Peace* (New York: Random House, 2012), xiii.

40. Leffler, *For the Soul of Mankind*, 150.

7. Black Appointees, Political Legitimacy, and the American Presidency

1. Condoleezza Rice, *No Higher Honor: A Memoir of My Years in Washington* (New York: Crown Publishers, 2011), 395–96.

2. Ibid.

3. "Obama: Racial Barrier Falls in Decisive Victory," *New York Times*, November 5, 2008, A1; "Obama Takes Oath, and a Nation in Crisis Embraces the Moment," *New York Times*, January 21, 2009, A1.

4. "Oh Mr. Wilson . . . ; A Lawmaker Loses It in More than One Sense," *Washington Post*, September 11, 2009, A27; "A Dispute over Obama's Birth Lives on in the Media," *New York Times*, July 25 2009, B2; "U.S. News: Obama Releases Full Birth Certificate," *Wall Street Journal Europe*, April 28, 2011, 7.

5. Kimberly A. Geaghan, "Forced to Move: An Analysis of Hurricane Katrina Movers," Social, Economic, and Housing Statistics Division, U.S. Census Bureau, June 2011.

6. Brian Williams of NBC News, in the oblique language common of our current racial moment, remembered after watching broadcasts from New Orleans after Katrina, "The fact that those people didn't qualify somehow for our help just

enraged me at the time—it still gets to me. If this happens again I worry about our cohesion, our ability to keep it together." "Brian Williams on What 'Enraged' Him about Katrina," NBC, available at www.nbcnews.com/nightly-news/brian-williams-what-enraged-him-about-katrina-n142971.

7. Steven M. Teles, "The Eternal Return of Compassionate Conservatism," *National Affairs* 1 (Fall 2009), available at www.nationalaffairs.com/publications/detail/the-eternal-return-of-compassionate-conservatism.

8. Roper Center, "How Groups Voted in 2000," available at www.ropercenter.uconn.edu/elections/how_groups_voted/voted_00.html.

9. Clarence Lusane, *Colin Powell and Condoleezza Rice: Foreign Policy, Race, and the New American Century* (Westport, CT: Praeger, 2006), 1.

10. This charge was leveled at the president by music producer and rap artist Kanye West during an NBC fundraiser for Hurricane victims. The moment eventually logged over seven million views on YouTube. Steven R. Weisman, "Rice Defends Bush's Race Record and Calls for Rebuilding Fairly," *New York Times*, September 13, 2005, A24.

11. Rice, *No Higher Honor*, 388–89.

12. For an excellent discussion of the contradictions and relative benefits of government employment in the late nineteenth century, particularly for black women, see Kate Masur, "Patronage and Protest in Kate Brown's Washington," *Journal of American History* 99 (March 2013): 1047–71.

13. Eric S. Yellin, *Racism in the Nation's Service: Government Workers and the Color Line in Woodrow Wilson's America* (Chapel Hill: University of North Carolina Press, 2013), 50; John Dittmer, *Black Georgia in the Progressive Era, 1900–1920* (Urbana and Champaign: University of Illinois Press, 1980), 92.

14. W. E. B. Du Bois, *The Autobiography of W. E. B. Du Bois*, 239, cited in Cedric Robinson, *Black Marxism: The Making of the Black Radical Tradition* (London: Zed Books, 1983), 275.

15. Mark Bauerlein, "Booker T. Washington and W. E. B. Du Bois: The Origins of a Bitter Intellectual Battle," *Journal of Blacks in Higher Education* (Winter 2004/2005): 110–11.

16. Yellin, *Racism in the Nation's Service*, 55.

17. Dittmer, *Black Georgia*, 92.

18. N. D. B. Connolly, *A World More Concrete: Real Estate and the Remaking of Jim Crow South Florida* (Chicago: University of Chicago Press, 2014), 90–92.

19. George Streator to W. E. B. Du Bois, April 29, 1935, available at http://credo.library.umass.edu/view/pageturn/mums312-b076-i213/#page/1/mode/1up.

20. Ira Katznelson, *Fear Itself: The New Deal and the Origins of Our Time* (New York: Liveright, 2013), 163–68.

21. Edgar G. Brown, "What the Civilian Conservation Corps (CCC) Is Doing For Colored Youth," Government Printing Office, Washington, D.C., 1941.

22. "Judge William Hastie, 71, of Federal Court, Dies," *New York Times*, April 15, 1976, 36.

23. Kenneth W. Mack, *Representing the Race: The Creation of the Civil Rights Lawyer* (Cambridge: Harvard University Press, 2012), 238.

24. Ira Katznelson describes Congress in this period as trapped in a "southern cage" from which, in his estimation, "there was no escape." Katznelson, *Fear Itself*, 16.

278 NOTES TO PAGES 129-132

25. "Judge Hastie Fought Army Segregation as Civilian Aide to Secretary of War 1940–1942," *Baltimore Afro-American*, November 20, 1976, 14A.

26. Kathleen L. Wolgemuth, "Woodrow Wilson and Federal Segregation," *Journal of Negro History* 44, no. 2 (April 1959): 163.

27. Yellin, *Racism in the Nation's Service*, 135.

28. Mack, *Representing the Race*, 242; Senate Committee on the Judiciary, *On Confirmation of the Nomination of Honorable William Henry Hastie, of the Virgin Islands, To Be Judge of U.S. Court of Appeals for the Third Circuit*, Hearing before the Committee on the Judiciary, 81st Cong. 2nd Sess., 1950, 64 (statement of William H. Hastie).

29. Eric Arnesen, "No 'Graver Danger': Black Anticommunism, the Communist Party, and the Race Question," *Labor: Studies in Working Class History of the Americas* 3, no. 4 (2006): 13–52; Carol Anderson, "'The Brother in Black Is Always Told to Wait': The Communist Party, African American Anticommunism, and the Prioritization of Black Equality—A Reply to Eric Arnesen," *Labor: Studies in Working Class History of the Americas* 3, no. 4 (2006): 67.

30. "Virgin Islands Governor to Address King of Club Forum," *Atlanta Daily World*, January 21, 1948, 4.

31. Robert Alan, "Paul Robeson: The Lost Shepherd," *Crisis* 58, no. 11 (November 1951): 569–73. Robert Alan was a pseudonym; the author was probably Roy Wilkins.

32. Ralph Johnson Bunche, *A Brief and Tentative Analysis of Negro Leadership* (New York: New York University Press, 2005), 154.

33. According to the FBI, Clifford Durr's National Lawyers Guild, which had written a letter in support of Hastie's appellate court nomination, was "a front organization" for the communist party. *On Confirmation of the Nomination of Honorable William Henry Hastie, of the Virgin Islands, To Be Judge of U.S. Court of Appeals for the Third Circuit*: Hearing before the Committee on the Judiciary, 81st Cong. 2nd Sess., 1950, 6.

34. *On Confirmation of the Nomination of Honorable William Henry Hastie, of the Virgin Islands, To Be Judge of U.S. Court of Appeals for the Third Circuit*: Hearing before the Committee on the Judiciary, 81st Cong. 2nd Sess., 1950, 16 (statement of Pat McCarran).

35. *On Confirmation of the Nomination of Honorable William Henry Hastie, of the Virgin Islands, To Be Judge of U.S. Court of Appeals for the Third Circuit*: Hearing before the Committee on the Judiciary, 81st Cong. 2nd Sess., 1950, 165 (Statement of Homer Ferguson).

36. *On Confirmation of the Nomination of Honorable William Henry Hastie, of the Virgin Islands, To Be Judge of U.S. Court of Appeals for the Third Circuit*: Hearing before the Committee on the Judiciary, 81st Cong. 2nd Sess., 1950, 88–90, 107.

37. Truxton King, "Truman Blasted for Hastie 'Maneuver,'" *Pittsburgh Courier*, October 22, 1949, 1.

38. Ibid., 5.

39. "Only One Dixiecrat Fights Hastie Okay," *Baltimore Afro American*, June 10, 1950, 2.

40. Carl Thomas Rowan, *Dream Makers, Dream Breakers: The World of Justice Thurgood Marshall* (Boston: Little Brown, 1993), 272.

41. Thurgood Marshall, *The Reminiscences of Thurgood Marshall*, Columbia Oral History Research Office, 1977, in Mark V. Tushnet, ed., *Thurgood Marshall: His Speeches, Writings, Arguments, Opinions, and Reminiscences* (Chicago: Lawrence Hill, 2001), 470.

42. Robert Kennedy and Earl Warren quoted in "'Just One More Vote for Frankfurter': Rethinking the Jurisprudence of Judge William Hastie," *Harvard Law Review* 117, no. 5 (March 2004): 1640.

43. "Just One More Vote for Frankfurter," 1646. The activist Esther Cooper Jackson contends, in fact, that Hastie's dissent in *United States v. Mesarosh* 223 F.2d 449 (1955) laid the logical foundation for the Warren Court to begin rolling back "Red Scare" prosecutions first carried out through the courts defense of the Smith Act. See "Interview with Esther and James Jackson by James V. Hatch, April 5, 1992," *Artist and Influence* 11 (1992): 164.

44. President Kennedy eventually appointed Byron White, Robert Kennedy's deputy attorney general, before President Lyndon Johnson appointed Marshall as the nation's first black Supreme Court justice in 1967.

45. Leah Wright Rigueur, *The Loneliness of the Black Republican: Pragmatic Politics and the Pursuit of Power* (Princeton: Princeton University Press, 2015), 10.

46. T. Millet Hand, "The Eisenhower Administration and the Negro," 100 Congressional Record House (1954), Extensions of Remarks, July 30, 1954, 1287; Simeon Booker, "Black Man in the White House," *Ebony*, April 1961, 79.

47. Clarence Lusane, *The Black History of the White House* (San Francisco: City Lights, 2011), 273. Simeon Booker wrongly claimed that "straw boss" described Morrow's "unbending nature." Booker, "Black Man in the White House," 79.

48. Ibid., 79.

49. Clifford P. Case, "First Negro Presidential Assistant," 103 Congressional Record House (1954), Extensions of Remarks, May 13, 1957, A3617.

50. Lusane, *Black History of the White House*, 274.

51. "Solons Predict Rights Action at Capital Press Club Fete," *Washington Afro-American*, May 27, 1958, 20.

52. Booker, "Black Man in the White House," 83.

53. E. Frederic Morrow, *A Black Man in the White House: A Diary of the Eisenhower Years by the Administrative Officer for Special Projects, the White House, 1955–1961* (New York: Coward-McCann, 1963), 221; Booker, "Black Man in the White House," 82–83.

54. Morrow, *Black Man in the White House*, 76.

55. Ibid., 110, 263–64.

56. Booker, "Black Man in the White House," 79.

57. Morrow, *Black Man in the White House*, 264.

58. Booker, "Black Man in the White House," 79.

59. Michael S. Mayer, "The Eisenhower Administration and the Desegregation of Washington, D.C.," *Journal of Policy History* 3, no. 1 (1991): 24–41.

60. Morrow, *Black Man in the White House*, 260.

61. Ibid., 261. See also "How the Negro Votes," *Lewiston Daily Sun*, April 22, 1959, 4.

62. Booker, "Black Man in the White House," 84.

63. "Louis Martin: From Chronicle Editor to Presidential Advisor," *Michigan Chronicle*, October 6, 2010.

64. "Atlanta Lone Bright Spot in Dixie for GOP," *Pittsburgh Courier*, November 19, 1960, 11.

65. James H. Meriwether, "'Worth a Lot of Negro Votes': Black Voters, Africa, and the 1960 Presidential Campaign," *Journal of American History* 95, no. 3 (December 2008): 737–63.

66. Martin's role on public accommodations was confirmed by Ramsey Clarke, the eventual attorney general under President Johnson. Alex Poinsette, *Walking with Presidents: Louis Martin and the Rise of Black Political Power* (Rowman and Littlefield, 2000), 111, 207.

67. Wendell E. Pritchett, *Robert Clifton Weaver and the American City: The Life and Times of an Urban Reformer* (Chicago: University of Chicago Press, 2008), 214, 271, 273.

68. "Louis Martin: A Voice for Civil Rights," *Focus*, May 1997, 3.

69. Robert C. Smith, "Black Appointed Officials: A Neglected Area of Research in Black Political Participation," *Journal of Black Studies* 14, no. 3 (March 1984): 374.

70. Yohuru Williams, "'A Red, Black, and Green Liberation Jumpsuit': Roy Wilkins, the Black Panthers, and the Conundrum of Black Power," in *The Black Power Movement: Rethinking the Civil Rights-Black Power Era*, ed. Peniel E. Joseph (New York: Routledge, 2006), 167–91.

71. William H. Hastie, quoted in Michael Lackey, ed., *The Haverford Discussions* (Charlottesville: University of Virginia Press, 2013), 10. This interaction is one that many close to Hastie would tell and re-tell. See Louis H. Pollak, "William Henry Hastie," *University of Pennsylvania Law Review* 125, no. 1 (November 1976): 4; Jonathan Scott Holloway, *Confronting the Veil: Abram Harris, Jr., E. Franklin Frazier, and Ralph Bunche, 1919–1941* (Chapel Hill: University of North Carolina Press, 2002), 253.

72. Michael C. Dawson, *Black Visions: The Roots of Contemporary African American Political Ideologies* (Chicago: University of Chicago Press, 2001), 40.

73. Flournoy A. Coles Jr., *Black Economic Development* (Chicago: Nelson-Hall, 1975).

74. Jakobi Williams, *From the Bullet to the Ballot: The Illinois Chapter of the Black Panther Party and Racial Coalition Politics in Chicago* (Chapel Hill: University of North Carolina Press, 2013), 172–78, 180–85; Kenneth O'Reilly, *Racial Matters: The FBI's Secret File on Black America, 1960–1972* (New York: Free Press, 1991).

75. Matthew J. Countryman, "'From Protest to Politics': Community Control and Black Independent Politics in Philadelphia, 1965–1984," *Journal of Urban History* 32, no. 6 (September 2006): 813–61; Andrew W. Kahrl, "Property Tax Discrimination and the Question of Fair Taxation," *History News Network*, January 27, 2011, available at www.hnn.us/article/135752.

76. "National Black Political Agenda" 1972, available at http://faculty.washington.edu/qtaylor/documents_us/gary_declaration.htm.

77. See for instance, Jessica Levy, "Selling Atlanta: Black Mayoral Politics from Protest to Entrepreneurialism, 1973 to 1996," *Journal of Urban History* (forthcoming).

78. George Derek Musgrove, *Rumor, Repression, and Racial Politics: How the Harassment of Black Elected Officials Shaped Post–Civil Rights America* (Athens: University of Georgia Press, 2012), 48.

79. Smith, "Black Appointed Officials," 373.

80. One of the most important accounts of the protection of the American political center (and the center's lingering racism) is Matthew D. Lassiter, *The Silent Majority: Suburban Politics in the Sunbelt South* (Princeton, NJ: Princeton University Press, 2006).

81. Mary Frances Berry, *And Justice for All: The United States Commission on Civil Rights and the Continuing Struggle for Freedom in America* (New York: Alfred A. Knopf, 2009), 3.

82. "The Post-Election Blues—Hurts," *Baltimore Afro-American*, November 15, 1980, 5.

83. Bill Clinton, *My Life* (New York: Alfred A. Knopf, 2004), 523–24.

84. "Embattled Van Jones Quits, but 'Czar' Debates Rage On," *New York Times*, September 9, 2009, available at http://www.nytimes.com/gwire/2009/09/08/08greenwire-embattled-van-jones-quits-but-czar-debates-rage-9373.html?pagewanted=all.

85. Ta-Nehisi Coates, "Fear of a Black President," *Atlantic Monthly*, September 2012, available at www.theatlantic.com/magazine/archive/2012/09/fear-of-a-black-president/309064/4/.

86. Shirley Sherrod, *The Courage to Hope: How I Stood Up to the Politics of Fear* (New York: Atria Books, 2013), 8. Coates, "Fear of a Black President."

87. Milton S. Katz, "E. Frederic Morrow and Civil Rights in the Eisenhower Administration," *Phylon* 42, no. 2 (1981): 143.

88. Lusane, *Colin Powell and Condoleezza Rice*, 2.

89. "C-Span: Barack Obama Speech at 2004 DNC Convention," available at www.youtube.com/watch?v=eWynt87PaJ0.

8. Presidents and the Media

1. Erving Goffman, *The Presentation of Self in Everyday Life* (New York: Doubleday, 1959), ch. 3.

2. Stephen Ponder, *Managing the Press: Origins of the Media Presidency, 1897–1933* (New York: Palgrave, 1998), xvi.

3. Marshall McLuhan was the most notorious articulator of technological determinism when he argued that "the medium is the message": that media content was irrelevant, it was the features of different communications technologies that made history. Some of his thinking has been revived in the wake of the digital revolution. McLuhan, *Understanding Media* (New York: McGraw Hill, 1964). Merritt Roe Smith and Leo Marx documented the prevalence of technological determinism in much media coverage of technological change. Smith and Marx, *Does Technology Drive History?* (Cambridge: MIT Press, 1994).

4. Ian Hutchby, *Conversation and Technology: From the Telephone to the Internet* (Cambridge, UK: Polity Press, 2001), ch. 2.

5. John F. Harris, *The Survivor: Bill Clinton in the White House* (New York: Random House, 2005), 36.

6. Ponder, *Managing the Press*, 1.

7. Ibid., 5–8.

8. Michael Emery and Edwin Emery, *The Press and America: An Interpretive History of the Mass Media*, 6th ed. (Englewood Cliffs, NJ: Prentice Hall, 1986), 234.

9. Ponder, *Managing the Press*, 14.

10. Ibid., 9–11.

11. T. J. Jackson Lears, *Fables of Abundance: A Cultural History of Advertising in America* (New York: Basic Books, 1994), ch. 6; Roland Marchand, *Advertising the American Dream* (University of California Press, 1986), ch. 7.

12. Ponder, *Managing the Press*, 18; Emery and Emery, *The Press and America*, 248.

13. Ponder, *Managing the Press*, 79.

14. Meirion Harries and Susie Harries, *The Last Days of Innocence: America At War, 1917–1918* (New York: Random House, 1997), 165.

15. Harries and Harries, *Last Days of Innocence*, 171.

16. Ponder, *Managing the Press*, 107.

17. Susan J. Douglas, "Media," in *Encyclopedia of American Political History*, ed. Jack P. Greene (New York: Charles Scribner's Sons, 1984), 826.

18. Doris Kearns Goodwin, *No Ordinary Time: Franklin and Eleanor Roosevelt: The Home Front in World War II* (New York: Simon & Schuster, 1994), 59.

19. Ponder, *Managing the Press*, 163; "White House Statement pm [*sic*] the National Emergency Council," American Presidency Project, available at www.presidency.ucsb.edu/ws/index.php?pid=14571.

20. Susan J. Douglas, *Listening In: Radio and the American Imagination* (New York: Times Books, 1999), 168; Neal Gabler, *Winchell: Gossip, Power, and the Culture of Celebrity* (New York: Alfred A. Knopf, 1995), 214.

21. Douglas, *Listening In*, 172–73.

22. Craig Allen, *Eisenhower and the Mass Media: Peace, Prosperity, and Prime-Time TV* (Chapel Hill: University of North Carolina Press, 1993).

23. Douglas, "Media," 827.

24. Cynthia Lowry, "Eisenhower's New TV Personality Is More Than Unplanned Change," *Miami Daily News*, March 21, 1954.

25. Douglas Larsen, "New Style Eisenhower Presented to Public by Robert Montgomery," *Milwaukee Journal*, April 21, 1954.

26. Michael Schudson, *Discovering the News* (New York: Basic Books, 1978), 170.

27. Sidney Kraus, "Winners of the First 1960 Televised Presidential Debate between Kennedy and Nixon," *Journal of Communication* 46, no. 4 (Autumn 1996).

28. James T. Graham, "Kennedy, Cuba, and the Press," *Journalism History* 24 (Summer 1998): 60–61.

29. Graham, "Kennedy, Cuba, and the Press," 68.

30. Kathleen Hall Jamieson, *Packaging the Presidency: A History of Presidential Campaign Advertising*, 3d ed. (New York: Oxford University Press, 1996), 233.

31. Jamieson, *Packaging the Presidency*, 262–64.

32. John Anthony Maltese, *Spin Control: The White House Office of Communications and the Management of Presidential News* (Chapel Hill: University of North Carolina Press, 1992).

33. Herbert Gans, *Deciding What's News: A Study of CBS Evening News, NBC Nightly News, Newsweek, and Time* (New York: Vintage Books, 1980), 147.

34. "Examining Carter's 'Malaise Speech' Thirty Years Later," NPR, July 12, 2009, available at www.npr.org/templates/story/story.php?storyId=106508243.

35. Mark Hertsgaard, *On Bended Knee: The Press and the Reagan Presidency* (New York: Farrar Straus & Giroux, 1988).

36. Stephen J. Farnsworth and S. Robert Lichter, *The Nightly News Nightmare: Media Coverage of U.S. Presidential Elections, 1988–2008* (New York: Rowman & Littlefield, 2011), xii.

37. Jacob Weisberg, "The White House Beast," *Vanity Fair*, September 1993, available at www.vanityfair.com/magazine/archive/1993/09/presscorps199309.

38. Robert W. McChesney, *Rich Media, Poor Democracy* (Urbana and Chicago: University of Illinois Press, 1999), 263–65.

39. Frank Rich, *The Greatest Story Ever Sold: The Decline and Fall of Truth from 9/11 to Hurricane Katrina* (New York: Penguin, 2006), 246–48.

40. Ibid., also *New York Times* article.

41. Rich, *Greatest Story Ever Sold*, 90. Elisabeth Bumiller, "Keepers of Bush Image Lift Stagecraft to New Heights," *New York Times*, May 16, 2003, available at www.nytimes.com/2003/05/16/us/keepers-of-bush-image-lift-stagecraft-to-new-heights.html.

42. Farnsworth and Lichter, *Nightly News Nightmare*, 60.

43. Kate Kenski, Bruce W. Hardy, and Kathleen Hall Jamieson, *The Obama Victory: How Media, Money, and Message Shaped the 2008 Election* (New York: Oxford University Press, 2010), 305–6.

9. The Making of the Celebrity Presidency

1. The author would like to thank Bruce Schulman, Brian Balogh, Lily Geismer, Steven Ross, and Donald Critchlow for their insights, critiques, and assistance with this article.

2. Austin Wehrwein, "Wisconsin Battle One of Contrasts," *New York Times*. February 21, 1960, 55. Advertisements for both the Nixon and Kennedy campaign can be found here: http://www.livingroomcandidate.org/commercials/1960.

3. For an examination of the emergence of "showbiz politics" see Kathryn Cramer Brownell, *Showbiz Politics: Hollywood in American Political Life* (Chapel Hill: University of North Carolina Press, 2014). For a discussion of "media-driven performative politics" in the California Democratic Party, see Jonathan Bell, *California Crucible: The Forging of Modern American Liberalism* (Philadelphia: University of Pennsylvania Press, 2012).

4. Lewis Gould, *The Modern American Presidency* (Lawrence: University of Kansas Press, 1996); Gary A. Donaldson, *The First Modern Campaign: Kennedy, Nixon, and the Election of 1960* (Lanham, MD: Rowman & Littlefield, 2007).

5. Marshall McLuhan, *Understanding Media: The Extensions of Man* (New York: McGraw-Hill, 1964).

6. For example, see Michael Schudson, *The Power of News* (Cambridge: Harvard University Press, 1996) and *Discovering the News: A Social History of American Newspapers* (New York: Basic Books, 1981); Paul Starr, *The Creation of the Media: Political Origins of Modern Communications* (New York: Basic Books, 2005). For a historical assessment of the politics behind the evolution of the telegraph and telephone, see Richard R. John, *Network Nation: Inventing American Telecommunications* (Cambridge: Harvard University Press, 2010).

7. Volumes have been written debating McLuhan and his theories. For an recent overview of these debates, see Bill Kovarik, *Revolution in Communications: Media*

History from Gutenberg to the Digital Age (New York: Continuum International Publishing Group, 2011).

8. Vicki Daitch, "Oral History Interview with Don Hewitt," in *Hollywood and Politics: A Sourcebook*, ed. Don Critchlow and Emilie Raymond (New York: Routledge, 2009), 31.

9. For a look at how mass media and advertising have contributed to voter apathy, see Theda Skocpol and Morris P. Fiorina, eds., *Civic Engagement in American Democracy* (Washington, DC: Brookings Institution Press, 1999); Robert Putnam, *Bowling Alone: The Collapse and Revival of American Community* (New York: Simon & Schuster, 2000). On television's role, see Stephen Ansolabehere, Roy Behr, and Shanto Iyengar, *The Media Game: American Politics in the Television Age* (New York: Macmillan, 1993); Kathleen Hall Jamieson, *Packaging The Presidency: A History and Criticism of Presidential Campaign Advertising*, 3d ed. (New York: Oxford University Press, 1996).

10. On presidential interactions with parties and extrapartisan organizations, see Daniel Galvin, *Presidential Party Building: Dwight D. Eisenhower to George W. Bush* (Princeton: Princeton University Press, 2010).

11. Art Buchwald, "Stars Turn Noses Up, Aid Campaign," *Los Angeles Times*, October 22, 1960, 6.

12. See Schudson, *Power of News*, 113–23.

13. Robert Dallek, *An Unfinished Life* (New York: Little, Brown, 2003), 227–96.

14. David Greenberg, *Calvin Coolidge* (New York: Times Books, 2006).

15. Brian Balogh, "'Mirrors of Desires': Interest Groups, Elections, and the Targeted Style in Twentieth-Century America," in *The Democratic Experiment: New Directions in American Political History*, ed. Meg Jacobs, William J. Novak, and Julian E. Zelizer (Princeton: Princeton University Press, 2003).

16. F. T. Birchall, "Where Heroes Can Be Made to Order," *New York Times*, May 6, 1934, 6.

17. "Repubs Frown on Pix Bureau," *Variety*, November 20, 1946, 17.

18. For a discussion of how World War II experiences and the Cold War environment shaped anxieties toward television, see David Greenberg, "A New Way of Campaigning: Eisenhower, Stevenson, and the Anxieties of Television Politics," in *Liberty and Justice for All? Rethinking Politics in Cold War America*, ed. Kathlene G. Donohue (Amherst: University of Massachusetts Press, 2012), 185–212.

19. Brownell, *Showbiz Politics*, 102–28.

20. "Distribution of Durable Consumer Goods in American Families," in *Post-War Economic Trends in the United States*, ed. Ralph Freeman, in John Patrick Diggins, *The Proud Decades: American in War and Peace, 1941-1960* (New York: W. W. Norton, 1989), 186.

21. John E. Hollitz, "Eisenhower and the Admen: The Television 'Spot' Campaign of 1952," *Wisconsin Magazine of History* 66 (1982); Edwin Diamond and Stephen Bates, *The Spot: The Rise of Political Advertising on Television*, 3d ed. (Cambridge: Massachusetts Institute of Technology Press, 1992); Greenberg, "New Way of Campaigning," 185–212.

22. For a discussion of Nixon's television triumphs in the 1950s, see David Greenberg, *Nixon's Shadow: The History of an Image* (New York: W.W. Norton, 2003), 36–72.

23. Hollitz, "Eisenhower and the Admen"; Stephen C. Wood, "Television's First Political Spot Ad Campaign: Eisenhower Answers America," *Presidential*

Studies Quarterly 20 (1990). Political advertisements for the 1952 election can be found here: http://www.livingroomcandidate.org/commercials/1952.

24. "Television Programming for Citizens TV," August 28, 1956, folder: "TV Scripts," box 6, Files of Y&R, Citizens for Eisenhower-Nixon, Staff Files, Dwight D. Eisenhower Library, Abilene, Kansas.

25. "Thoughts and Ideas in Connection with Television Programming for Citizens for Eisenhower-Nixon," #1, folder: "TV Scripts," box 6, Files of Y&R, Citizens for Eisenhower, Dwight D. Eisenhower Library, Abilene, Kansas.

26. Isabelle Shelton, "Be Yourself on TV, says Montgomery," *Washington Star*, February 16, 1957, folder: "Eisenhower Aides," box 334, News Clippings and Publications, Republican National Committee Files, Dwight D. Eisenhower Library, Abilene, Kansas.

27. Robert J. Pitchell, "The Influence of Professional Campaign Management Firms in Partisans Elections in California," *Western Political Quarterly* 11 (1958): 278–300. In his groundbreaking study on the impact of political consultants in American politics, Stanley Kelley Jr. also points to the influence of California politics in Stanley Kelley Jr., *Professional Public Relations and Political Power* (Baltimore: Johns Hopkins University Press, 1956).

28. Republican Associates News Letter, October 1956, folder: "Political, 1956," box 67: 10, Jack L. Warner Papers. University of Southern California Cinematic Library, Los Angeles, CA.

29. Memorandum re: Distribution, From Hollywood for Stevenson to Tom Durrance, September 22, 1952, folder: "Hollywood for Stevenson Sparkman II," box 371, Television and Radio Division, Democratic National Committee Records, John F. Kennedy Presidential Library, Boston, Massachusetts.

30. For a discussion of Stevenson's campaign in California, see Bell, *California Crucible*, 55–82.

31. W. H. Lawrence, "A Political Product to Market," *New York Times*, January 22, 1956, 226.

32. John Schneider, *The Golden Kazoo* (New York: Rinehart, 1956).

33. Stanley Kelley, *Professional Public Relations and Political Power*, 144–200.

34. Ibid., 155.

35. News clipping, Anthony Leviero, Eisenhower's TV Speeches are Major Productions, January 10, 1954. Eisenhower Aides, box 334, News Clippings and Publications, Republican National Committee Files, Dwight D. Eisenhower Library, Abilene, Kansas.

36. Galvin, *Presidential Party Building*, 46.

37. Stanley Kelley Jr., "P.R. Man: Political Mastermind," *New York Times*, September 2, 1956, 6.

38. Kelley, *Professional Public Relations and Political Power*, 199–200.

39. Media Strategy Outline, folder: "Media Campaign: Wisconsin Primary, 1/21/60–4/5/60," box 38, Political, Pre-Administration, Robert F. Kennedy Papers, John F. Kennedy Presidential Library, Boston, Massachusetts.

40. Austin Wehrwein, "Wisconsin Battle One of Contrasts," *New York Times*, February 21, 1960, 55.

41. Dallek, *Unfinished Life*, 43–44.

42. Carl Beauchamp, *Joseph P. Kennedy Presents: His Hollywood Years* (New York: Knopf, 2003), 372–90.

43. Media Strategy Outline, folder: "Media Campaign: Wisconsin Primary, 1/21/60–4/5/60," box 38, Political, Pre-Administration, Robert F. Kennedy Papers, John F. Kennedy Presidential Library, Boston, Massachusetts.

44. *Primary*, DVD, Directed by Robert Drew, 1960, New Video Group, Released on DVD 2003.

45. Wehrwein, "Wisconsin Battle One of Contrasts," 55.

46. Transcript, College News Conference, December 7, 1958, Theodore Sorensen Papers, box 25, Roosevelt, Eleanor, John F. Kennedy Presidential Library, Boston, Massachusetts. See also Allida Black, *Casting Her Own Shadow: Eleanor Roosevelt and the Shaping of Postwar Liberalism* (New York: Columbia University Press, 1996).

47. Wehrwein, "Wisconsin Battle One of Contrasts." 55.

48. For statistics concerning the financial expenditures, see Jamieson, *Packaging the Presidency*, 165–68.

49. For an account of the DNC, see Dallek, *Unfinished Life*, 229–66.

50. A more detailed description of Nixon's lack of media organizational experience can be found in Craig Allen, *Eisenhower and the Mass Media* (Durham: University of North Carolina Press, 1993), 150–89. For analysis of how the "savvy expert" had become "flatfooted and fallen behind the times," see Greenberg, *Nixon's Shadow*, 71.

51. Allen, *Eisenhower and the Mass Media*, 179–80.

52. "Television and the Voter," an address by Sig Mickelson, president of CBS News, October 28, 1959, folder: "TV arrangements, media plan summary," box 395, Radio and Television, Democratic National Committee Records, John F. Kennedy Presidential Library, Boston, Massachusetts.

53. Memo from J. Leonard Reinsch to Robert Kennedy, RE: TV, September 26, 1960, folder: "Media Campaign: Democratic National Committee, 8/22/60–10/28/60," box 37, General Subject File, Pre-Administration Political File, Robert F. Kennedy Papers, John F. Kennedy Presidential Library, Boston, Massachusetts.

54. Vicki Daitch, "Oral History Interview with Don Hewitt," 30.

55. Brownell, *Showbiz Politics*.

56. Gladwin Hill, "Election Pleases the Movie World," *New York Times*, November 11, 1960, 37.

57. Greenberg, *Nixon's Shadow*, 71.

58. Gladwin Hill, "Nixon Denounces the Press as Biased," *New York Times*, November 8, 1962, 1.

59. Michael Miles, "Reagan and the Respectable Right," folder: "Reagan: Articles Re: California Politics and Government," box 1, PPS 501, Ronald Reagan, Special Files, Research Files, Campaign 1968 Materials, Pre-Presidential Papers, Richard Nixon Library, Yorba Linda, California.

60. Michael Miles, "Reagan and the Respectable Right."

61. "Ronald Reagan: Here's the Rest of Him," *Ripon Forum*, June 1968, folder: "Reagan and California Politics and Government," box 1, PPS 501, Michael Miles, "Reagan and the Respectable Right." For a discussion of Nixon's "southern strategy," see Bruce Schulman, *The Seventies: The Great Shift in American Culture, Society, and Politics* (Cambridge: Da Capo Press, 2002), 102–17.

62. On Nixon's observations that Reagan reaches "the heart" with his speeches, see: Handwritten note by Richard Nixon in direct response to the memo from Pat

Buchanan to Richard Nixon, n.d. [1968] folder, Reagan, Speech Files III, box 1, PPS 501, Ronald Reagan, Special Files, Research Files, Campaign 1968 Materials, Richard Nixon Library.

63. Memorandum for Mr. Garment, Re; 1968 Presidential Election, folder: "Misc #2," box 69, Name File Box 3 of 29, 1968 Political Campaign, Garment, Len, White House Central Files, Richard Nixon Library, Yorba Linda, California.

64. Letter from Bill Gavin to Richard Nixon, n.d. [1967], folder: "Gavin, Bill" (2 of 3), box 69, Name File Box 3 of 29, 1968 Campaign File, Garment, Len, White House Central Files, Richard Nixon Library, Yorba Linda, California.

65. See Bill Gavin to Len Garment, n.d. [1967], folder: "Gavin, Bill" (2 of 3), box 69, Name File Box 3 of 29, 1968 Campaign File, Garment, Len, White House Central Files, Richard Nixon Library, Yorba Linda, California; Len Garment to Bill Gavin, Memo: re: soul, Folder, Gavin, Bill, 1 of 3, Box 69, Name File Box 3 of 29, 1968 Campaign File, Garment, Len, White House Central Files, Richard Nixon Library, Yorba Linda, California.

66. Joe McGinniss, *The Selling of the President: The Classic Account of the Packaging of a Candidate* (New York: Trident Press, 1969), 63.

67. Memorandum from Ellsworth to DC, Mitchell, Stans, Haldeman, Flanigan, Kleindienst, Garment, June 9, 1968, folder: "Strategy," box 81, Topical File Box 15 of 29, Garment, Len, White House Central Files, Richard Nixon Library, Yorba Linda, California. Nixon's television advertisements can be found at: www.livingroom candidate.org/commercials/1968.

68. Memorandum from Harry Treleavan, Re: Nixon for President Advertising in the Primary Campaigns, appendix, McGinniss, *Selling of the President*, 171–80.

69. McGinniss, *Selling of the President.*

70. On Nixon's attempts to "manage the news," see Greenberg, *Nixon's Shadow*, 126–79. On Nixon's efforts to institutionalize Hollywood production strategies in his administration, see Brownell, *Showbiz Politics*, 207–24.

10. Stand By Me

1. Ellis Hawley, "Herbert Hoover, the Commerce Secretariat, and the Vision of an 'Associative State,' 1921–1928" *Journal of American History* 61 (June 1, 1974); Cathie Jo Martin, *Shifting the Burden: The Struggle over Growth and Corporate Taxation* (Chicago: University of Chicago Press, 1991); Donald Brand, *Corporatism and the Rule of Law* (Ithaca, NY: Cornell University Press, 1988); Colin Gordon, *New Deals: Business, Labor and Politics 1920–1935* (New York: Cambridge University Press, 1994); Brian Balogh, "Meeting the State Half-Way," unpublished manuscript, 2013.

2. Benjamin Ginsberg and Martin Shefter, *Politics by Other Means* (New York: Basic Books, 1990); George Edwards, Andrew Barrett, and Jeffrey Peake, "The Legislative Impact of Divided Government," *American Political Science Review* 42 (April 1997): 545–63; David Mayhew, *Divided We Govern* (New Haven: Yale University Press, 1991).

3. Antagonistic competition between parties was strengthened with modern party reforms, which paradoxically both shifted power away from party bosses *and* weakened executive capacities for governance. See Sidney Milkis, *The President and the Parties* (New York: Oxford University Press, 1993).

4. Jeffrey Cohen, "Economic Perceptions and Executive Approval in Comparative Perspective," *Political Behavior* 26 (March 2004): 27–43.

5. Cathie Jo Martin and Duane Swank, *The Political Construction of Business Interests: Coordination, Growth and Equality* (New York: Cambridge University Press, 2012).

6. Even in the United States, private interest groups may contribute crucial support in policy battles between the executive and legislative branches. Martha Kumar and Michael Grossman, "The Presidency and Interest Groups," in *The Presidency and the Political System*, ed. Michael Nelson (Washington: Congressional Quarterly Press, 1984); Martin, *Shifting the Burden*; Brian Balogh, *A Government out of Sight* (New York: Cambridge University Press, 2009).

7. Jane Mansbridge, "A 'Selection Model' of Political Representation," *Journal of Political Philosophy* 17, no. 4 (2009): 369–98; Robert H. Mnookin and Lee Ross, "Introduction" in *Barriers to Conflict Resolution*, eds. Kenneth J. Arrow et al. (New York: W.W. Norton & Company, 1995).

8. Party systems crucially molded the early trajectories for national business organizations by shaping both the incentives of right party leaders to delegate policymaking to private associations and the motivations of opposing parties to block employers' demands for legislation. Before the consolidation of national economies, countries had rather similar pockets of local industrial coordination. At this point, in countries with multiparty systems (but not in two-party systems), right parties feared a left-center parliamentary coalition against them, created encompassing employers' associations, and delegated policymaking authority to private industrial relations channels. Cathie Jo Martin and Duane Swank, "The Political Origins of Coordinated Capitalism," *American Political Science Review* (May, 2008): 181–98; Martin and Swank, *The Political Construction of Business Interests*.

9. NAM, "Reports of Officers," *Proceedings of the Thirty-first Annual Convention of the National Association of Manufacturers of the United States of America* (New York: NAM, 1926); Richard Gable, "Birth of an Employers' Association," *Business History Review* 33, no. 4 (1959): 535–45; Cathie Jo Martin, "Sectional Parties, Divided Business," *Studies in American Political Development* 20, no. 2 (Fall 2006): 160–84.

10. NAM, "Reports of Officers," 61–62.

11. Evan Metcalf, "Secretary Hoover and the Emergence of Macroeconomic Management," *Business History Review* 49, no. 1 (Spring 1975): 64.

12. Herbert Hoover, "Report of the President's Conference on Unemployment" (Washington: Government Printing Office, 1921), 40, 90; Ellis Hawley, "Herbert Hoover, the Commerce Secretariat, and the Vision of an 'Associative State,'" 134.

13. Hoover, "Report of the President's Conference on Unemployment," 176.

14. Committee of the President's Conference on Unemployment, *Business Cycles and Employment* (New York: McGraw-Hill, 1923).

15. Robert Zieger, "Labor, Progressivism, and Herbert Hoover in the 1920s," *Wisconsin Magazine of History* 58 (Spring 1975): 196–208.

16. Hawley, "Herbert Hoover, the Commerce Secretariat, and the Vision of an 'Associative State,'" 118–23.

17. Zieger, "Labor, Progressivism, and Herbert Hoover in the 1920s," 201.

18. American Contractor, "Proposed Law Would Tend to Eliminate Seasonal Construction Slump," *American Contractor* (December 3, 1921): 29.

19. "Unemployment Bill Killed in the Senate: Kenyon's Last Measure Sent Back to Committee after Adoption of Amendment," *New York Times*, February 17, 1922,

3; Andrew Polsky and Olesya Tkacheva, "Legacies versus Politics: Herbert Hoover, Partisan Conflict, and the Symbolic Appeal of Associationalism in the 1920s," *International Journal of Politics, Culture, and Society* 16, no. 2 (Winter 2002): 218; Joseph Dorfman, *The Economic Mind in American Civilization* (New York: Viking, 1959), 36–37; "Another Effort to Rid Uncle Sam of Red Tapes," *New York Times*, August 30, 1925; Hawley, "Herbert Hoover, the Commerce Secretariat, and the Vision of an 'Associative State,'" 118–23, 138.

20. Hawley, "Herbert Hoover, the Commerce Secretariat, and the Vision of an 'Associative State,'" 139.

21. National Association of Manufacturers. "American Valuation Convention in Washington," *American Industries* 22 (February 7, 1922): 11.

22. National Association of Manufacturers, "American Valuation Convention in Washington," 8.

23. Hawley, "Herbert Hoover, the Commerce Secretariat, and the Vision of an 'Associative State,'" 57–65; Balogh, "Meeting the State Half-Way"; Gordon, *New Deals: Business, Labor and Politics*; Brand, *Corporatism and the Rule of Law*; Frances Perkins, "Why We Need a Minimum Wage Law," *Nation's Business* (July 1933): 23.

24. Hawley, "Herbert Hoover, the Commerce Secretariat, and the Vision of an 'Associative State,'" 57–65; Gordon, *New Deals: Business, Labor and Politics*; Brand, *Corporatism and the Rule of Law*; Balogh, "Meeting the State Half-Way."

25. Alfred Bindslev, *Konservatismens Historie i Danmark* (Odense: Kulturhistorisk forlag, 1936–1938); Asbjørn Sonne Nørgaard, *The Politics of Institutional Control: Corporatism in Danish Occupational Safety and Health Regulation & Unemployment Insurance, 1870–1995* (Aarhus, DK: Politica, 1997), 224–25.

26. Sophus Agerholm and Anders Vigen, *Arbejdsgiver Foreningen Gennem 25 Aar, 1896–1921* (Copenhagen: Langkjaers bogtrykkeri, 1921).

27. Italics in original, translated by Martin. Arbejdsgiverforeningen af 1896, "Til Bestyrelsen for," August 3, 1897, 1–2, DA – Korrespondance, General udgånde 1896 6 30 til 1899 9 21.

28. Agerholm and Vigen, *Arbejdsgiver Foreningen Gennem*; Martin and Swank, *The Political Construction of Business Interests*.

29. Jesper Due and Jørgen Steen Madsen, "Det danske Gent-systems storhed—og fald?" (Copenhagen: FAOS, 2007), 204–6, http://faos.ku.dk/pdf/artikler/videnska belige_artikler/2007/Det_danske_Gent-systems_storhed_0407.pdf/.

30. Nørgaard, *The Politics of Institutional Control*, 186–207; Daniel Levine, *Poverty and Society: The Growth of the American Welfare State in International Comparison* (New Brunswick: Rutgers Press, 1988), 93–94.

31. "Arbejdskonflikter i Danmark," 2004, Lexikon.org, http://www.leksikon. org/art.php?n=3342.

32. Harald Westergaard, *Economic Development in Denmark: Before and during the World War* (Oxford: Clarendon Press, 1922), 83–87.

33. Nørgaard, *The Politics of Institutional Control*, 208–17.

34. "Arbejdsanvisning og Arbejdsløshedsforsikring," *Arbejdsgiveren* 22, no. 43 (October 28, 1921): 345–47.

35. Nørgaard, *The Politics of Institutional Control*, 208–17.

11. Taking the Long View

1. Richard Neustadt, *Presidential Power* (1990; orig. ed. New York: Wiley, 1960).

2. George C. Edwards III, *At the Margins: Presidential Leadership of Congress* (New Haven: Yale University Press, 1989).

3. George C. Edwards III, "Campaigning Is Not Governing: Bill Clinton's Rhetorical Presidency," in *The Clinton Legacy*, ed. Colin Campbell and Bert A. Rockman (New York: Chatham House, 2000), 34. This argument is more fully developed in Edwards, *At the Margins*.

4. Terry Moe, "The Politicized Presidency," in *The New Direction in American Politics*, ed. John E. Chubb and Paul E. Peterson (Washington, DC: Brookings Institution, 1985); Terry Moe, "Presidents, Institutions, and Theory," *Researching the Presidency*, ed. George C. Edwards III, John H. Kessel, and Bert A. Rockman (Pittsburgh: University of Pittsburgh Press, 1993); Kenneth R. Mayer, *With the Stroke of a Pen: Executive Orders and Presidential Power* (Princeton: Princeton University Press, 2001); William G. Howell, *Power without Persuasion: The Politics of Direct Presidential Action* (Princeton: Princeton University Press, 2003).

5. Moe, "Politicized Presidency," 240–43.

6. Ibid., 242–43.

7. Stephen Skowronek, *The Politics Presidents Make: Leadership from John Adams to Bill Clinton* (Cambridge: Harvard University Press, 1997), 4.

8. Sidney M. Milkis, *The President and the Parties: The Transformation of the American Party System since the New Deal* (New York: Oxford University Press, 1993); Scott C. James, *Presidents, Parties, and the State* (New York: Cambridge University Press, 2000); Adam D. Sheingate, "Political Entrepreneurship, Institutional Change, and American Political Development," *Studies in American Political Development* 17, no. 2 (2003); Keith E. Whittington and Daniel P. Carpenter, "Executive Power in American Institutional Development," *Perspectives on Politics* 1, no. 3 (2003).

9. Benjamin Ginsberg and Martin Shefter, "The Presidency and the Organization of Interests," in *The Presidency and the Political System*, ed. Michael Nelson, vol. 2 (Washington, DC: Congressional Quarterly Press, 1988); M. Elizabeth Sanders, "Presidents and Social Movements: A Logic and Preliminary Results," in *Formative Acts: American Politics in the Making*, ed. Stephen Skowronek and Matthew Glassman (Philadelphia: University of Pennsylvania Press, 2007); Sidney M. Milkis and Daniel J. Tichenor, "Reform's Mating Dance: Presidents, Social Movements, and Racial Realignments," *Journal of Policy History* 23, no. 4 (2011); Jacob S. Hacker and Paul Pierson, "Presidents and the Political Economy: The Coalitional Foundations of Presidential Power," *Presidential Studies Quarterly* 42, no. 1 (2012).

10. Jeffrey Tulis, *The Rhetorical Presidency* (Princeton: Princeton University Press, 1987); Kevin J. McMahon, *Reconsidering Roosevelt on Race: How the Presidency Paved the Road to Brown* (Chicago: University of Chicago Press, 2004); Keith E. Whittington, *Political Foundations of Judicial Supremacy: The Presidency, the Supreme Court, and Constitutional Leadership in U.S. History* (Princeton: Princeton University Press, 2007).

11. On "formative acts," see Stephen Skowronek and Matthew Glassman, *Formative Acts: American Politics in the Making* (Philadelphia: University of Pennsylvania Press, 2007).

12. "Battering ram" comes from Skowronek, *Politics Presidents Make*, 28.

13. A "least-likely" case is "not expected to conform to the prediction of a particular theory. . . . If the case nonetheless conforms to the theory, this provides evidence against these rival hypotheses and, therefore, strong support for the theory." It relies on what Jack Levy calls "the Sinatra inference: If the theory can make it here, it can make it anywhere." Henry E. Brady and David Collier, *Rethinking Social Inquiry: Diverse Tools, Shared Standards* (Lanham, MD: Rowman & Littlefield, 2004); Levy, quoted in Andrew Bennett and Colin Elman, "Qualitative Research: Recent Developments in Case Study Methods," *Annual Review of Political Science* 9 (2006).

14. See, for example, "Campaign Plan" 1952, 1952—Campaign and Election, box 10, Robert Humphreys Papers, Dwight D. Eisenhower Library (hereafter DDEL); "Hall to the President," November 10, 1953, RNC (1)–(5), box 30, Whitman File, DDEL.

15. Handwritten notes, 1952, Campaign and Election (1)–(4), Humphreys Papers, DDEL.

16. See Alfred D. Chandler Jr., ed., *The Papers of Dwight David Eisenhower*, 21 vols. (Baltimore: Johns Hopkins University Press, 1970–2001), 14: 32n7 (hereafter *Eisenhower Papers*). William Edward Robinson's proposal was entitled "A Proposal for the Organization of a Public Opinion Division within the Republican National Committee," January 8, 1954, Ann Whitman Name File.

17. See "President to Robinson," November 19, 1953, in *Eisenhower Papers*, 14:680.

18. The exception is Cornelius P. Cotter, "Eisenhower as Party Leader," *Political Science Quarterly* 98, no. 2 (1983). On Eisenhower as a president "above party," see Ralph Ketcham, *Presidents above Party* (Chapel Hill: University of North Carolina Press, 1987), 231, 234. Other prominent works draw similar conclusions: John Bibby and Robert Huckshorn argue that Eisenhower was "generally oblivious to party affairs"; James Sundquist concludes that "there is no evidence that the Eisenhower administration gave any appreciable support to party-building"; and Philip Klinkner writes that "Eisenhower never made a serious attempt to recast the GOP in his own image of 'Modern (read moderate) Republicanism.'" Ralph Goldman similarly classifies Eisenhower as a "nonpartisan" president in "The American President as Party Leader: A Synoptic History," in Robert Harmel, ed., *Presidents and Their Parties: Leadership or Neglect?* (New York: Prager, 1984), 21. See John F. Bibby and Robert J. Huckshorn, "The Republican Party in American Politics," in Jeff Fishel, ed., *Parties and Elections in an Anti-Party Age* (Bloomington: Indiana University Press, 1978), 55; James L. Sundquist, *Dynamics of the Party System* (Washington, D.C.: Brookings Institution, 1983), 287; Philip A. Klinkner, *The Losing Parties: Out-Party National Committees, 1956–1993* (New Haven: Yale University Press, 1994), 42.

19. Theodore Lowi, *The Personal President* (Ithaca, NY: Cornell University Press, 1985), 74; see also David Broder, *The Party's Over* (New York: Harper & Row, 1972), 7.

20. Richard M. Pious, *The American Presidency* (New York: Basic Books, 1979), 124.

21. Lewis L. Gould, *Grand Old Party: A History of the Republicans* (New York: Random House, 2003), 334.

22. "President to Hauge," September 30, 1954, *Eisenhower Papers* 15: 1322.

23. Ambrose, Stephen E. *Eisenhower*, vol. 2 (New York: Simon and Schuster, 1983), 218; see also "Straining for Party Gain," *Washington Post*, November 1, 1954.

24. "Text of President Eisenhower's Talk Urging Election of Republican Congress," *New York Times*, October 29, 1954; see also "To Clifford Roberts," October 7, 1954, in *Eisenhower Papers* 15: 1335–36; and "To Clifford Roberts," October 30, 1954, in *Eisenhower Papers* 15: 1368–69; *Eisenhower Papers* 15: 1336n2.

25. "Diary," November 20, 1954, *Eisenhower Papers* 15: 1402–5.

26. Entry for December 7, 1954, in James C. Hagerty and Robert H. Ferrell, *The Diary of James C. Hagerty: Eisenhower in Mid-Course, 1954–1955* (Bloomington: Indiana University Press, 1983); Ambrose, *Eisenhower*, 220–21.

27. "To Paul Hoffman from Sherman Adams," November 22, 1954, RNC, box 709, White House Central Files (hereafter WHCF), Official File, DDEL, emphasis added.

28. Ibid.; see also "To Paul Gray Hoffman," November 23, 1954, in *Eisenhower Papers* 15: 1411–12.

29. "President to Adams," December 4, 1954, Adams, Sherman (5), box 1, Whitman File, DDEL.

30. Ibid.

31. Ibid.

32. Walter Williams and Mary Lord Oral Histories, DDEL; Bone, *Party Committees*, 29–31.

33. "Willis to Adams," February 10, 1955, RNC, box 709, WHCF Confidential File, Subject, DDEL.

34. "Willis to Adams," March 4, 1955, RNC, box 709, WHCF Confidential File, Subject, DDEL.

35. "Willis to Adams," May 20, 1955, RNC April–June '55, box 466, WHCF General File, DDEL.

36. Press Release, Citizens 1955, box 3, Whitman Campaign Series, DDEL.

37. Ibid.

38. "Division: Enrollment of New Republicans," Citizens 1955, box 3, Whitman Campaign Series, DDEL.

39. Ibid.

40. "President to Flenniken," December 3, 1953 in *Eisenhower Papers* 15: 727–28.

41. Ibid. See also, for example, "President to Alcorn," March 4, 1958, in *Eisenhower Papers* 19: 751–52; "President to Hall," April 26, 1956, in *Eisenhower Papers* 16: 2137.

42. "President to Alcorn," March 4, 1958, in *Eisenhower Papers* 19: 751–52; see also "President to Alcorn," April 1, 1959, in *Eisenhower Papers* 20: 1436. Eisenhower's efforts to invigorate the party through the recruitment of young Republicans were many. For a sampling, see "President to Alcorn," March 4, 1958, in *President Dwight D. Eisenhower's Office Files, 1953–1961, Part I: Eisenhower Administration Series, 64 Microfilm Reels*, ed. Robert E. Lester (Bethesda, Md.: University Publications of America, 1990). Henceforth *Office Files*. "President to McKay," June 4, 1956, in *Eisenhower Papers* 17: 2180–81; "President to Summerfield," June 13, 1957, in *Eisenhower Papers* 18: 258–59; "President to Whitney," March 12, 1956, in *Eisenhower Papers* 16: 2063–64.

43. See "President to Lampe and Fort," draft, November 24, 1958, *Office Files*.

44. "President to Lampe and Fort," in *Eisenhower Papers* 19: 1217–18. See a similar sentiment expressed to Lucius Clay, noted in "Diary, secret," November 20, 1954, *Eisenhower Papers* 15: 1402–5.

45. "Diary, secret," October 8, 1953, *Eisenhower Papers* 14: 568.

46. Sherman Adams, *Firsthand Report: The Story of the Eisenhower Administration* (New York: Harper, 1961), 28–29.

47. "Memorandum for the Record," November 20, 1954, *Office Files*; also in Dwight D. Eisenhower and Robert H. Ferrell, *The Eisenhower Diaries* (New York: Norton, 1981), November 20, 1954; also in "Diary, secret," November 20, 1954, *Eisenhower Papers* 15: 1402–5.

48. "President to Alcorn," August 30, 1957, in *Eisenhower Papers* 18: 396–97; "President to Jones," November 25, 1958, Republican Party, box 708, WHCF Official File, DDEL.

49. Paul Hoffman, "How Eisenhower Saved the Republican Party," *Collier's Magazine*, October 26, 1956.

50. Meade Alcorn Oral History, DDEL, 86.

51. "What If He Doesn't Run?" *National Review*, June 27, 1956, 5.

52. "President to Hazlett," November 2, 1956, in *Eisenhower Papers* 17: 2353–55.

53. "President to Paley," November 14, 1956, in *Eisenhower Papers* 17: 2392–93.

54. "President to Landers," November 23, 1956, Modern Republicanism, box 21, Whitman Name Series, DDEL.

55. Ibid.

56. "President to Alcorn," February 27, 1957, *Office Files*.

57. Ibid.

58. Godfrey Sperling Jr., "The Real Eisenhower Plan," *Christian Science Monitor*, May 21, 1957.

59. "Alcorn Sees Good Coming from GOP 'Differences,'" *Washington Post*, June 3, 1957.

60. Robert C. Albright, "Goldwater Hits 'Modern' GOP," *Washington Post*, April 9, 1957.

61. Lee Edwards, *The Conservative Revolution: The Movement That Remade America* (New York: Free Press, 1999), 84.

62. Quoted in David W. Reinhard, *The Republican Right since 1945* (Lexington: University Press of Kentucky, 1983), 140–42.

63. "Remarks by Alcorn, Republican National Conference: June 7, 1957, Washington, D.C.," in Paul L. Kesaris, ed., *Papers of the Republican Party, Part I: Meetings of the RNC, 1911–1980, Series A: 1911–1960, 51 Microfilm Reels* (Frederick, MD: University Publications of America, 1987, 1986). Henceforth, *PRP*.

64. Godfrey Sperling Jr., "GOP Rift 'Approved,'" *Christian Science Monitor*, May 18, 1957; see also "Address by the President, Republican National Conference, June 7, 1957, Washington, D.C.," *PRP*.

65. See Daniel J. Galvin, *Presidential Party Building: Dwight D. Eisenhower to George W. Bush* (Princeton: Princeton University Press, 2010), ch. 3.

66. "Straight Telegram," January 21, 1959, Alcorn, H. Meade, box 1, Whitman File, DDEL.

67. William M. Blair, "President Urged to Set Example for Active GOP," *New York Times*, January 23, 1959.

68. "President Tells GOP to Wake Up," *Los Angeles Times*, January 23, 1959.

69. John A. Andrew, *The Other Side of the Sixties: Young Americans for Freedom and the Rise of Conservative Politics*, Perspectives on the Sixties (New Brunswick, NJ: Rutgers University Press, 1997), 41.

70. Ibid., 47.

71. Daniel J. Galvin, "The Transformation of Political Institutions: Investments in Institutional Resources and Gradual Change in the National Party Committees," *Studies in American Political Development* 26, no. 1 (2012).

72. According to Stephen Shadegg, Goldwater's adviser. Cited in Andrew, *Other Side of the Sixties*, 37.

73. Reinhard, *Republican Right since 1945*; Andrew, *Other Side of the Sixties*; Rick Perlstein, *Before the Storm: Barry Goldwater and the Unmaking of the American Consensus* (New York: Hill and Wang, 2001).

74. Galvin, *Presidential Party Building*.

12. American Presidential Authority and Economic Expertise since World War II

1. See Robert M. Collins, "The Economic Crisis of 1968 and the Waning of the 'American Century,'" *American Historical Review* 101 (1996): 416, 418; Lloyd C. Gardner, *Pay Any Price: Lyndon Johnson and the Wars for Vietnam* (Chicago: I. R. Dee, 1995). Further appreciation of the aggressive dimensions Johnson envisioned for his reform agenda may be won from considering that in 1964 the *total* federal budget the president had put before the Congress was $98 billion. His OEO funding request two years later thus constituted by itself almost 30 percent of that figure. The growth in the food stamps component of the Aid to Families with Dependent Children (AFDC) program is also illustrative: $36 million in such stamps were distributed to approximately 600,000 people in 1965; within ten years the figures had grown to $4 billion allocated among 17 million persons. Similarly, public housing subsidies paid by the federal government rose from an annual total of $236 million to $1.2 billion in the same time period.

2. It cannot be emphasized enough that the conservative attack on Keynesianism relied to a very large extent on the specious comparison of government finance with household ledgers. For Keynes and his followers, however, the essential issue was that governments, given their virtually infinite time horizons, could indeed do what households could not—take on debt with an assurance that *in the long run* it could be liquidated. Indeed, assuming that future generations would be more prosperous (in no small part due to the inspired policy choices of their forebears), the burden of such liquidation would be proportionally smaller. Perhaps even more to the point, also forgotten in antideficit diatribes was the fact that the vast proportion of the national debt had been and is held by the public, to whom the United States Treasury paid and pays valuable interest payments in compensation for the risk it bears. In other words, the debt was and is an obligation even as it was and is an asset to millions of people and institutions. On the collapse of the "New Deal Order" owing, in part, to these transformations in the perceptions of state capabilities in finance, see Steve Fraser and Gary Gerstle, eds., *The Rise and Fall of the New Deal Order, 1930–1980* (Princeton: Princeton University Press, 1989).

3. On the president's fascination with the use of PPBS in the War on Poverty, see *Oral History Interview with Charles L. Schultze* (March 28, 1969, by David McComb, Washington, D.C.), Lyndon Baines Johnson Library, Austin, Texas, I-52; and *Oral History Interview with Robert Lampman* (May 24, 1983, by Michael L. Gillette, Madison, Wisconsin), Lyndon Baines Johnson Library, Austin, Texas, I-34–35.

4. See John Morton Blum, *Years of Discord: American Politics and Society, 1961–1974* (New York: Norton, 1991), 250–51; Collins, "Economic Crisis of 1968," 412; Robert Eisner, "Fiscal and Monetary Policy Reconsidered," *American Economic Review* 59 (1969): 897–905; as well as his "What Went Wrong?" *Journal of Political Economy* 79 (1971): 629–41. That the tax surcharge did little to stem the inflationary tide was also linked with an easing of monetary policy that took hold in 1968, which, adding insult to injury, had been implemented initially out of concern that fiscal restraint might overshoot its mark and generate excessive unemployment. Efforts to correct *that* problem, by raising the discount rate, only encouraged inflows of short-term funds from overseas (and efforts by banks to increase their loanable assets by borrowing on dollar accounts overseas). These international liquidity flows further frustrated efforts to use higher interest rates as a brake on the accelerating inflation of the late 1960s.

5. See Angus Maddison, "Economic Stagnation since 1973, Its Nature and Causes: A Six Country Survey," *De Economist* 131 (1983): 585–608; United States Council of Economic Advisers, *Economic Report of the President: 1984* (Washington, DC: U.S. Government Printing Office, 1984), selected tables; Stanley Legergott, *Manpower in Economic Growth: The American Record since 1800* (New York: McGraw-Hill, 1964), selected tables; Organization for Economic Cooperation and Development (OECD), *Labour Force Statistics: 1960–71* (Paris: OECD, 1973), 72–73; OECD, *Labour Force Statistics: 1966–77* (Paris: OECD, 1979), 78–79; and Michael A. Bernstein, *The Great Depression: Delayed Recovery and Economic Change in America, 1929–1939* (New York: Cambridge University Press, 1987), 200–14. The 1971 collapse of the Bretton Woods system of fixed exchange rates worsened the inflationary bias of economy then under way, but the real cost of imports, most especially fuel, rose further still.

6. On the powerful influence such rhetorical devices as the "misery index" brought to bear on political discussion during the 1970s, see Douglas A. Hibbs Jr., *The Political Economy of Industrial Democracies* (Cambridge: Harvard University Press, 1987).

7. From Alan S. Blinder, "The Fall and Rise of Keynesian Economics," *Economic Record* 64 (1988): 278.

8. The classical monetarism that Milton Friedman did so much to resurrect in governmental policy circles is perhaps best represented by his masterwork, coauthored with Anna J. Schwartz, *A Monetary History of the United States, 1867–1960* (Princeton: Princeton University Press, 1963). Also see his *Essays in Positive Economics* (Chicago: University of Chicago Press, 1953) as well as his presidential address to the American Economic Association, published as "The Role of Monetary Policy," *American Economic Review* 58 (1968): 1–22.

9. The "fallacy of composition," that a whole cannot be understood as merely the sum of its parts, framed much of Keynes's critique of prevailing doctrines in economics dating from the turn of the century. In his *General Theory* he noted, for example, that "rational" behavior on the part of individuals—say, saving substantial portions of their income during a recession—could generate "irrational" results in the aggregate, in this case, a reduction in total consumption spending that would merely make the recession worse.

10. It is now widely accepted that the "rational expectations" hypothesis first systematically emerged in R. F. Muth, "The Demand for Non-Farm Housing," in

The Demand for Durable Goods, ed. A. C. Hargerger (Chicago: University of Chicago Press, 1960), 29–96. Muth pursued the issue further in his "Rational Expectations and the Theory of Price Movements," *Econometrica* 29 (1961): 315–35. Its application to a "new macroeconomics" took form in the influential work of Robert E. Lucas Jr.—scholarship for which Lucas received the Nobel Prize in 1995. See, for example, Lucas, "An Equilibrium Model of the Business Cycle," *Journal of Political Economy* 83 (1975): 1113–44; Lucas, "Understanding Business Cycles," *in Stabilization of the Domestic and International Economy*, ed. Karl Brunner and Allan H. Meltzer (New York: North-Holland, 1977), 7–29, as well as his "Methods and Problems in Business Cycle Theory," in his *Studies in Business Cycle Theory* (Cambridge: MIT Press, 1980), 271–96.

11. On the exogenous nature of the 1970s inflation, see Alan S. Blinder, "The Anatomy of Double-Digit Inflations in the 1970s," *Inflation: Causes and Effects*, ed. Robert E. Hall (Chicago: University of Chicago Press, 1982). The most thorough narrative concerning the Watergate scandals is Stanley I. Kutler, *The Wars of Watergate: The Last Crisis of Richard Nixon* (New York: Norton, 1992).

12. California's Proposition 13, placed on the ballot in the wake of the tireless efforts of Howard Jarvis and Paul Gann, was a significant example of the links between the conservative offensives of the 1970s and 1980s and nonprofit organizations committed to conservative agendas. Independent-sector organizations like the American Enterprise Institute, the Cato Institute, and the Heritage Foundation all served (and continue to serve) to direct funding toward the political work of conservative activists and other social scientists embarked on an anti-Keynesian protocol.

13. See, for example, Anthony A. Campagna, *Economic Policy in the Carter Administration* (Westport, CT: Greenwood Press, 1995). As to the changing international contexts within which economic policy was implemented in the late twentieth century, see Harold James, *International Monetary Cooperation since Bretton Woods* (New York: Oxford University Press, 1996).

14. That the income tax reductions of the Program for Economic Recovery President Reagan put before the Congress were, in fact, a political contrivance to benefit the most privileged in the electorate is strikingly demonstrated in the memoirs of the president's director of the Office of Management and Budget, David Stockman. Stockman in particular referred to the budget strategy as a "Trojan horse" deployed on behalf of the rich. See his *Triumph of Politics: How the Reagan Revolution Failed* (New York: Harper and Row, 1986), 5–6, 8.

15. Another example of the sheer magnitude of the military spending strategies embraced by the Reagan administration is afforded by comparative data on proportionate commitments to defense. By the end of the 1980s, the United States distributed 6.1 percent of national product to defense. France, by comparison, allocated 3.5 percent; the Federal Republic of Germany, 3.1 percent; and Japan, a bit less than 1 percent.

16. See Proxmire to Okun, February 22, 1979; Okun to Proxmire, February 26, 1979; Okun to Proxmire, February 9, 1979; and Proxmire to Okun, February 1, 1979; all in the Papers of Arthur Okun, Lyndon Baines Johnson Library, Austin, Texas, Box 20B (folder "O P"). At the very time that supply-side theorists succeeded in condemning Keynesianism as a recipe for runaway deficit spending, the share of annual gross domestic product represented by the federal deficit fell from

6.3 percent in 1983 to 1.4 percent by 1996. In another telling demonstration of the hyperbole utilized in the discussion of contemporary public finance, it could be demonstrated that by 1989 the wealthiest five hundred thousand American households could have liquidated the entire national debt with the *increase* in their total wealth over the previous ten years. The striking inability of liberals to counter the rhetoric of supply-side theorists was at no time better demonstrated than during the presidency of Jimmy Carter. In this regard, see Bruce Schulman, "Slouching toward the Supply Side: Jimmy Carter and the New American Political Economy," in *The Carter Presidency: Policy Choices in the Post–New Deal Era*, ed. Gary Fink and Hugh Graham (Lawrence: University Press of Kansas, 1998).

17. In *The Business Response to Keynes: 1929–1964* (New York: Columbia University Press, 1981), Robert M. Collins vividly demonstrates how the American business community had once been entirely persuaded by Keynes's view of the interactions among enterprise, households, and individual behavior in the marketplace.

18. George H. W. Bush's travails as the nation's forty-first president provided a unique example of the "new classical economic chickens" coming home to roost. Within the first year of his term, it became obvious that federal tax cuts had so unbalanced the federal ledger that the nation's capital markets were at risk, given the enormous amounts of borrowing undertaken by the Treasury. Forced ultimately to ask for a tax increase, the president found himself hounded by the right wing of his own party as the 1992 campaign approached. Most analysts believe that these intra party struggles played a significant part in weakening Bush's bid for reelection. Bill Clinton's subsequent triumph, as the first Democrat to reach the White House in twelve years, was a striking representation, in the political realm, of the inherent contradictions to be found in a national fiscal policy recast by "Reaganism." See, in this regard, Peter Passell, "The Tax-Rise Issue: Bush Rationale vs Economists," *New York Times*, May 10, 1990, A14. No less an authority than Richard Darman, director of the Office of Management and Budget under President Bush, ultimately claimed that the combination of Reagan tax cuts and increased military spending constituted the largest and most undisciplined addition to federal debt in the nation's history. See his *Who's in Control? Polar Politics and the Sensible Center* (New York: Simon and Schuster, 1996).

19. In *Who's in Control?* Darman argues that the massive rise in the national debt during the 1980s was far more the result of increased military spending than it was due to the cost of social spending (especially antipoverty) programs. It is well worth noting that, at the same time, a rhetorical sleight of hand took place so subtle as to provoke little if any comment. Increasingly, politicians, economists, and voters alike spoke of what were once called "transfer-payments" (such as Medicare, Medicaid, Aid to Families with Dependent Children, Food Stamps, and Social Security) as "entitlements." The former label, of course, was freighted with operational and technical meaning drawn from the national income accounts themselves. By contrast, the latter evoked notions of engrossment at public expense by those possibly unworthy. Just as one could be "entitled" to something, one could just as arguably be "unentitled." Thus it became easier to speak of program elimination, zero-based budgeting, means-testing, and an array of efforts at fiscal contraction literally unthinkable a decade or more earlier. In such simple yet profound changes in word choice, conservatives found yet another weapon in their determination to disestablish the mixed

economy of the postwar era. See Gareth Davies, *From Opportunity to Entitlement: The Transformation and Decline of Great Society Liberalism* (Lawrence: University Press of Kansas, 1996).

20. In its most typical renditions, the proposed amendment would mandate a three-fifths majority in the Congress to pass any exceptions to a balanced budget in any given year—a legislative threshold that would effectively cripple any efforts toward deficit spending save for those during times of war. At the 1985 National Governors Association convention, it was Bill Clinton of Arkansas who stood as one of the most resolute Democratic supporters of the amendment proposal. His position changed quickly after his election as president.

21. For a particularly compelling discussion of the century's progress of American liberalism, framed more with reference to intellectual rather than political economic contexts, see Gary Gerstle, "The Protean Character of American Liberalism," *American Historical Review* 99 (1994): 1043–73. See also Alan Brinkley, *The End of Reform: New Deal Liberalism in Recession and War* (New York: Knopf, 1995).

22. See Joan Robinson, "Consumer Sovereignty in a Planned Economy," in *Collected Economic Papers* (Oxford: Blackwell, 1975), 3: 70–81.

13. The Changing Presidential Politics of Disaster

The author gratefully acknowledges the helpful resources of Brian Balogh, Edward D. Berkowitz, Martha Derthick, Hugh Heclo, James T. Patterson, and Bruce Schulman to earlier versions of this chapter.

1. *Washington Post*, July 23, 2012; *New York Times*, April 18, 2007; Gene Healy, *The Cult of the Presidency* (Washington, DC: Cato Institute, 2008), 2.

2. *Washington Post*, November 4, 2012 (citing Mississippi governor Haley Barbour).

3. For 'consoler in chief', see *Washington Post*, April 18, 2007.

4. *Christian Science Monitor*, June 29, 1957; *Baltimore Sun*, July 2, 1957; *Hartford Courant*, July 28, 1957.

5. In this section, I rely generally on John Barry, *Rising Tide* (New York: Touchstone, 1997).

6. For a selection of such entreaties, see reel 76–77, case file 124, Calvin Coolidge Papers, Library of Congress.

7. See Gareth Davies, "How Strong Was the Nineteenth Century State? The Case of Disaster Relief," *Journal of Policy History*, forthcoming.

8. For a detailed account, see Gareth Davies, "Shock Troops of Disaster," unpublished manuscript in possession of author.

9. Nan Elizabeth Woodruff, *As Rare as Rain: Federal Relief in the Great Southern Drought of 1930–31* (Urbana: University of Illinois Press, 1985).

10. See Gareth Davies, "From Shock Troops to Bureaucrats," unpublished manuscript in possession of author.

11. FDR's radio addresses are a conspicuous exception: Here, though, the president was seeking to reach the entire nation and not just a particular community.

12. On Hoover's general calculus, see Ellis Hawley, "Herbert Hoover, Associationalism, and the Great Depression Relief Crisis of 1930–1933," in *With Us Always:*

A History of Private Charity and Public Welfare, ed. Donald Critchlow and Charles Parker (Lanham, MD: Rowman and Littlefield, 1998), 161–90. In this case, Hoover coordinated an elaborate national response that involved governors, banks, railroads, and the Red Cross. See David Hamilton, "Herbert Hoover and the Great Drought of 1930," *Journal of American History* 68 (March 1982): 850–75.

13. In their 1936 platform, the Democrats declared: "The government in a modern civilization has certain inescapable obligations to its citizens, among which are protection of the family and the home, the establishment of a democracy of opportunity, and aid to those overtaken by disaster." Platform, dated June 23, 1936, downloaded from www.presidency.ucsb.edu on July 9, 2013.

14. Douglas Dacy and Howard Kunreuther, *The Economics of Natural Disasters: Implications for Federal Policy* (New York: Free Press, 1969), 33; David A. Moss, "Courting Disaster? The Transformation of Federal Disaster Policy since 1803," in *The Financing of Catastrophe Risk*, ed. Kenneth A. Froot (Chicago: University of Chicago Press, 1999), 327.

15. Calculated from Claire B. Rubin, ed., *Emergency Management: The American Experience, 1900–2005* (Fairfax, VA: Public Entity Risk Institute, 2007), 121 (table 5-1).

16. Press conference of June 12, 1952, downloaded from www.presidency.ucsb.edu on July 9, 2013.

17. Calculated from Rubin, ed., *Emergency Management*, 86 (tables 4–1), 96 (table 4-2).

18. Cited in David A. Moss, "Courting Disaster? The Transformation of Federal Disaster Policy Since 1803," in *The Financing of Catastrophe Risk*, ed. Kenneth A. Froot (Chicago: University of Chicago Press, 1999), 327. 1974 amendments to the 1950 disaster act increased the usual federal contribution to 75 percent. In 1989, Hurricane Hugo became the first disaster to stimulate the offer of 100 percent federal financing.

19. This section is again drawn primarily from contemporary newspaper coverage and from congressional debate. Also helpful is Edward F. Haas, "Victor H. Schiro, Hurricane Betsy, and the 'Forgiveness Bill,'" *Gulf Coast Historical Review* 6 (Fall 1990).

20. I rely here on "Transcript of New Orleans Remarks," http://www.lbjlib.utexas.edu/johnson/AV.hom/Hurricane/audio_transcript.shtm, downloaded on July 9, 2013.

21. Johnson, Remarks on Arrival in New Orleans, September 10, 1965, downloaded from www.lbjlib.utexas.edu on December 6, 2011.

22. Lady Bird Johnson, *A White House Diary* (1970; repr. Austin: University of Texas Press, 2007), 320.

23. Telephone conversation between Johnson and Phillips, September 14, 1965, downloaded from http://millercenter.org/scripps/archive/presidentialrecordings/johnson, on January 31, 2015 (the identifier for this conversation is WH9509.04 PNO 14). LBJ began by listing some fifteen agencies that had to liaise effectively together if the relief operation were to be successful.

24. Long had strongly supported Johnson's bid for reelection in 1964, despite the president's intense unpopularity in Louisiana, and Boggs had just cast a courageous vote in favor of the Voting Rights Act.

25. Brian Williams, "LBJ's Political Hurricane," *New York Times*, September 24, 2005; David Remnick, "High Water: How Presidents and Citizens Respond to Disaster," *New Yorker*, October 3, 2005.

26. George W. Bush, *Decision Points* (New York: Crown, 2010), 309.

27. See Kent B. Germany, "LBJ and the Response to Hurricane Betsy," which has a transcript of Johnson's conversation with Russell Long, available at http://whitehousetapes.net/exhibit/lbj-and-response-hurricane-betsy. See also the website of the Johnson library, which has recently transcribed audio tapes of some snippets of conversation that Johnson had with victims of Betsy during his visit to New Orleans, available at www.lbjlibrary.org.

28. Sidney Blumenthal, *The Permanent Campaign* (New York: Simon and Schuster, 1980); Jeffrey Tulis, *The Rhetorical Presidency* (Princeton: Princeton University Press, 1987); Samuel Kernell, *Going Public: New Strategies of Presidential Leadership* (Washington, DC: CQ Press, 1988); Theodore Lowi, *The Personal President: Power Invested, Promise Unfulfilled* (Ithaca, NY: Cornell University Press, 1985).

29. For the contribution of Theodore Roosevelt to this process, see Sidney Milkis, *Theodore Roosevelt, the Progressive Party, and the Transformation of American Democracy* (Lawrence: University of Kansas Press, 2009).

30. See Hugh Heclo, "Campaigning and Governing: A Conspectus," in *The Permanent Campaign and Its Future*, ed. Norman Ornstein and Thomas Mann (Washington, DC: AEI, 2000), 1–37.

31. The extracts from the Nixon tapes reproduced in this section are taken from Jules Witcover, *Very Strange Bedfellows: The Short and Unhappy Marriage of Richard Nixon and Spiro Agnew* (New York: Public Affairs, 2007), 156–61.

32. Stanley Kelly paid close attention to Nixon's 1950 Senate campaign in *Professional Public Relations and Political Power* (Baltimore: Johns Hopkins University Press, 1956). For an incisive recent account of this pattern, see Brian Balogh, "From Corn to Caviar: The Evolution of Presidential Electoral Communications, 1960–2000," in *America at the Ballot Box: Elections and American Political History*, ed. Gareth Davies and Julian Zelizer (Philadelphia: University of Pennsylvania Press, 2015).

33. I rely here on coverage in the *New York Times* and *Washington Post*. See especially *New York Times*, June 28, 1972; *Washington Post*, June 28, 1972, and July 3, 1972.

34. Nixon conversation with Charles S. Colson, No. 353-18A, June 24, 1972 (National Archives II, College Park, Maryland); *Washington Post*, June 25, 1972.

35. For example, see *Washington Post*, June 30, 1972, and August 9, 1972.

36. For OEP concern at the time of Betsy, see memo, Buford Ellington to Lee White, August 24, 1965, WHCF IS, box 5, and memo, Ellington to LBJ, October 11, 1965, WHCF LE/DI 6, box 35, Lyndon B. Johnson Presidential Library, Austin, Texas. For a task-force report on the need for community resilience, see Gilbert White, *A Unified National Flood Program for Managing Flood Losses* (August 1966), Lyndon B. Johnson Presidential Library.

37. *New York Times*, June 30, 1972.

38. *Washington Post*, July 15, 1972.

39. *New York Times*, July 1, 1972.

40. *New York Times*, July 12, 1972; *U.S. News and World Report*, July 24, 1972.

41. Most notably, an inaccurate Weather Bureau report that left residents of western Louisiana thinking that they had no immediate need to evacuate their homes.

42. *Washington Post*, August 8, 1972.

43. Ibid., August 9 and 10, 1972.

44. Oval Office tape 767-20, August 11, 1972.

45. *Washington Post*, September 5 and 9, 1972.

46. *New York Times*, September 9, 1972.

47. Walter LaFeber, *The Deadly Bet: LBJ, Vietnam, and the 1968 Election* (Lanham, MD: Rowman and Littlefield, 2005), 103.

Conclusion

1. Description comes from www.insidejobs.com/careers/presidential-historian, accessed July 30, 2013.

2. In fact, some analysts see this as a fundamental divide between political science and the discipline of history altogether. In 2002 Stephen Skowronek suggested that the "divergence of disciplinary interests" between political scientists and historians who study the presidency had grown so large that political scientists could no longer even expect historians to provide useful material for them to analyze. See Stephen Skowronek, "Presidency and American Political Development: A Third Look," *Presidential Studies Quarterly* 32, no. 4 (December 2002): 743–52.

3. To be sure, even some political scientists pushed back against Skowronek's formulation, seeing his views as too deterministic. See, for example, Douglas J. Hoekstra, "The Politics of *Politics*: Skowronek and Presidential Research," *Presidential Studies Quarterly* 29, no. 3 (September 1999): 657–71. While acknowledging the importance of Stephen Skowronek's 1993 book *The Politics Presidents Make*, Hoekstra advances an approach that leans more toward the "agency" side of the "structure-agency conflict," noting that Skowronek neglects to consider the importance of presidential character and political thought. However, he concludes by urging presidential scholars to incorporate into their explanations not only contingency but also critical theory, linguistics, and constructivism.

4. Hoekstra, "Politics of *Politics*."

5. Joseph Ellis, "Get a Life! Reflections on Biography and History," *Historically Speaking* 5, no. 5 (May/June 2004): 18–19.

6. Allen Kulikoff, "The Founding Fathers: Best Sellers! TV Stars! Punctual Plumbers!" *Journal of the Historical Society* 5, no. 2 (Spring 2005): 155–87.

7. Barbara Weinstein, "The Case of the Incredible Shrinking Historians?" *Perspectives on History* 45, no. 6 (September 2007), available at www.historians.org/perspectives/issues/2007/0709/0709pre1.cfm.

8. Ibid.

9. Sean Wilentz, "America Made Easy: McCullough, Adams, and the Decline of Popular History," *New Republic*, July 2, 2001, available at www.tnr.com/article/books-and-arts/90636/david-mccullough-john-adams-book-review.

10. Ibid.

11. Ibid.

12. Robert Self, *All in the Family* (New York: Hill & Wang, 2012); Lizabeth Cohen, *A Consumer's Republic* (New York: Vintage, 2004); Steven Fraser, *Every Man a Speculator* (New York: Harper Collins, 2005).

13. Jill Lepore, "Historians Who Love Too Much: Reflections on Microhistory and Biography," *Journal of American History* 88, no. 1 (June 2001): 141.

List of Contributors

Brian Balogh is Dorothy Danforth Compton Professor at the Miller Center of Public Affairs and professor in the Corcoran Department of History at the University of Virginia. The author of numerous publications including *A Government Out of Sight* (2012), Balogh directs the Miller Center's National Fellowship Program and cohosts *Backstory*, a nationally syndicated radio program.

Michael A. Bernstein is the senior vice president for academic affairs and provost at Tulane University, where he is also professor of economics and the John Christie Barr Professor of History. His books include *The Great Depression* (1987) and *A Perilous Progress: Economists and Public Purpose in Twentieth-Century America* (2001).

Kathryn Cramer Brownell is assistant professor of history at Purdue University and the author of *Showbiz Politics: Hollywood in American Political Life* (2014). She is currently writing a book about cable television and the transformation of American politics.

N. D. B. Connolly is assistant professor of history at Johns Hopkins University and the author of *A World More Concrete: Real Estate and the Remaking of Jim Crow South Florida* (2014). He is currently at work on a study of black capitalism.

Frank Costigliola is professor of history at the University of Connecticut. A prolific scholar, Costigliola has published numerous books, including *Awkward Dominion* (1984), *The Kennan Diaries* (2014), and *Roosevelt's Lost Alliances* (2012), for which he won the Ferrell Award of the Society for the Historians of American Foreign Relations.

Gareth Davies is a lecturer in American history and a fellow in St. Anne's College at the University of Oxford. His publications include *See Government Grow: Education Politics from Johnson to Reagan* (2007) and *From Opportunity to Entitlement: The Transformation and Decline of Great Society Liberalism* (1996). He is currently finishing a book on the politics of natural disasters in the United States.

Darren Dochuk is associate professor in the humanities in the John C. Danforth Center on Religion and Politics and in the Department of History at Washington University in St. Louis, Missouri. He is the author of *From Bible Belt to Sunbelt* (2011) and the coeditor of *Sunbelt Rising: The Politics of Space, Place, and Region* (2011).

Susan J. Douglas is the Catherine Neafie Kellogg Professor of Communication Studies at the University of Michigan and chair of the department. She is the author of *The Rise of Enlightened Sexism: How Pop Culture Took Us from Girl Power to Girls Gone Wild* (2010); *The Mommy Myth: The Idealization of Motherhood and How It Undermines Women* (2004); *Listening In: Radio and the American Imagination* (1999), *Where the Girls Are: Growing Up Female with the Mass Media* (1994; 1995) and *Inventing American Broadcasting, 1899–1922* (Johns Hopkins, 1987).

Daniel J. Galvin is an associate professor of political science and a faculty fellow at the Institute for Policy Research at Northwestern University. The author of *Presidential Party Building* (2010), Galvin has been the recipient of the "Emerging Scholar Award" from the American Political Science Association's Political Organizations and Parties section. He is currently at work on a book about Rust Belt Democrats.

William I. Hitchcock is Randolph Compton Professor at the Miller Center of Public Affairs and a professor in the Corcoran Department of History at the University of Virginia. He is the author of numerous publications, including *The Bitter Road to Freedom: A New History of the Liberation of Europe* (2008) and *The Struggle for Europe: The Turbulent History of a Divided Continent, 1945–Present* (2003). He is currently at work on a book about the Age of Eisenhower.

Cathie Jo Martin is professor of political science at Boston University and former chair of the Council for European Studies. She is the author of numerous publications in comparative politics and public policy, including *The Political Construction of Business Interests: Coordination, Growth, and Equality* (2012), *Stuck in Neutral: Business and the Politics of Human Capital Investment Policy* (2000), and *Shifting the Burden: The Struggle over Growth and Corporate Taxation* (1991).

Alice O'Connor is professor of history and United States public policy at the University of California, Santa Barbara. She is the author of *Social Science for What?* (2007) and *Poverty Knowledge* (2001), as well as the coeditor of *Urban Inequality* (2001) and *Poverty in the United States: An Encyclopedia of History, Policy, and Politics* (2004).

Bruce J. Schulman is the William E. Huntington Professor of History at Boston University. The author of three books and editor or coeditor of five others, he is currently completing a volume on the period 1896–1929 for the *Oxford History of the United States*.

Robert O. Self is the Royce Family Professor of Teaching Excellence and professor of history at Brown University. He is the author of *All in the Family: The Realignment of American Democracy since the 1960s* (2012) and *American Babylon* (2003), for which he won the James A. Rawley Prize of the Organization of American Historians and the Ralph J. Bunche Award of the American Political Science Association.

Stephen Skowronek is the Pelatiah Perit Professor of Political and Social Science at Yale University. His publications include *Building a New American State* (1982), *The Politics Presidents Make* (1997), *The Search for American Political Development* (2004, with Karen Orren), and *Presidential Leadership in Political Time* (2008). Skowronek cofounded the journal *Studies in American Political Development*, which he edited between 1986 and 2007, and he provided the episode structure and thematic content for the PBS miniseries *The American President*.

INDEX